Kerrie Meyler

Jason Sandys

Kenneth van Surksum

Michael Wiles

System Center 2012 R2 Configuration Manager

Supplement to System Center 2012 Configuration Manager (SCCM)

UNLEASHED

SAMS | 800 East 96th Street, Indianapolis, Indiana 46240 USA

System Center 2012 R2 Configuration Manager Unleashed

ISBN-13: 978-0-672-33715-4
ISBN-10: 0-672-33715-0

Library of Congress Control Number: 2014943440

Printed in the United States of America

First Printing: September 2014

Trademarks

All terms mentioned in this book that are known to be trademarks or service marks have been appropriately capitalized. Sams Publishing cannot attest to the accuracy of this information. Use of a term in this book should not be regarded as affecting the validity of any trademark or service mark.

Warning and Disclaimer

Every effort has been made to make this book as complete and as accurate as possible, but no warranty or fitness is implied. The information provided is on an "as is" basis. The authors and the publisher shall have neither liability nor responsibility to any person or entity with respect to any loss or damages arising from the information contained in this book or programs accompanying it.

Special Sales

For information about buying this title in bulk quantities, or for special sales opportunities (which may include electronic versions; custom cover designs; and content particular to your business, training goals, marketing focus, or branding interests), please contact our corporate sales department at corpsales@pearsoned.com or (800) 382-3419.

For government sales inquiries, please contact governmentsales@pearsoned.com.

For questions about sales outside the U.S., please contact international@pearsoned.com.

Editor-in-Chief
Greg Wiegand

Acquisitions Editor
Joan Murray

Development Editor
Keith Cline

Managing Editor
Kristy Hart

Senior Project Editor
Lori Lyons

Copy Editor
Keith Cline

Indexer
Erika Millen

Proofreader
Kathy Ruiz

Technical Editor
Steve Rachui

Editorial Assvistant
Cindy Teeters

Cover Designer
Mark Shirar

Compositor
Nonie Ratcliff

Contents at a Glance

Foreword.. x

Introduction... 1

Part I   Overview

1   People-Centric IT... 5

2   What's Changed Since Configuration Manager 2012 RTM.............. 19

Part II   Deep Dive

3   User Data and Profiles... 61

4   New Application Deployment Types.. 77

5   On-Premise Cross-Platform Support..117

6   What's New in Operating System Deployment..............................147

Part III   Journey to the Cloud

7   Using the Intune Connector...199

8   Mobile Device Management in Configuration Manager 2012 R2......243

Part IV   Appendixes

A   About Windows Intune..297

B   Reference URLs..315

C   Available Online...335

Index..337

Contents

Foreword x

Introduction 1

Part I   Overview

1   People-Centric IT 5

Microsoft's People-Centric IT Philosophy 6

Enabling Users for People-Centric IT 7

Unifying Your Environment for People-Centric IT 8

Protecting Your Data in a People-Centric IT World 9

People-Centric IT and ConfigMgr 2012 R2 with Windows Intune 9

Enabling Users with ConfigMgr 2012 R2 and Windows Intune 10

Unifying Your Environment with ConfigMgr 2012 R2
and Windows Intune 12

Protecting Your Data with ConfigMgr 2012 R2 and
Windows Intune 13

People-Centric IT and Windows Server 2012 R2 14

Enabling Users with Windows Server 2012 R2 14

Unifying Your Environment with Windows Server 2012 R2 16

Protecting Your Data with Windows Server 2012 R2 16

People-Centric IT and Microsoft Azure Active Directory 17

Summary 18

2   What's Changed Since Configuration Manager 2012 RTM 19

Administration Changes 19

Configuring Database Replication 20

Configuring Internet Proxy Server on Each Site System 24

Windows Intune Integration and Extensions for
Windows Intune 25

Software Update Points 25

Certificate Profiles 27

Client Settings 27

Security 28

Distribution Points (DPs) 28

Automatic Client Upgrade 31

Network Access Accounts 32

PowerShell Support 32

Assets and Compliance 34

    Collections 34

    Compliance Settings 37

Software Library 38

    Application Management 38

    Software Updates 39

    Operating System Deployment 41

Monitoring Changes 42

    Alerts 43

    Reporting 43

    Distribution Status 43

    Deployment Status 44

    Client Operations 44

Other Improvements 44

    Setup and Recovery 45

    Client and Client Experience 48

Summary 58

Part II   Deep Dive

3   User Data and Profiles   **61**

User Data and Profiles Overview 61

User Data and Profiles Prerequisites 62

Configuring User Data and Profiles 64

    Using Folder Redirection 64

    Using Offline Files 67

    Using Roaming User Profiles 70

    Roaming Profiles, Folder Redirection, and Offline Files

       in a Mash-Up 74

Deploying User Data and Profiles Configuration Items 75

Reporting User Data and Profiles Compliance 76

Summary 76

4   New Application Deployment Types   **77**

Application Overview 77

    Definition of an Application 77

    Defining Deployment Types 78

What's New for Applications Since ConfigMgr 2012 RTM 78

Support for Write Filters in Windows Embedded 79

Working with Virtual Applications 81

    Creating a Microsoft Application Virtualization 5

       Deployment Type 82

Using App-V Virtual Environments 83
Creating an App-V Virtual Environment 84
Deploying Applications to Mobile Devices 85
Creating Application Store Deployment Types 86
Sideloading Applications 93
Using VPN Profiles in Your Applications 104
Deploying Software to OS X, Linux, and UNIX Platforms 105
Deploying Applications to Apple OS X Computers 105
Deploying Software to Linux and UNIX 108
Deploying Web Applications 111
Best Practices for Working with Applications 112
Best Practices for Installing Software 112
Best Practices for Working with Applications in
Task Sequences 115
Summary 116

5 On-Premise Cross-Platform Support **117**
Supported Platforms 117
Cross-Platform Agent Architecture 119
Cross-Platform Agent Communication 120
Client Agent Settings 120
Cross-Platform Settings 121
Linux/UNIX Requirements 121
OS X Requirements 121
Firewall Ports 125
Downloading Client Agents 126
Cross-Platform Agent Deployment 126
Deploying the Linux/UNIX Client 127
Deploying the OS X Client 129
Uninstalling or Reinstalling Linux/UNIX 132
Uninstalling OS X 134
Cross-Platform Agent Components 134
Settings Management 134
Software Inventory 135
Hardware Inventory 136
Client Agent Commands 143
Troubleshooting with Log Files 143
Linux/UNIX Log Files 143
Verbose Logs 144
OS X Log Files 144
Summary 145

6   What's New in Operating System Deployment **147**

The Alphabet Soup of Prerequisites 148

    Operating System Version Support 149

    Boot Images 151

Windows Setup Support Change 155

Deployment Control 160

Deployment Monitoring 164

New Task Types 166

New Built-In Task Sequence Variables 175

UEFI Support 176

Virtual Hard Disks and Windows To Go 180

    Deploying to and Maintaining VHDs 180

    Deploying WTG Media 183

Other Improvements 185

    Offline Servicing 185

    Driver Package Export and Import 186

    Unknown Computer Cleanup 187

    Prestaged Media 188

    Content Prestaging 189

    Task Sequence Size Ceiling 190

Troubleshooting Hints and Tips 190

    Reviewing SMSTS.log 191

    Using SMSPXE.log 191

    SMSTSErrorDialogTimeout 192

    Power Scheme 193

    Pausing a Task Sequence 193

    Windows 8.1 Wireless Network Prompt 195

Summary 196

Part III   Journey to the Cloud

7   Using the Intune Connector **199**

Getting Started with the Intune Connector 199

Synchronizing AD with Microsoft Azure AD 200

    Creating a Windows Intune Instance and Azure
      AD Namespace 200

    Installing the Directory Synchronization Tool 204

MDM Prerequisites 209

    Managing Windows 8.1 Devices 210

    Managing Windows Phone 8.x Devices 212

    Managing iOS Devices 215

Installing the Windows Intune Subscription and Connector 220

Creating the Intune Subscription 220

Adding the Windows Intune Connector Site System Role 231

Confirming the Installation of the Subscription and
Connecter Role 232

Removing or Overriding an Existing Intune Subscription 236

Receiving Feature Updates Using the Extensions
for Windows Intune 238

Summary 241

8   Mobile Device Management in Configuration Manager 2012 R2 ....**243**

Understanding Mobile Device Management Challenges 244

Prerequisites of Mobile Device Management 246

Enrolling Mobile Devices 248

Enrolling Windows Phone 8 Devices 249

Enrolling Windows 8.1 Devices 251

Enrolling iOS Devices 252

Enrolling Android Devices 254

Inventorying Mobile Devices 254

Available Discovery and Inventory Data 255

Personal Versus Company-Owned Devices 259

Managing Mobile Device Settings 259

Configuration Items for Mobile Devices 260

Creating Custom Configuration Items for Mobile Devices 267

Remote Connection Profiles 267

Company Resource Access 271

Deploying Applications to Mobile Devices 281

Defining Application Information 282

Using the Company Portal 285

Retiring/Wiping Mobile Devices 288

Troubleshooting 290

Log Files on Site Server 291

Log File on iOS Devices 291

Log File on Windows Phone 8.x Devices 291

Log File on Android Devices 291

Troubleshooting Windows 8.1 OMA-DM Devices 293

Summary 293

Part IV   Appendixes

A   About Windows Intune **297**

Introduction to Windows Intune 297

    Intune Comes Into Focus 298

    Microsoft Strategic Direction Announcement 299

Mobile Device Management Features 300

    Device Management 301

    Device Inventory 301

    Policy Settings Management 303

    Application Distribution and the Windows Intune
      Company Portal 303

    Device Retirement and Remote Wipe 310

Windows Intune Licensing and Supported Architectures 311

    Unified Architecture 311

    Cloud-Only Architecture 312

The Windows Intune Connector and Subscription 314

B   Reference URLs **315**

General Resources 315

Microsoft's Configuration Manager Resources 322

Other Configuration Manager Resources 327

Blogs 331

Public Forums 332

Utilities 333

C   Available Online **335**

Setting SMSTSPreferredAdvertID 335

Creating an OfflineImageServicing Folder 335

Viewing the Current Drive Letter Set 336

Pausing a Task Sequence 336

Live Links 336

Index **337**

Foreword

Wow, that didn't take long. Less than two years after System Center 2012 Configuration Manager was released, the Enterprise Client Management team (formerly known as the Configuration Manager product group) released two new versions of the popular software. Service Pack (SP) 1 for Configuration Manager 2012 was released just nine months after the RTM version was released. The service pack added a number of new features to the Configuration Manager 2012 product, such as pull distribution points, the ability to expand a stand-alone primary site into a hierarchy, real-time client actions, support for non-Windows-based clients, as well as the first integration with the cloud-based Windows Intune service for managing mobile devices.

Only nine months after the release of System Center 2012 Configuration Manager SP 1, System Center 2012 R2 Configuration Manager was released. The primary update to the R2 version of Configuration Manager is the updated support for managing mobile devices when integrated with Windows Intune, but many additional features were added as well. In addition to the updated features for mobile device management, a great addition is role-based administration for reports.

As with most of our products, this product has undergone thorough testing—not only by the product group, but also by Microsoft IT, by numerous Technology Adoption Program (TAP) customers testing the beta release in their production environments, by our MVPs (a number of who are authors on this book), and by thousands of open beta customers testing in lab environments. So, we're very confident in the quality of Configuration Manager 2012 R2 and the features that it will provide in your own environments. Thanks to all of you who helped test the beta release and provided feedback to help improve the quality of this and future versions of Configuration Manager.

I want to offer a huge welcome to those of you who are just entering into the Configuration Manager world; it is a great product. If you are still using an earlier version of Configuration Manager, I urge you to give this new version a look. I think you'll find it a great update to what you already have in place today. It is easy to move from Configuration Manager 2007 to the latest release of Configuration Manager 2012. For those who are currently running Configuration Manager 2012, but not the R2 version, you will want to perform your upgrade as soon as you can, as great features await you!

I know all the authors and contributors on this book, and knowing their professionalism and knowledge, I am confident that you will find this book a great value to you in the process of your learning and experiencing System Center 2012 R2 Configuration Manager. The best of luck to you all, and again, thanks for your loyalty and trust in us.

Wally Mead, (former) Senior Program Manager
Enterprise Client Management Product Group
Microsoft Corporation
Now Principal Program Manager at Cireson

About the Authors

Kerrie Meyler, System Center MVP, is the lead author of numerous System Center books in the Unleashed series, including *System Center 2012 Configuration Manager Unleashed (2012)*, *System Center Configuration Manager 2007 Unleashed (2009)*, *System Center 2012 Operations Manager Unleashed (2013)*, *System Center 2012 Orchestrator Unleashed (2013)*, and *System Center 2012 Service Manager Unleashed (2014)*. She is an independent consultant with more than 17 years of Information Technology experience. Kerrie was responsible for evangelizing SMS while a Sr. Technology Specialist (TSP) at Microsoft. She was a member of the Management Insiders Group and has presented on System Center technologies at TechEd and MMS.

Jason Sandys, Enterprise and Client Management MVP, is a Technology Evangelist and Principal Consultant for Catapult Systems LLC, with just under 20 years of experience in a wide range of technologies, environments, and industries. He has extensive knowledge about implementing and supporting all things SMS and Configuration Manager beginning with SMS 2.0. He is a coauthor for *System Center Configuration Manager 2012 Unleashed (2012)*, a contributing author to *System Center Configuration Manager 2007 Unleashed (2009)*, and is a frequent presenter at Microsoft TechEd and MMS, as well as various other events and user groups nationwide. Jason blogs at blog.configmgrftw.com and is active in the online support community.

Greg Ramsey, Enterprise and Client Management MVP, is the Enterprise Tools Strategist at Dell, Inc. He has a B.S. in Computer Sciences and Engineering from Ohio State University. Greg coauthored *System Center Configuration Manager 2012 Unleashed (2012)*, *Microsoft System Center 2012 Configuration Manager: Administration Cookbook (Packt, 2012)*, and *System Center Configuration Manager 2007 Unleashed (2009)*. Greg is a cofounder of the Ohio SMS Users Group and the Central Texas Systems Management User Group.

About the Contributors

Dan Andersen, MCSE, MCTS, MCTIP, is a Senior Technology Specialist (TSP) for Windows Intune at Microsoft, where he has worked since 2001. He, along with his team, provides cloud-only and ConfigMgr-integrated Intune technical solutions for large-scale enterprise customers and partner technical development. Dan has held various technical subject matter expert roles at Microsoft and previously was a Management TSP where he helped to architect System Center solutions around configuration and operations management. He was a member of the Management Insiders Group and continues to be a regular speaker at Microsoft conferences and local user group meetings.

Panu Saukko, Enterprise Client Management MVP and MCT, is a consultant and trainer at ProTrainIT and is based in Finland. With more than 20 years of experience working with Microsoft technologies, Panu has been a MVP since 2003. Panu has worked with SMS and Configuration Manager beginning with SMS 1.2 and has created training courseware for multiple Microsoft products over the years. He frequently speaks at different seminars.

Kenneth van Surksum, MCT, is a trainer and System Center consultant at insight24, a company based in the Netherlands. With more than 10 years of experience, Kenneth has worked with SMS 1.2 and successive versions of the product and specializes in OS deployment. Kenneth was a contributing author to *System Center 2012 Configuration Manager Unleashed (2012)* and *System Center 2012 Service Manager Unleashed (2014)*, and coauthored *Mastering Windows 7 Deployment (Sybex, 2011)*. He blogs at http://www.vansurksum.com and is chief editor for several websites about virtualization and cloud computing, including http://www.virtualization.info and http://www.cloudcomputing.info.

Michael Wiles begin working with SMS 1.1 as a Microsoft support engineer in 1997 and was a Senior Premier Field Engineer (PFE) from 2005 to 2012. As a PFE, Michael worked with several large customers and the Configuration Manager Product Group through the TAP program to affect changes within the product. He now works for Dell, Inc., as a Configuration Manager Senior Advisor, leading the infrastructure team in Dell Services and servicing as an escalation point of any and all Configuration Manager-related issues within Dell.

Dedication

*To Wally, Microsoft's guiding force for Configuration Manager
to the community for so many years.*

Acknowledgments

Writing a book is an all-encompassing and time-consuming project, and this book certainly meets that description. Configuration Manager is a massive topic, and this book benefited from the input of many individuals. The authors and contributors would like to offer their sincere appreciation to all those who helped with *System Center 2012 R2 Configuration Manager Unleashed*. This includes John Joyner and Bob Longo of ClearPointe Technologies for dedicating lab resources, Wally Mead, and Steve Rachui.

We would also like to thank our spouses and significant others for their patience and understanding during the many hours spent on this book.

Thanks also go to the staff at Pearson; in particular, to Joan Murray and Neil Rowe.

We Want to Hear from You!

As the reader of this book, *you* are our most important critic and commentator. We value your opinion and want to know what we're doing right, what we could do better, what areas you'd like to see us publish in, and any other words of wisdom you're willing to pass our way.

We welcome your comments. You can email or write to let us know what you did or didn't like about this book—as well as what we can do to make our books better.

Please note that we cannot help you with technical problems related to the topic of this book.

When you write, please be sure to include this book's title and author as well as your name and email address. We will carefully review your comments and share them with the author and editors who worked on the book.

Email: consumer@samspublishing.com

Mail: Sams Publishing
         ATTN: Reader Feedback
         800 East 96th Street
         Indianapolis, IN 46240 USA

Reader Services

Visit our website and register this book at informit.com/register for convenient access to any updates, downloads, or errata that might be available for this book.

Introduction

As Wally Mead says in his Foreword, things have certainly moved quickly since Microsoft's 2012 release of System Center 2012 Configuration Manager! *System Center 2012 Configuration Manager Unleashed* (Sams, 2012) was completed shortly after Microsoft released Configuration Manager (ConfigMgr) 2012 to production; the company then released a service pack and R2 within a mere 18 months.

The fast and furious pace of releases to ConfigMgr 2012 has prompted the authors to write this supplement to bring you up to date on what has changed since its initial release and the publication of *System Center 2012 Configuration Manager Unleashed*. By definition of a *supplement*, this work does not cover material in the previous book; it delivers more than 300 pages of material discussing what has changed with Configuration Manager 2012 Service Pack 1 and R2.

Configuration Manager 2012 is most noteworthy in its orientation toward the user, not the device. Applications can now be distributed to users, empowering them to use the devices and applications they need, while maintaining the corporate compliance and control your organization requires. This layer of abstraction lets Configuration Manager assist in enabling your users to be productive with a unified infrastructure that delivers and manages user experiences across corporate and consumer devices. The timing of Microsoft's orientation toward the user is most appropriate, as the past few years have seen the need for Information Technology (IT) departments to become increasingly people centric. The explosion in mobile devices has led to many of the enhancements in ConfigMgr 2012 Service Pack 1 and R2, including its integration with Microsoft Intune. Yet, while mobile device management and Intune may be what first comes to mind when thinking about what's new, it's not to say that these are the only updates to Configuration Manager 2012. Support for cross-platform devices and enhancements to user and data profiles, application management, and OSD are also in Microsoft's bag of goodies, along with a number of performance enhancements, usability enhancements, and other updates covered throughout this book:

▶ The consumerization of IT and onset of people-centric IT means that the world is changing for system and ConfigMgr administrators—whether we like it or not. Chapter 1 introduces this new paradigm and Microsoft's mantra of *any user, any device, anywhere*. With the releases of Windows 8.1, Windows Server 2012 R2, Windows Intune, and System Center 2012 R2, Microsoft is helping IT enable users to be productive no matter where they are or what device they are using. Chapter 2 highlights the many enhancements in Service Pack 1 and R2.

▶ The next several chapters can be considered a deep dive into user and data profiles (Chapter 3), changes in application management (Chapter 4), on-premise management and cross-platform support (Chapter 5), and what's new in OSD (Chapter 6).

▶ Chapter 7 and Chapter 8 take you on Microsoft's journey to the cloud with Configuration Manager and Windows Intune, discussing the Intune connector and mobile device management (MDM) in ConfigMgr 2012 R2. Given the ongoing plethora of mobile devices and nonstop enhancements to Windows Intune, the authors plan to document updates to MDM in as timely a manner as possible by publishing content on the InformIT page for this book.

▶ Appendixes include a Windows Intune primer, a listing of web URLs discussing Configuration Manager, and add-on value through online content of scripts and live links in this book.

Disclaimers and Fine Print

As always, there are several disclaimers. The information provided is probably outdated the moment the book goes to print. A particular challenge when discussing Configuration Manager has been writing about mobile device management and Windows Intune, which seem to have updates faster than they can be written about.

In addition, the moment Microsoft considers code development on any product complete, they begin working on a service pack or future release. As the authors continue to work with the product, it is likely yet another one or two wrinkles will be discovered! The authors and contributors of *System Center 2012 R2 Configuration Manager Unleashed* have made every attempt to present information that is accurate and current as known at the time. Updates and corrections will be provided on the InformIT website. Look in particular for updates on InformIT regarding new functionality in MDM and Intune at http://www.informit.com/store/system-center-2012-r2-configuration-manager-unleashed-9780672337154.

Thank you for purchasing *System Center 2012 R2 Configuration Manager Unleashed*. The authors hope it is worth your while.

PART I

Overview

IN THIS PART

CHAPTER 1   People-Centric IT   5

CHAPTER 2   What's Changed Since Configuration
             Manager 2012 RTM   19

CHAPTER 1

People-Centric IT

IN THIS CHAPTER

▶ Microsoft's People-Centric IT Philosophy

▶ People-Centric IT and ConfigMgr 2012 R2 with Windows Intune

▶ People-Centric IT and Windows Server 2012 R2

▶ People-Centric IT and Microsoft Azure Active Directory

Attention Configuration Manager (ConfigMgr) administrators: *Your world is changing.* No longer can you expect users to accept the dictates of corporate Information Technology (IT) meekly. Many are familiar with environments where a user requests software on her computer, and IT obliges with standard processes to target that corporate workstation with the requested software. In a more advanced scenario, your users have the ability to visit an internal software portal for self-service application installation, greatly reducing IT overhead and eliminating the time lag for IT to install the software. This is actually described as the optimal implementation of the Infrastructure Optimization Model (http://www.microsoft.com/technet/infrastructure), where at the dynamic level IT achieves integration between users and data, desktops and servers, and the different departments and functions throughout the organization. Many companies dream of these highly managed environments, where all systems are in a managed state and owned by the company and where IT is a strategic asset aligned and managed according to business needs.

For years, you have understood that your computer is in fact a computer wholly owned by your organization. IT fully manages that system to ensure patch compliance, corporate software standards, and security compliance are met. Automated processes improved reliability, lowered costs, and increased service levels. The end user's experience was a secondary consideration, at best.

While security compliance and software standards are still paramount to a well-managed environment, the advent of bring your own device (BYOD) means that IT administrators must focus on people-centric management. This means doing your best to enable the business—enabling each user to do her job from any device, anywhere—which IT may or may not have total control over. This is a real paradigm shift.

Any user, any device, anywhere—This is Microsoft's mantra, and the goal of ConfigMgr administrators; and ConfigMgr 2012 R2 with Windows Intune integration is a big part of that enablement. With the advent of BYOD, users want to utilize their own devices and access corporate resources with those devices. This chapter helps explain the pieces of the Microsoft puzzle to enable users on any device, anywhere. It is important to state that traditional systems management is here to stay as well; but you can see the primary focus of Microsoft's release of 2012 R2 products (System Center 2012 R2, the latest release of Intune, Windows Server 2012 R2, and Windows 8.1) is to enable the end user and support the consumerization of IT.

Microsoft's People-Centric IT Philosophy

Microsoft believes that "People centric IT enables each person you support to work from virtually anywhere on the device of their choice and gives you a consistent way to manage and protect it all" (see http://www.microsoft.com/en-us/server-cloud/cloud-os/pcit.aspx#fbid=5bZ1uqqrqIt). The solutions from Microsoft for people-centric IT allow you (the administrator) to

▶ Keep end users productive

▶ Help with data protection and compliance

▶ Unify user and device management

NOTE: UNDERSTANDING THE CONSUMERIZATION OF IT AND PEOPLE-CENTRIC IT

Historically, IT has been responsible for defining the business standard for corporate notebooks and desktops. There is a new trend today, where information workers determine those devices, applications, and services to use to accomplish their jobs. This is referred to as the *consumerization of IT*. Smartphones and slates/tablets are now powerful enough to run applications that traditionally were run on notebooks and desktops. When applications aren't enabled for these modern devices, remote connectivity through Remote Desktop Services (RDS) or Virtual Desktop Infrastructure (VDI) can fill the gap, reducing the need for corporate-owned (and corporate-managed) assets.

Users are most productive when they can use their device of choice, and Microsoft believes the consumerization of IT should be embraced and implemented with an efficient people-centric IT administration, enabled with the latest wave of releases of Microsoft products.

As you explore this new paradigm, notice the focus has changed some from "protect and manage the device" to "protect the data." The device is still important, and you want to protect it when you can, but with the rise in BYOD and zero-trust networks, the device is less important. Protecting data is the core focus, and what is ultimately required for your business.

Millennials, Generation Y, *<insert other "cool" terms here>*—you've heard them all. The fact is that end users are getting smarter and smarter in relation to their ability to use computers. These "kids" were raised with a computer in their hand that far exceeds the computational power of the computers that put a man on the moon (see http://www. computerweekly.com/feature/Apollo-11-The-computers-that-put-man-on-the-moon and http://downloadsquad.switched.com/2009/07/20/how-powerful-was-the-apollo-11-computer/). As children become adults using smartphones, tablets, notebooks, and more, they are well versed in using their devices and are able to use them anywhere. These new users (as well as some of the old-timers) can find significant productivity improvements and satisfaction in the ability to leverage any device from anywhere to get the job done. For Microsoft not to miss the bus on BYOD, the company had to do an about-face on how it defined corporate computing and move from device-centric to people-centric IT. The challenges presented were as follows (see Figure 1.1):

- ▶ Users expect to be able to work in any location with access to all their work resources.

- ▶ The continuous proliferation of devices erodes the standards-based approach of corporate IT.

- ▶ Deploying and managing applications across multiple platforms is difficult.

- ▶ Users need to be productive while IT continues to maintain compliance and reduce risk.

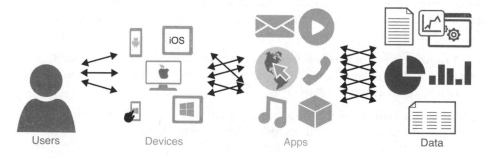

FIGURE 1.1   Challenges for today's IT.

The next sections describe Microsoft's vision of how to enable people-centric IT with Microsoft solutions.

Enabling Users for People-Centric IT

IT must enable users by allowing them to work on the devices of their choice and provide consistent access to corporate resources. Microsoft solutions provide the following:

▶ **Simplified registration and enrollment for BYOD:** Allowing users to easily register their devices to access corporate resources and enroll in Windows Intune to manage their devices and to install corporate applications through a consistent company portal.

▶ **Consistent access to company resources across devices:** Allowing users to use any device to access corporate resources—"Any user, any device, anywhere."

▶ **Support for modern work styles with Microsoft VDI:** Enabling users to leverage VDI to access a corporate desktop, applications, and data from their personal devices, from both internal and external locations, using an infrastructure running within the corporate data center.

▶ **Automatic connection to internal resources when needed:** Leveraging single sign-on and virtual private network (VPN) on-demand functionality to easily access corporate resources.

▶ **Cross-platform access to remote desktops and applications:** Microsoft now supports a Remote Desktop client application for Windows, Windows RT, iOS, OS X, and Android. This application (available through the app store for each device) allows access to a Remote Desktop Services (RDS) infrastructure, enabling access to personal or pooled/temporary virtual machines (VMs) and remote applications in the data center.

Unifying Your Environment for People-Centric IT

IT must unify the environment, enabling support and management of traditional on-premise systems as well as new devices from the cloud. The goal is to enable any user on any device, using corporate credentials, while allowing the IT administrator the ability to manage the devices easily through a single management console. Microsoft solutions provide the following:

▶ **Unified management of on-premise and cloud-based mobile devices:** Enabling IT administrators to extend ConfigMgr to integrate with Windows Intune, to enable cloud management of mobile devices.

▶ **Simplified, user-centric application management across devices:** Enabling the IT administrator to manage applications for all devices using a single console. When integrating ConfigMgr with Windows Intune, the administrator uses the ConfigMgr console to manage all devices, regardless of that device being a cloud device (managed by Windows Intune) or traditional device (managed by ConfigMgr).

▶ **Comprehensive settings management across platforms, including certificates, VPNs, and wireless network profiles:** Using the ConfigMgr console to apply policies to all devices and operating systems to meet corporate compliance, as well as provision certificates, VPNs, and Wi-Fi profiles.

Protecting Your Data in a People-Centric IT World

In moving from device-centric to people-centric IT, the focus changes slightly from protecting the device to protecting the data. Both are important, but in a BYOD scenario, IT is unable to "lock down" a personal device in the same manner it locked down traditional personal computers in the past. IT must provide flexible user models while protecting corporate resources from unauthorized access. Microsoft's solutions provide the following:

▶ **The ability to protect corporate information by selectively wiping apps and data:** IT can wipe corporate data and/or render it useless on the device (by revocation of a user/device certificate) when a device is lost, stolen, or retired.

▶ **Policy-based access control to corporate applications and data:** IT can set policy-based access control for compliance and data protection.

▶ **A common identity for accessing resources on-premises and in the cloud:** IT can better protect corporate data and mitigate risk by restricting access to corporate resources based on user, device, and location.

▶ **Identification of compromised mobile devices:** IT can leverage jailbreak and root detection, and then take appropriate action, such as selectively wiping the device.

People-Centric IT and ConfigMgr 2012 R2 with Windows Intune

ConfigMgr (previously known as Systems Management Server or SMS prior to 2007) has been the clear leader in systems management for more than a decade (see Gartner Group's positioning of Configuration Manager in their magic quadrant at http://www. itbl0b.com/2012/06/gartner-says-microsoft-is-leader-of.html#.U2_9-HkU_Gh and http://www2.managedplanet.com/downloads/Gartner%20Client%20Management%20 Magic%20Quadrant%202013.pdf for the article it references). With the release of ConfigMgr 2012, it is obvious that Microsoft is shifting focus to a more user-centric application deployment model. The introduction of "applications" in Configuration Manager 2012, as well as the Application Catalog, paved the way for things to come in ConfigMgr 2012 R2, an example being the company portal.

NOTE: DEFINITION OF A CONFIGMGR APPLICATION

Application is a specific type of object in ConfigMgr 2012. An application contains one or more *deployment types*, which are used to intelligently install software based on *requirement rules*, such as operating system (for example, iOS, Windows, Android), Active Directory organizational unit, and so on.

The greatest leap forward related to people-centric IT for Microsoft systems management occurred with the release of ConfigMgr 2012 SP 1. With SP 1, you can connect your on-premise ConfigMgr infrastructure to a cloud-based Windows Intune, and manage everything in Intune from your ConfigMgr console. Devices accessing the cloud are managed from the cloud using Intune, but once Intune is connected to ConfigMgr, all administration occurs from the ConfigMgr console.

The next sections describe how ConfigMgr 2012 R2 and Windows Intune enable people-centric IT.

Enabling Users with ConfigMgr 2012 R2 and Windows Intune

The company portal (available through both ConfigMgr 2012 R2 and Windows Intune) enables users to install corporate applications, as well as selectively wipe personal devices. ConfigMgr 2012 R2 and Windows Intune can also configure the corporate VPN on devices, as well as configure a corporate application to auto-trigger a VPN connection when launched.

Simplifying BYOD Registration and Enrollment with ConfigMgr 2012 R2 and Windows Intune

Users, once authorized, can easily enroll personal devices by downloading the Intune company portal application from the respective app store (Apple, Android, and Microsoft), and log in to the portal using their company domain credentials. Once logged in to the portal, users can perform the following actions:

▶ Install corporate-approved applications, including applications linked to the device app store, as well as internal line-of-business applications using the "sideloading" feature of the device. One great feature of the company portals is that the user only views software that is applicable to the device, as defined by the creator of the application in the ConfigMgr console.

▶ Selectively wipe corporate data from other personal devices owned by that user. This allows a user to deprovision a personal device, in the event the device is lost, stolen, or replaced with a new personal device.

▶ View information for how to contact IT via phone, email, or website.

Windows 8.x personal devices can also install the Intune company portal from the Microsoft app store and self-enroll as personal devices for your organization. In addition, Windows 8.x is supported as a full client in both Windows Intune (for stand-alone Intune management) and ConfigMgr. You should only install the Intune company portal on Windows 8.x if you plan to manage these devices as lightweight devices, because the user is limited to the features described in this section. For full management, install either the ConfigMgr client or Windows Intune client. Figure 1.2 shows the company portal from the Windows Start screen, at the bottom left of the screen.

Figure 1.3 shows the user interface for the Windows 8.x company portal. The company portal application provides a software portal that is very similar to the Windows Store.

FIGURE 1.2   The Windows 8.x Start screen.

FIGURE 1.3   The company portal modern application.

Enabling Consistent Access to Corporate Resources with ConfigMgr 2012 R2 and Windows Intune

Microsoft has also released a company portal for Windows 8.x for use with traditional clients. This allows an IT administrator to fully manage the Windows system, and provides the user a similar interface to the Intune company portals for installing software and managing personal devices. The company portal for ConfigMgr is a significant improvement over the Application Catalog originally released with ConfigMgr 2012, in that it presents available software to the user that is very similar to the Microsoft Store, and only displays software that can be installed on the device.

Automating How Users Connect to Internal Resources with ConfigMgr 2012 R2 and Windows Intune

ConfigMgr and Windows Intune can deploy policies and configuration information for VPN and Wi-Fi profiles, simplifying the user experience when connecting to corporate resources. In addition to configuring these settings, the administrator can configure specific applications to autotrigger VPN when launched on a device (Windows 8.1 and later). Figure 1.4 shows the basic configuration for configuring a VPN connection from ConfigMgr 2012 R2.

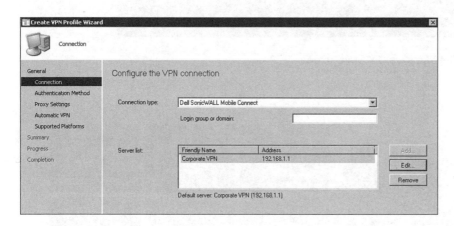

FIGURE 1.4   Creating a VPN connection profile with ConfigMgr 2012 R2.

Figure 1.5 shows how to configure an application to launch the VPN when the application is launched.

Remote connection profiles are also a new feature in ConfigMgr 2012 R2 and Windows Intune. Remote connection profiles allow your users to connect remotely to work computers from personal computers over the Internet by using the Intune company portal or by using Remote Desktop over a VPN connection. By deploying these settings, you give end users more flexibility with regard to how they connect to corporate resources.

Unifying Your Environment with ConfigMgr 2012 R2 and Windows Intune

Using ConfigMgr 2012 R2, administrators can consistently manage devices from a single console, regardless if the device is corporate-owned or a personal device. The following sections discuss how.

FIGURE 1.5   Using Auto-Trigger VPN to enable an automatic VPN connection for a modern application.

Targeting of Applications with ConfigMgr 2012 R2 and Windows Intune

With the integration of ConfigMgr and Intune, the ConfigMgr administrator can now target any user, on any device, anywhere, using a single console. The method of deploying software with ConfigMgr to these devices is smarter, allowing the administrator to deploy a single application that supports multiple types of devices.

Inventorying Mobile, Physical, and Virtual Assets with ConfigMgr 2012 R2 and Windows Intune

Whether the device is personal or corporate, workstation, or server, as long as it has access to corporate apps, the administrator has inventory in a single store (the ConfigMgr database). Personal devices are also classified properly in the database to allow for simplified asset tracking.

Enabling and Enforcing Device Settings with ConfigMgr 2012 R2 and Windows Intune

The ConfigMgr administrator can configure settings across device platforms, such as security and compliance settings (encryption and password/PIN certificates), as well as applications.

Integrating Active Directory with ConfigMgr 2012 R2 and Windows Intune

ConfigMgr can leverage Active Directory to target users and user groups with available applications. Because the enrollment of devices through the Intune company portal can use Active Directory information, ConfigMgr can target these users with software using Active Directory, regardless of whether the device is on-premise or in the cloud.

Unifying your environment allows users to have a common identity for accessing applications, regardless of device.

Protecting Your Data with ConfigMgr 2012 R2 and Windows Intune

Protecting your data is core to a successful BYOD implementation. IT must be able to protect data and maintain regulatory compliance. ConfigMgr 2012 R2 and Windows Intune protect your data by enabling the user (or administrator) to selectively wipe a device to protect corporate applications and data. See Chapter 8, "Mobile Device Management in Configuration Manager 2012 R2," for details.

Mobile devices are everywhere, and they are replaced (and lost) more often than traditional corporate notebooks. Allowing the user as well as the administrator the ability to wipe corporate data remotely is paramount to any BYOD solution.

People-Centric IT and Windows Server 2012 R2

Windows Server 2012 R2 provides many features that enable people-centric IT. Most of these features do not require a domain functional level for Server 2012 R2, but just 2012 R2 servers available to support the required roles.

Enabling Users with Windows Server 2012 R2

Windows Server 2012 R2 helps enable individuals to use their chosen devices at work, and provides consistent access to corporate resources. Workplace Join, the Web Application Proxy, and Active Directory Federation Services (ADFS) all work together to enable users to enroll and securely access corporate data easily.

Simplifying BYOD Registration and Enrollment with Windows Server 2012 R2

Windows Server 2012 R2 enables users to register their devices, creating a record in Active Directory that makes the device "known" to IT. This allows IT to use the device as part of the authentication and authorization policies. The following features help make this happen:

► **Workplace Join:** A new component of ADFS, Workplace Join is one of the new features of Windows Server 2012 R2. Workplace Join allows users to join devices to your organization that would not normally be joined to the domain, such as personal laptops, tablets, and smartphones. For additional information on Workplace Join, see http://technet.microsoft.com/en-us/library/dn280945.aspx.

► **Web Application Proxy:** This is a new Remote Access Role service in Windows Server 2012 R2, which allows users to access data and web applications from any device from outside the corporate network. Once enabled, the IT administrator can configure one or more applications to require a device be registered (through Workplace Join) before the user can gain access to published corporate applications or data from the internet on their personal device. Users access the data and applications through the new Web Application Proxy, using their trusted workplace-joined personal device. You can find additional information at http://technet.microsoft.com/en-us/library/dn280942.aspx.

Enabling Consistent Access to Corporate Resources with Windows Server 2012 R2

Enabling users to securely access their data from anywhere on any trusted device allows them to be more productive.

Work folders allow users to synchronize files between a personal sync share on their device with a corporate file server. IT can also integrate the share with Dynamic Access Control for automated classification and protection of documents based on content.

The Web Application Proxy and Workplace Join allow access, and enable IT to revoke rights on a personal device simply by un-enrolling it.

Delivering Windows Desktops and Applications with Microsoft Virtual Desktop Infrastructure with Windows Server 2012 R2

IT needs to provide a consistent, managed enterprise desktop to employees. VDI enables users to access corporate applications and desktops from their personal or corporate devices, from both internal and external locations:

► **Session shadowing:** This allows IT to shadow a user in a VDI session, enabling the service desk to view and remotely control a user's session.

► **Online disk deduplication:** In addition to SMB 3 and storage spaces, which are supported with Windows Server 2012, online disk deduplication is supported in Windows Server 2012 R2, which reduces the amount of space on disk that is consumed by VMs.

► **Storage tiering:** Storage tiering support enables IT to leverage solid state and spinning disks to optimize data access while reducing storage cost.

► **Remote Desktop Protocol (RDP):** RDP is improved in Windows Server 2012 R2, which significantly improves reconnection times and improves the performance of remote desktops over wide-area network (WAN) connections.

► **Remote applications (RemoteApp):** RemoteApp has been enhanced by displaying the correct thumbnail on the taskbar instead of a generic icon. The user experience with RemoteApp is nearly identical to a local application. With remote applications, also known as published apps, users can launch a single application instead of an entire virtual desktop.

► **Dynamic resolution change:** This enables full-screen remote desktop sessions to automatically resize when the endpoint resolution changes. For example, when undocking a notebook, the resolution may need to change, and now automatically resizes with Windows Server 2012 R2.

► **Remote desktop app support for BYO devices:** Windows Server 2012 R2 introduces a remote desktop application for Windows versions 8.x and RT, as well as iOS, OS X, and Android. (All apps are available from their respective app store.) This app can be used to launch personal or pooled VMs, session-based desktops, and RemoteApp programs.

Automating How Users Connect to Internal Resources with Windows Server 2012 R2

DirectAccess has been available for several years, and provides an "always on" connection for domain-joined Windows clients. The Remote Access role enables VPN connections from user devices to corporate resources.

The Web Application Proxy, when integrated with ADFS, allows IT to publish corporate resources to external users and trusted devices, even if the device is a personal device.

Auto-Trigger VPN is a new feature in Windows 8.1 that allows applications to trigger a defined VPN automatically on the user's behalf as an application is launched.

Unifying Your Environment with Windows Server 2012 R2

Windows Server 2012 R2 helps unify your environment by enabling single sign-on, enabling a common identity for accessing resources on-premise and in the cloud. Life was simpler for administrators when all devices were corporate owned and managed with enforced encryption, a standard antivirus client, and intrusion protection. As IT moves to a people-centric model, security becomes more complex. Proper access is managed best using a common identity that can access resources on-premise, in the cloud, and outside of the corporate network. Windows Server Active Directory in Windows Server 2012 R2 enables Workplace Join, which can allow users to join personal devices to the corporate directory, so that they are trusted, and allow the user to authenticate to the domain through the personal device. Windows Server Active Directory also integrates with Microsoft Azure Active Directory, to provide management and access control capabilities for cloud-based applications.

Protecting Your Data with Windows Server 2012 R2

In this people-centric IT world, administrators must provide flexible connectivity while preventing unauthorized access of corporate resources. IT must be able to secure, classify, and protect data based on the content it contains, while at the same time enabling users to access the data they need from any device, anywhere.

In addition to protecting your data, IT must also be able to audit against internal and regulatory requirements. Windows Server 2012 R2 can provide IT the control that helps them protect information and remain compliant, as well as enable users to get their work done:

- ▶ **Web Application Proxy:** This enables IT to publish resources selectively to users based on user, device, location, and application.

- ▶ **Active Directory Rights Management Services (RMS):** These services can help IT safeguard Microsoft Office documents and Exchange email by identifying the rights that a user has to the file, and preventing actions outside of those rights.

- ▶ **Dynamic Access Control:** This enables IT to encrypt documents automatically with Rights Management, based on defined access and classification policies. In addition, from an auditing perspective, Dynamic Access Control can audit and generate reports that detail which users have accessed classified information.

- ▶ **Work folders:** Work folders allow users to synchronize files in the data center with their devices, and IT can apply Dynamic Access Control policies to this data. Work folders could be published directly through a reverse proxy, or integrated with ADFS and published using the Web Application Proxy for conditional access policy enforcement.

People-Centric IT and Microsoft Azure Active Directory

Microsoft Azure Active Directory (Azure AD) is a cloud-based solution that enables enterprise-level identity and access management for the cloud. It provides directory services, advanced identity governance, and security and application access management. Azure AD enables people-centric IT by providing the following services:

▶ **Managing users and access to cloud services:** Uses the Microsoft Azure management portal to manage users' access centrally to Microsoft Azure and other online services such as Office 365.

▶ **Extending on-premise Active Directory to the cloud:** Allows users to authenticate with one set of corporate credentials. DirSync can be used to synchronize user attributes from the corporate domain to Azure AD.

▶ **Providing single sign-on across cloud applications:** Allows you to deliver a seamless, single sign-on experience for all Microsoft online services, as well as access to corporate resources.

▶ **Enabling multi-factor authentication for enhanced security:** Mobile applications, phone calls, and text messages can be used to allow a simple sign-on experience, while providing strong security procedures.

▶ **Offering authentication and access management solution for developers:** Enables developers to integrate identity management easily in their applications.

A new service, Microsoft Azure Active Directory Premium (Azure AD Premium), offers the following additional features:

▶ **User self-service password reset:** Self-service password reset for cloud applications.

▶ **Group-based application access:** Group-based provisioning and access management to software-as-a-service (SaaS) applications.

▶ **Company branding:** The Access Panel page can be branded with company logos and color schemes to improve the end-user experience.

▶ **Security reports:** Reports that display sign-in activity, anomalies, and potential threat areas.

Microsoft Azure Active Directory helps unify your environment by providing identity management and accessing control capabilities for cloud-based applications, by using the following features:

▶ IT can use cloud-based identity as the central authentication endpoint for all users and devices outside of the corporate environment, as well as for cloud and hybrid applications.

▶ IT can use federated connections from on-premise Active Directory to Microsoft Azure Active Directory, enabling IT to extend an organization's Active Directory easily into the cloud.

Summary

Microsoft has done a great job of enabling people-centric IT with the releases of Windows 8.1, Windows Server 2012 R2, Windows Intune, and System Center 2012 R2. Microsoft has enabled IT to enable the user, allowing access through personal devices to corporate applications and data, to utilize a scenario that allows modern information workers to be productive no matter where they are, or what device they are using.

In addition to allowing users to choose which devices to use, IT must ensure the following:

▶ Devices can be easily integrated into the corporate infrastructure.

▶ As long as devices are used for work, they must be configured to remain compliant with corporate access and security policies.

▶ IT must enable users to access applications and data consistently.

▶ Corporate applications must be protected and accessed only by compliant devices.

▶ IT must be able to remove corporate data and applications from devices when they are lost, stolen, or replaced.

The consumerization of IT has arrived. Now knowing the pieces of the puzzle, administrators must help define the way forward for people-centric IT. Administrators need to push forward to enable users to use any device, anywhere. Go forth and do good IT.

CHAPTER 2

What's Changed Since Configuration Manager 2012 RTM

IN THIS CHAPTER

▶ Administration Changes

▶ Assets and Compliance

▶ Software Library

▶ Monitoring Changes

▶ Other Improvements

In reviewing all the updates to System Center 2012 Configuration Manager (ConfigMgr) since its original November 2012 release, it appears that the ConfigMgr product team has been quite busy. While many community blogs discuss the updates to ConfigMgr that focus on integration with Intune, you can find more than enough new features for ConfigMgr itself.

This chapter highlights changes to ConfigMgr 2012 that are included with Service Pack (SP) 1 as well as R2. Some of these features are discussed further in other chapters of this book, while a significant number of smaller features are covered briefly in this chapter. The chapter first covers specific features that are new or improved, following their order in the ConfigMgr admin console. It then discusses additional items that are notable improvements but don't fit directly into a node in the console.

Administration Changes

Many features have been updated in the Administration node that can help make your job easier. Integration with Windows Intune is the most marketed administration feature, but even those of you not headed to the cloud anytime soon can also find some golden nuggets in the updated features.

Configuring Database Replication

As stressed in *System Center 2012 Configuration Manager Unleashed* (Sams, 2012), and by every Enterprise Client Management (ECM) MVP on the planet, you should reduce complexity of your infrastructure by choosing to install a central administration site (CAS) *only when absolutely necessary*. (See the Note in this chapter titled "Only Install a CAS When Absolutely Needed.") A CAS is a powerful role and is necessary in some scenarios, but due to the type of SQL replication used by ConfigMgr (SQL Service Broker—see http://social.technet.microsoft.com/wiki/contents/articles/6598.sql-server-service-broker-at-a-glance.aspx) between the CAS and primary sites, there are scenarios where having an advanced understanding of SQL replication would be greatly beneficial before implementing a CAS. Infrastructures with secondary sites also use database replication. (ConfigMgr 2012 secondary sites require a database and install SQL Express during initial installation, unless you perform a custom install configured to an existing instance of SQL Server.) So, unless you have a stand-alone primary site with no secondary sites, the next sections provide some new tips on features to improve SQL replication between sites.

Configure Replication for the SQL Server Database at a Site

With SP 1, you can now modify SQL Server replication configuration. Configure database properties from **Administration -> Site Configuration -> Servers and Site System Roles**, and select the server that contains the site database server role. Select **Properties** from the ribbon bar and review the settings, shown in Figure 2.1.

FIGURE 2.1   Site database server properties.

Alternatively, you could access the database properties from the Monitoring or Hierarchy node, then select Database Replication, and choose Parent Database Properties or Child Database Properties, and choose the Database tab. The properties are identical, regardless of how you access the Properties page. Verify the following options:

▶ **SQL Server Service Broker port:** This is the port used by SQL Service Broker replication. You can confirm the port configured in SQL Server by running the following SQL query from the site database:

```
SELECT name, protocol_desc, port, state_desc FROM sys.tcp_endpoints
   WHERE type_desc = 'SERVICE_BROKER'
```

▶ **Data compression:** Enable this check box so that ConfigMgr compresses SQL replication data that is being transferred between sites. This setting is especially helpful when sending initialization data between sites.

▶ **Data retention:** The default is 5 days, but you can specify a period of 1 to 14 days. Think of this setting as a maximum number of days to be able to send a delta of information, instead of a complete reinitialization. Also realize that the larger the number of days retention, the larger your database is by retaining the changes. Information on backup and recovery scenarios is at http://technet.microsoft.com/en-us/library/gg712697.aspx.

Schedule the Transfer of Site Data Across Replication Links

This setting applies to communications between primary sites and the CAS. (Secondary sites still use file-based replication to compress and send data to the primary site for processing data into the database.) You can access the database transfer scheduling properties from the Monitoring or Hierarchy node, then select Database Replication, choose Parent Database Properties or Child Database Properties, and choose the Database tab. The properties are identical, regardless of how you access the Properties page. Figure 2.2 shows the Schedule tab.

This figure provides an example of modifying the default schedule and only allowing replication of hardware inventory, software inventory, and software metering during off-business hours, while still allowing status messages to replicate at all times. This allows you to reduce replication traffic during the business day. Because collections are evaluated at primary sites, collections that depend on inventory or metering are not affected and process as normal. Note that delaying replication of this information affects what you see in queries and reports from the CAS; reports from the primary site would show the data immediately, whereas information on the CAS is constrained by replication schedules.

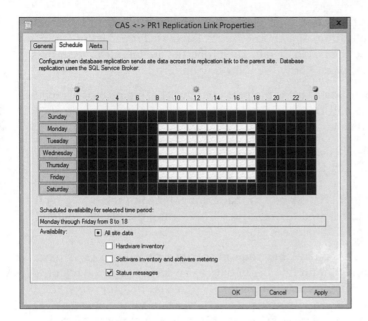

FIGURE 2.2   Replication link scheduling properties.

Support for Distributed Views

As mentioned in the previous section, because collections are evaluated at primary sites, it is not absolutely necessary to have the most up-to-date inventory information on the CAS. In fact, you can leverage distributed views and never send that data to the CAS. You can use distributed views to enable the CAS to directly access the data from the database of the primary site, instead of the primary site sending inventory and status message information to the CAS. Distributed views enable you to

▶ Reduce the CPU load on the CAS and primary sites for processing database changes (reduces the amount of data required for replication).

▶ Reduce amount of site data transferred from a primary site to CAS.

▶ Improve SQL Server performance on CAS (because there's less site replication data).

▶ Reduce disk space used by database at CAS. Hardware inventory, software inventory, metering, and status message information is a significant amount of data in the CAS database.

Figure 2.3 shows the options available for enabling distributed views. Notice that for each type of data configured for distributed views, that data is no longer available at the CAS.

Note the additional warnings shown in Figure 2.4, because these may prevent you from using distributed views.

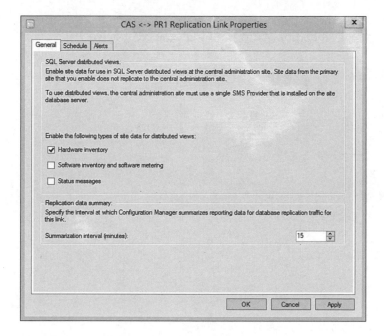

FIGURE 2.3   Configuring distributed views.

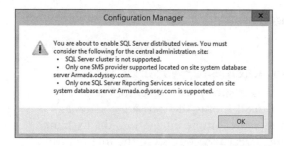

FIGURE 2.4   Warning when configuring distributed views.

Configure the Interval for Replication Data Summary

Figure 2.3 also shows where to configure the interval for replication data summary. This setting is used to modify the frequency of summarization of network traffic and affects the information you view in reports related to database replication. Leave the default of 15 minutes, or choose another value from 5 to 60.

Manage Replication Alerts

You can customize alerting for replication issues. If for example you are aware of inconsistent wide-area network (WAN) links in your environment that may cause replication to temporarily fail, you could modify the settings shown in Figure 2.5 to extend (or reduce) the number of retries before a replication link status is set to degraded or failed.

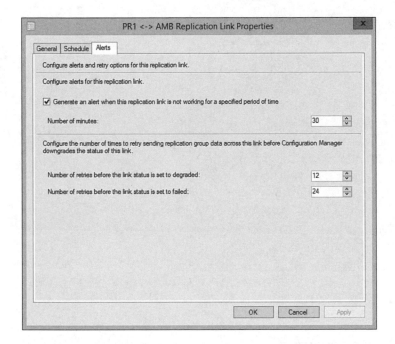

FIGURE 2.5   Database replication alerts configuration.

Configuring Internet Proxy Server on Each Site System

You can configure an Internet proxy server on each site system server for use by all site system roles installed on that server. Prior to SP 1, only the software updates and asset intelligence features accessed the Internet. Now, Intune integration, the Exchange server connector, and cloud distribution points (DPs) also connect to the Internet from ConfigMgr. Figure 2.6 shows that you can configure the Internet proxy for a site server. For additional information, see http://technet.microsoft.com/en-us/library/gg712282. aspx#BKMK_PlanforProxyServers.

Configure the proxy from **Administration -> Site Configuration -> Servers and Site System Roles,** then select the desired server, choose the **Site System** role in the Details pane, and select **Properties** from the ribbon bar.

NOTE: ONLY ONE PROXY CONFIGURATION PER SITE SERVER

The proxy server configuration is shared by all site roles on the site server. If you require different site roles to connect through different proxies, you must install the site system roles on different site servers.

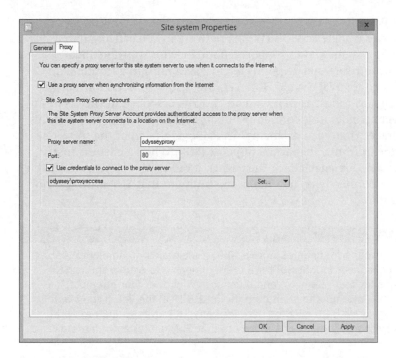

FIGURE 2.6   Configuring a site system proxy.

Windows Intune Integration and Extensions for Windows Intune

Device management moves at a faster pace than traditional client management. This is one of the main reasons that devices are managed through the cloud from Windows Intune. In addition to integrating Intune with ConfigMgr 2012, a new feature in R2 allows your ConfigMgr/Intune integration to take advantage of these features faster than you would normally receive traditional updates (or hot fixes) for ConfigMgr. Microsoft's Extensions for Windows Intune allows you to integrate new mobile device management capabilities into the Configuration Manager console, without the need for a ConfigMgr service pack, hot fix, or major release. For example, email profiles allow you to provision devices with settings to connect to corporate email. Chapter 7, "Using the Intune Connector," provides additional information about Extensions for Windows Intune.

Software Update Points

Many old-timers may recall a time when you installed the Software Update Services feature pack in Systems Management Server (SMS) 2.0. Software updates are now as core to the product as a steering wheel is to a car; there's no sense in having one without the other. The latest release of ConfigMgr takes what has been core to the product since SMS 2003 and improves its scalability and flexibility. You can find additional information about software update improvements at http://blogs.technet.com/b/configmgrteam/archive/2013/03/27/software-update-points-in-cm2012sp1.aspx.

Multiple Software Update Points

Prior to SP 1, Windows Server Update Services (WSUS) network load balancing (NLB) was required to support 100,000 systems and to support redundancy for software updates. Now, you can add multiple software update points (eight maximum) to a ConfigMgr primary site without the need for WSUS NLB. However, the failover process for multiple software update points is not as robust as that with an NLB. As described in the TechNet documentation (http://technet.microsoft.com/en-us/library/gg712696.aspx), think of this feature more as fault tolerance than load balancing. The failover design of the software update point (SUP) is different from a management point (MP). When a client is first installed (and software updates are enabled for the client), it randomly selects an available SUP, and after it establishes connectivity, maintains an affinity to that SUP until it is no longer able to connect to it.

> **NOTE: SUP AFFINITY**
>
> Once a client successfully scans for updates from a SUP, it maintains an affinity to that SUP until it can no longer connect to that SUP. If a client is unable to scan from its SUP, it retries every 30 minutes for four attempts, and if unsuccessful after four attempts, waits two minutes, and then attempts to scan from the next SUP in the list. If the client fails to scan four times again (with 30 minutes between retry), it moves to the next SUP. Once a client successfully scans, it maintains affinity to that SUP until it encounters a scan failure.

If this "fault-tolerant" failover does not meet the requirements for your environment, you can still use a SUP NLB (that uses a WSUS NLB). The ability to create the NLB no longer exists in the ConfigMgr admin console; use the Set-CMSoftwareUpdatePoint PowerShell cmdlet (documentation available at http://technet.microsoft.com/library/jj821938.aspx) to enable this feature. PowerShell support is now included with ConfigMgr; see the "PowerShell Support" section in this chapter for further information.

> **TIP: ADDITIONAL SUPS AT THE PRIMARY SITE SYNCHRONIZE WITH THE DEFAULT SOFTWARE UPDATE POINT**
>
> Only one SUP (known as the default SUP) from a primary site synchronizes with its parent, or with WSUS (if a stand-alone primary site). Additional SUPs at a primary site synchronize with the default SUP for the primary site.

Specify an Internal WSUS Server as the Synchronization Source

Prior to SP 1, the SUP on your CAS or stand-alone primary was required to synchronize with Microsoft's WSUS infrastructure on the Internet. This requirement proved to be a roadblock for some organizations. To alleviate this issue, you can now specify an internal WSUS server as the synchronization point for your top-level WSUS server (and SUP) in ConfigMgr.

Software Update Point Support in an Untrusted Forest

You can now create one or more SUPs at a site to support clients in an untrusted forest. To install a SUP in an untrusted forest, you must install and configure a WSUS server in that forest. You can then configure the SUP(s) in the untrusted forest to synchronize with the WSUS server in the same forest. The TechNet documentation at http://technet. microsoft.com/en-us/library/gg712696.aspx#BKMK_SUP_CrossForest provides additional information.

Certificate Profiles

Certificate profiles enable provisioning of authentication certificates for managed devices to enable users to access company resources from bring your own device (BYOD) systems. You can create and deploy a certificate profile to enable a user to initiate virtual private networking (VPN) and wireless connections. This new feature can provision and configure VPN and Wi-Fi certificates on Windows 8.1, Windows RT 8.1, iOS, and Android. You can also deploy trusted root certificate authority (CA) and intermediate certificates to configure a chain of trust on devices. You can find certificate profile documentation at http://technet.microsoft.com/en-us/library/dn248971.aspx.

Client Settings

You want to familiarize yourself with several new client settings. Some are introduced because of new features, whereas others have been created to adjust defaults that previously could not be modified:

▶ **PowerShell Execution Policy:** There is a new Computer Agent client setting that sets the default PowerShell execution policy to `AllSigned`, which means that by default ConfigMgr only runs scripts that are signed by a trusted publisher, regardless of the current Windows PowerShell configuration on the client computer. You can change this default setting, but a best practice would be to get your scripts signed.

▶ **Disable deadline randomization:** This is also a Computer Agent client setting that prevents deadline randomization. In the original release of ConfigMgr 2012, deadline randomization was enabled by default (and not configurable), to help reduce the risk of resource spikes in virtual machine (VM) farms. If you find you are targeting a large number of VMs in the same farm at the same time, consider enabling randomization.

▶ **Metered Internet Connections:** Use this setting to manage how Windows 8 systems transfer data over metered connections, as discussed in the "Metered Connections" section of this chapter.

▶ **Wake-Up Proxy Client Settings:** Starting with Configuration Manager 2012 SP 1 clients, you can supplement the Wake on LAN site setting for unicast packets by using the wake-up proxy client settings. This combination helps wake up computers on subnets without the requirement to reconfigure network switches. For more information about wake-up proxy, see http://technet.microsoft.com/en-us/library/gg712701.aspx#BKMK_PlanToWakeClients.

▶ **User Data and Profiles:** This new configuration item contains settings that manage folder redirection, offline files and folders, and roaming profiles for users on Windows 8 (and newer) systems in your ConfigMgr hierarchy. These settings can be used to enable users to access data in many scenarios, such as a Virtual Desktop Infrastructure (VDI) environment, as well as maintain user data in a protected, backed-up location in your data center. Chapter 3, "User Data and Profiles," describes scenarios for using these settings, as well as how to configure each of them.

Security

Company Resource Access Manager is a new security role available in ConfigMgr R2. This role grants permissions to create, manage, and deploy company resource access profiles such as Wi-Fi, VPN, and certificate profiles to users and devices.

Distribution Points (DPs)

DPs have always been a vital component in any ConfigMgr infrastructure; with each release, service pack, and cumulative update, they become more efficient, consistent, and resilient. Following is a brief review of improvements to DPs since ConfigMgr 2012 RTM (release to manufacturing, the original release).

Cloud-Based Distribution Point

Beginning with SP 1, you can create a cloud DP in Windows Azure for your ConfigMgr infrastructure. Cloud-based DPs support both intranet and Internet-based clients, and automatically enable BranchCache on the DP to help you reduce content transfer from your cloud-based DP. See http://technet.microsoft.com/en-us/library/b2516212-e524-4031-9a1f-7b768084304d#BKMK_PlanCloudDPs for more information about cloud DPs. CoreTech also provides an overview of cloud DPs at http://blog.coretech.dk/kea/configmgr-cloud-distribution-points/. You can find additional information at http://blogs.technet.com/b/configmgrteam/archive/2013/01/31/new-distribution-points-in-configuration-manager-sp1.aspx.

Pull Distribution Points

Pull DPs, added in ConfigMgr 2012 SP 1, improve scalability of ConfigMgr content distribution. Each primary and secondary site supports up to 250 traditional DPs, but you can scale up to a total of 2,250 with 2,000 of them configured to be pull DPs, as these are considered a client connection when accessing another DP to obtain content. For traditional DPs, content is pushed from the site server to each DP. For pull DPs, the site server sends instructions (via Windows Management Instrumentation [WMI]) to the DP, which then does all the work, downloading content in the same manner that a client would download using Background Intelligent Transfer Service (BITS).

NOTE: MAXIMUM OF 5,000 DISTRIBUTION POINTS PER PRIMARY SITE

Each primary site supports a total of 5,000 DPs, including all DPs at the primary site, and all DPs for secondary sites that report to the primary site.

Pull DPs perform the same functions as traditional DPs, with the following exceptions:

▶ A cloud-based DP cannot be configured as a pull DP.

▶ A DP on a site server cannot be configured as a pull DP.

▶ A pull DP configured to support prestaged content does not pull content that is marked for prestage.

▶ Rate limits are not enabled for a pull DP, since a pull DP relies on pulling content using BITS. You can alter the BITS configuration on the pull DP with group policy to throttle BITS.

▶ Retry settings are not configured like a traditional DP. The TechNet documentation at http://technet.microsoft.com/en-us/library/gg712321.aspx discusses the automatic retry settings for a pull DP.

▶ If the pull DP is in a remote forest from the source DP, it must have a ConfigMgr client agent installed so that the Network Access account can be used to download content. (By default, a pull DP uses the Local System account to access source DP content.)

▶ Pull DPs send DP status back to the primary site through a MP. This causes less load on the site server than the alternative, in which distribution manager (on the primary site) queries for information from the DP.

TIP: PULL DPS ARE LOW OVERHEAD

A pull DP communicates like a ConfigMgr client when it accesses another DP to obtain content.

You can specify multiple source DPs for a pull DP. New in ConfigMgr 2012 R2, you can also assign a priority to each DP, to specify a preference for the pull DP to download content. When the pull DP needs to download content, it starts with the DP with the lowest priority number in the list. If content is not available it proceeds to the next-priority DP in the list.

Another feature new in ConfigMgr 2012 R2 for pull DPs is the processing path of DP status messages from pull DPs. In SP 1, the distribution manager (on the site server) had to remotely poll each Pull DP periodically to update DP status. With R2, the pull DP forwards the status information to a site MP, which reduces the overhead previously required by distribution manager on the site server. The following steps walk through the process of creating a new pull DP:

1. Navigate to **Administration -> Site Configuration -> Sites** and select **Create Site System Server** from the ribbon bar to start the Create Site System Server Wizard.

2. Enter the server (or workstation) name, and select the desired site code for the site to manage the pull DP, as shown in Figure 2.7.

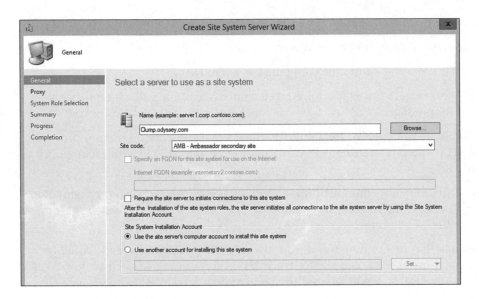

FIGURE 2.7   Configuring a pull DP.

3. Choose **Distribution Point** as the site role for this server.

4. Choose the appropriate options on the Distribution Point tab, as shown in Figure 2.8. (Notice the new Description field, which you can use to describe your obscurely named DPs to improve your ability to troubleshoot faster.)

5. Choose your corporate standard drive configuration for the Drive Settings tab, and then proceed to the next step.

6. On the Pull Distribution Point tab, choose to **Enable the DP to pull content**, as well as add one or more source DPs for the system configuration.

7. Continue through the rest of the wizard and modify the remaining settings as required.

Two additional optimizations are introduced in ConfigMgr 2012 R2 to improve deployment of content to DPs:

▶ **Smarter selection of DP priority for traditional (non-pull) DPs:** Each time ConfigMgr sends content to a DP, it records the speed of the transfer. This information is used for the next content deployment, so the DPs that receive the content the fastest are targeted first. This maximizes the number of DPs that receive content in the shortest period of time.

▶ **More efficient validation of content:** ConfigMgr previously used a single WMI call to a DP for each file to verify content. As some content source for an application can easily exceed 1,000 files (and it is not too-uncommon to see a source with more than 10,000 files), remote WMI calls for every single file would take a considerable amount of time. With ConfigMgr 2012 R2, ConfigMgr now validates up to 50 files during each WMI call to a DP.

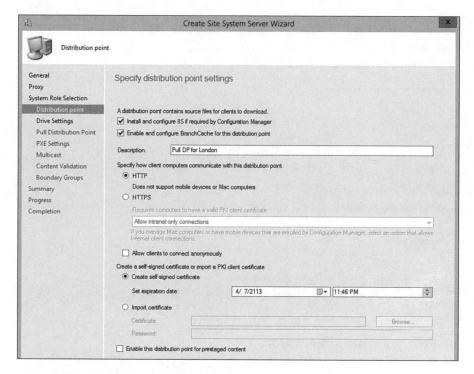

FIGURE 2.8   Configuring a pull DP and instructions.

Automatic Client Upgrade

Automatic client upgrade was introduced with the initial release of ConfigMgr 2012, but never really worked as intended. With ConfigMgr 2012 SP 1, ConfigMgr can automatically upgrade ConfigMgr 2007 and 2012 clients to the version of the ConfigMgr 2012 assigned site, and this is supported as the main method to upgrade clients.

> **TIP: CLIENT SYSTEMS MUST BE IN A FAST BOUNDARY**
>
> Clients in slow or unreliable boundaries are not upgraded automatically.

To configure automatic upgrade, go to the CAS if you have one (otherwise, your stand-alone primary site), and navigate to **Administration -> Site Configuration -> Sites**, and choose **Hierarchy Settings** from the ribbon bar. Review the Automatic Client Upgrade tab, shown in Figure 2.9.

Notice the default of 7 days to automatically upgrade clients. This means that all clients needing to be upgraded in the hierarchy are upgraded randomly over the next 7 days. Also, note that only clients in a boundary designated as "Fast" automatically upgrade.

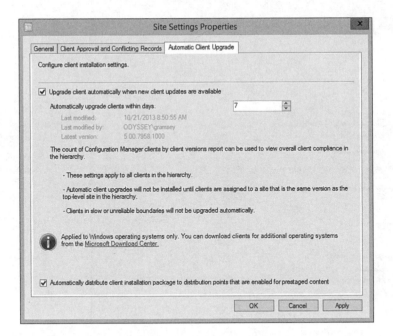

FIGURE 2.9   Configuring automatic client upgrade.

Network Access Accounts

Prior to ConfigMgr 2012 R2, a primary site could only have one Network Access account. Up to 10 Network Access accounts per primary site are now supported, removing another reason for having multiple primary sites.

> **NOTE: ABOUT THE NETWORK ACCESS ACCOUNT**
>
> A Network Access account is used by the ConfigMgr client to access content on a DP when the local computer account is unable to authenticate. This is a common scenario for workgroup clients, operating system deployment in the WinPE phase, and DPs in nontrusted domains.

PowerShell Support

PowerShell support was introduced in ConfigMgr 2012 SP 1. Although PowerShell could be used to access ConfigMgr through WMI prior to SP 1, you now have a full PowerShell provider for ConfigMgr. As of the R2 release, there are 560 cmdlets for ConfigMgr. (The cmdlet reference is at http://technet.microsoft.com/en-us/library/jj821831(v=sc.20).aspx.) With these cmdlets, you can create collections, add devices (or users) to a collection, deploy software, update software, create email subscriptions for alerts, and more. PowerShell and automation is the key to the future, so invest the time in learning more about how you can leverage PowerShell in ConfigMgr to handle frequent, repetitive tasks, as well as take the usability of the product to the next level.

The ConfigMgr admin console must be installed to access the PowerShell provider for ConfigMgr. From the console, click the blue icon in the upper-left corner and select **Connect via Windows PowerShell**. The ConfigMgr PowerShell provider uses the same rights as you have in the console. As shown in Figure 2.10, the prompt displays the site code for the site from which the PowerShell prompt was launched. In this case, the site code is CAS.

FIGURE 2.10   The PowerShell command prompt for ConfigMgr.

The following command, run from the PowerShell prompt, displays all ConfigMgr cmdlets in the PowerShell module:

```
Get-Command -Module ConfigurationManager | Out-Gridview
```

`Out-Gridview` is optional; it is a handy feature to be able to pipe (with |) information to a grid view so that you can easily sort and filter.

The following script creates a device collection and adds a system to that collection:

```
#Create a new Collection named TestWorkstations,
#limited to All Systems, and configured with incremental updates.
New-CMDeviceCollection -Name "TestWorkstations"
  -LimitingCollectionName "All Systems" -RefreshType ConstantUpdate

#Get resource information on computer named "Divot" and store in $Resource
$Resource = Get-CMDevice -Name "Divot"

#Adding Divot to TestWorkstations collection, with a direct membership rule
Add-CMDeviceCollectionDirectMemberShipRule -CollectionName
  "TestWorkstations"
  -ResourceID $Resource.ResourceID

#Deploy the 7-Zip 9.20 application as a simulation to the
#TestWorkstations collection.

Start-CMApplicationDeploymentSimulation -CollectionName
  "TestWorkstations" -Name "7-Zip 9.20" -DeployAction Install
```

The script shows that the process to create a collection, add a member, and deploy an application simulation is fairly straightforward. The cmdlet names are somewhat long, so use tab completion to ensure that you type them correctly.

ConfigMgr 2012 R2 adds approximately 100 additional PowerShell cmdlets, as well as support for native x64 for almost all cmdlets. At the time of this writing, almost all cmdlets are supported in a native x64 environment (see http://support.microsoft.com/kb/2932274).

Assets and Compliance

The Assets and Compliance node is the hub of targeting systems for application installation and software updates, as well as configuring and deploying compliance settings. ConfigMgr 2012 SP 1 and R2 expand on Assets and Compliance, providing the ability to control roaming profiles, as well as manage certificates, Wi-Fi profiles, and VPN configuration. The next sections discuss new and enhanced features in the Assets and Compliance node.

Collections

If you've installed any Microsoft application, you have probably seen a prompt that asks if you want to send anonymous feedback to Microsoft for the product, usually known as the Customer Experience Improvement Program (CEIP). Over the years, Microsoft has reported that ConfigMgr administrators and operators spend the majority of their time in the console working on collections, and based on this CEIP feedback, Microsoft continues working on collections to make your job easier. Some of the new features make that process easier, but many new features in collections just may make you spend a bit more time in this area, for very good reasons.

Resultant Client Settings

ConfigMgr 2012 did a great job of allowing you to deploy more granular client settings, targeting specific collections with unique settings. This can be challenging in some environments, as you may have one system in multiple collections, receiving multiple client settings. You can now select Resultant Client Settings from the Configuration Manager console to view the effective client settings to be applied to the selected device. The resultant client setting accounts for the prioritization or combination of attributes where multiple client settings have been deployed to the same device. Right-click a user or device in a collection and select **Client Settings -> Resultant Client Settings**; this shows a read-only view of the effective settings applying to that client (see Figure 2.11).

Maintenance Windows for Software Updates

You now can create maintenance windows that only apply to software updates, task sequences, or to all deployments. As the patching team is often separate from the software distribution team, having only one type of maintenance window can cause additional challenges and coordination. Now, as shown in Figure 2.12, you can create maintenance windows for device collections that are strictly for software updates.

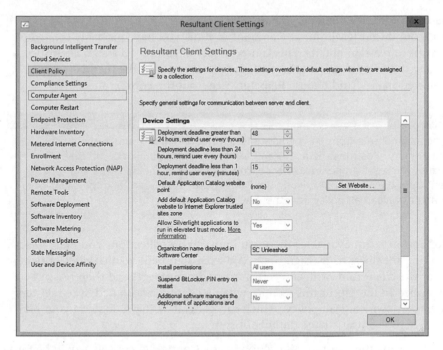

FIGURE 2.11   Resultant Client Settings page.

FIGURE 2.12   Maintenance window for software updates.

Reassign Clients to a Different ConfigMgr Primary Site

If you have been around ConfigMgr for any amount of time, you have probably created (or searched for) a script to reassign clients. This is now a native feature. To assign clients to a different site, view the members of a collection and select one or more members. Next, right-click the selected names, and choose **Reassign Site** from the context menu.

TIP: REASSIGNING CLIENTS

You can only reassign clients from one primary site to another primary site in the same hierarchy. Both primary sites must be active and healthy to reassign clients with this method. Note that the reassignment experience from the client is the same as changing site assignment from the client—all existing ConfigMgr policy is deleted, and the client must register and download all policy from the new primary site.

The Reassign Site option is not available when you right-click a collection. You must select the specific collection members to reassign them. After reassignment is initiated, ConfigMgr creates a policy for the client to download on its next polling interval and then reassigns the client. As described in the Tip in this section, when a client is reassigned, it re-registers with the new site and downloads all policy, which can generate a heavy load on your MPs and site database when targeting a large number of systems.

An ideal scenario for using the Reassign Site action in the ConfigMgr console would be for a small number of systems that were incorrectly assigned to the wrong site. Now you (or any other administrator with the proper role-based administration) can reassign the site code, without the need (or rights) to log in to the server and manually change the site code.

Client Notification

Triggering ConfigMgr machine policy refresh is a frequent task that administrators look to add to ConfigMgr via community right-click extensions. This is now a native feature in the console, as shown in Figure 2.13.

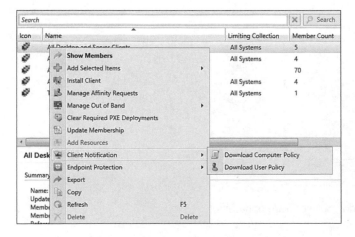

FIGURE 2.13   Client Notification for Download Computer and User Policy.

You can immediately initiate a download of computer or user policy, as well as initiate a malware scan for System Center Endpoint Protection (SCEP) clients. Client notification uses TCP Port 10123 by default to connect to the desired client, and this is configurable at the primary site. You can review the status of initiated operations from Monitoring -> Client Operations view, as shown in Figure 2.14.

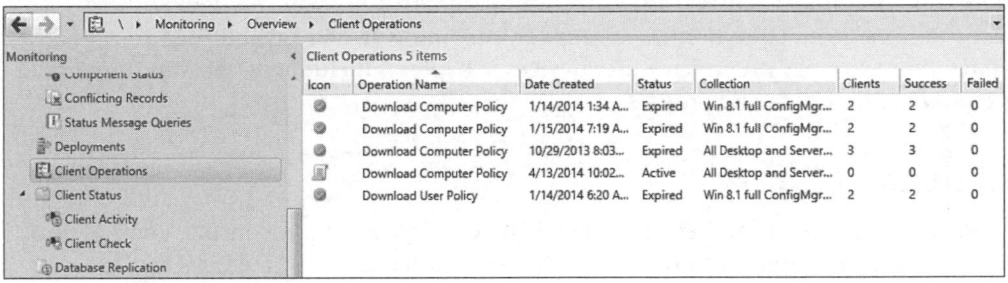

FIGURE 2.14 Display results of Client Notification in the Monitoring -> Client Operations node.

Compliance Settings

Compliance settings is another area in ConfigMgr that has significant integration with Windows Intune. In addition to the full Windows client, compliance settings can now enforce settings for Android, iOS, OS X, Windows Phone, and Windows RT devices. The supported features vary, depending on the targeted device. Following are some of the most popular features available:

▶ File encryption on mobile device

▶ Minimum password length

▶ Password complexity

▶ Password quality

▶ Disable/enable camera

▶ Idle time before device is locked

For more information, see Chapter 8, "Mobile Device Management in Configuration Manager 2012 R2."

Remote Connection Profiles

You can also configure Remote Connection Profiles to enable users to start a remote desktop connection to their primary devices. See Chapter 8 for more information.

Company Resource Access

This feature is used to deploy certificates, as well as configure wireless and VPN connections. Six virtual private network (VPN) vendors are supported, in addition to standard

VPN protocols. Email profiles can also be deployed with this method, so that users who provision a device through the company portal are automatically configured for email on that device. This is discussed further in Chapter 8.

User Data and Profiles

Previously group policy objects (GPOs) were required to manage roaming user profiles, offline files, and folder redirection. With ConfigMgr 2012 R2, you can deploy these settings to a targeted collection in ConfigMgr, providing greater flexibility in how you manage these settings on primary user devices. Chapter 3 includes detailed information for managing user data and profiles.

Software Library

The Software Library is another key node in the ConfigMgr admin console, and has also received significant upgrades since the release of ConfigMgr 2012. This is where you create and deploy applications, software updates, and operating system deployment task sequences. Changes are discussed in the following sections.

Application Management

The Application Management area manages all items for software deployment, including applications and packages, as well as supporting items such as approval requests, global conditions, App-V virtual environments, and Windows sideloading keys. An overview of updated (or newly released) items since the original release of ConfigMgr is described in the next sections. Chapter 4, "New Application Deployment Types," focuses on managing applications.

Managing Applications

Applications are the new type of software deployment mechanism in ConfigMgr 2012. Applications have deployment types, requirement rules, and detection methods. Since the initial release of ConfigMgr 2012, deployment types have been added for Linux and OS X (both covered in Chapter 5, "On-Premise Cross-Platform Support"), as well as devices that are managed through Intune, such as iOS, Android, and Windows Phone, as shown in Figure 2.15.

Windows 8.x applications and app bundles enable the administrator to deploy full applications from ConfigMgr, with no need for Internet access from the client. Windows app packages from the Windows Store allow you to present Windows Store applications to a user through the Application Catalog or through the company portal. As shown by the list of application types in Figure 2.15, when ConfigMgr is integrated with Windows Intune you can manage just about any popular device that's available in the market, reinforcing the idea that Microsoft is "all in" for supporting any user on any device, anywhere. Following are several additional features that further the mantra *any user, any device, anywhere*:

▶ Web Applications are a new deployment type allowing you to deploy a shortcut to a web-based application on user devices.

▶ You can enable an application as a featured application, making it available in the Featured section of the device's company portal.

▶ You can configure an application to automatically open a VPN connection if a VPN profile has been configured.

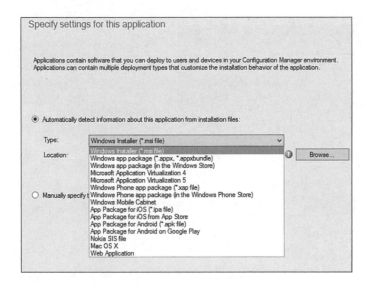

FIGURE 2.15   The Create Application Wizard.

App-V Virtual Environments

In addition to new support for Microsoft Application Virtualization (App-V) 5.0, ConfigMgr now supports App-V virtual environments. Virtual environments allow multiple virtual applications to share file system and Registry information instead of running in an isolated space. This feature allows you to separate your middleware virtual application from your line-of-business virtual application, enabling you to simplify the update process of one application or the other.

Windows Sideloading Keys

Windows sideloading keys can be imported into ConfigMgr, allowing you to deploy internally developed Windows 8.x applications (as well as other applications not in the Windows Store) to managed systems.

Review Chapter 4 to understand how to take advantage of all the new features for managing applications on devices, as well as Windows 8.x applications on your highly managed Windows 8.x systems.

Software Updates

Software updates play a critical role in the monthly operations of systems management. Following is a list of the most important updates to the software updates feature:

▶ **Enable systems to fall back to Windows Update for content:** As shown in Figure 2.16, you can authorize a client to download content directly from Microsoft Updates. This is a great feature for systems in remote locations, as well as those one-off types of updates, where perhaps only three systems in your entire organization need the update.

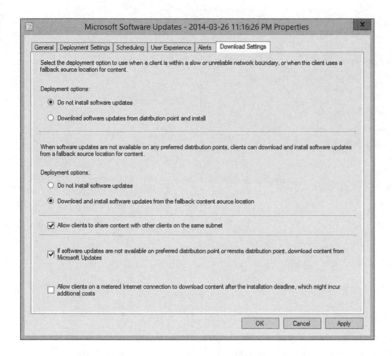

FIGURE 2.16   Enable clients to download from Microsoft Updates.

▶ **Support for Endpoint Protection updates multiple times per day:** Prior to ConfigMgr 2012 R2, Microsoft recommended updating definition updates for Endpoint Protection once daily, but Microsoft updates definitions three times a day. ConfigMgr now supports the deployment of definition updates three times per day.

▶ **Auto deployment rules:** Automatic deployment rules (ADRs) are used to automatically deploy updates to a target collection, based on defined rules for product, classification, release date, and other update attributes. Following are several improvements to ADRs:

▶ **New templates:** When creating a new ADR, there are templates for Patch Tuesday and Definition Updates. These templates help you build the appropriate ADR.

▶ **Change the package source:** Previously, you could not change the update package for an ADR and had to re-create the ADR. You now have the ability to change the package sources for an existing ADR. This helps prevent the deployment package from getting too large.

▶ **Preview software updates that meet the criteria for your ADR:** Clicking the Preview button on the Software Updates page, shown in Figure 2.17, lets you preview updates. Previously, you didn't know if you built the criteria correctly until you ran the ADR, which could cause a bit of churn while testing.

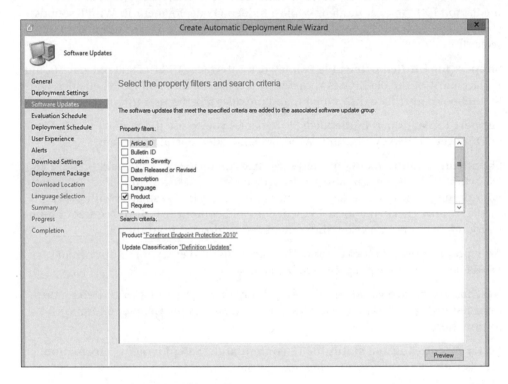

FIGURE 2.17   Preview ADR configuration.

Operating System Deployment

Operating system deployment (OSD) is a key feature of ConfigMgr, and has been updated significantly since the original release of ConfigMgr 2012. Most OSD administrators are familiar with the *normal* ConfigMgr hot fix required when a new operating system version becomes supported. (This hot fix adds the new platform to the GUI, so that you can choose to include or exclude programs and application deployment types for the new platform.) Following is a brief list of other significant updates for OSD. Chapter 6, "What's New in Operating System Deployment," provides full detail:

▶ **Support for Windows PowerShell in WinPE:** PowerShell support in WinPE is a significant improvement. You can now leverage PowerShell in addition to VBScript and HTML applications (HTAs).

▶ **Support for WinPE boot images based on WinPE 3.1:** This enables support of older computer hardware.

▶ **Ability to add optional components to WinPE from the admin console:** This replaces the previous manual process of mounting the boot.wim file using DISM.

▶ **Control the visibility of an OS deployment targeted to a collection:** You can choose whether to make the deployment visible in Software Center, from boot media and PXE only, or hidden. While a hidden OS deployment in WinPE sounds strange, you can use task sequence variables in a prestart (pre-execution) script to select it.

▶ **Support for Unified Extensible Framework Interface (UEFI):** UEFI one day should replace most of the old BIOSes with which you are familiar with. UEFI enables SecureBoot, larger hard disk support, and provides a better user interface.

▶ **Support for Windows Embedded:** SP 1 enables you to use the familiar ConfigMgr OSD process to deploy a custom Windows Embedded operating system.

▶ **Significant enhancements to prestaged media:** Previously, you could prestage an OS .wim file. Now you can also specify applications, packages, and driver packages to your prestaged media. The task sequence (TS) process is also smarter with prestaged media. It now checks the local TS cache for valid content first; if the content cannot be found or has been revised, the content is downloaded from the DP.

▶ **New preprovision BitLocker task:** This can be used to encrypt the drive from WinPE and only encrypt space used by data.

▶ **New task sequence variables:** There are many new TS variables to give you more information, as well as make your TS more flexible. Review Chapter 6 for more information.

▶ **Better monitoring and status for TS content and TS deployment information:** This is viewable in the Monitoring node of the ConfigMgr console.

▶ **New task sequence steps:** New steps like Run PowerShell Script, Check Readiness, and Set Dynamic Variables provide more flexibility in your TS.

▶ **Create virtual hard disk (VHD):** You can create VHDs from the admin console.

▶ **Support for Windows To Go:** You can use ConfigMgr to provision Windows To Go (WTG) USB drives.

Monitoring Changes

Monitoring enables you to easily keep an eye on content distribution, deployments, infrastructure health and alerts, client health, and Endpoint Protection status. The next sections focus on the updates to Monitoring since the initial release of ConfigMgr 2012.

Alerts

Email alert subscriptions are now supported for all features, not just Endpoint Protection. You can browse and select the desired alert, and click **Create Subscription** from the toolbar.

Reporting

ConfigMgr reports are now fully enabled for role-based administration. The data for all reports included with ConfigMgr is filtered based on the permissions of the administrative user who runs the report. Administrative users with specific roles can only view information defined for their roles. For more information, see the "Planning for Role-Based Administration for Reports" section at http://technet.microsoft.com/en-us/library/7ca322fc-bbbf-42c8-82c9-6fc8941ef2e6#BKMK_RoleBaseAdministration. Santos Martinez also created a detailed walk-through to help you build reports that support role-based administration; his blog post is available at http://blogs.technet.com/b/smartinez/archive/2013/11/28/how-to-create-a-rba-capable-report-for-configmgr-r2.aspx.

TIP: REPORTING PERFORMANCE

Role-based-enabled reports require additional processing time and can slow down report rendering. If you're more concerned with the speed of rendering reports than filtering results based on user role, you can set the following Registry value: `HKEY_LOCAL_MACHINE\SOFTWARE\Microsoft\SMS\SRSRP\EnableRBACReporting = 0`.

You can also review DP utilization on a daily basis to determine the utilization of a DP in a location. The report displayed in Figure 2.18 shows how many clients connected and how many bytes were downloaded.

Distribution point usage summary
⊞ Description

Time Period (Start)	Time Period (End)	Clients Accessed (Unique)	Requests Processed	Bytes Sent (MB)
4/13/2014 12:00:01 AM	4/13/2014 11:59:59 PM	3	110	0
4/12/2014 12:00:01 AM	4/12/2014 11:59:59 PM	5	155	8
4/11/2014 12:00:01 AM	4/11/2014 11:59:59 PM	2	100	0

FIGURE 2.18   DP usage summary.

Distribution Status

The Distribution Status node has become more user friendly, allowing you to cancel a distribution that is In Progress from the Content Status details pane, as shown in Figure 2.19. You also have the ability to redistribute failed package content from the Error tab.

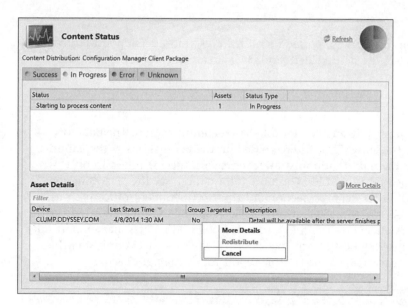

FIGURE 2.19   Cancel a content distribution from the Monitoring -> Content Status tab.

Deployment Status

Previously, viewing individual steps in a task sequence required that you open a web report to view the information. Now you can navigate to deployment status, right-click the desired device name, and select **More Details** to view the steps (and success of each step), as shown in Figure 2.20.

Client Operations

This is a new node in the Monitoring section of the console, and displays the status of client notification actions. Figure 2.14 previously displayed an image of Client Operations status. For added value, add the Created By column to the view, so you can identify which administrator initiated an action against a collection.

Other Improvements

In addition to all the changes evident in the ConfigMgr console, many other enhancements can either improve your experience as an administrator or enable you to enhance the end-user experience for your organization. These changes, which fall into the categories of setup and recovery and client and client experience, are discussed in the remainder of this chapter.

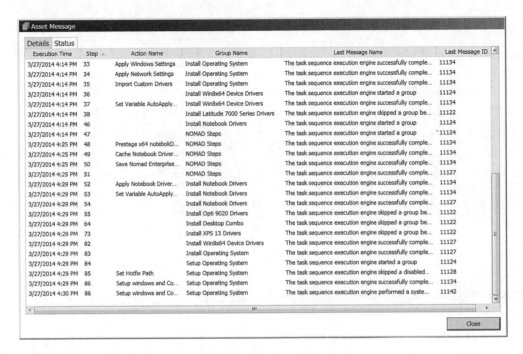

Execution Time	Step	Action Name	Group Name	Last Message Name	Last Message ID
3/27/2014 4:14 PM	33	Apply Windows Settings	Install Operating System	The task sequence execution engine successfully comple...	11134
3/27/2014 4:14 PM	34	Apply Network Settings	Install Operating System	The task sequence execution engine successfully comple...	11134
3/27/2014 4:14 PM	35	Import Custom Drivers	Install Operating System	The task sequence execution engine successfully comple...	11134
3/27/2014 4:14 PM	36		Install Win8x64 Device Drivers	The task sequence execution engine started a group	11124
3/27/2014 4:14 PM	37	Set Variable AutoApply...	Install Win8x64 Device Drivers	The task sequence execution engine successfully comple...	11134
3/27/2014 4:14 PM	38		Install Latitude 7000 Series Drivers	The task sequence execution engine skipped a group be...	11122
3/27/2014 4:14 PM	46		Install Notebook Drivers	The task sequence execution engine started a group	11124
3/27/2014 4:14 PM	47		NOMAD Steps	The task sequence execution engine started a group	11124
3/27/2014 4:25 PM	48	Prestage x64 notebokD...	NOMAD Steps	The task sequence execution engine successfully comple...	11134
3/27/2014 4:25 PM	49	Cache Notebook Driver...	NOMAD Steps	The task sequence execution engine successfully comple...	11134
3/27/2014 4:25 PM	50	Save Nomad Enterprise...	NOMAD Steps	The task sequence execution engine successfully comple...	11134
3/27/2014 4:25 PM	51		NOMAD Steps	The task sequence execution engine successfully comple...	11127
3/27/2014 4:29 PM	52	Apply Notebook Driver...	Install Notebook Drivers	The task sequence execution engine successfully comple...	11134
3/27/2014 4:29 PM	53	Set Variable AutoApply...	Install Notebook Drivers	The task sequence execution engine successfully comple...	11134
3/27/2014 4:29 PM	54		Install Notebook Drivers	The task sequence execution engine successfully comple...	11127
3/27/2014 4:29 PM	55		Install Opti 9020 Drivers	The task sequence execution engine skipped a group be...	11122
3/27/2014 4:29 PM	64		Install Desktop Combo	The task sequence execution engine skipped a group be...	11122
3/27/2014 4:29 PM	73		Install XPS 13 Drivers	The task sequence execution engine skipped a group be...	11122
3/27/2014 4:29 PM	82		Install Win8x64 Device Drivers	The task sequence execution engine successfully comple...	11127
3/27/2014 4:29 PM	83		Install Operating System	The task sequence execution engine successfully comple...	11127
3/27/2014 4:29 PM	84		Setup Operating System	The task sequence execution engine started a group	11124
3/27/2014 4:29 PM	85	Set Hotfix Path	Setup Operating System	The task sequence execution engine skipped a disabled...	11128
3/27/2014 4:29 PM	86	Setup windows and Co...	Setup Operating System	The task sequence execution engine successfully comple...	11134
3/27/2014 4:30 PM	86	Setup windows and Co...	Setup Operating System	The task sequence execution engine performed a syste...	11142

FIGURE 2.20   Task sequence deployment status information.

Setup and Recovery

The next sections focus on enhancements related to initial evaluation and setup, upgrade scenarios, and recovery scenarios. These include support for new operating systems, database configuration, and scalability enhancements.

Support for New Operating Systems

All site system roles are now supported on Windows Server 2012 and Windows Server 2012 R2, and the Distribution Point role is also supported on Windows 8 and Windows 8.1.

Database Configuration

When installing ConfigMgr 2012 RTM, the database files and transaction logs were created using the default SQL locations for the file types. You now can designate the database and transaction log location during setup, as shown in Figure 2.21.

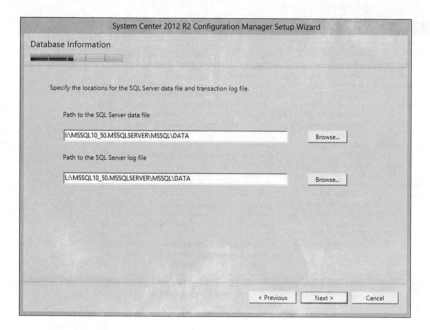

FIGURE 2.21   Database configuration during setup.

Scalability Enhancements

ConfigMgr scalability continues to improve. The current highlights follow:

▶ Each primary and secondary site now supports up to 250 DPs. Each primary and secondary site supports up to 2,000 additional DPs configured as pull DPs. For example, a single primary site supports 2,250 DPs when 2,000 of those DPs are configured as pull DPs.

> **NOTE: PULL DPS DOWNLOAD CONTENT LIKE A CLIENT**
>
> A pull DP is considered to be a client when it accesses another DP to obtain content.

▶ Each DP supports connections up to 4,000 clients.

▶ Each primary site supports a combined total of 5,000 DPs, including all DPs at the primary site and all that belong to secondary sites of the primary site.

▶ Each DP supports a combined total of up to 10,000 packages and applications (including software update packages, operating system images driver packages, and operating system boot disks).

▶ A software update point installed on a server that is remote from the primary site server supports up to 100,000 clients when the remote computer meets the WSUS requirements to support this number.

▶ Each primary site now supports multiple software update points for use on the intranet and on the Internet. Beginning with Configuration Manager 2012 SP 1, the Configuration Manager console does not support configuring software update points as NLB clusters. (You can still use the Configuration Manager software development kit [SDK] to configure a software update point on a NLB cluster; for information, review the documentation for the PowerShell cmdlet `Set-CMSoftwareUpdatePoint` at http://technet.microsoft.com/library/jj821938.aspx.)

▶ A stand-alone primary site supports up to 100,000 clients.

▶ The CAS supports 400,000 clients; the database must use SQL Server Enterprise edition for total client counts exceeding 50,000 systems.

Upgrade Path

You can upgrade from ConfigMgr 2012 SP 1 to ConfigMgr 2012 R2. There are no other supported upgrade configurations. When upgrading to ConfigMgr 2012 R2, you must manually uninstall the Windows Assessment and Deployment Toolkit (ADK) for Windows 8, and install the latest version (currently for Window 8.1), available at http://www.microsoft.com/en-us/download/details.aspx?id=39982.

Migration Capabilities

With Configuration Manager 2012 Service Pack 1 and newer, you can migrate (or merge) data from one or more hierarchies running the same version of ConfigMgr software. This feature allows you to easily collapse multiple infrastructures into one, as well as easily migrate objects from your nonproduction environment to your production environment.

Adding a Central Administration Site

Prior to SP 1, you were required to install a CAS before any primary sites. Many administrators elected to install a CAS whether it was needed at the time or not, in case one might be needed at a later time. You now have the capability to add a CAS to an existing stand-alone primary site, as shown in Figure 2.22.

NOTE: ONLY INSTALL A CAS WHEN ABSOLUTELY NEEDED

There is no longer a good reason to install a CAS "just in case" your company might need it in the future. While the CAS is a completely supported role in ConfigMgr, it adds additional complexity and may require more experience in troubleshooting various types of SQL replication. Role-based administration, pull DPs, and additional capacity support for a primary site reduce the need to implement a CAS.

Recovering a Secondary Site

You can recover a secondary site by using the Recover Secondary Site action from the Sites node in the Configuration Manager console. During recovery, the secondary site files are installed on the destination computer and the secondary site data is then reinitialized with data from the primary site. The secondary site you recover must have the same

FQDN and meet all secondary site prerequisites, and you must configure appropriate security rights for the secondary site.

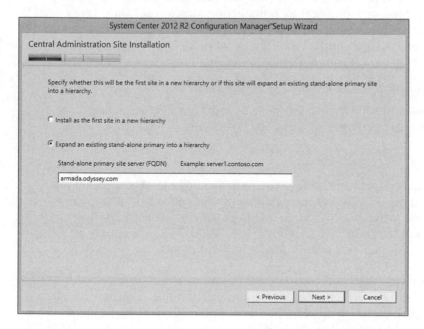

FIGURE 2.22   Adding a central administration site to a stand-alone primary site.

During recovery, ConfigMgr verifies the content library exists and has the appropriate content. Once verified, the content is reinitialized for use by the secondary site. If the verification process fails, you must redistribute content or use the prestage content process. You can verify status of the recovery by selecting Show Install Status from the Sites node in the console.

> **TIP: VERIFY SQL SERVER HEALTH BEFORE RECOVERING SECONDARY SITE**
>
> The secondary site recovery process does not install (or reinstall) SQL. Verify the health of SQL Server before starting the recovery process. If unhealthy, reinstall the same version of SQL Server (Enterprise, Standard, or Express) and the same instance as previously installed.

Client and Client Experience

ConfigMgr has come a long way since the release of ConfigMgr 2012 in terms of cross-platform support and improved client experience. In fact, most of this book focuses on users and how they can leverage different devices to be more productive.

OS X Support

OS X support was added in ConfigMgr 2012 SP 1. You can install the Configuration Manager client agent on computers that run OS X. You can then manage the OS X client by using compliance settings, deploying software, and collecting hardware inventory. R2 improved the experience with the Mac Computer Enrollment Wizard. For more information, see Chapter 5.

Linux and UNIX Systems

ConfigMgr 2012 SP 1 added Linux and UNIX support. You can install the Configuration Manager client on servers that run a supported version of Linux or UNIX. You can then manage this client by using software deployment and by collecting hardware inventory. For more information, see Chapter 5. Chapter 5 also lists all Linux and UNIX distributions that are currently supported.

Windows Embedded Support

Windows Embedded is a special type of operating system that is designed for embedded (or purpose-built) systems. Although you may not see it, Windows Embedded is all around you. You can find Windows Embedded in ATMs, point of sale devices, car "infotainment" systems, kiosks, and ticket scanners at your favorite sports game or music venue. For more information about Windows Embedded, see http://www.microsoft.com/windowsembedded.

SCEP supports Windows Embedded. To properly enable virus definition updates, create custom client device settings (as shown in Figure 2.23), and enable the option that reads **For Windows Embedded devices with write filters, commit Endpoint Protection client installation (requires restarts)**.

With the client installed, be advised of the following items specific to Windows Embedded and support with ConfigMgr:

▶ You can choose to run Windows Embedded with the write filter disabled, in which case all ConfigMgr client features are supported natively. Write filters are a big reason for choosing Windows Embedded over a traditional workstation operating system, so permanently disabling write filters is not a normal configuration.

▶ The ConfigMgr Power Management features are not supported on Windows Embedded.

▶ The Application Catalog is not supported on any Windows Embedded device.

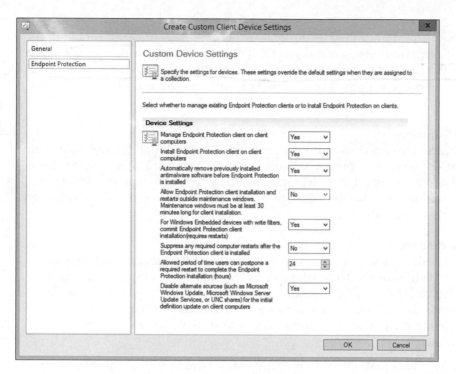

FIGURE 2.23 System Center Endpoint Protection settings for Windows Embedded.

Software deployment to Windows Embedded systems is similar to traditional Windows operating systems. While walking through the deployment wizard for applications, packages, and software updates, enable the check box to **Commit changes at deadline or during a maintenance window (requires restarts)**, as shown in Figure 2.24.

ConfigMgr handles the tedious steps of disabling the write filter, rebooting, installing the desired software, rebooting (if necessary), enabling the write filter, and rebooting a final time.

TIP: USE MAINTENANCE WINDOWS

Remember that safety doesn't take a holiday! Leverage maintenance windows on Windows Embedded systems to reduce the risk of surprise software installations at undesired times.

Windows 8.x Support

ConfigMgr 2012 supports new features in Windows 8.x. The next sections focus on these features, and how ConfigMgr can take advantage of these features.

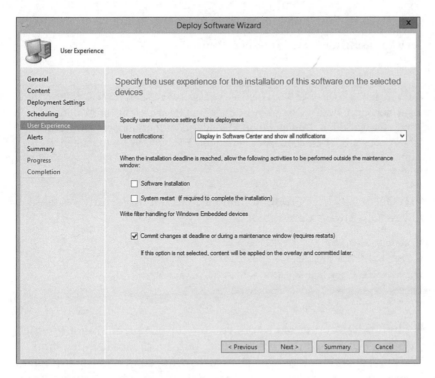

FIGURE 2.24   Configuring a deployment to commit changes to Windows Embedded at deadline or during a maintenance window.

Always On, Always Connected   Always On, Always Connected (also referred to as connected standby) is a new power model in Windows 8 to provide an instant-on, always-connected experience, similar to smartphones. There are several requirements for a computer model running Windows 8 to support connected standby. You can find information about connected standby at http://msdn.microsoft.com/en-us/library/windows/hardware/dn481224(v=vs.85).aspx.

Starting with ConfigMgr 2012 SP 1, the client can detect power states for devices that support Always On, Always Connected, which can enable the ConfigMgr client to delay client actions to run at alternate times, maximizing performance and preserving battery life for the device. The Configuration Manager client can detect the following states on an Always On, Always Connected device:

▶ Whether networking is turned on or off

▶ Whether the device is running on battery power or plugged in

▶ The battery power remaining

▶ Whether the device is in idle mode

▶ Whether the device is in its Windows Automatic Maintenance window

▶ Whether the device is using a metered Internet connection

NOTE: ALWAYS ON, ALWAYS CONNECTED FEATURE FOR X86 AND X64 ONLY

Configuration Manager supports Always On, Always Connected devices that run Windows 8 versions on x86 and x64 platforms. Configuration Manager does not support Always On, Always Connected for Windows 8 RT devices. As a reminder, RT can only be managed as a device through Intune.

Use the following WMI Query Language (WQL) to build a collection to identify systems that are capable of Always On, Always Connected:

```
select SMS_R_SYSTEM.ResourceID,SMS_R_SYSTEM.ResourceType,
  SMS_R_SYSTEM.Name,SMS_R_SYSTEM.SMS_UniqueIdentifier,
  SMS_R_SYSTEM.ResourceDomainORWorkgroup,SMS_R_SYSTEM.Client from
  SMS_R_System where SMS_R_System.IsAOACCapable = "True"
```

Metered Connections   In this well-connected world, you often pay a premium for Internet access. Whereas free Wi-Fi is becoming more prevalent at your favorite local coffee shop, your users may use a 4G broadband card, or even share data connection off a smartphone while on the go at airports or other locations around the globe. As an administrator, it's in your best interest to not deploy the latest Windows service pack to a user while connected to that high-cost data connection.

Metered connections allow you manage how Windows 8.x client computers communicate with ConfigMgr sites while on a metered connection. By default, Windows sets mobile broadband networks to metered, while Wi-Fi networks are configured as non-metered. Ethernet network connections cannot be set to metered. To enable or disable a metered network, go to **Start - > PC Settings - > Network**, select your desired network, and modify the Data usage setting, as shown in Figure 2.25.

You must also configure and deploy the client setting for Metered Internet Connections (see Figure 2.26). Three options are available when you configure this setting:

▶ **Allow:** All client communications are allowed over the metered Internet connection unless the client device is using a roaming data connection.

▶ **Limit:** Limit client communications to the following:

  ▶ Client policy retrieval

  ▶ Client state messages sent to site server

  ▶ Required deployments, when the deadline is reached

▶ **Block:** The ConfigMgr client does not communicate with ConfigMgr site roles while on a metered network. This is the default value.

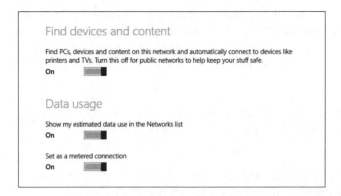

FIGURE 2.25   Enabling a metered connection for Wi-Fi connection.

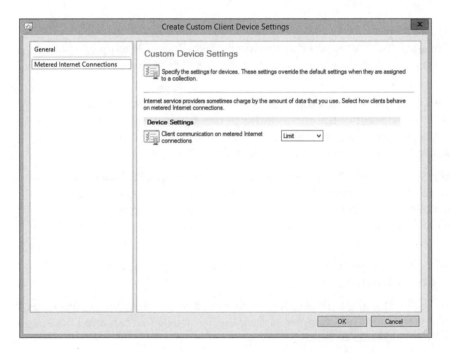

FIGURE 2.26   Enabling the metered connection network client setting.

NOTE: USER-INITIATED INSTALLATIONS ARE NEVER BLOCKED

User-initiated software installations from Software Center, Application Catalog, or the company portal are always permitted, regardless of metered Internet connection settings.

Windows 8.x Modern Applications   ConfigMgr 2012 SP 1 introduced support for Windows 8.x modern applications (also known as "metro" applications). ConfigMgr can deploy privately created modern applications, as well as make Windows Store applications available in the Application Catalog and company portal. Chapter 4 discusses deploying modern applications.

Windows To Go   ConfigMgr 2012 SP 1 supports automated configuration and deployment of WTG to your supported USB stick. See Chapter 6 for additional information.

Device Support Through Intune

Windows Intune is the most significant feature added to ConfigMgr 2012. With Intune integration, you can enroll and manage mobile devices that run Windows Phone 8, Windows RT, Android, and iOS. For more information, see Chapter 7 and Chapter 8. In addition, Chapter 1, "People-Centric IT," discusses the path that Microsoft is taking to enable *any user, any device, anywhere.*

Client Setup/Upgrade

Starting with ConfigMgr 2012 SP 1, you can specify the following CCMSetup.exe properties as installation options when you use client push, as well as with command-line installations:

- ▶ **/forcereboot:** Configures CCMSetup to force a reboot of the client computer if required, after installation of the client. If this option is not specified, ccmsetup.exe runs until it determines a restart is necessary, and then exits. Once the system has been rebooted, CCMSetup continues after the restart.

- ▶ **/skipprereq:** Specifies that CCMSetup must not install the specified prerequisite program(s) during client installation. For example, `/skipprereq:silverlight.exe` prevents installation/upgrade of Silverlight. Use a semicolon to separate multiple items to exclude (for example, `CCMSetup.exe /skipprereq:dotnetfx40_client_x86_x64.exe;Silverlight.exe`).

- ▶ **/logon:** This argument specifies that CCMSetup.exe should stop if any version of ConfigMgr 2012 is detected.

- ▶ **/BITSPriority:** Specifies the BITS priority for download of the client installation files over an http connection (for example, `/BITSPriority:HIGH`). You can also choose FOREGROUND, NORMAL, or LOW.

- ▶ **/downloadtimeout:** Specifies the length of time (in minutes) that CCMsetup attempts to download the client installation files before it gives up. The default is 1,440 minutes (1 day).

- ▶ **/forceinstall:** Specifies that a client is uninstalled first, and then the new client installed.

A new property is added to CCMSetup.exe: `/ExcludeFeatures:<feature>`. Use this argument to prevent a feature from being enabled during a ConfigMgr client installation on Windows. Currently, `ClientUI` is the only feature that can use the command-line

argument. Run CCMSetup.exe with your normal command-line parameters, and add
/ExcludeFeatures:ClientUI to prevent Software Center from being installed on target
systems. Using this option in conjunction with /skipprereq allows you to deploy
ConfigMgr without the Software Center GUI and reduces the requirement to install
prerequisites (like Silverlight) on targeted systems.

Client Experience

The client (end-user) experience has also evolved and improved since the initial release
of ConfigMgr 2012. The user experience has moved to be a first class citizen for the traditional ConfigMgr client, and integration with Intune has created a unified experience for
secondary devices such as Android, IOS, Windows RT, and Windows Phone.

Traditional Client Experience Improvements   Much of Microsoft's development focus has
been on mobile devices, and this book dedicates Chapters 7 and 8 to integrating mobile
devices with ConfigMgr. Microsoft has also done a great job of improving the client experience for your domain-joined clients.

Company Portal for Windows 8.x   Chapter 8 provides a full dive into all the company
portals; Microsoft has gone "all in" for support of Android, IOS, Windows RT, and
Windows Phone in terms of a company portal (accessed through Intune). Microsoft has
also gone the extra mile for your traditional, fully featured clients. Chapter 8 provides
installation and configuration information. The company portal for Windows 8.x (see
Figure 2.27, also shown in Chapter 8) provides a modern app-friendly user experience and
should become your standard for presenting applications to users.

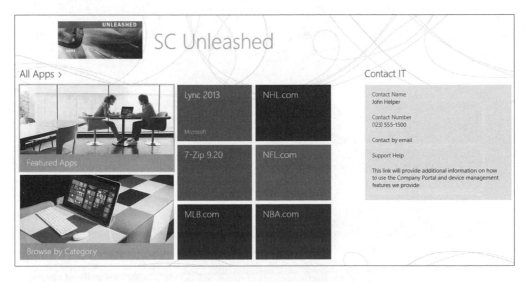

FIGURE 2.27   Windows 8.x company portal for full ConfigMgr clients.

NOTE: APPLICATIONS ARE SUPPORTED IN THE COMPANY PORTAL

Similar to the company portals for secondary devices, the company portal supports applications deployed to users. Packages/program task sequences, software updates, and applications that are targeted to systems (instead of users) are not supported in the company portal. Review the sidebar "Software Center, Application Catalog, and Company Portal: What's the Difference?" and Table 2.1 for additional information.

Multiselect in Software Center

The user can use Software Center to select one or more applications, task sequences, software, updates and package/programs for installation, as shown in Figure 2.28.

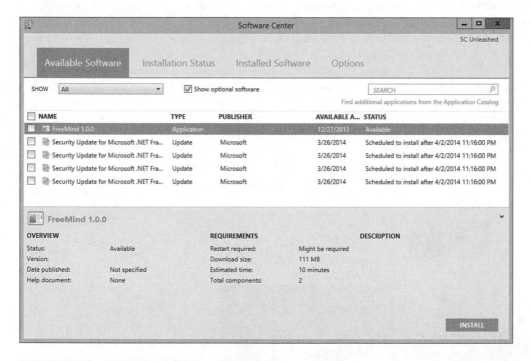

FIGURE 2.28   Multiselect in Software Center.

SOFTWARE CENTER, APPLICATION CATALOG, AND COMPANY PORTAL: WHAT'S THE DIFFERENCE?

If you're like the authors of this book, you may be wondering why a company portal was introduced for Windows systems. The company portal provides the best user experience. Unfortunately, it is one more place that users may need to visit to install software. If you can make all of your deployments based on applications targeted to users, the company portal can be the one-stop shop for your users. If you need to deploy task sequences, package/programs, and software updates optionally to systems, you may need to leverage the Application Catalog or Software Center. Table 2.1 provides a summary of features for each experience.

As the table shows, your users may need to visit more than one interface to install specialty software. Whenever possible, target users rather than devices and leverage the company portal to provide the best end-user experience.

TABLE 2.1   Software Center, Application Catalog, and Company Portal

Feature	Software Center	Application Catalog	Company Portal
Machine Targeted	✓		
User Targeted		✓	✓
Supports Application Uninstall	✓		
Supports Deployment of Task Sequence	✓		
Supports Deployment of Software Updates	✓		
Limits View of Available Software Based on Operating System Platform	✓		✓
Supports Windows 7	✓	✓	
Supports Windows 8.x	✓	✓	✓
Supports Package/Program	✓	✓	
Supports Applications (Application Model)	✓	✓	✓
Supports Optional Modern (Metro) Applications		✓	✓
Supports Featured Application Setting			✓

Required Deployment to Devices   Devices that run Windows RT, iOS, and Android now support a deployment purpose of Required. This allows you to deploy apps to devices according to a configured schedule. Note that installation for a required deployment on a device does not force the install, but notifies the user that a required deployment is pending. Chapter 8 provides additional information.

Selective Wipe   Wipe and retire functions now include the option to only remove company content from devices. The table at http://technet.microsoft.com/en-us/library/2c6bd0e5-d436-41c8-bf38-30152d76be10#bkmk_dev shows what company content is removed.

BranchCache - Resume Download   Clients that use Windows BranchCache to download content and have a download interrupted now resume the download where it left off, without having to restart the download from the beginning. This is a significant improvement for a mobile, disconnected world.

Wake-Up Proxy   With Configuration Manager SP 1 clients, you can supplement the Wake on LAN site setting for unicast packets by using the wake-up proxy client settings. This combination helps wake up computers on subnets without needing to reconfigure network switches. For more information about wake-up proxy, see http://technet. microsoft.com/en-us/library/gg712701.aspx#BKMK_PlanToWakeClients.

Configuration Manager 2012 Servicing Extension

A brand new feature for ConfigMgr (in beta as this book is being completed) is the ConfigMgr 2012 Servicing Extension. This extension allows you to be more aware of the versions of ConfigMgr running in your infrastructure, as well as released hotfixes. Following is a brief overview of the key capabilities:

▶ **Site updates:** Notifies you of updates to ConfigMgr as they become available, and allows you to filter according to major releases.

▶ **Site versions:** Displays the last major ConfigMgr version installed on all sites, as well as the most recently installed cumulative update.

▶ **Client targeting:** This view shows you updates that are available for a specific service pack and cumulative update. You can click the Create Query link under the Monitoring tab to create a query to view those systems that have that update or require it (you choose which query to create when you select the Create Query link).

   After creating and verifying the query, you can create a collection based on the WQL query, so you can target an updated ConfigMgr installation to a collection if desired.

To fully leverage this feature, ensure that your admin console has access to the Internet.

Summary

The list of updates since ConfigMgr 2012 RTM is quite significant. Microsoft invested significantly in the integration between ConfigMgr and Windows Intune, as well as in new features for ConfigMgr itself. As the remainder of this book discusses, just about every aspect of ConfigMgr 2012 has been upgraded since its initial release.

The next chapter discusses managing user data and profiles settings in ConfigMgr.

PART II
Deep Dive

IN THIS PART

CHAPTER 3 User Data and Profiles   61

CHAPTER 4 New Application Deployment Types   77

CHAPTER 5 On-Premise Cross-Platform Support 117

CHAPTER 6 What's New in Operating System
           Deployment   147

User Data and Profiles

IN THIS CHAPTER

▶ User Data and Profiles Overview

▶ User Data and Profiles Prerequisites

▶ Configuring User Data and Profiles

▶ Deploying User Data and Profiles Configuration Items

▶ Reporting User Data and Profiles Compliance

A*ny user, any device, anywhere.* As Information Technology (IT) continues to embrace people-centric IT, you can expect to hear this phrase more and more. The more IT can enable a user to be productive, regardless of his location, the more successful your business can be.

System Center 2012 Configuration Manager (ConfigMgr) Service Pack (SP) 1 introduced a new type of configuration item (found under Compliance Settings in the console) called User Data and Profiles. This new configuration item contains settings that manage folder redirection, offline files and folders, and roaming profiles for users on Windows 8 (and newer) systems in your ConfigMgr hierarchy. These settings can be used to enable users to access data in many scenarios, such as a Virtual Desktop Infrastructure (VDI) environment, as well as maintain user data in a protected, backed-up location in your data center. This chapter describes scenarios for using these settings and how to configure each of them.

User Data and Profiles Overview

While roaming profiles, offline files, and folder redirection have been around for a while in Active Directory group policy objects (GPOs), these settings are new to ConfigMgr 2012 SP 1 (and thus, R2), and are handled differently in ConfigMgr. In fact, ConfigMgr only supports Windows 8/ Server 2012 and newer systems for management of these settings. This section covers the basics of using the User Data and Profiles feature on these newer platforms.

Following is a brief overview of each of the features for User and Data Profiles:

▶ **Roaming User Profiles:** Roaming user profiles redirect the entire user profile to a file share. When enabled, this feature copies the entire profile from the specified share at each login, and synchronizes all changes to the specified share at each logoff. While this can be the most resource-intensive option (copying an entire profile over WAN can be costly, whereas folder redirection makes the files available without copying locally), it provides the user a consistent experience, as all user-specific settings are preserved on the specified profile share.

▶ **Offline Files:** Offline files make network files available to a user, even when a network connection to the server is not available. Specified folders in a network location are configured to synchronize to the local system.

▶ **Folder Redirection:** This enables redirection of the path of one or more folders to a different location on the local disk or a specified file share. For example, the Documents folder could be redirected to a network location, such that the user always has access to documents regardless of the system logged in to.

Each of these features could be used alone, or could be leveraged to provide the best user experience. For example, you can enable a roaming user profile with folder redirection for the user's Documents folder. This keeps documents out of the user profile, which helps to improve sign-on times as well as keep the user profile smaller.

User Data and Profiles Prerequisites

To leverage user data and profiles in ConfigMgr, the following prerequisites must be met:

▶ Install Windows 8 (or later) on the target system.

▶ Enable user data and profiles for client settings. This is a ConfigMgr client agent setting that must be configured and deployed to Windows systems supporting user data and profiles configurations.

Because it is unlikely that you want to leverage user data and profiles for all your managed systems, the authors recommend building a dynamic collection of systems that should use this feature. Perform the following steps to enable user and data profiles for client settings for a custom collection named Managed User Data and Profiles:

1. In the ConfigMgr console, navigate to **Administration -> Client Settings**, and select **Create Custom Client Device Settings** from the ribbon bar.

2. On the Create Custom Client Device Settings page, enter a descriptive name, such as **Enable User and Data Profiles**, and enable the Compliance Settings check box.

3. Click the **Compliance Settings** group and configure both settings to **Yes**, as shown in Figure 3.1. Click **OK** to save your changes.

4. From the Client Settings node, select the new custom client setting, and click **Deploy** from the ribbon bar.

5. Browse to select the Managed User and Data Profiles collection, verify the Member Count column looks accurate (see Figure 3.2), and click **OK**.

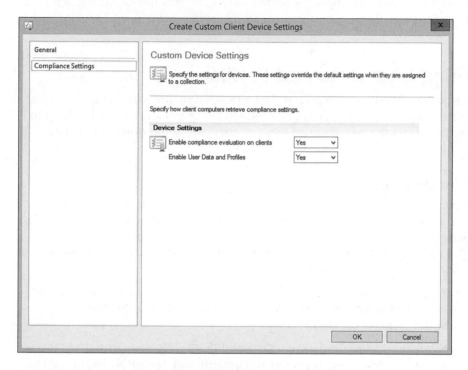

FIGURE 3.1   Enabling user and data profiles in Compliance Settings.

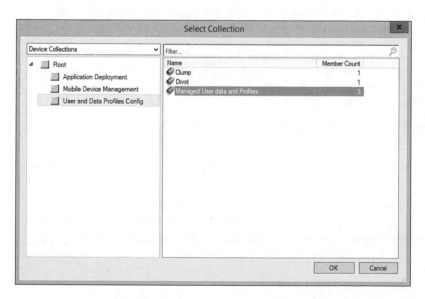

FIGURE 3.2   Deploying the Managed User Data and Profiles custom setting.

Client systems automatically download and apply the configuration change at the next machine polling cycle, or you could initiate the Machine Policy Retrieval & Evaluation Cycle action on a test system to apply the setting faster. The remainder of this chapter describes the various scenarios for configuring and deploying user data and profiles settings.

Configuring User Data and Profiles

The next sections describe how to configure folder redirection, use roaming user profiles, and offline files. For clarity, each type is described separately in this chapter, but keep in mind that these features can be combined into one user data and profiles configuration item.

Using Folder Redirection

Folder redirection allows administrators to redirect the path of one or more user profile folders to a new location, which can be a local folder or a network location. For example, if you enable folder redirection for the user's Documents folder to a network share, the user can easily access documents from any computer on the network. Follow these steps to configure the folder redirection configuration item:

1. In the ConfigMgr console, navigate to **Assets and Compliance -> Compliance Settings -> User Data and Profiles**. Click **Create User Data and Profiles Configuration Item** on the ribbon bar.

2. On the General page of the Create user Data and Profiles Configuration Item Wizard, enter a name like **Folder Redirection of Documents and Favorites**, and check the Folder Redirection check box, shown in Figure 3.3.

3. On the Folder Redirection page shown in Figure 3.4, configure the options as required for your environment.

   The drop-down for Folder redirection applicability selection has three options, allowing you to choose how targeted devices determine applicability of the redirection rule. Based on the drop-down, you can choose to apply the redirection rule in one of the following three scenarios:

   ▶ **On any device:** Forces folder redirection on any device that is logged on by the user.

   ▶ **Only on primary devices:** Forces folder redirection on any device that is associated in ConfigMgr as the primary user of the device.

   ▶ **Folder redirection on any device; caching on primary devices only:** Similar to the first option, redirect the specified folders on any device, but also cache (using offline folders) the redirected folders on the user's primary device(s).

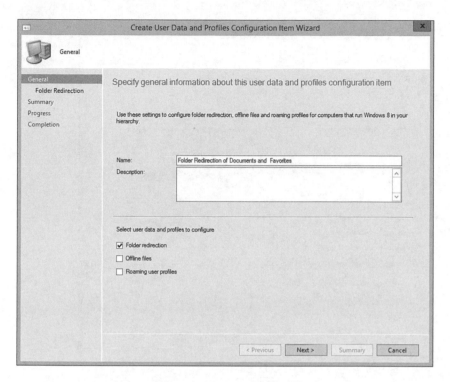

FIGURE 3.3   Specifying folder redirection in the Create User Data and Profiles Configuration Item Wizard.

The Folders to redirect selection allows you to choose individual settings for the following folders:

▶ Desktop

▶ Start menu

▶ Documents

▶ Music

▶ Videos

▶ Favorites

▶ Contacts

▶ Downloads

▶ Links

▶ Searches

▶ Saved games

▶ Application data

▶ Pictures

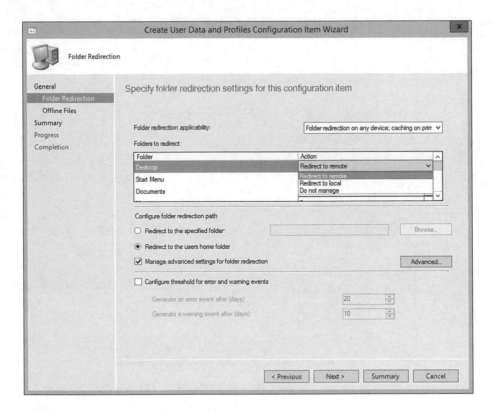

FIGURE 3.4   Configuring folder redirection settings.

Settings for these folders follow:

▶ **Do not manage:** Do nothing with content stored in this folder.

▶ **Redirect to remote:** Enforce use of the specified redirection path (either user's home folder or a specified folder) to store content.

▶ **Redirect to local:** Enforce use of the local folder for the specified content.

Options for the Configure folder redirection path follow:

▶ **Redirect to the specified folder:** Specify a folder for redirection.

▶ **Redirect to the users home folder:** Use the home drive (defined in Active Directory).

The Folder Redirection dialog contains two additional check boxes:

▶ **Manage advanced settings for folder redirection:** The Advanced button displays additional settings (see Figure 3.5).

▶ **Configure threshold for error and warning events:** This setting allows you to specify when error and warning events should be forwarded to ConfigMgr.

4. Click **Next** to review the Summary information, and **Next** and then **Close** to complete the wizard.

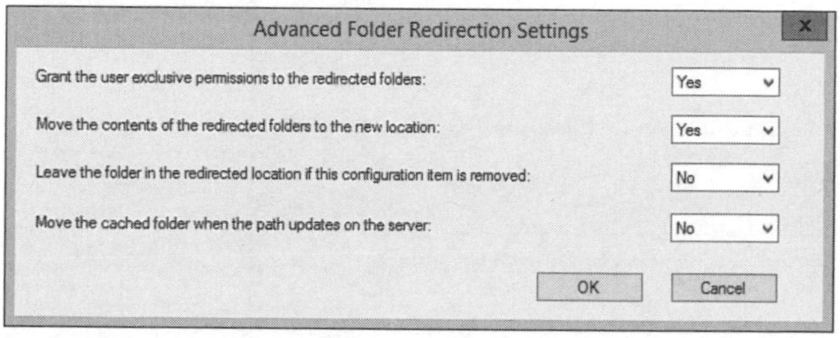

FIGURE 3.5   Advanced Folder Redirection Settings.

Using Offline Files

Using offline files enables a mobile worker to access network files locally offline, even when folder redirection is configured. While a user is connected to the local-area network (LAN), files are accessed from the network location. When working offline, files are retrieved from the Offline Files folder on the local system. A computer switches to offline mode when any of the following events occur:

▶ Always Offline mode has been enabled.

▶ The system is unable to access the redirected folders share.

▶ The network connection is slower than a configurable threshold in group policy.

▶ The user clicks the Work offline button in Windows Explorer.

Perform the following steps to configure the offline files configuration item:

1. In the ConfigMgr console, navigate to **Assets and Compliance -> Compliance Settings -> User Data and Profiles**. Click **Create User Data and Profiles Configuration Item** on the ribbon bar.

2. On the General page of the Create User Data and Profiles Configuration Item Wizard, enter a name like **Offline files**, and check the **Offline files** check box, as shown in Figure 3.6.

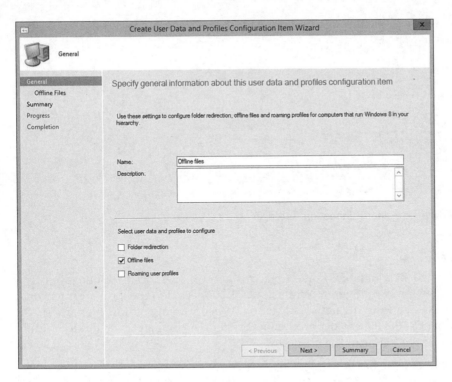

FIGURE 3.6   Specifying offline files in the Create User Data and Profiles Configuration
Item Wizard.

3. On the Offline Files page, choose the option to **Enable offline files**, as shown in
Figure 3.7, and configure the remaining settings as required for your environment.
A brief description of each setting follows:

▶ **Enable background synchronization in work offline mode:** Choose
from Enabled, Disabled, and Not Configured in the drop-down. Note that
when you configure this option to Enabled, there are default configuration
settings for this option that can be modified in group policy under Computer
Configuration -> Administrative Templates -> Network -> Offline Files ->
Configure Background Sync.

▶ **Allow file synchronization on metered network connections:** Choose
from Enabled, Disabled, and Not Configured in the drop-down. Starting with
Windows 8, a user can specify a network connection as a metered connection, which could be used to limit activity over that connection, as metered
connections generally are more expensive. For example, when tethering
your phone to your notebook for Internet access, you want to minimize
data download to reduce data transfer charges. For more information on
metered networks, see http://windows.microsoft.com/en-US/windows-8/
metered-internet-connections-frequently-asked-questions.

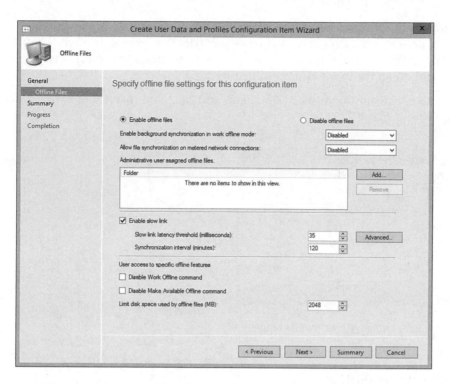

FIGURE 3.7   Specifying offline file settings.

▶ **Administrative user assigned offline files:** This setting coincides with the Specify Administratively assigned offline files group policy setting. Use this setting to specify a network folder that is always available for offline use. For example, if you have a human resources team share, you could enable this setting to enable the share for offline use on all HR employees.

▶ **Enable slow link:** This setting coincides with the Configure Slow Link group policy setting. Configure this setting to set a threshold value at which Offline Files considers a network connection to be slow.

When enabled, the default setting of 35 milliseconds is a good starting point. When latency is more than 35 milliseconds, file synchronization occurs every 120 minutes. Click the Advanced button for more granularity. As shown in Figure 3.8, you can configure different latency thresholds for different shares.

▶ **User access to offline features:** This section allows the administrator to control whether the user can disable the features that allow a user to select additional folders to make available offline, as well as the ability to initiate the action to work offline.

▶ **Limit disk space used by offline files (MB):** The final section of the configuration page shows a default configuration of 2048MB for the maximum amount of disk space used for offline files use. This affects how much space can be used on the user's PC for offline files.

4. Click **Next** to review the Summary information, and **Next** and then **Close** to complete the wizard.

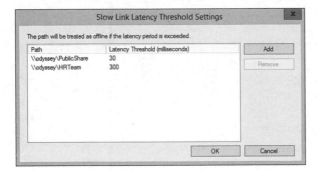

FIGURE 3.8   Slow Link Latency Threshold Settings.

Using Roaming User Profiles

Roaming user profiles redirect the entire user profile to a file share, enabling the user to receive the same operating system and application settings configuration on multiple computers. Each time a user logs in to a computer with an account enabled for roaming profiles, his profile is downloaded to the local computer and merged with the local profile. The updated user profile is synchronized back to the profile share when the user logs off. To configure the roaming user profile configuration item, follow these steps:

1. In the ConfigMgr console, navigate to **Assets and Compliance -> Compliance Settings -> User Data and Profiles**. Click **Create User Data and Profiles Configuration Item** on the ribbon bar.

2. On the General page of the Create User Data and Profiles Configuration Item Wizard, enter a name like **Roaming Profiles**, and check for **Roaming user profiles** check box.

3. On the Roaming Profiles page, choose the option to **Allow roaming profiles on any device**, as shown in Figure 3.9, and configure the remaining settings as required for your environment. A brief description of each setting follows:

   ▶ **Allow roaming profiles on any device:** This default setting enables roaming profiles for any device logged in to by the user (regardless of whether it is a primary device).

   ▶ **Allow roaming profiles only on the users' primary devices:** This setting prevents roaming profile usage on a user's nonprimary devices.

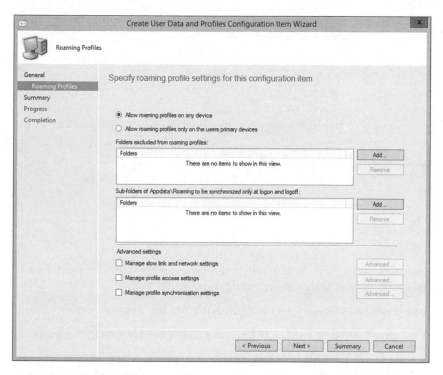

FIGURE 3.9   Specifying roaming profile settings in the Create User Data and Profiles Configuration Item Wizard.

▶ **Folders excluded from roaming profiles:** By default, the History, Local Settings, Temp, and Temporary Internet Files folders are excluded from synchronizing with a roaming profile. Add additional folders, as shown in Figure 3.10, such as Downloads, Dropbox, and OneDrive. Note that the path is relative to *%UserProfile%*. For example, the path *%UserProfile%*\OneDrive is simply entered as OneDrive in this dialog.

FIGURE 3.10   Specifying folders excluded from roaming profiles.

▶ **Sub-folders of Appdata\Roaming to be synchronized only at logon and logoff:** Add application folders in this group that should be synchronized at logon and logoff. This setting is used in conjunction with Folder Redirection to help resolve issues with applications that do not work well with Offline Files while the user is online. This setting prevents periodic synchronization of specified folders, and only synchronizes at logon/logoff.

▶ **Manage Slow link and network settings:** The Advanced button allows you to configure options, as shown in Figure 3.11.

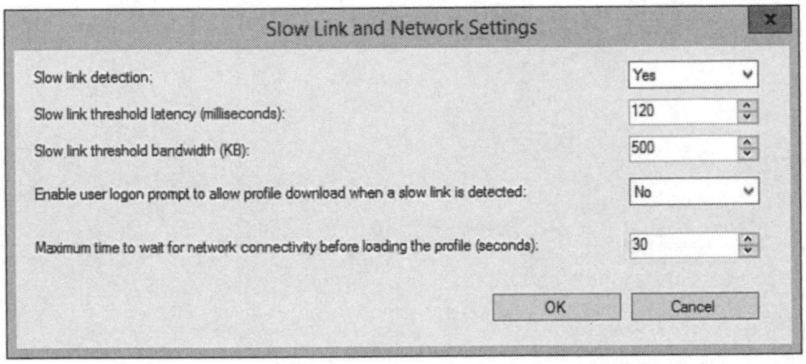

Slow Link and Network Settings

Slow link detection:	Yes
Slow link threshold latency (milliseconds):	120
Slow link threshold bandwidth (KB):	500
Enable user logon prompt to allow profile download when a slow link is detected:	No
Maximum time to wait for network connectivity before loading the profile (seconds):	30

OK   Cancel

FIGURE 3.11   Specifying slow link and network settings.

Slow link detection: Slow link is calculated between the user's computer and the remote server that stores the roaming user profile.

Slow link threshold latency (milliseconds): Enter the desired latency value.

Slow link threshold bandwidth (KB): Enter the desired bandwidth threshold.

Enable user logon prompt to allow profile download when a slow link is detected: When enabled, this setting allows a user to enable a check box on the login screen to enable profile download over a slow network. If this setting is not enabled, the system uses a local copy of the user profile when a slow link is detected.

Maximum time to wait for network connectivity before loading the profile (seconds): This setting controls how long Windows waits for a response from the network before logging on a user without a remote home directory, and without synchronizing roaming user profiles. Setting this value to zero causes Windows to proceed without waiting for the network.

▶ **Manage profile access settings:** The Advanced button enables you to configure the settings shown in Figure 3.12:

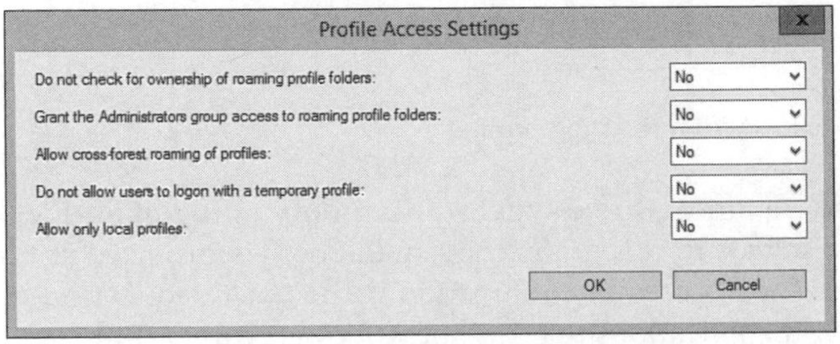

Profile Access Settings

Do not check for ownership of roaming profile folders:	No
Grant the Administrators group access to roaming profile folders:	No
Allow cross-forest roaming of profiles:	No
Do not allow users to logon with a temporary profile:	No
Allow only local profiles:	No

OK   Cancel

FIGURE 3.12   Specifying profile access settings.

Do not check for ownership of roaming profile folders: Enabling this setting disables the Windows check for proper permissions on an existing roaming profile folder for the user. By default, Windows checks for folder ownership by either the user or the administrator's group, if ownership is incorrect it does not allow the profile to synchronize, and the user gets a temporary profile.

Grant the Administrators group access to roaming profile folders: By default, only the user has rights to the roaming profile share. Enable this option to grant the Administrators group full control of the user's profile folder.

Allow cross-forest roaming of profiles: This setting allows roaming user profiles across forests. This policy configures the Allow cross-forest user policy and roaming user profiles group policy, which also controls user-based policy and user object logon scripts.

Do not allow users to logon with a temporary profile: By default, if a user's profile is corrupt or unreadable, Windows creates a temporary local profile so that the user can log on. Enable this setting to prevent a roaming user from logging on with a temporary profile.

Allow only local profiles: Use this setting to prevent a roaming profile from being used on a system. For example, you could enable this setting on a server, so that in the event that a roaming profile user logs in to a server, the user's profile is not synchronized.

▶ **Manage profile synchronization settings:** The Advanced button enables you to configure the following settings, as shown in Figure 3.13:

Specify time for background upload of the user hive (hours): Allows the administrator to set a specific time (local to the computer) to upload the user Registry hive to the roaming profile. This option is used to upload the user Registry hive while the user is logged on, and does not affect the synchronization that occurs when the user logs off. Think of this as a way to synchronize the profile on an interval, even though the user never logs off the system.

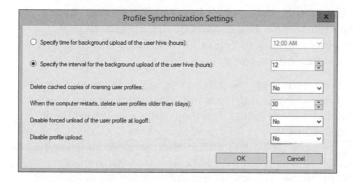

FIGURE 3.13   Specifying profile synchronization settings.

Specify the interval for the background upload of the user hive (hours):
Use this interval to specify an interval based on the user login time. For
example, if the interval is set to 6 hours, the user Registry hive is uploaded
every 6 hours after the user logs on. Similar to the previous setting, this interval does not affect the normal logoff synchronization.

Delete cached copies of roaming user profiles: Enable this setting to delete
the local copy of the user's profile when the user logs off, and synchronization
to the network profile is complete.

When the computer restarts, delete user profiles older than (days): Use this
setting to delete local profiles that have not been used for the specified number
of days (default 30).

Disable forced unload of the user profile at logoff: When enabled, Windows
does not forcefully unload the user's Registry at logoff. Windows unloads the
Registry when all open handles to that user's Registry keys are closed. Use
this setting with caution, because it may prevent the upload synchronization of a user profile hive. In most cases, it is best to leave this disabled, so
that Windows forces unloading the hive and the hive can be successfully
synchronized.

Disable profile upload: By default, when a user logs in, the roaming profile
is synchronized to the local system, and when the user logs off, the roaming
profile is synchronized back to the profile share. Enable this setting to prevent
the synchronization of the profile back to the profile share. This setting could
be used on test systems, or other testing scenarios where you don't want the
two-way synchronization of the user profile.

4. Click **Next** to review the Summary tab, and **Next** and then **Close** to complete the
   wizard.

Roaming Profiles, Folder Redirection, and Offline Files in a Mash-Up

To get the most from User Data and Profiles, consider using multiple options. For
example, you could enable roaming profiles, but leverage folder redirection for documents, pictures, and other normal user folders. This enables the user profile to load much
faster than having everything in folder redirection. You can also leverage offline files for
mobile workers, to enable them to take work on the go easily.

Combining these settings provides even more of a way to enable any user, on any device,
anywhere. Imagine saving a document on your notebook in the morning (folder redirection and offline files), connecting into a kiosk virtual desktop from a conference room
at noon (roaming profile and folder redirection), and even editing that document on
the train that evening, using your favorite tablet device with a virtual desktop (roaming
profile and folder redirection). Finally, at night connect back to work with your notebook,
to easily synchronize that document (folder redirection and offline files).

Deploying User Data and Profiles Configuration Items

Recall that the Enable User and Data Profiles client settings must be enabled for any of these settings to take effect (refer to the "User Data and Profiles Prerequisites" section earlier in this chapter). Unlike traditional configuration items, there is no need to add User Data and Profile configurations to a baseline to deploy. Follow these steps to deploy a User Data and Profiles configuration to a collection of users:

1. In the ConfigMgr console, navigate to **Assets and Compliance -> Compliance Settings -> User Data and Profiles**. Select the desired configuration in the Details pane, and select **Deploy** from the ribbon bar.

2. Review the deployment details dialog, as shown in Figure 3.14:

   ▶ Target a user collection.

   ▶ Enable the **Remediate noncompliant rules when supported** and **Allow Remediation outside the maintenance window** to enforce settings.

   ▶ Choose to generate a ConfigMgr alert if compliance is below the desired percentage, based on the specified date and time.

   ▶ Choose whether to generate System Center Operations Manager alerts.

   ▶ Choose the desired schedule to reevaluate (and re-enforce) the setting.

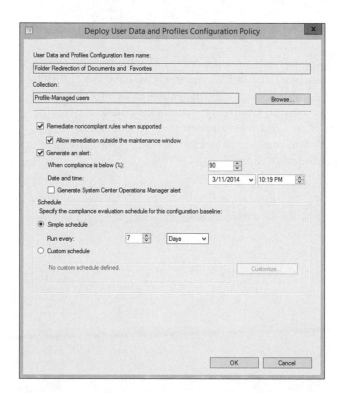

FIGURE 3.14   Deploying user data and profiles configuration policy.

3. Click **OK** to complete the Deploy User Data and Profiles Configuration Wizard.

You can verify successful application of the configuration policy from the Monitoring node in the ConfigMgr console. Select **Deployments**, and search for the configuration policy.

Reporting User Data and Profiles Compliance

New reports were added for user data and profiles. From your reporting point, select the **User Data and Profiles Health** folder. The following reports are available:

- ▶ **User Data and Profiles Heath Report - Summary:** This report shows the summary of health status for folder redirection and roaming user profiles.

- ▶ **User Data and Profile Health Report - Details:** This report shows the details of error or warning messages for folder redirection or roaming user profile.

- ▶ **Roaming User Profiles Health Report - Details:** This report shows the details of health state of roaming user profiles, for a specific user.

- ▶ **Folder Redirection Health Report - Details:** This report shows the details of health state for folder redirection for each of the redirected folders for a given user.

Summary

Microsoft has done a great job of helping to enable people-centric IT with the additional feature of User Data and Profiles. As demonstrated in this chapter, you have the ability to help enable any user, on any device, anywhere. By using this feature in ConfigMgr, you can target groups of users and systems based on ConfigMgr criteria instead of controlling by GPO. This capability provides you as an administrator with more granular control for targeting the configuration of user data and profiles, reducing the risk of configuring/ linking the wrong group policy object to production.

The next chapter covers application management.

CHAPTER 4

New Application Deployment Types

IN THIS CHAPTER

▶ Application Overview

▶ What's New for Applications Since ConfigMgr 2012 RTM

▶ Support for Write Filters in Windows Embedded

▶ Working with Virtual Applications

▶ Deploying Applications to Mobile Devices

▶ Deploying Software to OS X, Linux, and UNIX Platforms

▶ Deploying Web Applications

▶ Best Practices for Working with Applications

A major enhancement of Service Pack (SP) 1 for Configuration Manager (ConfigMgr) 2012 was support for non-Microsoft clients. The SP introduced support for installing agents on OS X, UNIX, and Linux computers, and introduced support to manage Windows Phone 8, Windows RT, iOS, and Android through the Windows Intune connector. SP 1 also included many new deployment types for use within applications, this being a new way to deliver software first introduced with Configuration Manager 2012. This chapter discusses changes to application management in SP 1 and Release 2 (R2) of System Center 2012 Configuration Manager.

Application Overview

System Center 2012 Configuration Manager Unleashed (Sams, 2012) previously discussed creating, managing, deploying, and monitoring applications. SP 1 and R2 build on application management with support for new deployment types. The following sections summarize the application concept introduced with System Center 2012 Configuration Manager.

Definition of an Application

An *application* is a container used to deliver software. It contains basic information for the application, such as name, version, application owner, and localization information that describes how the application is displayed in the Application Catalog. It also provides information regarding the distribution settings that are used and to which distribution points (DPs) and DP groups the content for the application is distributed. It includes any references/dependencies for other applications, as well as whether the application replaces an existing application or is part of a virtual environment. The application is the shell; installing software requires a deployment type, which is the key component of the application.

When comparing Configuration Manager applications to packages and programs, consider an application as an enhanced way to deliver software to a user or computer. An application is a container that may contain multiple methods of installation, based on user state or computer state. Similar to packages, applications are used to distribute software, but contain additional information to support smart deployment to different devices and different deployment scenarios.

Defining Deployment Types

Deployment types (DTs) are a major component of a ConfigMgr application. You can almost compare a DT to a program, used with packages in ConfigMgr 2012 and earlier versions. Just as a program contains the installation command line and any platform requirements (such as Windows 7 x86), a DT contains this same basic information, and much more.

An application can have multiple deployment types. For example, say you have software with different installations for x86, x64, or different versions of Windows. Once the DT is built properly and the application deployed, the DTs are evaluated to determine which is appropriate to install. (For example, an x86 Windows 7 DT only installs the x86 version of the software.) Although this is a very basic example, it helps to convey the process. Requirement rules for deployment types are flexible and can leverage just about anything on a system, as well as SQL or LDAP queries, primary user information, and more. Applications are deployed to a user or a group of users, who get the correct deployment type installed depending on the type of device being used and where that device is situated at that time.

What's New for Applications Since ConfigMgr 2012 RTM

Microsoft released System Center 2012 Service Pack 1 on January 15, 2013. The service pack included changes to application management and introduced two new concepts:

▶ **Deep linking:** Identifies an application that you want to deploy in a vendor's application store. Deep linking points the device directly to the correct location in the application store used by the device.

▶ **Sideloading:** This is the process of deploying in-house or custom applications to mobile devices managed by Configuration Manager.

SP 1 also extended the number of deployment types from 5 to 14, introducing support for

▶ **Windows Application Packages:** Through .appx files via sideloading and the Windows Store via deep linking

► **Windows Phone Applications:** Through .xap files and .appx or .appxbundle files for Windows Phone 8.1 via sideloading and through the Windows Phone Store via deep linking

► **Application Package for Apple iOS:** Through .ipa files via sideloading and through the Apple App Store via deep linking

► **Application Package for Android:** Through .apk files and the Google Play Store

 ► **Mac OS X Applications:** Through .dmg, .mpkg, .pkg and .app files, and using a .cmmac manifest file

 ► **Microsoft Application Virtualization version 5:** Through .appv files, the new file format for App-V

Along with support of App-V version 5, Microsoft introduced the concept of App-V virtual environments, discussed in the "Working with Virtual Applications" section of this chapter. Microsoft also introduced support for Windows 8 features such as metered Internet connections, Always On, Always Connected, hosting a DP on Windows Azure, and built-in support for write filters used in Windows Embedded.

NOTE: WHAT'S NEW WITH SERVICE PACK 1 AND RELEASE 2

For more information about what changed with SP 1 and R2, see Chapter 2, "What's Changed Since Configuration Manager 2012 RTM."

Microsoft made System Center 2012 R2 generally available on October 18, 2013. In terms of application management, R2 introduced the concept of deploying web applications and support for the newly introduced .appxbundle package format introduced with Windows 8.1.

When an application is created, you can specify that it be featured, meaning the application is placed more prominently in the different company portals. You also can specify a privacy link for each application that could point to information users should read before installing the software. In addition, an application can open a virtual private network (VPN) connection automatically if a VPN profile has been configured.

Support for Write Filters in Windows Embedded

Windows Embedded is an operating system designed for use in embedded systems; these are devices that have an all-in-one functionality. Microsoft makes Windows Embedded available for original equipment manufacturers (OEM) to preload on embedded devices.

For operational reasons, it might be undesirable to write to storage media in Windows Embedded devices. By redirecting all write requests to either a separate disk partition or RAM, a write filter allows the runtime image to maintain the appearance of a writable runtime image without committing changes to the storage media. When the filter is enabled, changes made to the system are discarded when the device restarts; this is also true for any software installation that occurred while the write filter is enabled.

With ConfigMgr 2012 Service Pack 1, Microsoft included support for write filters out of the box. Prior to SP 1, either third-party software or complex installation procedures were required to install software on devices with write filters enabled. These procedures would disable the write filter, restart the device, install the software, reenable the write filter, and restart the device once more. These procedures were complex to manage and error prone.

Now with write filter support in ConfigMgr, the entire process is covered out of the box, with the only noticeable change an additional option (enabled by default) in the Deploy Software Wizard. This is the Commit changes at deadline or during a maintenance windows (requires restart) option, shown in Figure 4.1.

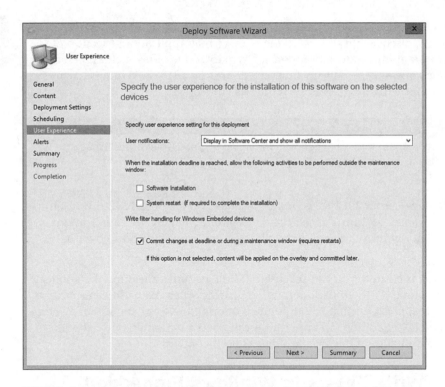

FIGURE 4.1   The commit changes option in the Deploy Software Wizard.

When enabled, this option installs the software either when the deadline is reached, or when the device enters a maintenance mode timeframe defined by the collection settings of which it is a member, known as *forced persist*. If not enabled, ConfigMgr assumes you have another process that is capable of committing the software; this is called *opportunistically persist*.

When ConfigMgr disables the write filters, it puts the device in a servicing lock mode, allowing only members of the Administrators group to log in to the machine. Figure 4.2 shows a Windows Embedded device in servicing mode.

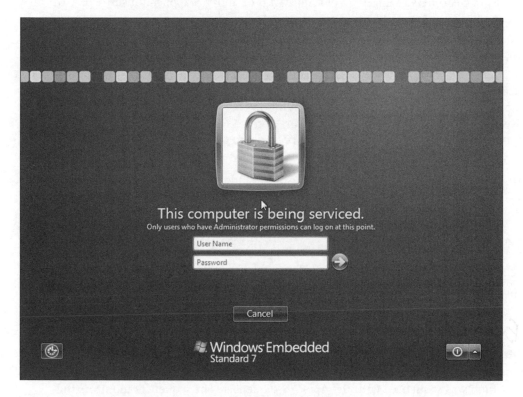

FIGURE 4.2   Windows Embedded device in servicing mode.

> **NOTE: ADDITIONAL INFORMATION ABOUT MANAGING WINDOWS EMBEDDED WITH WRITE FILTERS**
>
> For more information about managing devices with write filters enabled using ConfigMgr, see the TechNet article "Managing Embedded Devices with Write Filters in Configuration Manager Service Pack 1," at http://blogs.technet.com/b/configmgrteam/archive/2012/ 11/26/managing-embedded-devices-with-write-filters-in-configuration-manager-service-pack-1.aspx.

Working with Virtual Applications

System Center 2012 Configuration Manager included support for version 4.6 of Microsoft App-V. With Microsoft Application Virtualization version 5, released in late 2012, Microsoft completely rewrote the App-V product, dropping SFT, ICO, OSD, and manifest

.xml files and introducing the APPV file format that contains all the information in those previously mentioned files. Because of this major rewrite of the product, Microsoft now supports App-V 4.6 and App-V 5 virtual applications coexisting on the same system. This allows customers to migrate from App-V 4.6 to App-V 5 applications in a phased approach, because App-V 4.6 applications have to be converted or resequenced to make them available in the App-V 5 format.

System Center 2012 Configuration Manager SP 1 includes support for App-V 5 and App-V 5 SP 1. Microsoft App-V 5 SP 2 is supported on Configuration Manager 2012 SP 1 for Cumulative Update (CU) 4 and Configuration Manager 2012 R2 for CU 1 and later versions. App-V 5.0 SP 2 adds support for Windows 8.1, Windows Server 2012 R2, and the Office 2013 suite using the App-V sequencer. App-V 5 SP 2 also improves the virtual application upgrade experience, as it no longer prompts to close the running virtual application, postponing the upgrade to when the virtual environment is not in use.

With App-V 5, the ConfigMgr client now uses a Windows PowerShell module to manage App-V objects such as virtual applications, connection groups, and dynamic configuration files.

> **NOTE: MORE INFORMATION ABOUT INTEGRATING APP-V 5 WITH CONFIGMGR**
>
> For additional information about how to integrate App-V into ConfigMgr, see the whitepaper "Integrating Virtual Application Management with App-V 5 and Configuration Manager 2012 SP1," available at http://www.microsoft.com/en-us/download/details.aspx?id=38177.

ExacqVision?

Creating a Microsoft Application Virtualization 5 Deployment Type

The example in this section creates an App-V 5 deployment type for the 7-Zip application, which was sequenced with the App-V 5 sequencer. The sequencer monitors the installation and setup process for an application, and records the information necessary for the application to run in a virtual environment. The output of the sequencing should be copied to a share on the server hosting the ConfigMgr application sources from the sequencing computer. Complete the following steps to create the App-V 5 deployment type:

1. In the ConfigMgr console, navigate to **Software Library -> Application Management -> Applications**. Select the application for which you want to add the Windows Store deployment type, and click **Create Deployment Type** on the ribbon bar to open the Create Deployment Type Wizard.

2. On the General page of the Create Deployment Type Wizard, select **Microsoft Application Virtualization 5** as the type in the drop-down list.

3. Supply the UNC path to the location of the .appv file, created by the App-V sequencer while saving the sequenced application (in this case, **\\armada\source\ applications\7-Zip\App-V 5.0 SP1\7-Zip 9.20\7-Zip 9.20.appv**). Click **Next** to continue to the next page of the wizard.

4. Verify the Import Succeeded in the Import Information page of the Create Deployment Wizard. Click **Next** to continue.

5. On the General Information page, you can modify the name that is already filled in to one that suits your organization's needs. You can also supply administrator comments and select the languages that are included in this deployment type. Click **Next** to continue.

6. Use the Requirements page to specify the requirements. Click **Add** to open the Create Requirement dialog, and select those requirements that must be met to start this application. An example could be a global condition check of whether the App-V 5.0 client is installed on the client. Click **OK** to select the necessary requirement, and click **Next** in the Create Deployment Type Wizard.

7. On the Dependencies page, you can select dependencies by configuring a dependency group containing the applications on which this application depends. An example of an application that could be defined here is the App-V client installation. Note that if you create a requirement based on a global condition that specifies whether the App-V 5 client is installed, the deployment type dependencies is never reached and the App-V 5 client, even though specified as a dependency, is never installed and the deployment type is not started.

After creating the dependency group, click **OK** to close the Add Dependency window. Click **Next** to continue.

8. On the Summary page of the Create Deployment Wizard, review the information and click **Next** to create the deployment type.

9. Follow the progress and verify that the deployment type was successfully created in the Completion page. When successful, click **Close** to close the wizard.

Using App-V Virtual Environments

You can use App-V's virtual environment functionality to define App-V connection groups in ConfigMgr; these are the follow-up to the dynamic suite composition (DSC) functionality previously available in App-V. Defining interaction between two or more applications using DSC includes editing the OSD file to add a reference to the GUID of the other application, which is error-prone.

Applications residing in the same connection group can share the file system and Registry on client computers, enabling them to interact with each other. For example, Microsoft Outlook and a third-party add-in for Outlook could be delivered separately from each other. You can give priority to applications within the connection group, allowing their file system or Registry changes to take precedence over an application with less priority. The next section describes how to create an App-V Virtual Environment for FreeMind, a mind-mapping tool that requires the Oracle Java framework to run.

Creating an App-V Virtual Environment

The scenario in this section uses two App-V packages created using the App-V 5 sequencer:

▶ **FreeMind version 1.0.0:** This application is capable of creating mind maps, and depends on Java to be installed on the machine on which it runs

▶ **Java Runtime Environment:** In this case, Java JRE version 7 update 45.

Both applications were sequenced on the App-V sequencing machine and imported using the procedure described earlier in the "Creating a Microsoft Application Virtualization 5 Deployment Type" section of this chapter. After both applications with their App-V deployment types have been created, create a dependency between the FreeMind deployment type and the deployment type that was created for Java. Follow these steps:

1. In the ConfigMgr console, navigate to **Software Library** -> **Application Management** -> **App-V Virtual Environments**. Select **Create Virtual Environment** to define a new App-V connection group; this opens the Create Virtual Environment page.

2. On the Create Virtual Environment page, specify a name and provide a description for the connection group. In this case, specify **Java 7 Update 45 with FreeMind 1.0.0** as the name and use **Connection Group for FreeMind 1.0.0**.

3. Click **Add** to open the Add Applications page. Here you must provide a group name, which in this case is **Java 7 update 45**. Click **Add** to open the Specify Application page.

4. On the Specify Application page, select the **Java JRE 7 Update 45 - Microsoft Application Virtualization 5** deployment type and click **OK** to close the Specify Application page. Click **Add** again and select an additional application if needed, in the case that more than one virtual application can be used. This creates an OR statement for the specified applications. Click **OK** when finished.

5. Back on the Create Virtual Environment page, click **Add** to again open the Add Applications page. Specify a group name, which in this case is **FreeMind 1.0.0**. Click **Add** to open the Specify Application page.

6. On the Specify Application page, select the **FreeMind 1.0.0 - Microsoft Application Virtualization 5** deployment type and click **OK** to close this page. To select an additional application if needed, you can click **Add** again; this creates an OR statement for the specified applications. Click **OK** when finished.

7. You now see the two virtual applications added as App-V deployment types on the Create Virtual Environment page (see Figure 4.3).

   Notice the AND statement, which states in this case that FreeMind 1.0.0 and Java 7 update 45 can run in the same virtual environment.

8. Click **OK** to close the Create Virtual Environment page; the Java 7 update 45 with FreeMind 1.0.0 connection group has been created.

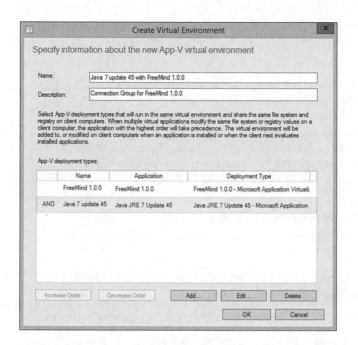

FIGURE 4.3 Specifying information about a new App-V virtual environment.

With the App-V virtual environment is specified, you can create a deployment for the FreeMind 1.0.0 application. Although you created the App-V virtual environment, you also need to specify that the FreeMind 1.0.0 - Microsoft Application Virtualization 5 deployment type is dependent on the Java 7 update 45 - Microsoft Application Virtualization 5 deployment type.

You can check whether the connection group is active on the client by using the Get-AppVClientConnectionGroup PowerShell cmdlet, available on each App-V client after importing the AppvClient.psd1 module and changing the execution policy.

Deploying Applications to Mobile Devices

System Center 2012 SP 1 Configuration Manager introduces the capability to integrate ConfigMgr with Microsoft's hosted Windows Intune device management solution. This makes it possible to manage mobile devices that are connected to Windows Intune from the ConfigMgr console. Microsoft refers to managing mobile devices through Windows Intune as *unified device management*. For information about integrating ConfigMgr with Windows Intune, see Chapter 7, "Using the Intune Connector," which explains how to set up the integration between Windows Intune and System Center 2012 R2 Configuration Manager, and Chapter 8, "Mobile Device Management in Configuration Manager 2012 R2," which discusses Configuration Manager mobile device management (MDM) when integrated with Windows Intune.

After configuring your Microsoft-based, Android-based, or Apple mobile devices through Windows Intune to be managed by ConfigMgr, you can deploy applications to those devices using deep linking or sideloading.

Creating application store deployment types for mobile devices is quite easy; in most cases, you browse to the application in the application store of the manufacturer and select the application you want to install. Sideloading applications requires different procedures depending on the manufacturer of the operating system (OS) on which the mobile device runs. The process of sideloading applications is described in the "Sideloading Applications" section of this chapter; creating deployment types for application store deployment types is described in the next sections.

Creating Application Store Deployment Types

The following sections discuss creating deployment types for various types of devices, including the following

▶ Windows devices running a version of Windows 8 or Windows 8 RT that obtain their applications from the Windows Store

▶ Windows Phone devices that get their applications from the Windows Phone Store

▶ Apple iPad and iPhone devices that get their applications from the Apple App Store

▶ Devices running Android that obtain their applications from the Google Play Store

Although most steps for creating deployment types are similar, some steps differ depending on the particular application store. All procedures assume that an extra deployment type is created for an already existing application.

Creating a Windows Store Deployment Type

When you define a deployment type for the Windows Store, you must browse to a computer with the application from the Windows Store already installed. To browse the remote computer, you need to configure Windows Remote Management (WinRM) and Windows PowerShell remoting on the Windows computer on which the application is installed. Follow these steps:

1. Log on to the computer to which you want to browse for the application.

2. Start a Windows PowerShell session as Administrator on the computer.

3. Start by configuring WinRM and typing `winrm qc`. When the program asks to make the changes, type `Y` to confirm the changes. Verify that WinRM has been updated to receive requests.

4. Enable PowerShell remoting by typing `enable-psremoting`. When asked whether you want to continue, type `A` (this stands for Yes to All). Also, specify `A` when the installation wants to execute the `Set-PSSessionConfiguration` cmdlet, which lets selected users remotely run Windows PowerShell cmdlets on the computer. Verify that the outcome of both commands is successful.

5. Verify that WinRM is configured correctly by typing `winrm enumerate winrm/config/listener`. Verify port 5985 is used, and the Enabled option is set to True.

Using the Windows 8 machine that already has the application installed and configured, you can start creating the deployment type. Complete the following steps:

1. In the ConfigMgr console, navigate to **Software Library** -> **Application Management** -> **Applications**. Select the application for which you want to add the Windows Store deployment type and click **Create Deployment Type** on the ribbon bar to open the Create Deployment Type Wizard.

2. On the General page of the Create Deployment Type Wizard, select **Windows app package (in the Windows Store)** from the drop-down list.

3. Click **Browse** to open the Browse Windows App Packages dialog box. Type the name of the machine on which you enabled Windows Remote Management and Windows PowerShell remoting, in this example the machine name is **clump**. Click **Connect** to connect to the machine.

4. Select the **Microsoft.LyncMX** application from the list (see Figure 4.4) and click OK to return to the wizard. Verify that the Location field is filled (in this case, with **ms-windows-store:PDP?PFN=Microsoft.LyncMX_8wekyb3d8bbwe**). Click **Next**.

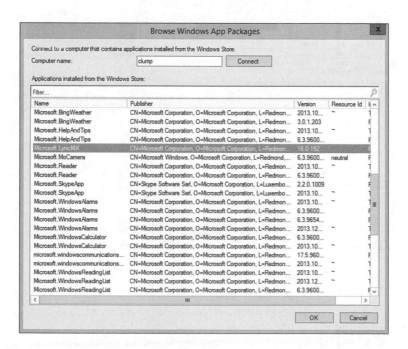

FIGURE 4.4   Selecting Lync 2013.

5. Confirm that the Import Succeeded on the Import Information page of the wizard. If not, select **Previous** and verify that the URL in the Location field on the General page is correct. Click **Next** to continue.

6. On the General Information page, you can modify the name that is already filled in. You can also supply administrator comments and select the languages to include in this deployment type. Click **Next** to continue.

7. Notice some requirements are already listed on the Requirements page. In this case, the OS should be one of All Windows 8 (64-bit), All Windows 8.1 (64-bit), All Windows Server 2012 (64-bit), and All Windows Server 2012 R2 (64-bit). In addition, the Global Condition Windows Store Inactive selection should not be equal to 1, meaning that the store is active on the machine, as shown in Figure 4.5.

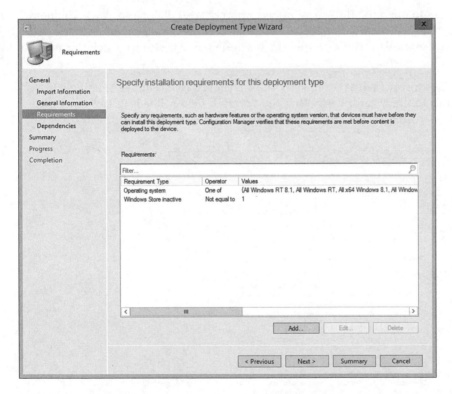

FIGURE 4.5   Lync Windows app package installation requirements.

8. On the Dependencies page, select the dependencies you have by configuring a dependency group containing the applications on which this deployment type depends. There are no known dependencies in this case; click **Next** to continue.

9. On the Summary page, review the information and click **Next** to create the deployment type.

10. On the Completion page, verify that the deployment type was created successfully. When successful, click **Close** to close the Create Deployment Type Wizard.

Creating a Windows Phone Store Deployment Type

The procedure in this section shows how to create a deployment type that provides a link to the Windows Phone Store. Clicking the link takes users directly to the application in the Windows Phone Store, where they can decide to install the application. Complete the following steps:

1. In the ConfigMgr console, navigate to **Software Library -> Application Management -> Applications**. Select the application for which you want to add the Windows Phone Store deployment type and click **Create Deployment Type** on the ribbon bar to open the Create Deployment Type Wizard.

2. On the General page of the wizard, select **Windows Phone app package (in the Windows Phone Store)** as the type from the drop-down list.

3. You now have to supply the URL in the Windows Phone Store to the application that you want to specify. If you know the URL you can paste it in the Location field; if not, click **Browse** to open the Windows Phone app package Browser.

4. Type the name of the application you want to add in the search field, in this case **Lync 2013**, and click the magnifying glass icon to start the search for the Lync 2013 app.

5. Select the Lync 2013 application from the search results; this brings you to the correct location for the Lync 2013 application (shown in Figure 4.6). Click **OK** to select Lync 2013 and close the Windows Phone app package Browser.

6. Notice that the URL in the location field at the General page of the wizard contains the Windows Phone Store location. Click **Next** to continue.

7. Verify that the Import Succeeded in the Import Information page of the Create Deployment Wizard. If not, click **Previous** and check the URL you filled in on the Location field on the General page is correct. Click **Next** to continue.

8. On the General Information page of the wizard, you can modify the Name that is already filled in to one that suits your organization's needs. You can also provide Administrator comments and select the languages included in this deployment type. Click **Next** to continue.

9. On the Summary page, review the information and click **Next** to create the deployment type.

10. Follow the progress and verify that the deployment type was successfully created in the Completion page of the Create Deployment Type Wizard. When successful, click **Close** to close the wizard.

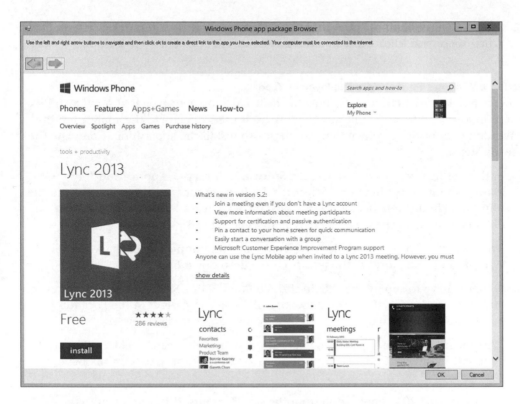

FIGURE 4.6   Lync 2013 in the Windows Phone app package Browser.

Creating an Apple App Store Deployment Type

The procedure in this section discusses how to create a deployment type that provides a link to the Apple App Store. Clicking the link takes users directly to the application in the Apple App Store, where they can decide whether to install the application. In some cases, different links may be available for the same application, depending on whether it is an iPhone or an iPad. You can specify requirements to ensure the deployment type is applicable to either the iPhone or the iPad. Follow these steps:

1. In the ConfigMgr console, navigate to **Software Library -> Application Management -> Applications**. Select the application for which you want to add the Apple App Store deployment type and click **Create Deployment Type** on the ribbon bar to open the Create Deployment Type Wizard.

2. On the General page of the wizard, select **App Package for iOS from App Store** as the type from the drop-down list.

3. Supply the URL in the Apple store to the application that you want to specify. If you already know the URL, you can paste it in the Location field; otherwise click **Browse** to open the App Package for iOS Browser.

4. In this case, typing the name of the Application that you want to add in the search field does not provide the desired result. Therefore, click **Business** to select the business category in the App Store. Select the letter **M**; somewhere around page 17, you should find Microsoft Lync 2010 for iPad and Microsoft Lync 2010 for iPhone.

5. Click **Microsoft Lync 2010 for iPad** to bring up the dialog box shown in Figure 4.7. Click **OK** to select this application and close the App Package for iOS Browser page.

FIGURE 4.7   Lync 2010 for iPad in the App Package for iOS Browser window.

6. Notice that the URL in the location field on the General page of the wizard now contains the Apple Store location. Click **Next** to continue.

7. Confirm the import was successful in the Import Information page of the Create Deployment Wizard. If not, select **Previous** and verify that the URL on the Location field on the General page is correct. Click **Next** to continue.

8. On the General Information page, you can modify the name that is provided to one that suits your organization's needs. You can also enter administrator comments and select the languages to include in this deployment type. Click **Next** to continue.

9. On the Requirements page of the wizard, you can specify the requirements. Click **Add** to open the Create Requirement dialog box. In this case, you can select the iPad

page to select iOS5, iOS6, and iOS 7 as the platform on which this application can be run. Click **Next** to continue in the Create Deployment Type Wizard.

10. On the Summary page, review the information and click **Next** to create the deployment type.

11. On the Completion page, verify that the deployment type was successfully created. When successful, click **Close** to close the Create Deployment Type Wizard.

Creating a Google Play Store Deployment Type

This section shows how to create a deployment type that provides a link to the Google Play Store. Clicking the link takes users directly to the application in the Google Play Store, where they can decide to install the application. Complete the following steps:

1. In the ConfigMgr console, navigate to **Software Library** -> **Application Management** -> **Applications**. Select the application for which you want to add the Google Play Store deployment type and click **Create Deployment Type** on the ribbon bar to open the Create Deployment Type Wizard.

2. On the General page of the wizard, select **App Package for Android on Google Play** as the type from the drop-down list.

3. Provide the URL in the Google Play Store to the application that you want to specify. If you already know the URL, you can paste it in the Location field; otherwise, browse for the URL using an external browser session.

   ▶ Using an external browser is recommended by the authors, as when using the App Package Browser for Android, the App Package Browser window doesn't show the search Play Store options that you can see in an external browser session. Open a web browser and type the following URL to go to the Google Play application store: http://play.google.com. In the Search Play Store field, type **Lync 2013** and click the magnifying glass to start the search. Select the Lync 2013 application from the search results and copy the URL of the page to your Clipboard, as shown in Figure 4.8.

   ▶ Supply the URL you just copied in the Location field on the General page of the Create Deployment Type Wizard.

   Click **Next** to continue.

4. Confirm that the import was successful in the Import Information page of the wizard. If not, select **Previous** and verify that the URL on the Location field on the General page is correct. Click **Next** to continue.

5. On the General Information page of the Create Deployment Type Wizard, you can modify the name that is already filled in to one that suits your organization's needs. You could also provide administrator comments and select those languages included in this deployment type. Click **Next** to continue.

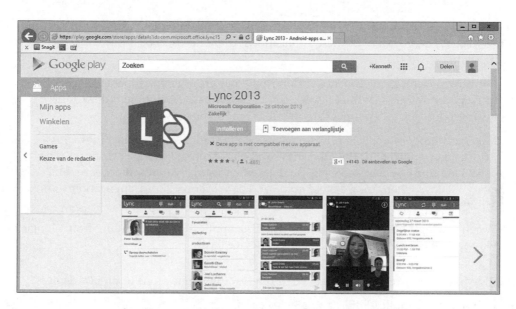

FIGURE 4.8   Lync 2013 in the Google Play Store using a web browser session.

6. On the Summary page of the wizard, review the information and click **Next** to create the deployment type.

7. Follow the progress and verify that the deployment type was successfully created in the Completion page of the Create Deployment Type Wizard. When successful, click **Close** to close the wizard.

Sideloading Applications

When a company wants to install custom applications on their users' mobile devices, they could buy that software from a software development company that develops the application, or use in-house developers to create the application.

For each type of application, the OS manufacturer provides a development environment:

▶ Microsoft provides Microsoft Visual Studio as a development platform for developing Windows modern applications and applications for Windows Phone.

▶ The Apple development platform is called Xcode.

▶ Google provides an Android Developer Tools plug-in for Eclipse, which is a platform for developing open source software.

Other third-party development environments are also available for developers to write software for devices.

Microsoft and Apple provide methods for developers to test their applications on devices. To prevent mass deployment of these applications, there needs to be a way to restrict running them.

▶ Running development applications on Apple requires the developer to register the universally unique identifier (UUID) of the device as a development device for testing purposes; a developer can only register 100 devices per year.

▶ Microsoft modern applications can be tested on domain-joined machines with a Registry key enabled, or the machines can be provisioned using a certificate. The certificate must be renewed every 30 days when using a Microsoft account, and every 90 days when using a Store account. For Windows Phone application testing, Microsoft provides an emulator that is available with Visual Studio.

▶ When testing Android applications, installing applications not coming from Google Play can be enabled or disabled on a per-device basis.

The following scenarios are supported when sideloading applications to mobile devices:

▶ Deploying an application as available to users.

▶ Deploying an application as required to users and devices. Note that this is not supported on Windows Phone and that user consent is required for iOS and Android devices.

▶ Uninstalling an application deployed to users and devices. This is not supported on Windows Phone 8; Android devices require user consent.

Sideloading Applications for Windows and Windows RT Devices

Sideloading applications is supported on the following editions of Windows:

▶ Windows RT 8 and Windows RT 8.1

▶ Windows 8 and Windows 8.1, Enterprise or Pro editions

▶ Windows Server 2012 and Windows Server 2012 R2

When you have a Windows 8/8.1Enterprise or Windows Server 2012/2012 R2 computer that is domain-joined, you can enable sideloading of trusted applications using the group policy item Allow all trusted applications to install. Sideloading applications also require that the application is signed with a trusted certificate where the publisher name in the certificate matches the publisher name in the package. The certificate can be distributed to your domain-joined clients using group policy or by using the Certificate Profiles option in ConfigMgr.

When Windows devices are not joined or cannot be joined to a domain, Windows RT devices being an example, you must acquire an enterprise sideloading key. Windows 8 and 8.1 Pro, which can be domain-joined, also require a sideloading key. These requirements were changed with Windows 8.1 Update, as domain-joined Pro editions no longer require a sideloading key.

The sideloading key must be applied to the device and the Windows installation on the device should be reactivated. As of May 1, 2014, Microsoft customers in certain volume licensing programs are provided enterprise sideloading rights at no additional cost. Other customers can purchase enterprise sideloading rights for an unlimited number of devices for as little as $100. (See http://microsoft-news.com/you-can-buy-windows-8-1-enterprise-sideloading-rights-for-an-unlimited-number-of-devices-for-100/ and the volume licensing reference guide at 9439A928-A0D1-44C2-A099-26A59AE0543B/Windows_8-1_Licensing_Guide.pdf for details.) You can find additional information at http://blogs.windows.com/windows/b/springboard/archive/2014/04/03/windows-8-1-sideloading-enhancements.aspx.

Use the slmgr.vbs script for activation with the ConfigMgr client. When managing the client with Windows Intune, you can upload the sideloading key to the ConfigMgr console; the key is enrolled during the next maintenance window.

> **TIP: HOW TO FIND SIDELOADING KEYS**
>
> Microsoft refers to sideloading keys with an internal code of J7S-00005. Searching for this code on the Internet provides you with purchase options for sideloading keys.

To distribute applications to Windows devices, the application must be signed by a certification authority that is trusted by the device in use. You can obtain a public certificate from a non-Microsoft authority or use your internal organization public key infrastructure (PKI) to generate the code-signing certificate. The certificate can be distributed using the Certificate Profiles functionality in ConfigMgr.

Defining the Policy to Enable Sideloading on Domain-Joined Machines

This scenario deploys a Windows app to your Windows 8.1 Enterprise domain-joined machines. You configure the necessary group policy object (GPO) setting and distribute the certificate to the machines using the Certificate Profile option in ConfigMgr.

To enable installation of the custom Windows app, modify an already existing group policy, which is applied to your Windows agents. Follow these steps:

1. Start the Group Policy Management Console (GPMC) and browse for the GPO to which you are adding the new policy setting. Right-click the object and select **Edit**.

2. Browse to **Computer Configuration -> Policies -> Administrative Templates -> Windows Components -> App Package Deployment**. Double-click **Allow all trusted apps to install** and modify its setting to **Enabled**.

3. Close the GPMC.

You can verify if the policy was applied correctly by opening the local group policy editor on your target machine and browsing for the setting of the group policy you just set using the GPO. Figure 4.9 shows the expected outcome.

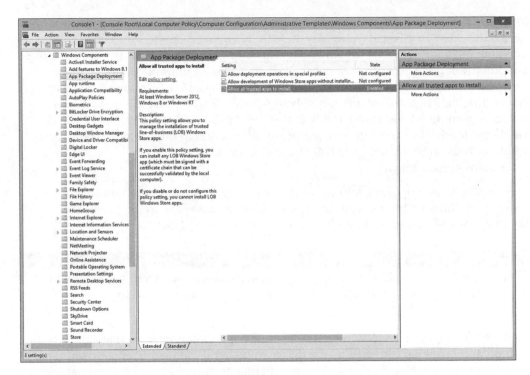

FIGURE 4.9   Set the Allow all trusted apps to install policy setting to Enabled.

Creating and Deploying a Certificate Profile

This section creates a certificate profile, which is distributed to your agents using the compliance settings feature of ConfigMgr.

Note that if you want to deploy a certificate to OMA-DM (Open Mobile Alliance-Device Management) clients managed through MDM, you can also upload the certificate to the ConfigMgr console for the certificate to be automatically installed at enrollment time or during the next maintenance window. Complete the following steps:

1. In the ConfigMgr console, navigate to **Assets and Compliance** -> **Compliance Settings** -> **Company Resource Access** -> **Certificate Profiles**. Click **Create Certificate Profile** on the ribbon bar to start the Create Certificate Profile Wizard.

2. On the General page of the wizard, provide a Name for the Certificate Profile and an optional description. Confirm that the Trusted CA certificate radio button is selected. Click **Next** to continue.

3. On the Trusted CA Certificate page, provide the path to the location where the certificate is stored. In this example, this is **\\armada\source\Applications\ reversi\Reversi_0.1.0.0_AnyCPU_Debug_Test\Reversi_0.1.0.0_AnyCPU_ Debug.cer**. Verify that the Computer certificate store - Root radio button is selected

and that the Certificate thumbprint field is filled after selecting the certificate. Click **Next** to continue.

4. On the Supported Platforms page, confirm that Windows 8.1 is selected, which includes All Windows RT 8.1, All Windows 8.1 (64-bit), and All Windows 8.1 (32-bit), and click **Next**.

5. On the Summary page of the Create Certificate Profile Wizard, review the information and click **Next** to create the certificate profile.

6. Follow the progress and verify that the certificate profile was successfully created in the Completion page of the Create Certificate Profile Wizard. When successful, click **Close** to close the wizard.

You can now deploy the certificate profile to a collection containing all Windows 8.1 Enterprise devices, so that they receive the policy. After the machines have installed the policy with the deployment, installation of the certificate is executed during the next scheduled compliance evaluation.

You can check whether the certificate was installed successfully by verifying whether the configuration baseline is compliant on the Configuration tab of the ConfigMgr control panel applet, or you could open the Local Computer certificates and browse to Trusted Root Certification Authorities -> Certificates. The code-signing certificate should be in the list. Use the serial number as the unique identifier to verify the certificate is there.

Sideloading Windows Modern Applications

With the GPO and certificate profile created and verified as successfully applied, you can create the deployment type to distribute the application to users of your Windows 8.1 machines. Follow these steps:

1. In the ConfigMgr console, navigate to **Software Library -> Application Management -> Applications**. Select the application for which you want to add the Windows Store deployment type and click **Create Deployment Type** on the ribbon bar to open the Create Deployment Type Wizard.

2. On the General page of the wizard, select **Windows app package (*.appx, *appxbundle)** as the type from the drop-down list.

3. Provide the UNC path to the location of the .appx file (in this case, **\\armada\ source\applications\reversi\Reversi_0.1.0.0_AnyCU_Debug_Test\Reversi_0.1.0.0_ AnyCPU_Debug.appx**). Click **Next** to continue.

4. Confirm that the Import Succeeded in the Import Information page of the Create Deployment Wizard. If not, click **Previous** and verify the specified information. Click **Next** to continue.

5. On the General Information page, you can modify the Name that is already filled in to one that suits your organization's needs. You can also provide administrator comments, publisher information, software version, optional reference, and specify administrative categories. Click **Next** to continue.

6. On the Requirements page, the operating systems supported for sideloading are already specified. To add additional requirements, click **Add** to open the Create Requirement dialog box. Click **Next** to continue in the wizard.

7. Define any dependencies on the Dependencies page. An example could be that Adobe Flash is needed to view the application. Specify the necessary Adobe Flash deployment types in a dependency group name if needed, and click **Next** to continue.

8. On the Summary page of the Create Deployment Wizard, review the information and click **Next** to create the deployment type.

9. On the completion page displayed in Figure 4.10, verify that the deployment type was successfully created. When successful, click **Close** to close the Create Deployment Type Wizard.

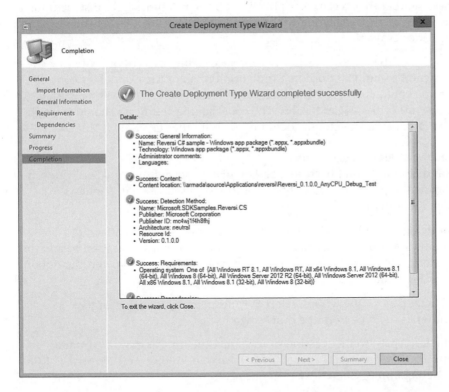

FIGURE 4.10   Completing the Create Deployment Type Wizard for a Windows app package.

After the deployment type is created, the application can be deployed to a user collection. If a user is member of the collection and receives a new user policy, the application becomes available or is installed for the user (depending on the deployment settings). Figure 4.11 shows the Reversi application loaded on a Windows 8 device.

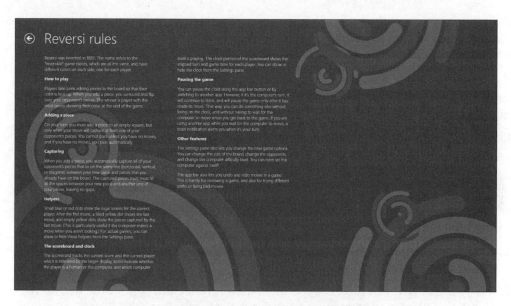

FIGURE 4.11   Reversi App started on the Windows 8.1 Enterprise machine.

If the application installation fails, you can check the AppEnforce.log log file, located in the \Logs folder under the ConfigMgr agent installation folder.

TIP: TROUBLESHOOTING APPLICATION DEPLOYMENT ON MDM-MANAGED WINDOWS CLIENTS

Session PCIT-B323 from TechEd North America 2014 provides information for troubleshooting application deployment on MDM-managed Windows devices. See http://channel9.msdn.com/Events/TechEd/NorthAmerica/2014/PCIT-B323#fbid= for more information. You may also want to read the Technet blog article at http://blogs.technet.com/b/configmgrteam/archive/2013/03/13/troubleshooting-windows-rt-client-software-distribution-issues.aspx.

Sideloading Applications for Windows Phone Devices

Sideloaded applications for Windows Phone must be code-signed. This requires a code-signing certificate, which must be purchased from Symantec. You can purchase certificates at http://www.symantec.com/verisign/code-signing/windows-phone after joining the Windows Phone Dev Center at https://dev.windowsphone.com/en-US/join.

TIP: TESTING WINDOWS PHONE APP DEPLOYMENTS

To test application deployments to Windows Phone devices, Microsoft provides the Support Tool for Windows Intune Trial Management for Windows Phone 8 and Windows Phone 8.1. This tool contains a script that populates a sample application enrollment token in the Configuration Manager 2012 environment, a sample Windows Phone 8 company portal app, and three sample applications that can be used for Windows Phone 8 software distribution scenarios. You can find the tool at http://www.microsoft.com/en-us/download/details.aspx?id=39079.

To create a deployment type within an application for sideloading on Windows Phone devices, perform the following steps:

1. In the ConfigMgr console, navigate to **Software Library -> Application Management -> Applications**. Select the application for which you want to add the Windows Phone Store deployment type and click **Create Deployment Type** on the ribbon bar to open the Create Deployment Type Wizard.

2. On the General page, select **Windows Phone app package (*.apk file)** as the type in the drop-down list.

3. Provide the UNC path to the .apk file (**armada\source\applications\Windows Phone Sample Apps\Shapes.xap**, in this case). Click **Next** to continue.

4. Verify the import was successful on the Import Information page of the wizard. If not, select **Previous** and confirm a valid .apk file is specified. Click **Next**.

5. On the General Information page, you can modify the name that is already filled in to one that suits your organization's needs. You can also provide administrator comments, publisher information, software version, optional reference, and specify administrative categories. Click **Next** to continue.

6. On the Summary page of the Create Deployment Wizard, review the information and click **Next** to create the deployment type.

7. On the Completion page displayed in Figure 4.12, verify that the deployment type was successfully created. When successful, click **Close** to close the wizard.

NOTE: WINDOWS PHONE 8.1 ADOPTS .APPX FORMAT

With the release of Windows Phone 8.1, Microsoft introduces support for the .appx file format. The "Sideloading Applications for Windows and Windows RT Devices" section previously discussed deploying appx-type applications. Note that the application developer still must compile the application on the specific platform.

Sideloading Applications for Apple iPhone, iPod, and iPad Devices

Apple iPhone and iPad devices run the iOS operating system. These iOS devices must be contacted by the Apple Push Notification service (APNs) to check for policy. An APN certificate is required to communicate with Apple's APNs. When a new policy for iOS devices is created, Intune contacts the APNs for those devices, and the devices in turn check with Intune for their new policy. Configuring APNs for use with Windows Intune is described in Chapter 7.

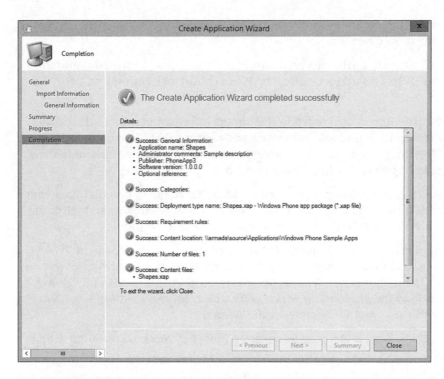

FIGURE 4.12   Completing the Create Application Wizard for Windows Phone app package.

NOTE: APPLE ENTERPRISE DEVELOPER LICENSE

Distributing iOS applications created in-house requires an Apple Developer License. Alternatively, you could buy applications in volume using Apple's Volume Purchase Program (VPP). Sideloading applications for iOS devices is accomplished by importing an .ipk file, an application archive that stores the application for the iOS device. The .ipk file is encrypted using Apple's Fairplay DRM technology. The Apple Enterprise Developer License costs $299 per year. For information about this license, see http://developer. apple.com/programs/ios/enterprise.

Once you enroll an iOS device, a provisioning profile is installed on the iOS device, connecting the device to the company's enterprise program membership. Each device has a special profile for the Apple App Store, which cannot be changed. Any application that is installed on the device is matched against this profile; if profiles do not match, the application is not installed.

Before starting, you need an .ipa file and a manifest file .plist. Follow these steps:

1. In the ConfigMgr console, navigate to **Software Library -> Application Management -> Applications**. Select the application for which you want to add the Apple App Store deployment type and click **Create Deployment Type** on the ribbon bar to open the Create Deployment Type Wizard.

2. On the General page of the wizard, select **App Package for iOS (*.ipa file)** as the type from the drop-down list.

3. Provide the UNC path to the .ipa and .plist files (in this case, **\\armada\source\ applications\WireLessAdHocDemo\iOS\WireLessAdHocDemo.ipa**). Click **Next** to continue.

4. Confirm that the Import Succeeded in the Import Information page of the Create Deployment Wizard. If not, select **Previous** and confirm that the correct path is supplied. Note that a .plist file must also exist besides the .ipa file containing the application to be installed. Click **Next** to continue.

5. On the General Information page, you can modify the Name to one that suits your organization's needs. You can also provide Administrator comments and select the languages included in this deployment type. Click **Next** to continue.

6. Specify requirements on the Requirements page of the Create Deployment Type Wizard. Click **Add** to open the Create Requirement dialog box. In this case, you can select either the iPhone or the iPad section or select specific versions of iOS (iOS5, iOS6, or iOS 7) as the platform on which you can run this application. Click **Next** to continue with the Create Deployment Type Wizard.

7. On the Summary page, review the information and click **Next** to create the deployment type.

8. On the Completion page, verify that the deployment type was successfully created as shown in Figure 4.13. When successful, click **Close** to close the wizard.

In contrast to Windows Modern, Windows Phone, and Android sideloaded applications that are offered from the company portal, installing sideloaded applications for iOS requires the user to access the web version of the company portal. The user should start Safari and browse to http://m.manage.microsoft.com to log in with his Windows Intune account and access the portal. From there, the user can see and choose to install those applications available for installation on his iOS device.

Sideloading Applications for Android Devices

By default, Android devices can only install applications from the Google Play Store. You can modify the settings of each Android device to enable installation of applications from any source, enabling installation of applications using sideloading. To define applications for sideloading, complete the following steps:

1. In the ConfigMgr console, navigate to **Software Library -> Application Management -> Applications**. Select the application for which you want to add the Google Play Store deployment type and click **Create Deployment Type** on the ribbon bar to open the Create Deployment Type Wizard.

2. On the General page of the wizard, select **App Package for Android (*.apk file)** as type from the drop-down list.

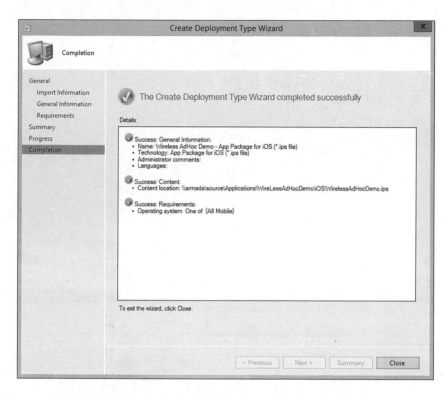

FIGURE 4.13   Completing the Create Deployment Type Wizard for iOS.

3. Provide the UNC path to the .apk file (**\\armada\source\applications\Citrix ShareFile\Android\v2.3.8_mdm_unsigned_ShareFileTablet.apk**, in this case). Click **Next** to continue.

4. Verify the import was successful in the Import Information page of the wizard. If not, click **Previous** and confirm that the correct path is supplied to a location where the .apk file is located Click **Next**.

5. On the General Information page, you can modify the name to one that suits your organization's needs. You can also supply administrator comments and select the languages included in this deployment type. Click **Next** to continue.

6. Specify a requirement on the Requirements page; in this case, a requirement is already specified: Minimum operation system version, which should be greater than or equal to 11. For Android applications, you can only add a requirement based on device ownership. Click **Next** to continue.

7. Review the information on the Summary page and click **Next** to create the deployment type.

8. Verify that the deployment type was created successfully in the Completion page (see Figure 4.14). Click **Close** to close the wizard.

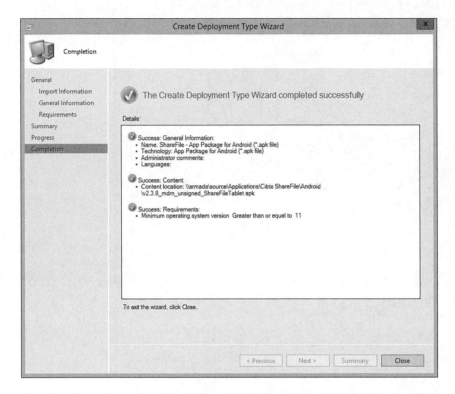

FIGURE 4.14   Completing the Create Deployment Type Wizard for an Android app package.

Using VPN Profiles in Your Applications

Defining VPN profiles in ConfigMgr enables deploying VPN settings to different types of devices. The VPN profiles are supported for devices running the following operating systems:

- ▶ Windows 8.1 (32- and 64-bit)

- ▶ Windows RT 8 and Windows RT 8.1

- ▶ Windows Phone 8.1

- ▶ iPhone and iPad devices running iOS 5, iOS 6, and iOS 7

When you create a Windows app package, you can specify the option to Use an automatic VPN connection (if configured), as shown in Figure 4.15. This lets the application open the VPN connection automatically.

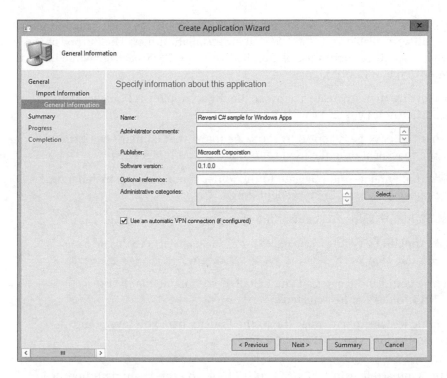

FIGURE 4.15   The Use an automatic VPN connection (if configured) option.

Deploying Software to OS X, Linux, and UNIX Platforms

Most organizations use non-Windows platforms; these must be supported using a device management solution. To support mobile devices running these operating systems, ConfigMgr uses the Windows Intune connector and manages the devices through Windows Intune; for in-company devices, ConfigMgr can also support OS X, Linux, and UNIX flavors. The next sections describe how to create applications for Apple OS X, and how to use ConfigMgr packages and programs functionality to install software on Linux and UNIX devices.

Deploying Applications to Apple OS X Computers

ConfigMgr 2012 SP 1 and later support the following Apple OS X packages:

▶ Apple Disk Image (*.dmg file)

▶ Meta Package File (*.mpkg file)

▶ Mac OS X Installer Package (*.pkg)

▶ Mac OS X Application (*.app)

Before deploying these app packages, you must gather some application information using the CMAppUtil utility, available with the OS X client installation files. The output of the CMAppUtil is a .cmmac file, which must be supplied with the OS X package while importing the deployment type in ConfigMgr.

Complete the following steps to create a .cmmac file for an Apple Disk Image file that you can use to install Microsoft Lync 2011 with Service Pack 1:

1. Confirm that the package is copied to the same folder that contains the extracted files from the macclient.dmg file used to install the ConfigMgr client.

2. Open a terminal window and navigate to the folder containing the installer.dmg and the extracted files from the macclient.dmg.

3. Create a subfolder to store the .cmmac file by typing `mkdir mac-lync-2011`.

4. Execute CMAppUtil by typing `./CMAppUtil -C /users/sysadmin/Downloads/ mu_lync_for_mac_2011_with_service_pack_2_842710.dmg -o mac-lync-2011`.

   Executing the command creates a Lync Installer.pkg.cmmac file in the mac-lync-2011 folder you just created.

5. Copy the Lync Installer.pkg.cmmac file to the folder where you save your application sources for Lync 2011 for OS X.

After creating the .cmmac file using the CMAppUtil tool, you can begin defining the application deployment type for Mac OS X. Follow these steps:

1. In the ConfigMgr console, navigate to **Software Library -> Application Management -> Applications**. Select the application for which you want to add the Mac OS X deployment type and click **Create Deployment Type** on the ribbon bar to open the Create Deployment Type Wizard.

2. On the General page, select **Mac OS X** as the type from the drop-down list.

3. Provide the UNC path to the .cmmac file (in this case, **\\armada\source\ applications\microsoft_lync\lync_for_mac_2011_sp2\Lync Installer.pkg. cmmac**). Click **Next** to continue.

4. Confirm that the import succeeded in the Import Information page. If not, select **Previous** and verify that the correct path is supplied. Click **Next** to continue.

5. On the General Information page of the Create Deployment Type Wizard, you can modify the name already filled in to one that suits your organization's needs. You can also provide administrator comments and select the languages that are included in this deployment type. Click **Next** to continue.

6. Use the Requirements page to specify the requirements. Click **Add** to open the Create Requirement dialog box. In this case, you can select the Mac OS X section to select Mac OS X 10.6, Mac OS X 10.7, Mac OS X 10.8, or a combination as the platform on which you can run this application. Click **Next** to continue.

7. On the Summary page of the wizard, review the information and click **Next** to create the deployment type.

8. In the Completion page of the Create Deployment Type Wizard, verify that the deployment type was successfully created, as shown in Figure 4.16. When successful, click **Close** to close the wizard.

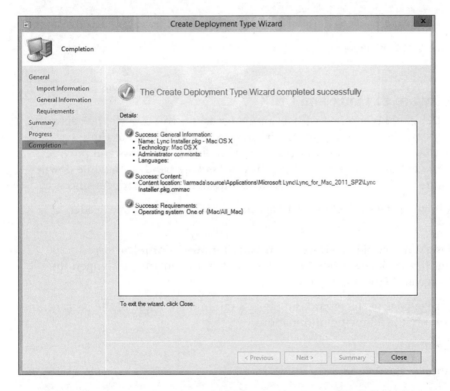

FIGURE 4.16   Completing the Create Deployment Type Wizard for Mac OS X.

After a deployment is created to the OS X computer, the user receives a pop-up that new software is available for installation. The user can install the software at that time or install the software at the specified deadline as shown in Figure 4.17. You can use the CCMClient.log file on that system to troubleshoot any issues.

FIGURE 4.17   Lync 2011 available as new software on OS X.

Deploying Software to Linux and UNIX

If a Linux or UNIX system is enrolled with a ConfigMgr agent, you can use the packages and programs software distribution functionality to deploy applications to those systems. The software distribution functionality works with maintenance windows and provides status messages for centralized reporting. Throttling of network bandwidth while downloading the software is also supported; this can be configured using Client Settings.

Complete the following steps to define a package and a program for Adobe Reader version 9.5.5-1:

1. In the ConfigMgr console, navigate to **Software Library -> Application Management -> Packages**. Click **Create Package** on the ribbon bar to open the Create Package and Program Wizard.

2. On the Package page of the wizard, supply at a minimum a name of the package. In this case, supply the following information:

   ▶ **Name: Reader**

   ▶ **Manufacturer: Adobe**

   ▶ **Language: EN-US**

   ▶ **Version: 9.5.5-1**

3. Select **This package contains source files** and click **Browse** to open the Set Source Folder dialog box. Confirm that the radio button for the Network Path (UNC name) is selected and provide the UNC path to the folder where the .rpm file is located (in this case, **\\armada\source\applications\adobe reader\Linux**). Click **OK** to close the Set Source Folder dialog box, and click **Next** to continue.

4. On the Program Type page, select whether you want to create a Standard program (for a client computer), a Program for device (of a device), or if you do not want to create a program. Confirm **Standard Program** is selected and click **Next** to continue.

5. On the Standard Program page of the Create Package and Program Wizard, provide the information for this specific program, at a minimum, a name and command line. In this case, the following is provided:

▶ **Name: Install Adobe Reader 9.5.5-1 using RPM**

▶ **Command Line: rpm -ivh AdbeRdr9.5.5-`_i486linux_enu.rpm**

▶ **Startup folder:** <none>

▶ **Run: Normal**

▶ **Program can run: Whether or not a user is logged on**

▶ **Run mode: Run with administrative rights**

▶ **Allow users to view and interact with the program installation:** <not selected>

▶ **Drive Mode: Runs with UNC name**

6. Click **Next** on the Standard Program page to continue.

7. On the Requirements page, specify whether you want to run another program first, which is not necessary in this case. You can also specify the platform requirements. Select **This program can run only on specified platforms** and select the x64 versions of every Linux supported guest OS in the list. Also specify the estimated disk space, which is **60 MB**, and the maximum allowed runtime, which is **15** minutes in this scenario. When finished, click **Next** to continue.

8. On the Summary page of the Create Package and Program Wizard, verify the information you entered; if everything looks correct, click **Next** to continue.

9. On the Completion page, verify that the package and program were created successfully (see Figure 4.18). When successful, click **Close** to close the wizard.

With the package and program created, you can distribute the files to the DPs and deploy the program to a custom collection containing the hosts to which you want to install Adobe Reader.

On the Linux client, you can use the scxcm.log file for troubleshooting package deployment issues. If installation was successful, Adobe displays under the Office submenu of Applications, in this case on CentOS 6.4 (shown in Figure 4.19).

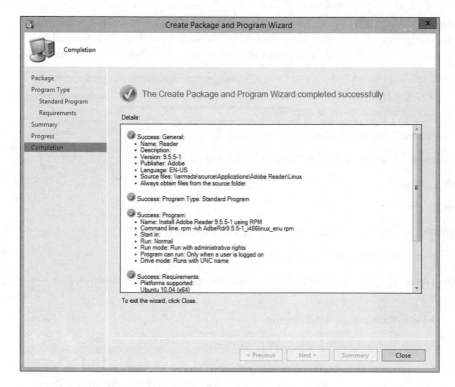

FIGURE 4.18   Completing the Create Package and Program Wizard.

FIGURE 4.19   Adobe Reader installed on Linux.

Deploying Web Applications

Creating a web application consists of defining a link to a URL pointing to an intranet or Internet location. With more and more applications now accessible through a web browser, the ability to deploy web applications has become a common requirement. The link is deployed as a shortcut for Windows, as a web clip for iOS, and as a widget for Android devices. For Windows Phone 8.x, you can launch the link from the company portal. Complete the following steps to deploy a web application:

1. In the ConfigMgr console, navigate to **Software Library** -> **Application Management** -> **Applications**. Select the application to add the Web Application deployment type for and click **Create Deployment Type** on the ribbon bar to open the Create Deployment Type Wizard.

2. On the General page, select **Web Application** from the drop-down list.

3. Supply the URL to the webpage hosting the application, and click **Next** to continue the wizard.

4. On the Import Information page, verify the import was successful. If not, select **Previous** and confirm that the URL you provided for the Location field on the General page is correctly formatted. Click **Next** to continue.

5. On the General Information page, you can modify the name with one that suits your organization's needs. You can also provide administrator comments and select the languages included in this deployment type. Click **Next** to continue.

6. On the Requirements page of the wizard, specify the requirements. Click **Add** to open the Create Requirement dialog box and specify any requirements. Click **Next** to continue the Create Deployment Type Wizard.

7. On the Dependencies page, define any dependencies. This could be that Microsoft Silverlight is needed to view the web application. Specify the necessary Microsoft Silverlight deployment types in a dependency group name if needed and click **Next** to continue.

8. Review the information on the Summary page and click **Next** to create the deployment type.

9. On the Completion page, verify that the deployment type was successfully created (shown in Figure 4.20). When successful, click **Close** to close the wizard.

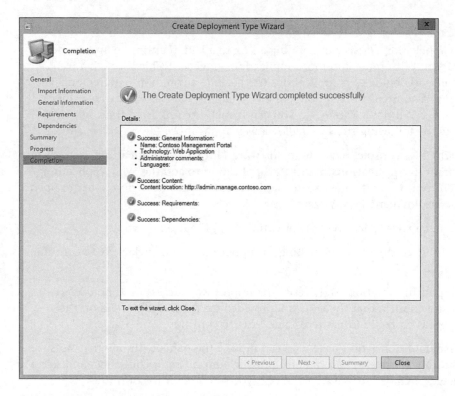

FIGURE 4.20   Completing the Create Deployment Type Wizard for a web application.

Best Practices for Working with Applications

A common misconception about installing applications using a software distribution platform like ConfigMgr is that the platform is capable of supporting each installation procedure. This actually is not true; there are some prerequisites regarding software installations for ConfigMgr to successfully distribute and install them on remote clients. The next sections discuss some best practices for working with applications, including installing software and working with applications in task sequences.

Best Practices for Installing Software

Most software installed with Configuration Manager uses an installer; this could be a Windows installer (.msi) or third-party installation method such as installers from InstallShield, Wise, Nullsoft, Inno, and many others. You can also install software using script methods:

▶ If the installer is capable of installing the software unattended (without any user interaction), it could be used within ConfigMgr as either a deployment type within an application, or as a program within a package—making it suitable for installation on many machines.

▶ If the software cannot be installed with an installer but can be installed unattended or requires company-specific modifications, the software goes through a process referred to as repackaging. This is the process of capturing a software installation procedure, modifying it, and repackaging the installation process in such a way that it is repeatable for large-scale rollouts. While Microsoft provides a tool known as Orca to perform some minor adjustments to its Windows Installer .MSI installers, most companies doing software repackaging use third-party tools from companies like InstallShield or Wise. Repackaging software is not new; this has been done since early versions of Systems Management Server (SMS)/ConfigMgr.

CAUTION: BE CAREFUL WHEN REPACKAGING MSI FILES

When repackaging MSIs, take extra care not to change detection settings, uninstallation options, and installation results; these could lead to real problems when deploying these applications using ConfigMgr.

Before trying to distribute software with ConfigMgr, the authors recommend you first use a test machine to test the ability to install unattended. After confirming that an unattended installation is possible, you can define the deployment type in ConfigMgr.

NOTE: COMMUNITY INFORMATION ABOUT UNATTENDED SOFTWARE INSTALLATION

Testing whether software can be installed unattended is often a matter of finding the right command line parameters to use when executing the software installer. The Internet has a valuable community-driven source that provides a forum where users who have to deal with this task share their experiences. Previously known as AppDeploy.com, the community now goes by the name of IT Ninja. You can find the website at http://www.itninja. com.

Before ConfigMgr executes a deployment type on a machine, it checks whether the application is already installed, which is why you must specify a detection method. While in most cases, the detection method is the unique identifier of the Windows installer MSI, you may need to define other methods, such as a Registry key or particular file version. Checking to see if the application is already installed prevents the deployment type from executing unnecessarily. After installation, ConfigMgr performs the same check again to verify that the detection method validated successfully. This makes it important that you specify the detection method correctly, and that you fully understand the process before deploying software to remote agents.

When ConfigMgr installs software, the following occurs:

1. ConfigMgr executes the command line specified in the deployment type.

2. ConfigMgr then monitors the process ID of the executable. When the process ID is no longer active, ConfigMgr uses the return code from that installation to determine whether installation was successful, and whether a reboot is needed. The Maximum

allowed runtime value specifies how long the installation may run; this is available for both deployment types and programs. Return codes are specified based on the MSI known return codes, which are as follows:

- ▶ **0:** Successful installation, no reboot is necessary.

- ▶ **1707:** Successful installation, no reboot is necessary.

- ▶ **3010:** Soft reboot required.

- ▶ **1641:** Hard reboot needed.

- ▶ **1618:** Fast retry, meaning that another installation is already running.

3. If a reboot is required, issuers are presented with a pop-up window asking if they want to reboot the machine. Keep in mind that you should configure your software installation in such a way that it utilizes the information that a reboot is needed. Do not let the application reboot the system, since that fails the application installation from a ConfigMgr perspective.

CAUTION: POTENTIAL ISSUES WITH SOFTWARE INSTALLATION WRAPPERS

Some organizations use so-called *installation wrappers*, which can be command files or scripts. These typically provide basic logging and determine the required environment for the installation to occur. The wrapper is provided as a template, meaning the individuals creating these applications need only fill in the necessary information for the installation.

With packages and programs, wrappers typically weren't a problem and could be used to install a 32-bit version of the software on 32-bit systems or install the 64-bit version of the software on 64-bit systems. However, installation wrappers often would return to ConfigMgr only the return code of the last action performed (such as writing to a log file) and not take into account the return code of the installer that was executed or return that information. For example, if the wrapper did some logging to a log file as its last action, which was successful, the wrapper would return a return code of success to ConfigMgr even if the installation failed!

This approach can have serious consequences in ConfigMgr 2012. The detection method executed afterward would determine that the application actually is not installed, causing the installation to eventually fail from a ConfigMgr perspective.

Because ConfigMgr executes the command line specified in the deployment type or the program, waits for the process to finish, and determines whether the installation was successful based on return codes, there is a period of time when ConfigMgr logging is unavailable during software installation. The authors of this book recommend you either enable logging on the installation command line or on a global level on a machine basis. If logging is enabled, you can determine why an installation failed; this can help with troubleshooting application installation failures.

TIP: SAMPLE APPLICATIONS FROM THE SOFTWARE DEVELOPMENT KIT

The software development kit (SDK) for System Center 2012 Configuration Manager includes the Application Model Kit. This contains a set of exported applications demonstrating the use of various features of the application model. You can import the Application Model Kit by importing the provided ZIP file, which creates sample applications in addition to some custom global conditions.

The latest version of the SDK is the System Center 2012 R2 Configuration Manager SDK, available for download at http://www.microsoft.com/en-us/download/details.aspx?id=29559.

Best Practices for Working with Applications in Task Sequences

Although Microsoft recommends you deploy applications for users, applications could also be included within a task sequence during operating system deployment (OSD). Consider Microsoft Office: This is an application commonly deployed in a task sequence, because it not only provides application components such as Word and Excel to end users, but also serves as a type of middleware for many other applications.

Because of the way the task sequence runs, it is necessary to take extra precautions when installing applications in a task sequence, because

- ▶ The task sequence runs in the context of the Local System account.

- ▶ The explorer.exe task is not running during a task sequence.

- ▶ The installer must be fully unattended and no user interaction is allowed. If the installer requires any interaction, the task sequence would fail.

You can install user-targeted applications just after the task sequence finishes by following these steps:

1. Define a user device affinity (UDA) filling the SMSTSUdaUsers variable with the user account of the user who is using the machine. You can prompt for the value of this variable by using a pre-hook execution command or by creating an empty SMSTSUdaUsers variable on the computer object or collection.

2. While deploying the application and specifying the deployment settings, ensure that the purpose is set to Required and that the Pre-deploy software to the user's primary device option is checked, as shown in Figure 4.21.

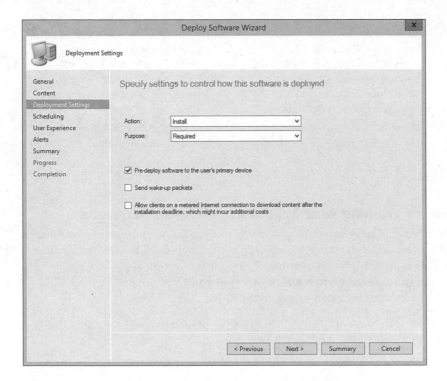

FIGURE 4.21   Deployment settings in the Deploy Software Wizard.

Summary

This chapter discussed changes to ConfigMgr applications since their introduction in Configuration Manager 2012 RTM. It discussed how to handle enabled write filters effective on embedded versions of Windows, working with virtual applications, and using the newly introduced Virtual Environments feature. It described deploying applications using deep linking and sideloading to mobile devices; for some selected platforms, you can also use VPN profiles to set up a VPN connection while executing the application on the end user's device. The chapter also covered deploying applications to OS X, Linux, and UNIX systems, along with deploying web applications. The chapter also discussed some best practices on how to work with the new application model.

The next chapter covers on-premise management and cross-platform support.

CHAPTER 5

On-Premise Cross-Platform Support

IN THIS CHAPTER

▶ Supported Platforms

▶ Cross-Platform Settings

▶ Cross-Platform Agent Deployment

▶ Cross-Platform Agent Components

▶ Client Agent Commands

▶ Troubleshooting with Log Files

Something that has been missing from System Center Configuration Manager (ConfigMgr) is support of non-Windows clients. Customers have been requesting this feature ever since Microsoft removed Macintosh support from the product back in Systems Management Server (SMS) 2.0. Microsoft has considered this feedback and has developed a cross-platform model that allows support of some non-Windows-based clients. Configuration Manager 2012 Service Pack (SP) 1 adds that support for a limited set of versions of OS X, Linux, and UNIX operating systems. The R2 version goes the extra mile and adds support for even more versions. Although cross-platform functionally is now somewhat limited in certain areas, it should be enhanced in future versions.

This chapter explains how System Center 2012 Configuration Manager R2 allows you to manage these non-Windows assets; it also discusses what is needed for client installation, installing the client on these systems, inventory, client agent commands, and some troubleshooting techniques for when things don't go just right.

Supported Platforms

To get started with on-premise cross-platform support, Microsoft first had to determine what they would support. Due to the vast nature of the many different flavors of the OS X, Linux, and UNIX operating systems, Microsoft was unable to support many of them, because this would have required countless weeks and months of setup and testing. Microsoft picked the more popular flavors that you would see in a typical heterogeneous business environment and chose to support those versions. Currently, that set of platforms is pretty well set. As newer versions are released and tested by Microsoft, they are added to the list.

Table 5.1 shows the current list of platforms that are supported.

TABLE 5.1   Cross-Platform Operating System Versions

Platform	Version
AIX	Version 5.3 (Power)*
	Version 6.1 (Power)*
	Version 7.1 (Power)*
CentOS	Version 5 (x86/x64)*
	Version 6 (x86/x64)*
Debian	Version 5 (x86/x64)*
	Version 6 (x86/x64)*
	Version 7 (x86/x64)**
HP-UX	Version 11iv2 (IA64 and PA-RISC)*
	Version 11iv3 (IA64 and PA-RISC)*
OS X	Version 10.9 (Mavericks)**
	Version 10.8 (Mountain Lion)*
	Version 10.7 (Lion)
	Version 10.6 (Snow Leopard)
Oracle Linux	Version 5 (x86/x64)*
	Version 6 (x86/x64)*
Red Hat Enterprise Linux (RHEL)	Version 4 (x86/x64)
	Version 5 (x86/x64)
	Version 6 (x86/x64)
Solaris	Version 9 (SPARC)
	Version 10 (x86/SPARC)
	Version 11 (x86/SPARC)*
SUSE Linux Enterprise (SLES)	Version 9 (x86)
	Version 10 SP 1 (x86/x64)
	Version 11 (x86/x64)
Ubuntu	Version 10.4 (LTS x86/x64)*
	Version 12.4 (LTS x86/x64)*

Supported in ConfigMgr 2012 SP 1 Cumulative Update (CU) 1 and later

**Only supported in ConfigMgr 2012 R2*

Cross-Platform Agent Architecture

Microsoft has worked hard in the open source community to create standards and processes for the cross-platform agent, and this work has come together to help create multiproduct agents. Linux Integration Services is now part of the default installation for several versions of Linux, which allows the products to install and perform better when installed in a Microsoft virtual environment. Microsoft's effort over the past few years has helped create a common platform to build upon, and this platform has evolved into the current cross-platform agent included in ConfigMgr 2012 R2. This agent acts very much like the Windows-based agent; it has multiple layers with communication between each layer that ends up talking with a normal ConfigMgr management point (MP) and distribution point (DP). The agent works with a web-based enterprise management (WBEM) type database called open management infrastructure (OMI) and even has a common root/cimv2 namespace. Similar to the Windows-based agent, this database is used to collect hardware inventory information, store client policy, and other client information. Figure 5.1 shows the detailed components used in the cross-platform agent.

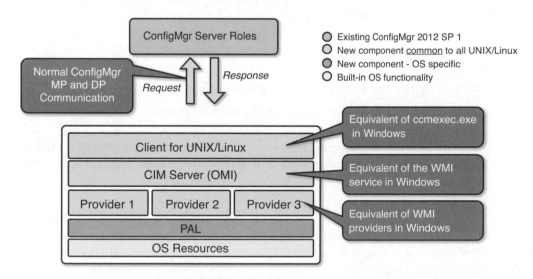

FIGURE 5.1   Detailed cross-platform architecture.

In this architecture, the agent is a fully functional agent with the ability to have custom providers that leverage the common information model (CIM) server and has the ability to report back customized inventory to the ConfigMgr server. The architecture also lends itself to easier troubleshooting when the need arises, because of the similar working structure of the Windows-based client with which most folks are familiar.

Cross-Platform Agent Communication

System Center 2012 Configuration Manager has always used HTTP traffic for clients to communicate with their MPs and DPs. The cross-platform agent uses the same method that the Windows-based agents use—port 80 for HTTP communication, and port 443 for HTTPS communication.

NOTE: SUPPORT FOR THE FALLBACK STATUS POINT ADDED

Service Pack 1 and Cumulative Update 1 added support for the cross-platform agent to send back fallback status messages to the fallback status point (FSP) if the agent is installed using the -fsp command-line option.

Cross-platform agents cannot use Background Intelligent Transfer Service (BITS) as Windows agents do; however, you can still manage bandwidth control on these agents by changing the BITS settings in client agent settings for these agents. The SP 1 CU 1 Linux/UNIX agent now makes use of the BITS settings in client agent settings. You can use these settings to manage the HTTP request chunk size and inter-chunk delay. The agent can use the following settings once it gets the policy setting Limit the maximum network bandwidth for BITS background transfers to yes:

▶ Throttling window start time

▶ Throttling window end time

▶ Maximum transfer rate during throttling window (Kbps)

▶ Maximum transfer rate outside the throttling windows (Kbps)

Because these are global settings, you should create custom client device settings for the global settings, and then deploy that custom setting to a collection of Linux/UNIX agents.

Client Agent Settings

Because the cross-platform agents are limited in functionality, they cannot use all the default client agent settings. The agent has the intelligence to ignore client agent settings that it doesn't use. For example, if you have the default settings for software inventory set to run every day, the Linux/UNIX agent just ignores that setting because software inventory is not supported on those platforms.

Following are the client management capabilities supported on the Linux/UNIX platform:

▶ Collections, queries, and maintenance windows

▶ Hardware inventory

▶ Software deployment (packages and programs only)

▶ Monitoring and reporting

These client management capabilities are supported on the OS X platform:

▶ Hardware inventory

▶ Compliance settings

▶ Application management (you would use this to apply software updates)

Cross-Platform Settings

Similar to Windows agents, the cross-platform agent has certain prerequisites that must be met for a successful deployment of the agent. There are two types of on-premise cross-platform agents, discussed in the following sections.

Linux/UNIX Requirements

In the Linux/UNIX agent, programs are installed as part of a package. Certain packages must be in place for the cross-platform agent to install correctly. The agent makes external calls to these packages to run specific programs. Because so many different versions of Linux/UNIX are supported and each of these different versions has different packages, Microsoft created a matrix that outlines these requirements. The table at http://technet.microsoft.com/en-us/library/da15f702-ba6a-40fb-b130-c624f17e2846#BKMK_ClientDeployPrereqforLnU provides in-depth information on each of these versions and packages. In most all the versions used, these packages are considered standard and are installed as part of the operating system (OS) when it is installed. Chances are that you do not need to install anything, but you should check to be sure.

Nothing extra is needed in ConfigMgr for the Linux/UNIX agent to install correctly.

OS X Requirements

The OS X cross-platform agent requirements differ significantly from the Linux/UNIX agent requirements. The OS X agent is treated like an Internet-based client; therefore, it only communicates with the MP and DPs via a certificate. The next sections explain the types of certificates and where these certificates are placed for a successful install of the OS X agent.

Certificates Needed for OS X

Because ConfigMgr treats the OS X cross-platform agent like an Internet-based client, you need two certificates: a server authentication certificate and a client authentication certificate. The server-based certificate is used on all MPs and DPs with which the OS X agent would communicate. The client-based certificate is installed and used only on the OS X client. You can find in-depth information on these certificates at http://technet.microsoft.com/en-us/library/gg699362.

Configuring the ConfigMgr Server, DPs, and MPs

Once you have the server authentication certificate, you need to install it in the personal store within the computer certificate store on the site server and on each machine using a site role that the OS X agent would talk to, for example the MP, DP, and enrollment point (EP). Follow these steps to install the server authentication certificate in the personal store:

1. Installing the certificate in the personal store requires the MMC Certificate snap-in. Using the snap-in, you can request the correct server authentication certificate and have it added to the correct stores in each machine running the ConfigMgr site roles. See Figure 5.2 as an example.

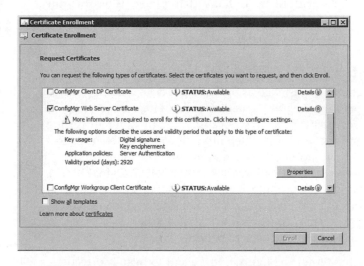

FIGURE 5.2   Certificate enrollment examples.

2. After it is installed in the personal store, you must configure Internet Information Services (IIS) to use that certificate. Edit the site binding in the default website in IIS. Figure 5.3 shows an example of the binding for HTTPS.

3. Ensure that the fully qualified domain name (FQDN) is set correctly on each of the site systems the OS X agent would communicate with. You can check this by looking at the site system properties in the ConfigMgr console. Make sure that the machine's FQDN is set under the Specify an FQDN for this site system for use on the Internet section.

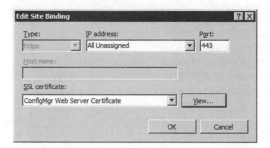

FIGURE 5.3   IIS Edit Site Binding for default website.

HTTPS Site Roles

With the certificate installed, you must make sure that your DP and MP site roles are using HTTPS for the OS X clients to communicate with. For your DP role, verify that you have HTTPS selected and then choose the appropriate drop-down item as it relates to the use of the type of clients communicating with this DP. Figure 5.4 shows the correct setup for a DP with both intranet and Internet clients talking to it.

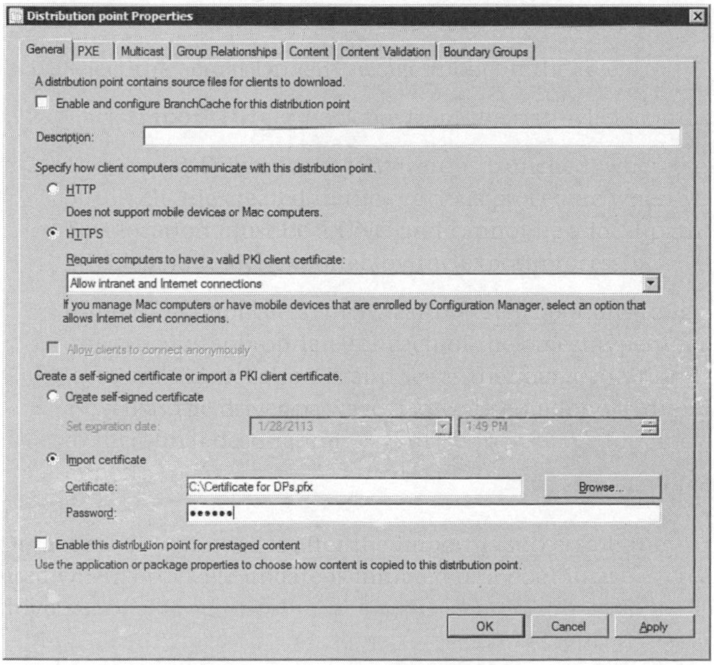

FIGURE 5.4   Distribution point Properties dialog.

> **TIP: DISTRIBUTION POINT CERTIFICATE INFORMATION**
>
> When using HTTPS on a DP, you must import a certificate for the DP to use when it communicates with other site systems. The "Deploying the Client Certificate for Distribution Points" section at http://technet.microsoft.com/en-us/library/230dfec0-bddb-4429-a5db-30020e881f1e#BKMK_clientdistributionpoint2008_cm2012 explains more about this certificate and how to create it with the correct properties for the private key to be exported out.

Next, look at the properties of the MPs with which the agent would communicate. The MP doesn't need to have any certificate configured in its properties, but does need to be set to use HTTPS, allow intranet connections, and have the check box enabled to allow OS X computers to use it. Figure 5.5 shows an MP with the correct settings for OS X client communication.

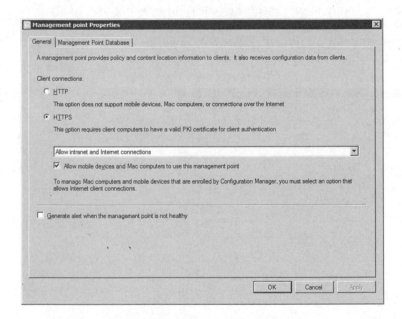

FIGURE 5.5   Management point Properties dialog.

Client Enrollment

OS X clients must have the client authentication certificate installed to be able to use HTTPS to communicate with the MP and DP. This is accomplished by using the EP and the enrollment proxy point (EPP). The EP uses the certificates for ConfigMgr to complete the enrollment process for mobile devices and OS X agents. The EPP manages the enrollment requests from mobile devices and OS X agents and forwards those requests to the EP so that they can be completed. There is no additional configuration needed past the default values. Both these roles can be installed by using the ConfigMgr console.

Now configure the client settings to allow a user to enroll the OS X agent. Follow these steps:

1. In the client settings, select **Enrollment**; change User Settings to say **Yes** for "Allow users to enroll mobile devices and Mac computers."

2. Click **Set Profile** and choose **Create**.

3. On the Edit Enrollment Profile page, give it a name, make sure that your site code is set correctly, and then add in the correct certificate authority certificate. Now select the client authentication certificate that was created for the OS X client.

4. Click **OK** three times to save your changes.

Figure 5.6 shows a proper enrollment profile.

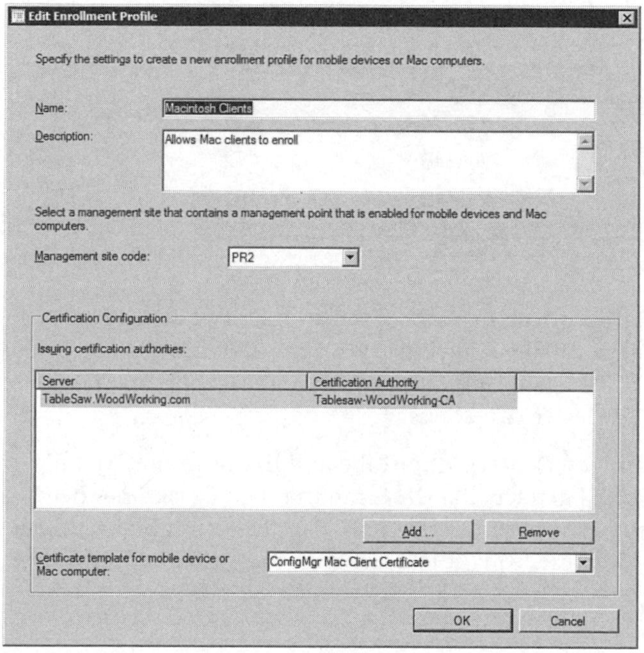

FIGURE 5.6   Enrollment profile.

Firewall Ports

The Linux/UNIX agent uses port 80 to communicate with its MP and DPs, the OS X agent uses port 443 to communicate with MPs and DPs. Both of these ports must be open on the client side for outbound traffic. Because these are the default ports, if you have changed any of the client communication properties to use different ports, you should make sure that those ports are opened for outbound communication on the client.

Downloading Client Agents

The Linux/UNIX and OS X client agents are not included with the installation files for ConfigMgr. You must download the appropriate agent from the Microsoft Download Center:

▶ For ConfigMgr 2012 SP 1, download the agent from http://www.microsoft.com/en-us/download/details.aspx?id=36212.

▶ For R2, the client agent can be downloaded from http://www.microsoft.com/en-us/download/details.aspx?id=39360.

Clicking **Download** presents you with several files to download. Table 5.2 shows that list for ConfigMgr 2012 R2.

TABLE 5.2   ConfigMgr 2012 R2 Cross-Platform Client Agent Downloads

File Name	Size
ConfigMgr Clients for Linux.exe	46.7MB
ConfigMgr Clients for AIX.exe	115.7MB
ConfigMgr Clients for HP-UX.exe	49.0MB
ConfigMgr Clients for Solaris.exe	57.2MB
ConfigMgrMacClient.msi	5.4MB

For Linux/UNIX clients, download the correct .exe and then run that .exe on a Windows system. The .exe is a self-extracting executable and extracts out the TAR file and the install script needed to install the Linux/UNIX agent. After you have the files, copy them to a network share that your Linux/UNIX device can access.

For OS X clients, download the ConfigMgrMacClient.msi file and then run that MSI file on a Windows-based machine. The MSI extracts the DMG file that OS X machines need into the *%ProgramFiles(x86)%*\Microsoft\System Center 2012 Configuration Manager Mac Client folder. Once you have this DMG file, copy it to a network share that your OS X client can access.

Cross-Platform Agent Deployment

Cross-platform agent deployment is different than Windows-based agent deployments. You cannot deploy via an automatic method like client push; the deployment must be done in a manual fashion with the installation scripts and agent files that Microsoft provides. Each agent installation is a bit different, but once the agent is installed it communicates back to the MP in the same manner as the Windows-based agents. As noted earlier in the "Cross-Platform Agent Communication" section, ConfigMgr 2012 SP 1 CU 1 now supports the use of the -fsp install command-line parameter so that the agent can communicate with the fallback status point during installation. The authors recommend using this setting for reporting purposes.

Deploying the Linux/UNIX Client

Installing the Linux/UNIX agent is a manual process. With ConfigMgr 2012 SP 1 CU 1 and later, you now have a universal agent to replace many of the specific client installation packages. If the version of Linux/UNIX that you are using is not listed as one of the specific download packages in Table 5.2, you can use the universal agent from the ConfigMgr Clients for Linux.exe download. After you have the TAR file and the install script on a network share, copy those files to the local Linux/UNIX machine. The TAR file contains all the client agent files. The Linux/UNIX install does not connect to the MP to download any additional files as do the Windows-based agents.

The install script used to install the agent has several command lines that can be used with it depending on what options you need. The full list of options is located at http://technet.microsoft.com/en-us/library/jj573939.aspx.

Follow these steps to deploy the Linux/UNIX client:

1. The install script must be run as a program and also be run as the superuser root. Once you open a terminal window, make sure you run the command `su root` and enter the password. This allows you to run as the root superuser.

2. You need to allow the install script to run as a program, so enter the following command:

   ```
   chmod +x install
   ```

3. Now, you are ready to run the actual client install. The basic command line for the install is this:

   ```
   ./install -mp <mp fqdn> -sitecode <sitecode> -fsp <fsp fqdn > name of install
   package
   ```

   Figure 5.7 shows the command line used to install the agent on CentOS and the results.

4. The client is now installed and sends the MP_ClientRegistration record to the MP. This is logged in the MP_RegistrationManager.log file on the MP. You should also be able to see the client in the All Systems collection of the site that you used in the command line in step 3.

   If the agent does not show up in the All Systems collection as a client, verify that you have approved the client for use in the site. You can do this by right-clicking the client and choosing **Approve**. If you have many Linux/UNIX clients to install, you might want to change the approval setting in the site settings properties to **Automatically approve all computers (not recommended)**. Figure 5.8 shows that setting.

5

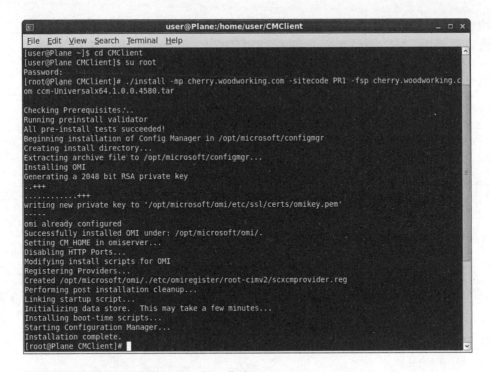

FIGURE 5.7   Linux/UNIX agents installation.

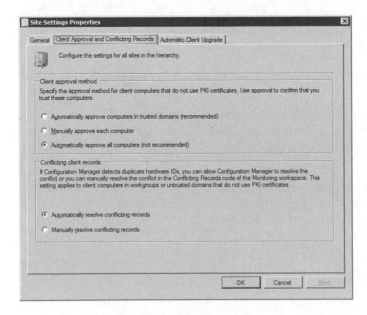

FIGURE 5.8   Approval site settings.

NOTE: AUTOMATING THE LINUX/UNIX CLIENT INSTALL

System Center Orchestrator is a great tool that allows you to automate many tasks. One of those tasks is the client install on a Linux/UNIX system. The use of runbooks inside Orchestrator allows getting away from the manual and tedious install that comes with installing the client across many Linux/UNIX systems and enables deploying the client on a large scale if needed. For information on the process and sample runbooks to download, see http://blogs.technet.com/b/neilp/archive/2012/10/17/system-center-2012-automating-configuration-manager-client-deployment-to-linux-systems.aspx.

Deploying the OS X Client

Deploying the OS X agent is a manual process. Follow these steps:

1. Copy the macclient.dmg file over to the OS X computer.

2. On the OS X system, run that DMG file, which expands into a folder on the desktop. The DMG file is like a Zip file in Windows.

3. Copy that folder (7958shipbin) to a local folder on the OS X.

4. Verify that you have the ccmsetup program, the CMClient.pkg package, and a Tools folder, as shown in Figure 5.9.

5. Next, install the agent. Open a terminal window and navigate to the folder shown in Figure 5.9. Run the ccmsetup program using this command:

```
sudo ./ccmsetup
```

FIGURE 5.9   OS X agent folder.

You are prompted for a password. This is the password to the superuser account. Figure 5.10 shows the command line and the finished result.

TIP: DO NOT REBOOT

It states in the screen shot in Figure 5.10 that the install requires a reboot. If using ConfigMgr 2012 SP 1 CU 1, do not reboot at this time.

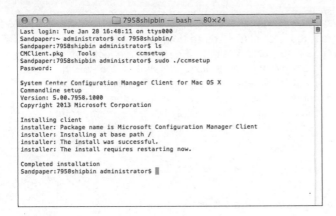

```
● ○ ○              🖥 7958shipbin — bash — 80×24
Last login: Tue Jan 28 16:48:11 on ttys000
Sandpaper:~ administrator$ cd 7958shipbin/
Sandpaper:7958shipbin administrator$ ls
CMClient.pkg    Tools              ccmsetup
Sandpaper:7958shipbin administrator$ sudo ./ccmsetup
Password:

System Center Configuration Manager Client for Mac OS X
Commandline setup
Version: 5.00.7958.1000
Copyright 2013 Microsoft Corporation

Installing client
installer: Package name is Microsoft Configuration Manager Client
installer: Installing at base path /
installer: The install was successful.
installer: The install requires restarting now.

Completed installation
Sandpaper:7958shipbin administrator$ ▉
```

FIGURE 5.10   OS X agent install.

The certificate needs to be enrolled on the OS X system. If using ConfigMgr 2012 SP 1 CU 1 or earlier, use the CMEnroll program in the Tools folder of the 7958shipbin folder, discussed in the following section. If you are using ConfigMgr 2012 R2, reboot, and the OS X Computer Enrollment Wizard appears after the reboot.

Running CMEnroll

The CMEnroll tool is a manual process to install the certificate on an OS X system. Run the tool in the terminal window with the following command line:

```
sudo ./CMEnroll -s <enrollment proxy server name> -ignorecertchainvalidation
  --u <'user name'>
```

When you run CMEnroll, it asks for two passwords:

▶ The first is the password to run as a superuser account.

▶ The second password is for the user account to connect back to the enrollment proxy server.

Figure 5.11 shows the CMEnroll program being run with this command line.

Using the OS X Computer Enrollment Wizard

New with ConfigMgr 2012 R2 is the ability to use a wizard to complete the enrollment for the OS X agent. This wizard allows you to enroll without having to use a terminal window and a command line. Once the client is installed, if you reboot, the wizards automatically start after a login. To launch the wizard manually, click the **Enroll** button on the OS X agent client window. To enroll using the wizard, complete the following steps:

1. After launching the wizard, you see a page that allows you to start the process (see Figure 5.12).

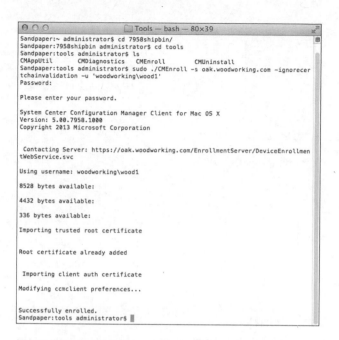

FIGURE 5.11   Running the CMEnroll tool.

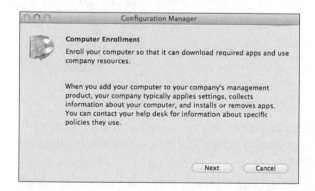

FIGURE 5.12   Enrollment Wizard welcome page.

2. After you click **Next**, the wizard asks for your username, password, and the enrollment server name, as shown in Figure 5.13.

3. After you fill in the information and click **Next**, the wizard begins the enrollment process, and you see a progress bar. When it finishes the enrollment, you see the page shown in Figure 5.14.

   If this process fails, look at the enrollment point logs to see why the failure occurred.

FIGURE 5.13   Enrollment Wizard user information page.

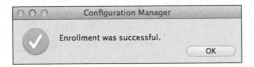

FIGURE 5.14   Enrollment Wizard successful page.

Uninstalling or Reinstalling Linux/UNIX

You might sometimes need to reinstall the client. You have several options available to do so. You could reinstall on top of the existing client, keeping the existing database of client information. You use the same command line as you would when installing but when it runs you are presented with several new options (see Figure 5.15):

▶ Install, but keep the existing database

▶ Delete all existing data then install

▶ Exit installer

If you choose to keep the existing database, the client retains the same GUID, certificate store, and local OMI information. If you choose to delete all the existing data, it wipes out the client and starts an install of the agent.

There may be a time when you just need to uninstall the agent. This can be accomplished by using the uninstall utility located in the /opt/microsoft/configmgr/bin folder on the client. To start the uninstall, use this command line from a terminal window with su (root superuser) access:

```
/opt/microsoft/configmgr/bin/uninstall
```

When running the command, you are presented with three options, as shown in Figure 5.16:

▶ **Completely Uninstall:** ConfigMgr and OMI

▶ **Partial Uninstall:** Remove ConfigMgr, Keep OMI

▶ **Exit installer:** Exit the installer

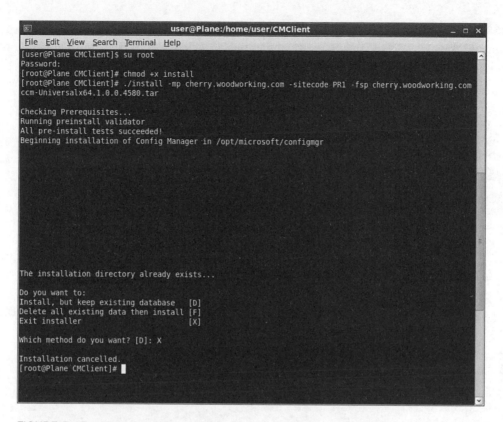

FIGURE 5.15   Linux reinstall options.

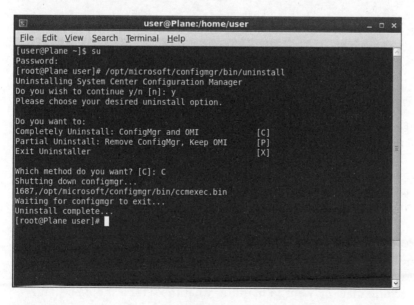

FIGURE 5.16   Linux agent uninstall.

Uninstalling OS X

To uninstall the OS X agent, open a terminal window and change into the Tools folder that is located in the 7958shipbin folder. To start the uninstall, use this command line:

```
Sudo ./CMUninstall -c
```

The -c command-line option is optional. If you do not use it, the client logs and client crash logs are not deleted. The authors recommend that you always use the -c option so that when the client is reinstalled it is not confusing when you look at the logs. Figure 5.17 shows the results when running the command-line using the -c option.

FIGURE 5.17   OS X agent uninstall.

Cross-Platform Agent Components

The cross-platform agent would not be very useful without a set of meaningful components to manage the non-Windows machine. Microsoft understands this, and includes a limited set of the Windows-based agent components. This limited set still has considerable functionality and provides more than just the basics. This set enables you to retrieve the hardware inventory and the installed applications, and find out when the machine drifts out of compliance with certain settings.

Settings Management

Settings Management is available on the OS X platform only. This component operates in the same way as the Windows-based component. You start out with a configuration item (CI) that defines the setting that you want to monitor, what the setting should be, and how to remediate it when it drifts out of compliance. Once you have the CI defined, you must attach it to a configuration baseline (CB). That CB is then deployed to a collection of machines; in this case, that collection would contain your OS X clients. On the client side, the agent downloads the policy from the MP, reads the CI and verifies it is in compliance, and reports back the status to the MP. If the CI is not in compliance, remediation occurs, forcing the machine into compliance with that information then sent back to the MP. Reporting on the compliance state for OS X clients is the same as Windows-based agents, through the Monitor node of the ConfigMgr console.

> **NOTE: YOU CANNOT MIX PLATFORM CONFIGURATION ITEMS**
>
> When creating the settings rule, you must select a platform for the rule. You cannot mix OS X and Windows rules in the same CI.

Software Inventory

Traditional software inventory is not supported with the cross-platform agent as it is with the Windows-based agent. You cannot launch Resource Explorer and go to the Software section to see a list of the installed software. Software inventory for cross-platform clients is found in the Installed Applications section of hardware inventory within the Resource Explorer. The inventory (displayed in Figure 5.18) shows a list with the display name, product ID, install date, and version.

FIGURE 5.18   Cross-platform agent software inventory.

Hardware Inventory

Hardware inventory is supported on both the Linux/UNIX and the OS X cross-platform agents. It operates much like the Windows-based agent. The database of hardware information is queried and the results reported back to the MP.

What Is OMI

In the Windows world, hardware inventory is taken from the web-based enterprise management (WBEM) database. In the Linux/UNIX and OS X world, this database of information is called open management infrastructure (OMI). This statement is taken from The Open Group website, http://www.opengroup.org/software/omi:

OMI is an open source project to further the development of a production quality implementation of the DMTF CIM/WBEM standards. The OMI CIMOM is also designed to be portable and highly modular. In order to attain its small footprint, it is coded in C, which also makes it a much more viable CIM Object Manager for embedded systems and other infrastructure components that have memory constraints for their management processor. OMI is also designed to be inherently portable. It builds and runs today on most UNIX® systems and Linux. In addition to OMI's small footprint, it also demonstrates very high performance.

OMI runs on non-Windows operating systems. The software is similar to the WBEM software that runs on Windows operating systems. It contains a CIM server, schema, and protocols allowing the server and the client to communicate. The CIM server, with the use of a provider, allows a client application to perform certain operations on managed resources. Some of these operations are as follows:

▶ **GetInstance:** Gets a single instance from the server

▶ **EnumerateInstances:** Enumerates instances of a given CIM class

▶ **CreateInstance:** Creates an instance of a CIM class

▶ **DeleteInstance:** Deletes an instance

▶ **ModifyInstance:** Modifies the properties of an instance

▶ **Associators:** Finds instances associated with a given instance

▶ **References:** Finds references that refer to a given instance

▶ **Invoke:** Invokes a method on a given instance or class

The provider uses the protocol to communicate between the client request and the CIM server. The CIM server gathers the information requested and sends it to the client application requesting the information.

You can find more in-depth information about OMI and how it works at https://collaboration.opengroup.org/omi/.

Default Classes

The cross-platform agent uses a default subset of the classes that a Windows-based agent uses. These classes are populated in the same manner as the Windows base classes are; the hardware inventory provider queries the OMI database and returns the values that it finds. There are several differences between the Linux/UNIX agent and OS X agent. Figure 5.19 shows what is found inside the Resource Explorer for default hardware inventory on a Linux/UNIX machine, and Figure 5.20 shows the default hardware inventory for the OS X agent.

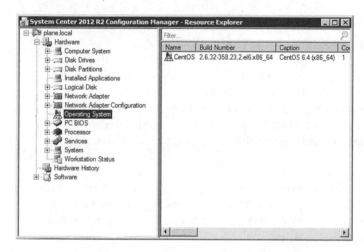

FIGURE 5.19   Linux/UNIX default hardware inventory.

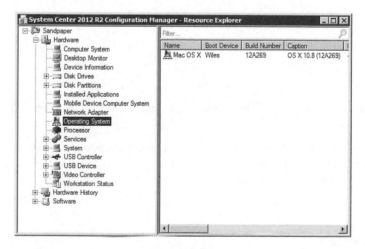

FIGURE 5.20   OS X default hardware inventory.

Creating Custom Classes

Sometimes you just want to collect more information than what is returned in the default classes. Just as with the Windows-based agent, this can be accomplished by creating a custom class that contains the information you need and have hardware inventory return that information to the database. To create the custom class and have the information reported back to the ConfigMgr database is a somewhat complex process consisting of the following steps:

▶ Create a custom inventory provider.

▶ Configure the non-Windows machines to use the custom provider.

▶ Enable the ConfigMgr site to support the new provider.

Microsoft has written a detailed instruction guide that can lead you through the process. This guide, *OMI Getting Started*, can be downloaded at https://collaboration.opengroup. org/omi/documents.php. This link also allows you to download the OMI source application necessary to create the custom inventory provider. Use this guide to install the OMI source application. The application must be installed to create a custom provider.

Creating a Custom Inventory Provider

As an example of creating a custom inventory provider, suppose that you want to collect information about any printers that might be attached to your Linux/UNIX machines. Your first step in creating this new printer provider is to develop a schema.mof file. An example of what that mof file might look like this:

```
#pragma namespace("\\\\.\\root\\cimv2")
.[Description("Printer Information")]
 class XYZ_Printer
 {
 [Key] string Name; // the name of the Printer
 string Location; // the location of the Printer
 string Model; // the model of the Printer
 };
```

Next, you need to create the provider source. This done using a command line, as shown in Figure 5.21.

Once the source is created, you need to add the information you want returned into the Class_Provider.cpp file. For this example, this would the XYZ_Printer_Class_Provider.cpp file. ConfigMgr only supports the Load, Unload, and EnumerateInstances. Your edits should look like Figure 5.22.

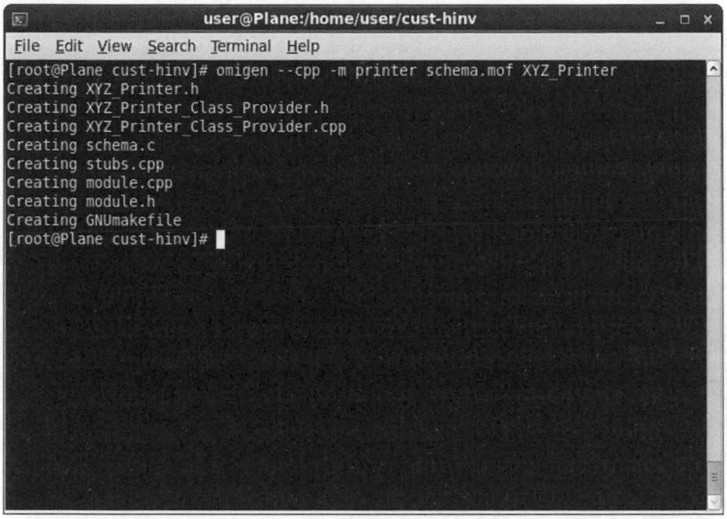

```
user@Plane:/home/user/cust-hinv                    _ □ ×

File  Edit  View  Search  Terminal  Help
[root@Plane cust-hinv]# omigen --cpp -m printer schema.mof XYZ_Printer
Creating XYZ_Printer.h
Creating XYZ_Printer_Class_Provider.h
Creating XYZ_Printer_Class_Provider.cpp
Creating schema.c
Creating stubs.cpp
Creating module.cpp
Creating module.h
Creating GNUmakefile
[root@Plane cust-hinv]#
```

FIGURE 5.21   Creating the provider source.

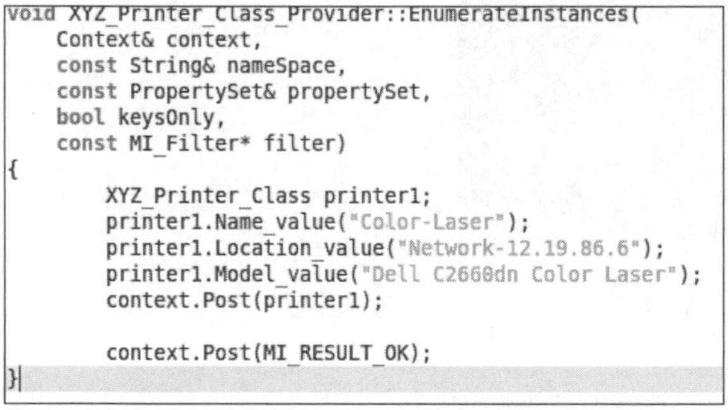

```
void XYZ_Printer_Class_Provider::EnumerateInstances(
    Context& context,
    const String& nameSpace,
    const PropertySet& propertySet,
    bool keysOnly,
    const MI_Filter* filter)
{
        XYZ_Printer_Class printer1;
        printer1.Name_value("Color-Laser");
        printer1.Location_value("Network-12.19.86.6");
        printer1.Model_value("Dell C2660dn Color Laser");
        context.Post(printer1);

        context.Post(MI_RESULT_OK);
}
```

FIGURE 5.22   The EnumerateInstances provider.

The next step in the process is to compile the provider with the edits shown in Figure 5.22. This is done using gmake, shown in Figure 5.23.

Configure the Non-Windows Machine to Use the Custom Provider

When the provider is compiled, a runtime file is created. You can see the name of this runtime in the last line of Figure 5.23, where it is called libprinter.so. This runtime file must be copied over to the ConfigMgr installation folder. Once there, it needs to be registered with ConfigMgr. The commands to accomplish this are as follows and are shown in Figure 5.24:

```
[root@Plane cust-hinv]# cp libprinter.so /opt/microsoft/omi/lib
[root@Plane cust-hinv]#
[root@Plane cust-hinv]# /opt/microsoft/omi/bin/omiserver -s
/opt/microsoft/omi/bin/omiserver.bin: stopped server
```

```
[root@Plane cust-hinv]#
[root@Plane cust-hinv]# /opt/microsoft/omi/bin/omireg -n root/cimv2
/opt/microsoft/omi/lib/libprinter.so
Created /opt/microsoft/omi/./lib/libprinter.so
Created /opt/microsoft/omi/./etc/omiregister/root-cimv2/printer.reg
[root@Plane cust-hinv]#
[root@Plane cust-hinv]# /opt/microsoft/omi/bin/omiserver &
[1] 42158
[root@Plane cust-hinv]#
```

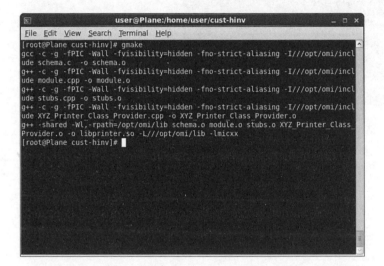

FIGURE 5.23   Compiling the provider with gmake.

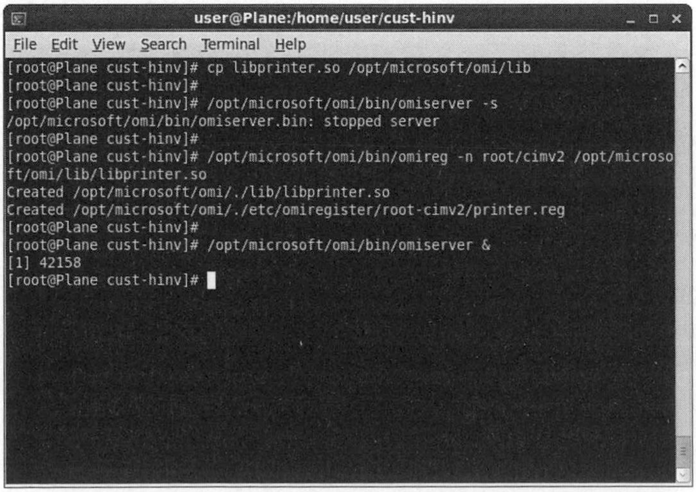

FIGURE 5.24   Registering the provider with ConfigMgr.

At this point, everything should be working correctly and the data is now in OMI. You can use the OMI client tool to view this data. The command to view the data and the results follows and are shown in Figure 5.25:

```
[root@Plane cust-hinv]# /opt/microsoft/omi/bin/omicli ei root/cimv2 XYZ_printer
instance of XYZ_Printer
{
    [Key] Name=Color-Laser
     Location=Network-12.19.86.6
     Model=Dell C2660dn Color Laser
}
 [root@Plane cust-hinv]#
```

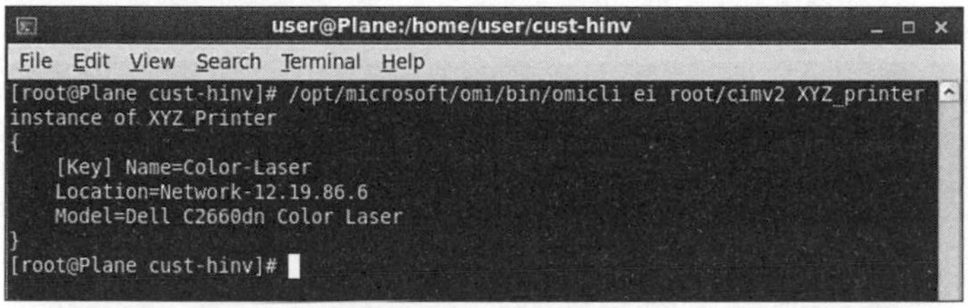

FIGURE 5.25 Viewing the data with the OMI client.

Enabling the ConfigMgr Site to Support the New Provider

You must add the contents of that schema.mof file to the hardware inventory classes for ConfigMgr to collect that information. There are several ways to accomplish this but the easiest is to use the Mofcomp program in Windows on the ConfigMgr site server. Follow these steps:

1. Copy over the schema.mof file to the site server, open a CMD window as Administrator, and run the tool using mofcomp schema.mof (see Figure 5.26).

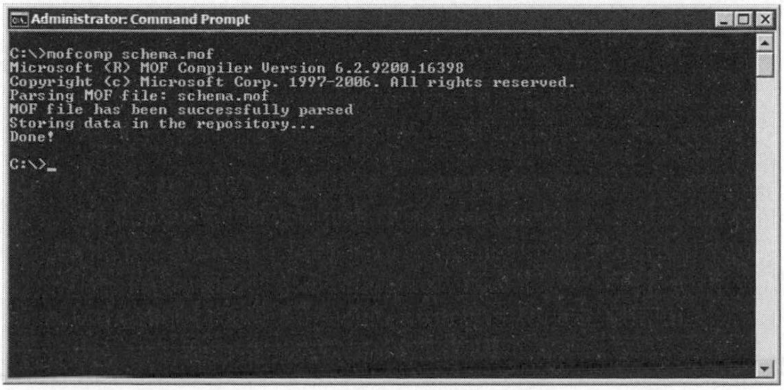

FIGURE 5.26 Running mofcomp on the ConfigMgr site server.

2. Next, in the ConfigMgr console under the Client Settings, open up the hardware inventory and choose **Set Classes**.

3. Now choose **Add**, click **Connect**, and connect to the machine that you ran the mofcomp on.

4. Once connected, scroll through the list until you find the inventory that you added; in this example, that is XYZ_Printer. Check the **Class** box, and then choose **Edit**.

5. Under Display Name, give it a friendly name, and then click **OK** twice.

6. Confirm that all the boxes are checked that you want to collect inventory for (see Figure 5.27), and click **OK** to save your changes.

7. A policy is created and sent to the clients to collect this information during the next hardware inventory cycle.

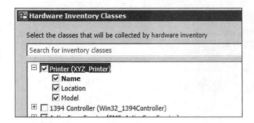

FIGURE 5.27   Enabling the new class.

Viewing Results

When the Linux/UNIX agent runs hardware inventory again, the new class is collected and added to the ConfigMgr database. This new information can be viewed in Resource Explorer. Figure 5.28 shows the printer information used in the example.

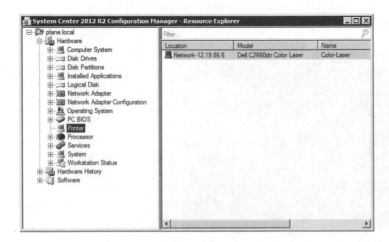

FIGURE 5.28   Custom inventory in Resource Explorer.

Client Agent Commands

You can use several commands to force the client to do different things right away and not wait for the timed interval to occur on Linux/UNIX clients. All the following commands must be run as the root superuser.

▶ To force a policy refresh, run this command:

```
/opt/microsoft/configmgr/bin/ccmexec -rs policy
```

▶ To force hardware inventory to run, use this command:

```
/opt/microsoft/configmgr/bin/ccmexec -rs hinv
```

▶ To view the inventory data on the client you can use the OMI Client tool. This example returns the information associated with the processor:

```
/opt/microsoft/omi/bin/omicli ei root/cimv2 SCXCM_Processor
```

▶ If you need to find the client version, you can use this command:

```
/opt/microsoft/configmgr/bin/ccmexec -v
```

Troubleshooting with Log Files

When problems occur, one of the first places to look for what might be wrong is in the console. If that doesn't point you in the right direction, the next place is the client logs.

Linux/UNIX Log Files

The Linux/UNIX agent logs everything into one log file called SCXCM.log. This file is located at /var/opt/microsoft/scxcm.log.

This is the only log file for all client activity. Multiple components write to this log, which makes it more difficult to look for the issue that you are experiencing. This log can be viewed on the Linux/UNIX client by using the gedit program. It shows as plain text, and looks similar as to when using notepad on a Windows-based client. There is no cmtrace program for the Linux/UNIX agent. Gedit works for a quick look, but to go in-depth in the log you would want to copy the log file to a Windows-based machine and use cmtrace to view it. The format of the log makes it viewable with cmtrace.

There is a second log file that may be of interest; this is the scxcmprovider.log file, located at /opt/microsoft/omi/scxcmprovider.log.

This is the log file for the CIM server service, and has entries for all the providers that are used to collect information from the OMI database. Again, this log can be viewed with the gedit program, but to make the most use of it copy it over to a Windows-based machine and use the cmtrace program to view it.

There is also a program in the Linux/UNIX world called tail. You can use this program to view the last 10 lines of the log file in real time. An example of using the tail program follows:

```
tail -f /var/opt/microsoft/scxcm.log
```

Verbose Logs

The default logging provides all the errors that show up. In certain instances you might need to see more detailed information. You need to be aware of four logging levels:

▶ **Error:** Shows problems that require attention; default value

▶ **Warning:** Shows possible problems that might need attention

▶ **Info:** Detailed logging that indicates the status of various events

▶ **Trace:** Verbose logging showing as much detail as possible

The detail of the logging can be changed by modifying the scxcm.conf file, located at /opt/microsoft/configmgr/etc/scxcm.conf.

This file can be changed with any text editing program like gedit. The file only has a few lines and is very easy to modify. The contents of this file follow:

```
FILE (
PATH: /var/opt/microsoft/scxcm.log
MODULE:  WARNING
MODULE: scx.client WARNING
)
```

To change the logging levels just change the two MODULE items to the new log level. The Linux/UNIX agent does not have any rollover logging like the Windows-based agent does. After you change the logging level, collect the information you are looking for in the log file and change the level back as soon as possible; otherwise, you might lose the information that you are looking for.

OS X Log Files

The OS X agent is similar in logging to the Linux/UNIX agent, most client activity is logged into one file. This file is located at /Library/Application Support/Microsoft/CCM/Logs/Client-DATE-TIME.log.

The naming conventions for this file have the date as the actual year, month, day, and the time is in 24-hour format. The log size is set at 1MB and rolls over to another log file, saving the old one when that size is reached. The file can be viewed with any text editor on the OS X machine, but most likely needs to be viewed with cmtrace on a Windows machine for in-depth viewing.

The OS X agent creates the three additional logs listed in Table 5.3.

TABLE 5.3   OS X Client Logs

Log Filename	Purpose
CCMAgent-DATE-TIME.log	Contains information about user logon and logoffs
CCMNotification-DATE-TIME.log	Contains information about ConfigMgr notifications displayed on the OS X computer
CCMPrefPane-DATE-TIME.log	Contains information about the preferences dialog box and general status and errors

Each of the above logs is found in the same folder on the OS X computer, ~/Library/Logs.

By default in OS X 10.7 and OS X 10.8, this folder is hidden from the user. You can still view the folder from the terminal window as the superuser or if you remove the hidden flag on the folder. The logs are the same as other logs, viewable with any text editor on OS X but more readable if copied to a Windows-based system and viewed with cmtrace.

Summary

This chapter covered the on-premise cross-platform support agents for Linux/UNIX and OS X. It looked at the supported operating systems, the cross-platform architecture, and at how the agent handles communications. It covered in-depth how each agent installs and the requirements to install the agent. It described the agent components and covered step by step custom inventory. The chapter also looked at commands you can use to force client actions, the log files created by the agents, where they are located, and how to view them.

5

CHAPTER 6

What's New in Operating System Deployment

IN THIS CHAPTER

▶ The Alphabet Soup of Prerequisites

▶ Windows Setup Support Change

▶ Deployment Control

▶ Deployment Monitoring

▶ New Task Types

▶ New Built-In Task Sequence Variables

▶ UEFI Support

▶ Virtual Hard Disks and Windows To Go

▶ Other Improvements

▶ Troubleshooting Hints and Tips

Operating system deployment (OSD) is arguably one of the most important features within System Center 2012 R2 Configuration Manager (ConfigMgr), particularly for those enterprises desiring to move from the Windows XP platform, which is now past its end of life and end of support date. As its name implies, the OSD feature set enables deploying operating systems to compatible devices. However, OSD functionality is limited to deploying Microsoft Windows to Windows-compatible devices; it does not include Windows RT or any other non-Windows operating system (OS) supported by ConfigMgr 2012 R2 such as OS X or Linux. While many things are possible with some hard work and knowledge (including deploying Linux, see http://blogs.msdn.com/b/steverac/archive/2014/01/02/osd-for-linux-imaging-yes-really.aspx for a discussion), these are not discussed in this chapter or supported by Microsoft.

> **NOTE: WINDOWS XP END OF LIFE**
>
> April 8, 2014 marked the official end of life date for Windows XP. Technically, this date was for Windows XP Service Pack (SP) 3 support, because SP 2 has been end of life since July 13, 2010. After this date, Microsoft no longer supports anything related to Windows XP and makes no guarantees about its use, functionality, or security (unless you pay Microsoft a premium price for extended support).
>
> End of life for XP also affects other products that support it, such as ConfigMgr; ConfigMgr 2012 (all versions) does not "officially support" Windows XP after the XP

end of life date. This means that Microsoft no longer accounts for any scenarios that are Windows XP specific, or fixes any XP-specific issues in any of its products (or Windows XP itself). However, this does not mean there is a time bomb in ConfigMgr such that things related to Windows XP stop working.

This chapter covers the changes introduced to OSD in ConfigMgr 2012 SP 1 and ConfigMgr 2012 R2 since ConfigMgr 2012's initial release to manufacturing (RTM). For a complete discussion of OSD, see *System Center 2012 Configuration Manager Unleashed* (2012). Many of the changes to OSD are not OSD specific; instead, they enable other technologies or account for changes in the Windows ecosystem, including changes to Windows setup.

The Alphabet Soup of Prerequisites

OSD at its core is an automation engine, typically referred to as a *task sequence engine* because it uses task sequences to define the tasks it performs. Under the covers, the actions performed in OSD primarily utilize the tools provided by Windows itself, Windows setup, and the various toolkits released by Microsoft to automate Windows setup. For ConfigMgr 2012 R2, these prerequisite tools are as follows:

▶ User State Migration Toolkit (USMT) 8.1

▶ Windows Preinstallation Environment (PE) 5

▶ Windows deployment tools

These tools are included in the Windows Automated Deployment Kit (ADK) for Windows 8.1 (http://www.microsoft.com/en-us/download/details.aspx?id=30652) as a single download and install from Microsoft. The ADK includes other tools not required for ConfigMgr, such as the Application Compatibility Toolkit (ACT) and Windows Performance Toolkit. The three prerequisite tools must be installed on the top-level site in your hierarchy; this is either a primary site or a central administration site (CAS). You must also install Windows PE and the Windows deployment tools on every primary site server and on site systems hosting the SMS provider role. The SMS provider is often overlooked, as that role is traditionally installed on the site server.

> **CAUTION: APPLICATION COMPATIBILITY KIT REQUIRES A SQL DATABASE**
>
> ACT requires a SQL Server database and installs a local instance of SQL Server Express. Because this can lead to confusion and failures during ConfigMgr setup, do not install ACT on a ConfigMgr site server system unless you truly know how to manage separate instances of SQL Server or configure ACT to use the same SQL instance used by ConfigMgr. As either approach requires some forethought and planning, it is best to avoid installing a SQL Express instance on a ConfigMgr primary site server.

Operating System Version Support

OSD in ConfigMgr 2012 R2 supports deploying every version of Windows supported by ConfigMgr 2012 R2, which includes Windows XP SP 3, Windows Vista SP 2, Windows 7, Windows 8, and Windows 8.1. Technically speaking (although not from a formal support perspective), support for Windows XP SP 3 is maintained even after its April 2014 end of life because Microsoft has no intention of crippling or removing this capability. However, deploying Windows XP does require additional configuration; this is discussed in the "Down-Level Boot Images" section of this chapter.

Each version of Windows includes a new version of the prerequisite tools discussed in the previous section. The tools generally don't change much other than adding support for the newest iteration of Windows and officially dropping support for older versions of Windows, which could create a possible hurdle for those still supporting older versions such as Windows XP. The statement from the Windows team is that their tools support N-2 versions, meaning that each iteration of the tool supports the version of Windows it was launched with (N) and two previous versions. This means that the latest incarnation of these tools released in conjunction with Windows 8.1 also support Windows 8 (N-1), and Windows 7 (N-2), but explicitly do not support Windows Vista or XP. This leads to both a support and technical dilemma if you were deploying Windows XP in your environment before XP's end of life, or still must after its end of life. Interestingly, the latest version of the tools can be installed on Windows Vista (N-3), although they don't deploy or maintain Windows Vista images.

TIP: ABOUT VERSION NUMBERING

Be wary of version numbers used in the various tools, as they are not necessarily incremented by one for new versions and many now use version numbers that match the OS version they were released with. For example, the latest version of USMT is now 8.1; what happened to versions 6 and 7 is anyone's guess. This is possibly even more confusing because the tools included within USMT, namely scanstate and loadstate, are now version 6.3, which matches the internal version of Windows 8.1 and gives some order to this if you take a step back and match them up.

Supporting Windows XP deployments requires creating and importing your own Windows PE 3.1 images into ConfigMgr, which requires installing the Windows Automated Installation Kit (WAIK) for Windows 7 and the WAIK Supplement for Windows 7 SP 1 to a separate system. This could be an administrative workstation, a "tools" server, or any system that is not a ConfigMgr site server or site system. Do not consider this a temporary installation, as you may need to maintain these Windows PE 3.1 boot images in the future. Creating, maintaining, and importing Windows PE 3.1-based boot images into ConfigMgr is covered in the "Down-Level Boot Images" section of this chapter.

USMT and state migration also present versioning challenges. While installing ConfigMgr 2012 R2 (or upgrading from 2012 SP 1), the installer automatically creates a package for USMT 8.1. This does not affect or upgrade any previous versions of USMT that you may have packages for, and does not prevent you from creating new packages for older versions of USMT. This is important, because similar to Windows PE, you must use a down-level version of USMT for task sequences involving Windows XP.

NOTE: WINDOWS ADK FOR WINDOWS 8.1 UPDATE

Along with the Windows 8.1 update in April 2014, officially known as Windows 8.1 Update, Microsoft released an update to the ADK for Windows 8.1 that includes an update to Windows PE 5.0 and USMT.

Windows PE 5.1 introduces a handful of very small changes that do not impact deploying Windows or are required to deploy Windows 8.1 Update. In fact, attempting to add a Windows PE 5.1-based boot image to ConfigMgr is currently problematic at best and should not done at all.

The update for USMT includes a handful of bug fixes and is recommended for installation and use with ConfigMgr 2012 R2. Installing the updated ADK on your site server(s) updates the existing installed USMT, which is directly referenced by the USMT package created by ConfigMgr during installation or upgrade. After updating USMT with the ADK's installer, update the existing USMT package by selecting it and choosing **Update Distribution Points** from the ribbon bar or right-click context menu.

The supported method for migrating from Windows XP to Windows 8.1, while preserving user data, suffers from the support limitations previously discussed in this section and involves the use of two task sequences:

▶ The first task sequence captures state in Windows XP. It uses USMT 5.0 and is run within the existing Windows XP instance—no reboots or boot images are used or required. This task sequence should only contain the following tasks:

  ▶ Request State Store

  ▶ Capture User State

  ▶ Release State Store

▶ The second task sequence deploys Windows 8.1 and restores the state using USMT 8.1. As with all Windows 8.1 deployment task sequences, this one uses a Windows PE 5.0 boot image. It is a standard Windows 8.1 deployment task sequence in all respects.

Other than using a different version of USMT, this is nearly identical to a replace scenario involving the two separate task sequences. One other major caveat is that USMT 8.1 can only restore the user settings defined in miguser.xml from state captured using USMT 5.0. This means that in the Capture User State task in the first task sequence and the Restore User State task in the second task sequence, you must specify the **Customize how user profiles are restored** option and then specify only **miguser.xml** in the Configuration Files dialog that appears when you click the Files button shown in Figure 6.1.

Although other permutations may work, such as using a single task sequence for the entire procedure, the process in this section is the recommended and supported procedure. For an explicit walk-through, see http://blogs.technet.com/b/configmgrteam/archive/2013/09/12/how-to-migrate-user-data-from-win-xp-to-win-8-1-with-system-center-2012-r2-configmgr.aspx.

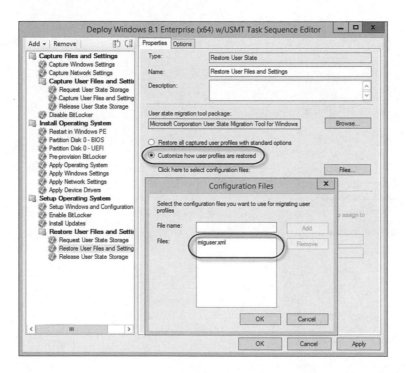

FIGURE 6.1   Setting a custom configuration file for a Restore User State task.

Boot Images

New boot images based on Windows PE 5.0 are created when you install ConfigMgr 2012 R2 or upgrade from SP 1 to R2. If you are upgrading from SP 1, existing boot images are not upgraded to Windows PE 5.0. While you could continue to use these Windows PE 4.0-based boot images, they are officially unsupported in ConfigMgr 2012 R2 and might cause problems. One of the first post-upgrade tasks to thus perform is to transition all your task sequences to the new default boot images or new Windows PE 5.0-based boot images. As discussed in the "Down-Level Boot Images" section, there are also potential problems with the new Windows PE 5.0-based boot images on older hardware and virtual machines (VMs).

In addition, while down-level boot images remain in the console, they cannot be modified from the ConfigMgr console. Specifically, you cannot add or remove drivers, customize these images, or modify any optional components; the respective tabs for these activities are not even available in the Properties dialog for these down-level boot images (shown in Figure 6.2).

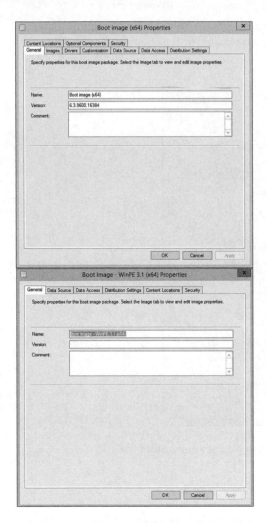

FIGURE 6.2   Comparing the current and down-level boot image properties dialogs.

Down-Level Boot Images

This section discusses creating a down-level Windows PE 3.1-based boot image. In addition to supporting Windows XP deployments (mentioned in the "Operating System Version Support" section), supporting older hardware could also require a down-level boot image. A new requirement introduced with Windows 8 was for CPUs to support Physical Address Extension (PAE), the NX processor bit (NX), and Streaming SIMD Extensions 2 (SSE2). Depending upon the motherboard, you may need to explicitly enable some of these features in the BIOS. See http://windows.microsoft.com/en-US/windows-8/what-is-pae-nx-sse2 for information on these processor capabilities and their requirements in Windows 8.

Many older processors (and even several newer ones) do not include support for these processor features, meaning they cannot support Windows 8 or newer versions. Because

Windows PE 5.0 is directly based on Windows 8.1, boot images based on Windows PE 5.0 also cannot be used on these older systems that do not support Windows 8 even if you are deploying an older version of Windows. With ConfigMgr 2012 R2, the straightforward workaround is to use Windows PE 3.1 boot images as needed to support these older systems. This removes the need for Windows 8 support.

Note that ConfigMgr 2012 R2 does not support other down-level versions of Windows PE such as 3.0 or 4.0.

NOTE: HYPERVISOR SUPPORT

Hypervisors, by definition, are simply a layer of hardware virtualization and thus must provide the processor requirements listed in this section to support Windows 8, Windows 8.1, and Windows PE 5.0. Microsoft's Hyper-V hypervisor (all versions) fully supports these requirements. However, older versions of VMware's various hypervisor products that are still commonly used do not (this includes ESX, ESXi, and VMware Workstation). For full support, upgrade to the latest versions of these products or use a Windows PE 3.1 boot image.

For other hypervisor products, please check with their manufacturer regarding support.

As mentioned in the "Operating System Version Support" section of this chapter, creating a down-level Windows PE 3.1 boot image should occur on an alternate, non-R2 site server system. This system should remain available in the future, because you may need to later modify or re-create these down-level boot images. Another approach for maintaining down-level boot images is to use an alternate, nonproduction installation of ConfigMgr 2012 SP 1. You would use this "tools" installation explicitly for creating and managing the down-level boot images, without having to perform the manual tasks listed next in this section. The boot images could be exported as needed from this tools installation and imported into the actual, production installation.

To manually create and maintain Windows PE 3.1 images for use in ConfigMgr 2012 R2, complete the following steps:

1. Download and install the WAIK 3.0 from http://www.microsoft.com/en-us/download/details.aspx?id=5753. This large ISO file must be mounted, burned to media, or extracted using a tool like 7-zip. Initiate the install using wAIKAMD64.msi (for 64-bit systems) or wAIKX86.msi (for 32-bit systems), and follow the steps in the wizard.

2. Download and install the WAIK 3.1 Supplement from http://www.microsoft.com/en-us/download/details.aspx?id=5188. This is also a large ISO file. Unfortunately, the contents of this ISO are just the raw files needed for the supplement and it does not include a setup routine.

   To install the supplement, copy the entire contents of the ISO (after it is mounted, burned, or extracted) over the top of the WAIK 3.0 installation from step 1. The recommended method for copying the contents is to run `xcopy E:\"%ProgramFiles% \Windows AIK\Tools\PETools" /ERDY` from a command prompt where E: is the drive letter of the mounted ISO or media (or path to the extracted files if they were extracted). This also assumes WAIK 3.0 is installed to the default folder of %*ProgramFiles*%\Windows AIK\Tools\PETools in step 1; adjust accordingly if not the case.

3. Open the Deployment Tools Command Prompt from the Start menu or start screen.

4. See the steps at http://technet.microsoft.com/en-us/library/dd744533(WS.10).aspx to create the new Windows PE image and add the following three required components to the boot image:

> ▶ WinPE-Scripting

> ▶ WinPE-WMI

> ▶ WinPE-WDS-Tools

5. Follow the steps at http://technet.microsoft.com/en-us/library/dd744355(v=WS.10). aspx#AddDriverDISM to add any optional drivers to the Windows PE image. As this image is based on Windows PE 3.1, which is in turn based on Windows 7 SP 1, you must add Windows 7 SP 1 compatible drivers to it.

6. The boot image is now ready to import into ConfigMgr for use with your task sequence. Copy the created WIM file to your usual software repository location; from here it is imported and directly referenced by ConfigMgr. Do not move or delete the WIM file, as you may need to modify and reuse it in the future. The location you copy the WIM file to must be accessible via UNC; ConfigMgr uses the system account of the server hosting the SMS provider to access this content.

7. Navigate to **Software Library -> Overview -> Operating Systems -> Boot Images** in the console. From the ribbon bar or right-click context menu of the Boot Images node, select **Add Boot Image** and follow the Add Boot Image Wizard.

A complete, step-by-step walk-through for these steps is also available at http://technet. microsoft.com/en-us/library/dn387582.aspx.

Optional Components Within Boot Images

Windows PE, by design, is a componentized version of Windows. By default, Windows PE boot images do not contain all possible components, although those needed by ConfigMgr are automatically injected by ConfigMgr.

There may be occasion to add additional components to support custom or nondefault functionality within your boot images. ConfigMgr 2012 R2 lets you easily accomplish this on any Windows PE 5.0 boot image imported into ConfigMgr (see Figure 6.3). For Windows PE 3.1 boot images, you must manually add the required components per the instructions in the "Down-Level Boot Images" section of this chapter. Complete the following steps to add additional components to Windows PE 5.0 boot images:

1. Click the starburst on the Optional Components tab to open the Select optional components dialog shown in Figure 6.3.

This dialog shows all available optional components and the size each adds to the boot image. The additional size is significant because it increases the time required for the boot image to download to the target system during the OSD process, which in turn may affect your decision to use that component.

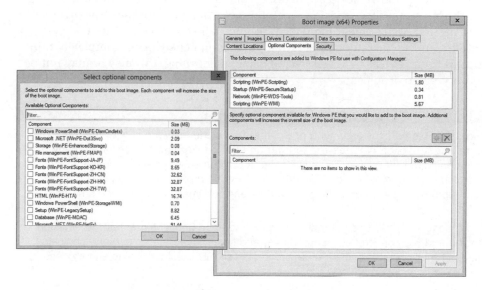

FIGURE 6.3   Select optional components dialog.

2. Choose the components you want to add and click **OK**.

    If any components have dependencies, a confirmation box appears to add these additional components; as an example, the Windows PowerShell (WinPE-DismCmdlets) component also requires the Microsoft .NET (WinPE-NetFx) and Windows PowerShell (WinPE-PowerShell) components.

3. As with all other changes to a boot image within the console, after clicking Apply or OK on the boot image's properties dialog, you are prompted to initiate an update of the boot image to the distribution points (DPs) to which it is distributed. You should confirm this update to ensure that your changes are available as soon as possible, subject to your intentions, the change control process in your environment, and the network speed.

Windows Setup Support Change

Starting with ConfigMgr 2012 SP 1, Microsoft supports directly using the install.wim image file from Windows source media and this now works correctly within a ConfigMgr task sequence. Previously, direct use of this image file installed Windows to the logical D: drive (rarely desired). This was often a technical challenge because administrators and applications normally assume the C: drive is used. To account for this when directly using the image.wim file, you must properly set the OSDPreserveDriveLetter task sequence variable as discussed later in this section.

Directly using image.wim means you could completely skip building a reference image for your deployments. However, this has security implications as this base image is not current with latest Windows security updates; if you do not build a reference image, you should use the built-in offline servicing capabilities of ConfigMgr (or the Deployment Image Servicing and Management tool/DISM) to inject all applicable security updates directly into the image file before using it in a production deployment. Completely thin images such as these do lead to longer overall deployment times; this may or may not be of concern in your environment.

NOTE: USING THIN VS. THICK IMAGES

The discussion (sometimes argument) of whether to include software in your reference image, making it thicker, or to leave it to layer on after deployment has occurred many times by many different people. There is no right or wrong answer here, although generally using a thin (or at least thinner) image is preferred and often recommended because it reduces upfront image creation time as well as ongoing image maintenance time and effort.

Part of the beauty of OSD and the task sequence model in ConfigMgr is that the decision is up to you and your preferences, constraints, and goals; there are no actual technical implications other than deployment time and security. OSD is a true, end-to-end process that the image is only part of.

Using the install.wim image file is now preferred for build and capture task sequences. Starting with ConfigMgr 2012 SP 1, the built-in Create Task Sequence Wizard forces you to choose an operating system image. This change now aligns ConfigMgr with Windows setup supportability requirements that were not strictly followed by previous versions of ConfigMgr in certain scenarios. Combined with the offline servicing feature, directly using image.wim reduces the complexity and time it takes to run your build and capture task sequences when generating (or regenerating) your reference images.

Alternatively, using the operating system source files (the default for build and capture task sequences in previous versions of ConfigMgr) requires changing the default Apply Operating System task within the wizard-generated task sequence to reference an operating system installer instead of an operating system image (see Figure 6.4).

TIP: OPERATING SYSTEM SOURCE FILES

Operating system source files are directly imported into ConfigMgr from the operating system installation media as an Operating System Installer package. This package contains the entire contents of the operating system installation media and performs a classic full setup of Windows.

This classic full setup, as of Windows Vista, is similar in nature to OSD in that it first prepares the target system and then applies an image, specifically the image.wim from the media itself. However, you could apply the image.wim directly and not use the full classic setup to accomplish the same task. While technically valid, using the complete set of operating system source files is a legacy concept that should no longer be used unless deploying a legacy operating system such as Windows XP.

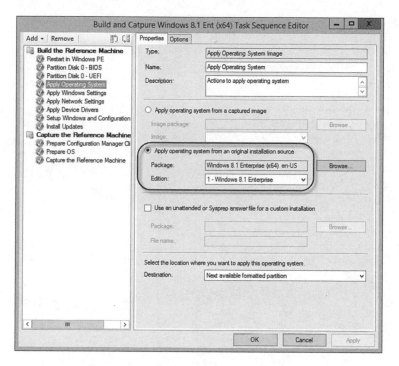

FIGURE 6.4   Default Apply Operating System task.

Using a build and capture task sequence is generally recommended because the offline servicing feature cannot inject all update types into the image. There are also other valid changes that make sense to put directly into your image. These include items that apply to all of your systems including the Visual C++ runtimes, the .NET Framework, and the Windows Management Framework (which includes an updated version of PowerShell).

To directly use a Windows 8.x or Windows 7 install.wim file in your task sequence and have Windows installed properly to the C: drive, complete the following steps to change the task sequence:

1. Add a Set Task Sequence Variable task to the task sequence from the General fly-out menu under the Add menu of the task sequence editor. Place this task anywhere before the Apply Operating System task.

2. Rename this task to **Set OSDPreserveDriveLetter Task Sequence Variable** or some other suitable name to uniquely identify it and its purpose during the task sequence.

3. For the Task Sequence Variable field, enter **OSDPreserveDriveLetter**.

4. For the Value field, enter **False**. Figure 6.5 shows a completed example.

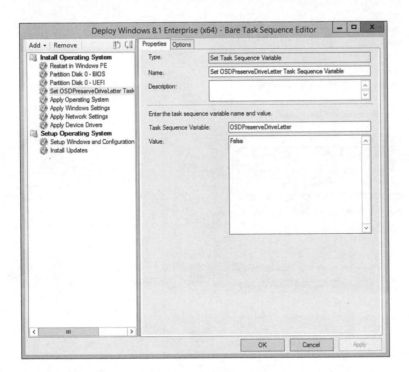

FIGURE 6.5   Set OSDPreserveDriveLetter Task Sequence Variable task.

5. Review and edit any Partition Disk tasks; specifically, verify that any volumes appearing before the Windows volume in the Volume list box at the bottom (see Figure 6.6) have the **Do not assign a drive letter to this partition** option selected (shown in Figure 6.7).

REAL WORLD: UPGRADING WINDOWS 8 TO WINDOWS 8.1

Upgrading from Windows 8 to Windows 8.1 is a new challenge for ConfigMgr. Microsoft designed this Windows upgrade experience to be seamless, fast, and painless; it was also designed using in-place upgrades as the preferred choice to preserve existing settings, applications, and user data, and to minimize the disruption for those that have already moved to Windows 8.

However, ConfigMgr has never supported direct, in-place Windows upgrades. Using the traditional refresh method within a task sequence adds complexity and time to a process that already works well out of the box, and should be unnecessary.

When Microsoft's internal Information Technology (IT) group undertook the challenge of upgrading their internal user base from Windows 8 to Windows 8.1, they chose to leverage a hybrid approach where a ConfigMgr application directly runs the Windows 8.1 setup. The whitepaper at http://www.microsoft.com/en-us/download/details.aspx?id=40811 describes this undertaking at a high-level level, and the whitepaper at http://www.microsoft.com/en-us/download/details.aspx?id=41965 provides explicit details. This in-place upgrade is now fully supported after the live-fire testing Microsoft performed on its user base, although it is not supported or recommended for any other type of Windows upgrade.

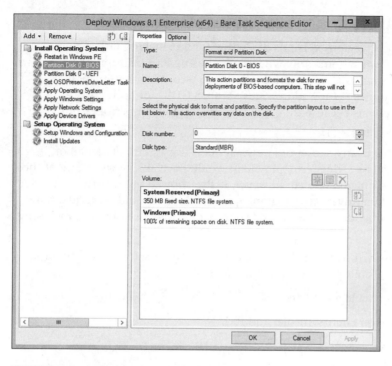

FIGURE 6.6   Volume list box of a Default Partition Disk task.

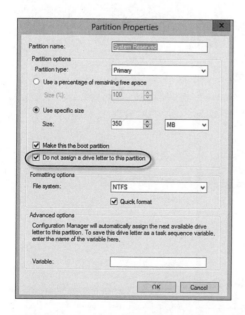

FIGURE 6.7   Do not assign a drive letter to this partition option.

Deployment Control

A common challenge with previous versions of ConfigMgr was making task sequences generally available to known systems only when booted using PXE or from media. Known systems are those that a site has a corresponding resource record for that includes a system's Media Access Control (MAC) address, it's SMBIOS GUID, or both. This is not a problem for unknown systems because they don't receive deployments from ConfigMgr unless PXE or media booted.

Deploying a task sequence to any subset of known systems was essentially an all or nothing proposition. The task sequence deployment would be available when any of those known systems was PXE or media booted; however, it also showed up in Software Center (or the ConfigMgr 2007 Run Advertised Program applet), where it could be accidentally triggered by users. Workarounds for this had side effects that were not obvious, including inaccuracies in reporting.

ConfigMgr 2012 SP 1 resolved this issue by introducing four new, self-explanatory task sequence deployment availability types (shown in Figure 6.8):

▶ Only Configuration Manager clients

▶ Configuration Manager clients, media, and PXE

▶ Only media and PXE

▶ Only media and PXE (hidden)

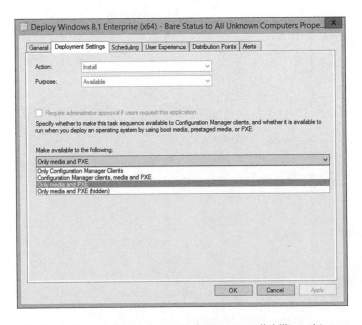

FIGURE 6.8   Task sequence deployment availability subtypes.

These availability types are applicable for both required and available task sequence deployments. The only option needing any additional explanation is the last one in the list: Only media and PXE (hidden). This option, as implied by "hidden," creates a task sequence deployment that can never be selected by an interactive user from the Task Sequence Wizard when a system is PXE or media booted, because it is hidden.

Deployments with this availability type can only be initiated by setting the value of the SMSTSPreferredAdvertID task sequence variable to the deployment's deployment ID. This is applicable for Available and Required deployments, where the only difference is the level of user interaction during the initial part of the task sequence: In a Required deployment, the task sequence automatically initiates and executes without any user involvement. This could be dangerous; use this option with caution and appropriate safeguards to avoid wiping and reloading systems that should not be wiped.

Setting SMSTSPreferredAdvertID can be accomplished in several ways (none being specific to hidden task sequence deployments):

▶ **Scripting:** You could use a script that sets this variable appropriately, then run the script using a pre-start command set directly in a boot image (on the Customization tab shown in Figure 6.9) or during the creation of boot media (see Figure 6.10). The logic in the script is up to you and can be as complex or simple as necessary, as long as the value of the variable is set properly.

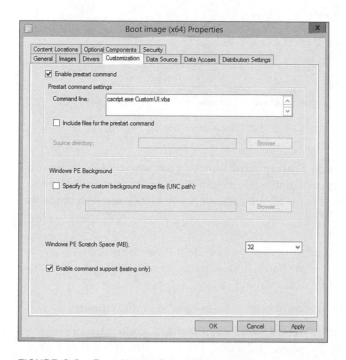

FIGURE 6.9   Boot image Customization tab.

▶ **Hard-coding the variable:** By hard-coding the value of this variable when creating boot media (also on the Customization page shown in Figure 6.10), you essentially create boot media tied to this one specific hidden task sequence deployment. This could be your secret USB key that allows only you to run a specific or special task sequence.

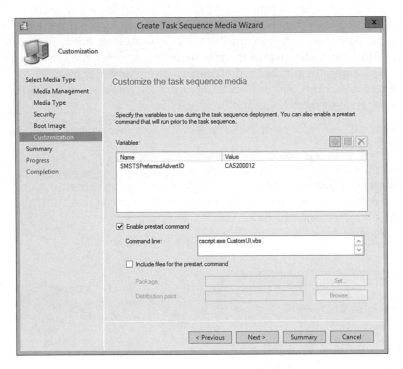

FIGURE 6.10   Customization page of the Create Task Sequence Media Wizard.

▶ **Setting the value directly when dealing with known computers:** Setting the value on a collection using a collection variable (see Figure 6.11) enforces a specific, task sequence deployment on the systems in the collection when they are PXE or media booted.

To determine a deployment's deployment ID, use one of the following console procedures or PowerShell commands that immediately follow these procedures—each finds the deployment ID. For the first procedure, follow these steps:

1. Within the console, navigate to **Monitoring -> Overview -> Deployments**.

2. Right-click the column header of the deployment list in the Details pane. This shows a list of all available columns; Software, Collection, Purpose, Action, Feature Type, Compliance %, and Date Created are shown by default and are selected in the list shown. Choose **Deployment ID** to add this column to those shown.

FIGURE 6.11   Collection Variables tab.

3. Find the applicable deployment by using the search functionality in the console, sorting, scrolling, or any combination of these. The deployment ID is displayed in the Deployment ID column and has eight characters: the first three are your site code, followed by a 2, followed by four hexadecimal-based digits.

Alternatively, you could follow the steps in this procedure:

1. Within the console, navigate to **Monitoring -> Overview -> Operating Systems -> Task Sequences**.

2. Select the applicable task sequence in the Details pane on the left, and then select the **Deployments** tab in the bottom pane.

3. Similar to step 2 in the previous procedure, add the Deployment ID column to those shown by right-clicking the column headers and selecting **Deployment ID**. You shouldn't have to search, sort, or scroll very far to find your target deployment, as only the deployments for this task sequence are shown.

An additional, possibly quicker, and easier way is using PowerShell. Two possible examples follow. Just replace Collection Name or Deploy* appropriately for your environment:

```
Get-CMDeployment -CollectionName "Collection Name" | Select-Object SoftwareName,
  DeploymentID
Get-CMDeployment | Where-Object {$_.SoftwareName -like "Deploy*"} | Select-Object
  SoftwareName, DeploymentID
```

Listing 6.1 is a sample script that could be used in a prestart command to set the SMSTSPreferredAdvertID. The script prompts the user to supply the deployment ID. You can use it to make an USB key that runs any task sequence deployment, including those that are hidden. The task sequence must still be deployed to the system booted from PXE or media, but since the task sequence is hidden, you can deploy it to all known and unknown systems without any negative ramifications. For production use, add error handling and input validation as appropriate. This script is available as online content for this book; see Appendix C, "Available Online," for details.

LISTING 6.1   Set SMSTSPreferredAdvertID

```
Option Explicit
Dim tsEnv
Dim result
Dim prompt, title, defaultID
set tsEnv = CreateObject("Microsoft.SMS.TSEnvironment")
prompt = "Please enter a valid Task Sequence Deployment ID to execute."
title = "Deployment ID"
defaultID = "ONE20002"
result = InputBox (prompt, title, defaultID)
tsEnv("SMSTSPreferredAdvertID") = result
```

REAL WORLD: HIDDEN TASK SEQUENCES

An additional real-world example of using hidden task sequences is to provide custom logic that limits task sequence availability to servers or desktops or potentially some other environment-specific criteria like location. This is accomplished using a pre-start script that queries Windows Management Instrumentation (WMI) or some other facility such as a database or Active Directory, and then presents a list of appropriate task sequences to the interactive user. The script then sets SMSTSPreferredAdvertID for the task sequence chosen by the user. The actual code for this script is specific to the scenario and thus left as an exercise for the reader.

Deployment Monitoring

At a basic level, monitoring task sequence deployments is similar to monitoring other ConfigMgr deployments, and is unchanged since ConfigMgr 2012 RTM.

To check the status of a task sequence deployment in the console, follow these steps:

1. Navigate to **Monitoring -> Deployments** and use the console's search functionality to find the deployment you want to monitor.

2. The Details pane shows completion statistics; to view a detailed breakdown of which systems are in each of the deployment status types (Success, In Progress, Error, Requirements Not Met, Unknown), click the View Status link in the Details pane or

right-click the deployment and select View Status to open the Deployment Status view for the deployment. This has tabs for each of the deployment status types at the top and a list of each of the systems within that status in the Asset Details pane at the bottom.

3. For further details of a system's status for the deployment, right-click that system and select **More Details** to display an Asset Message dialog for the system.

4. New with ConfigMgr 2012 R2 is a Status tab on the resulting Asset Message Dialog (see Figure 6.12). This tab lists all status messages for the system specific to this task sequence deployment.

The Status tab provides a task-by-task summary of the execution of the task sequence enabling more detailed analysis; it is nearly identical in content to the advertisement status view in ConfigMgr 2007 used to monitor task sequence execution and perform initial troubleshooting when things went wrong within a task sequence. However, the dialog is not a true Windows dialog: It is not resizable, and it is difficult to view all the information presented; so, although it contains the needed and relevant information, it can be challenging to use effectively.

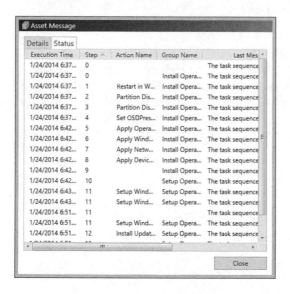

FIGURE 6.12   Asset Message Status tab.

Built-in reports provide the best approach for detailed monitoring and tracking of task sequences within ConfigMgr 2012, even though there are no new reports in SP 1 or R2. Specifically, use the History of a task sequence deployment on a computer report within the Task Sequence - Deployment Status folder. This report shows the same information shown on the Asset Message Status tab (see Figure 6.12) but in a friendlier, easier to work with format. If you are familiar with the status message view in ConfigMgr 2007, you could follow the procedures at http://www.scconfigmgr.com/2014/02/27/monitor-osd-with-status-message-queries-in-configmgr-2012/ to achieve the same results with the status message viewer.

New Task Types

OSD (in its current form) was introduced with ConfigMgr 2007, but Microsoft did not include any new built-in task types until ConfigMgr 2012 R2. ConfigMgr 2012 R2 marks another significant milestone: It is the first release of ConfigMgr after the ConfigMgr product team took ownership of the Microsoft Deployment Toolkit (MDT). These two milestones are tightly related.

> **NOTE: ABOUT THE MICROSOFT DEPLOYMENT TOOLKIT**
>
> MDT is a free and fully supported solution from Microsoft that is both a complete stand-alone solution for deploying Windows and an add-on to base functionality of ConfigMgr OSD. As an add-on for OSD, it provides a great deal of commonly needed functionality and makes the deployment process both dynamic and database driven. In general, MDT is not discussed in this chapter; however, MDT does not conceptually change any of the information presented, it merely extends and supplements it.

To decrease complexity and increase supportability, Microsoft is slowly integrating MDT functionality into the native ConfigMgr OSD feature set, which may eventually obviate the need for integrating MDT into ConfigMgr at all. ConfigMgr 2012 R2 includes the first baby steps for this effort in the form of three new task types; these are available under the Add -> General menu in the task sequence editor (see Figure 6.13). These new task types are effectively direct imports of tasks or capabilities from MDT, making them formal parts of the ConfigMgr task sequencer:

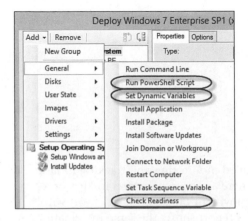

FIGURE 6.13   New task sequence tasks.

▶ **Run PowerShell Script:** This task type, shown in Figure 6.14, runs a predefined PowerShell script. It differs little in capability from a Run Command Line task type, other than facilitating easy input of all information required to run the script. You can use this task in any type of task sequence and anywhere within the task sequence as long as PowerShell is actually available:

    ▶ For portions of the task sequence executing within Windows PE, the boot image in use must have PowerShell enabled.

    ▶ For portions of the task sequence executing within Windows, that instance of Windows must have PowerShell installed.

Although no specific version of PowerShell is required for this task, the commands, syntax, and cmdlets used within the script must fit the version of PowerShell available at the time the script is executed.

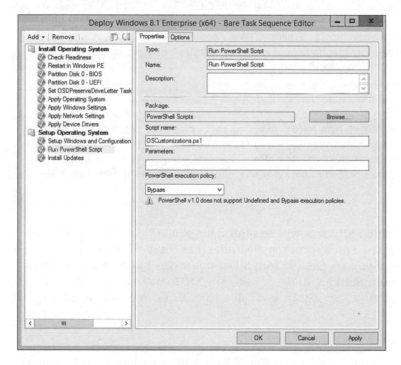

FIGURE 6.14   Run PowerShell Script task.

The following parameters are available to configure this task:

▶ **Package:** This parameter specifies the package where the actual PowerShell script file is stored and from where it is accessed. Using a package (defined under Software Library -> Overview -> Application Management -> Packages) is consistent with the rest of the ConfigMgr content distribution methodology and procedures, and enables the task sequence to retrieve the script from the nearest DP without being concerned about permissions or other related accessibility issues.

▶ **Script Name:** This is the filename of the script itself as stored in the package specified in the Package parameter.

▶ **Parameters:** These are additional command-line parameters passed to the script for use during execution. See http://technet.microsoft.com/en-us/magazine/jj554301.aspx for a discussion on using PowerShell command-line parameters in your scripts.

▶ **PowerShell execution policy:** This parameter overrides the target system's execution policy for PowerShell scripts for the execution of the script specified (and only for the execution of this script). This is equivalent to using the `-ExecutionPolicy` switch when invoking a script from the command line.

NOTE: THE POWERSHELL EXECUTION POLICY

The PowerShell execution policy is a default mechanism to help prevent unwanted scripts from running on systems accidentally. Similar to User Account Control (UAC), it is not intended as an actual security mechanism; it is an inhibiter that forces the user or administrator to make explicit decisions about what to allow.

By default, PowerShell execution policies allow only signed scripts to execute. However, most internal IT organizations do not have a code-signing certificate or wish to use one, as this could increase the maintenance overhead and complexity of what is often a simple script. Code-signing certificates also have a recurring cost unless the organization has a suitable internal public key infrastructure (PKI) to issue this type of certificate. For information on the PowerShell execution policy, see http://4sysops.com/archives/powershell-execution-policy/?utm_source=feedburner&utm_medium=feed&utm_campaign=Feed%3A+4sysops+(4sysops).

▶ **Set Dynamic Variables:** This task type sets the value of a task sequence variable (or set of variables) based on a set of supplied rules that check the target system against those rules. If you are familiar with MDT, this task is functionally similar to customizing the customsettings.ini file or using the MDT database to set the values of variables dynamically. Task sequence variable types that can be set include the following:

   ▶ Built-in variables (that are not read-only)

   ▶ Action task sequence variables (action task sequence variables are those that set the value of a property in one of the standard tasks)

   ▶ Custom task sequence variables

When you click the Add Variable button and select Existing variables from the fly-out menu, the task provides a handy browser dialog (shown in Figure 6.15) where you can choose any of the documented, standard built-in or action task sequence variables.

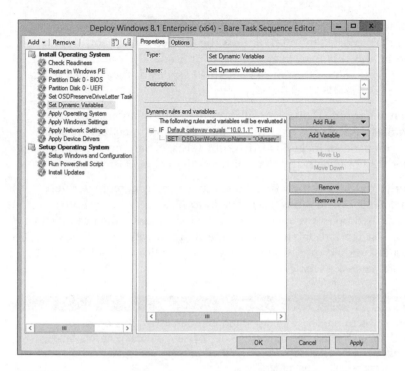

FIGURE 6.15   A Set Dynamic Variables task example.

The custom variable option from the Add Variables fly-out menu lets you specify the name of any task sequence variable, including ones not yet defined. Adding a variable by selecting **Add Variables** places the variable into the list box in the middle (see Figure 6.15), which can be selected to define its desired value. When setting the value of a variable, there is a check box to make the value Secret. Secret values are not exported when a task sequence is exported. Some default variables, like OSDCaptureAccountPassword, are automatically configured as Secret. The values set are only assigned when a task is executed if the rules set within the task evaluate to true. Four rule types are possible:

▶ **Computer:** This rule type is for matching against a specific computer. You can identify a specific computer using one of four possible criteria: asset tag, UUID, serial number, or MAC address. Only one of these must be supplied, and only one (if more than one is defined) needs to match. This rule type is very specific and used only when you have a small set of predefined computers that require something very specific performed during the task sequence.

▶ **Location:** This rule compares the default (IPv4) gateway against a set value. The gateway is usually indicative of the location of a system.

▶ **Make and Model:** This rule compares the make and model names of the target system (as reported by WMI) against the defined values. Both values must match for this rule to evaluate to true. Unfortunately, you cannot use wildcards for these values; they must be defined exactly as they appear in the `Win32_ComputerSystem` WMI class.

▶ **Task Sequence Variable:** This rule compares the value of an existing task sequence variable against the predefined value. Multiple operators are available for the comparison, including exists, not exists, equals, not equals, greater than, greater than or equals, less than, and less than or equals.

You can add multiple rules to a single task, but cannot directly combine or nest the rules to form complex evaluations. Each rule in turn can set one or more task sequence variables, based upon the evaluation of the rule at task sequence run-time on a target system. The Options tab lets you define complex conditional logic to determine when a task should run; this enables setting additional conditions that are evaluated before the task executes.

NOTE: MDT STAND-ALONE

Although MDT functionality is to be slowly incorporated into ConfigMgr, this does not affect the future of MDT when used as a stand-alone deployment solution. At this time, Microsoft and the ConfigMgr product group are committed to maintaining MDT as a stand-alone solution that does not require ConfigMgr.

▶ **Check Readiness:** This task type does as implied, checks the system where the task sequence is run for readiness; Figure 6.16 shows an example. The task is intended primarily for use in refresh scenarios where a clean operating system is installed on a user's existing hardware. Checking system readiness for this cleanly installed operating system before affecting the currently installed operating system is important, as it prevents data loss or user disruption if the system does not meet specified minimum requirements. The task could also be used in other scenarios, but provides somewhat reduced value depending upon your goals. In addition, this task is best used at the beginning of the task sequence before any changes are made to the target system.

This task can optionally check four self-explanatory criteria, depending on configuration:

▶ Ensure minimum memory (MB)

▶ Ensure minimum processor speed (MHz)

▶ Ensure minimum free disk space (MB)

▶ Ensure current OS to be refreshed is "Client" or "Server"

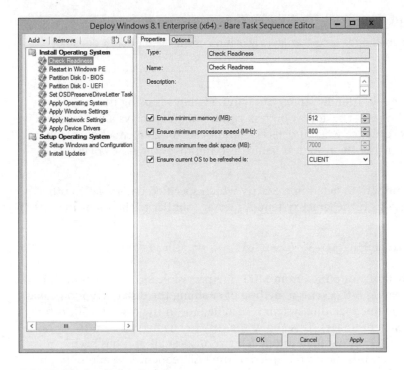

FIGURE 6.16   Check Readiness task.

If any of the criteria selected and specified are not met, the task fails with an error code of 0x80004005. If Continue on error on the Options tab for this task is not selected or this task is not a member of a group that has this option selected, the entire task sequence fails also. This failure is rather abrupt and provides no information to the interactive user about why it failed, other than a standard task sequence failure message and the error code in Figure 6.17.

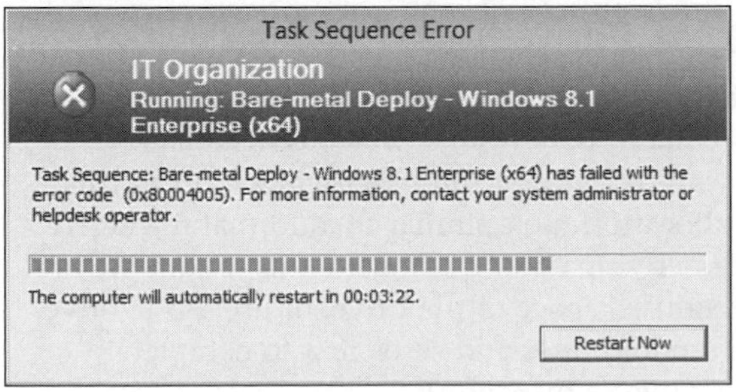

FIGURE 6.17   Check Readiness task failure.

> **NOTE: MEANING OF 0X80004005 ERROR CODE**
>
> 0x80004005 is a Windows error code that literally means unspecified error; it does not mean access denied.

A better or perhaps more user-friendly strategy to handle failures is using the return code of this task in a follow-on task. This follow-on task conditionally displays a message and gracefully exits the task sequence when it detects a failure. Sending an email or somehow notifying support personnel of the readiness failure also improves the user's overall experience.

Unfortunately, there is no way to determine exactly which specified criteria failed other than to check the smsts.log on the target system. A message similar to the following appears within the log:

```
Memory requirements validation failed. (Required: 512 MB, Found: 384 MB)
```

SP 1 added another new task, not ported from MDT: Pre-provision BitLocker (shown in Figure 6.18). Pre-provisioning BitLocker is a method of enabling the disk encryption capabilities of BitLocker before the operating system is installed (or in the case of OSD, before applying the operating system image). This allows the disk to be encrypted on the fly as content is written to the disk, rather than in one fell swoop after all of it has been written. Using this task increases the overall speed of the task sequence. In addition, pre-provisioning BitLocker within a task sequence encrypts only the used space of a volume and leaves free space unencrypted. This dramatically increases the speed of enforcing BitLocker on a volume, increasing the overall speed of the task sequence.

To use the Pre-provision BitLocker task within a task sequence the following must all be true:

▶ The task sequence uses a Windows PE 5.0 boot image.

▶ The task sequence deploys Windows 7 or above. Windows 7 does not directly support "used space only" encryption that is enforced when using this task, as it does not and cannot correctly reflect the fact that only the used space is encrypted. Nevertheless, only used space is truly encrypted when Windows 7 is the target operating system, even though this is not correctly reported. Be aware that the free space, which is not encrypted, may actually contain data from a previous installation, and this data is not protected in any way; although ConfigMgr wipes a drive, this drive wiping simply removes the file allocation table similar to a normal file delete and does not physically remove the underlying data. Do not use this task if you are concerned about what may be on the unused space of the drive, or use a true drive-wiping tool that overwrites data with random ones and zeros first to completely clear the data and eliminate the risk of anyone recovering it.

▶ A trusted platform module (TPM) must be supported and enabled on the target system. The only check box on this task's configuration page enables the task sequence to skip the task gracefully if a TPM does not exist or is not enabled on the target system.

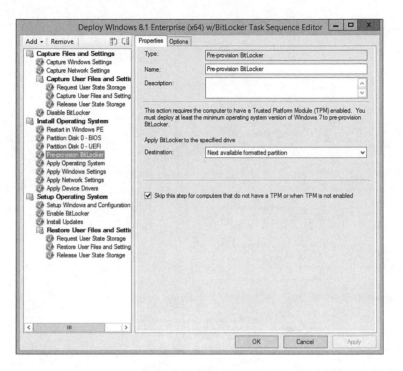

FIGURE 6.18   The Pre-provision BitLocker task.

▶ The task must be run during the initial Windows PE portion of the task sequence, before the Apply Operating System task, and after any applicable disk partitioning tasks.

▶ An Enable BitLocker task is placed after the Setup Windows and ConfigMgr task that sets the protector for the drive. This must be done because the pre-provision task uses a randomly generated clear protector, which is therefore unsecure. The Enable BitLocker task sets a secure protector for the volume.

If you use the Create a New Task Sequence Wizard (recommended by the authors), it automatically adds the appropriate tasks to pre-provision and enable BitLocker in the generated task sequence if you check the Configure task sequence for use with BitLocker check box on the Install Windows page of the wizard (see Figure 6.19).

SP 1 also includes a small addition to the Enable BitLocker task; this is the ability to use TPM and PIN for key management on the target system (see Figure 6.20).

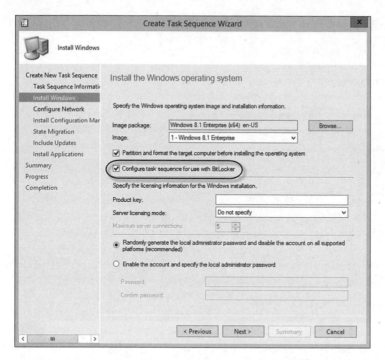

FIGURE 6.19   Configure task sequence for use with BitLocker check box.

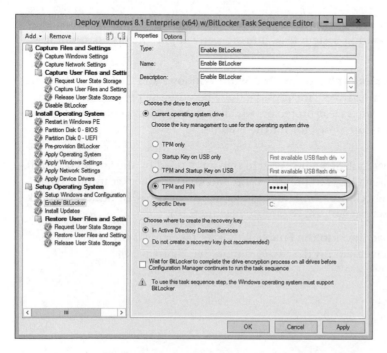

FIGURE 6.20   The new TPM and PIN choice in the Enable BitLocker task.

New Built-In Task Sequence Variables

In addition to new task types, ConfigMgr 2012 SP 1 and R2 introduce a handful of new built-in task sequence variables. As with the built-in variables that shipped with RTM, these new variables come in two flavors: read-only and writable.

▶ The new read-only variables provide some information about the task sequence itself and are used to make conditional choices during the task sequence. Read-only is indicated by an initial underscore in the name of the variable.

▶ Setting the values of the new writable variables controls various aspects of the task sequence.

The following list enumerates all the new variables, followed by a brief discussion of several notable or interesting ones. For a complete list of all available built-in variables and their purpose, see http://technet.microsoft.com/en-us/library/hh273375.aspx.

▶ _TSAppInstallStatus

▶ _SMSTSBootUEFI

▶ _SMSTSWTG

▶ SMSTSAssignmentsDownloadInterval

▶ SMSTSAssignmentsDownloadRetry

▶ SMSTSDownloadProgram

▶ SMSTSDownloadRetryCount

▶ SMSTSDownloadRetryDelay

▶ TSErrorOnWarning

▶ SMSTSLanguageFolder

▶ SMSTSMPListRequestTimeout

▶ SMSTSPersistContent

▶ SMSTSPostAction

▶ OSDPreserveDriveLetter

OSDPreserveDriveLetter, discussed in the "Windows Setup Support Change" section, enables direct use of the image from the Windows media within task sequences.

Using SMSTSPostAction, you can execute any valid command or command-line immediately following the completion of the task sequence. A simple and possibly useful example of using this variable is to shut down a system at the end of a task sequence. To do so, set the value of this variable to `shutdown.exe /s /t 0 /f`.

SMSTSAssignmentsDownloadInterval and SMSTSAssignmentsDownloadRetry effectively enable a retry mechanism within the task sequence engine any time it attempts to locate applicable policies for the current client. This can be problematic in environments with slower networks, Dynamic Host Configuration Protocol (DHCP) issues, Domain Name System (DNS) issues, or other random or unexplainable behavior that prevents the task sequence engine from initially retrieving policy successfully.

Similarly, SMSTSDownloadRetryCount and SMSTSDownloadRetryDelay add a retry mechanism for the content download process during a task sequence. Content download can fail for many reasons and is often beyond the control of ConfigMgr and the task sequence engine; however, a simple retry often succeeds. These seemingly random failures are often indicated in the logs by an error code of 0x80072ee2.

> **NOTE: MEANING OF 0X80072EE2 ERROR CODE**
>
> 0x80072ee2 is a Windows HTTP protocol error code that literally means the operation timed out.

UEFI Support

Unified Extensible Firmware Interface (UEFI) is a relatively new specification that is quickly being adopted by hardware manufacturers to replace Basic Input/Output System (BIOS) firmware interfaces. BIOS interfaces have existed since the inception of the personal computer and have begun to limit severely the flexibility and capabilities that hardware and operating system manufactures can implement. Compared to UEFI, BIOS is slow, insecure, and fragile; UEFI offers many advantages such as drastically reduced boot times, larger hard drive support, and Secure Boot. For a complete discussion of UEFI, see http://en.wikipedia.org/wiki/Unified_Extensible_Firmware_Interface and http://technet. microsoft.com/en-us/library/hh824898.aspx.

UEFI is an ever-evolving specification and has had its issues. Most UEFI-enabled systems include a BIOS compatibility mode called Compatibility Support Module (CSM). Because of the various issues encountered in enterprise environments, such as older operating systems not supporting it and PXE boot not working correctly, many shops continue to operate their systems using the CSM of the hardware, referred to as legacy BIOS-compatibility mode. Hardware manufacturers have worked their way through most of these issues though, and the current UEFI-based systems are generally problem-free.

You cannot change between UEFI and CSM mode after you load an OS onto a system, so this decision must be made before deploying the OS. This implies that your OS deployment tool is also UEFI-aware and able to prepare a system for the UEFI requirements, which include drive partition type and layout. Specifically, UEFI requires the use of GUID partition table (GPT) drive volumes and the three following volumes in this order on the primary boot disk:

▶ **Extensible Firmware Interface System Partition (ESP):** This is the main boot partition that a UEFI system boots into, and contains the hardware abstraction layer (HAL), the loader, and other boot critical files. The ESP partition should be formatted with the FAT32 file system and be at least 100MB in size and have no other files placed on it.

▶ **Microsoft Reserved Partition (MSR):** This is a special partition containing OS-specific data, previously stored in hidden sectors on MBR disks. As GPT disks do not allow hidden sectors, Microsoft needed a new partition type to store this information. Every GPT disk requires an MSR partition that must be created at initial disk partitioning time. Its size is always 128MB for disks bigger than 16GB. The MSR must have no other files placed on it.

▶ **Windows Partition:** This is effectively a data partition that contains all the files needed to run the Windows OS; this becomes the C: drive in most Windows installations. This partition must be at least 20GB on x64 systems and 16GB on x86 systems; it must also be formatted with the NTFS file system.

For more in-depth details and discussions of these partitions, see http://technet.microsoft.com/en-us/library/hh824839.aspx and http://msdn.microsoft.com/en-us/library/windows/hardware/gg463525.aspx.

As of SP 1, ConfigMgr 2012 knows about, detects, and supports UEFI systems and creating the listed partitions during a task sequence. Although UEFI is a major change for hardware and OS vendors, proper creation of the disk partitions is all that is required. If you plan to deploy Windows to a UEFI-enabled system, start out with a default, wizard-generated deployment task sequence; this adds all the necessary steps and information required, and accounts for non UEFI-enabled systems or systems in legacy BIOS-compatibility mode.

The default task sequences created using the Create Task Sequence Wizard automatically include an additional disk-partitioning task to format the drives properly when the target system is UEFI-enabled. The wizard itself does not reflect any changes, but the resulting task sequences do, as shown in Figure 6.21.

To detect a UEFI enabled system, Microsoft introduced the new built-in, read-only task sequence variable _SMSTSBootUEFI. This variable is set to true automatically by the task sequence engine if a UEFI capable system is detected. The Partition Disk 0 - BIOS and Partition Disk 0 - UEFI (shown in Figure 6.21) tasks within the default wizard-generated task sequence are conditionally executed based upon this variable (along with _SMSTSClientCache, _SMSTSMediaType, and _OSDMigrateUseHardlinks). These two tasks also create the necessary and required partitions along with a recovery partition in the case of the UEFI-specific partition task. The recovery partition is not strictly required but recommended; its purpose is to contain BitLocker-specific files and an instance of the Windows Recovery Environment (RE) to perform recovery tasks.

6

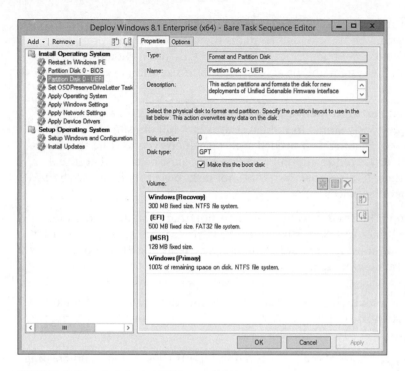

FIGURE 6.21   A default UEFI-aware task sequence.

A major limitation of deploying to a UEFI-enabled system is that the boot image used must match the architecture of the target system. This means that those organizations deploying multiple Windows OS architectures can no longer use a single boot image for all task sequence deployments, as a x86-boot image must be assigned to task sequences deploying an x86 edition of Windows and an x64-boot image to task sequences deploying an x64 edition of Windows. There are several major ramifications:

▶ You can no longer use a single task sequence that deploys multiple Windows architectures. This was a relatively uncommon practice as it complicated task sequences and now is not possible at all with UEFI.

▶ Using DHCP scope options (which were never recommended or explicitly supported by Microsoft in the first place) to enable cross-subnet (or more technically accurate, cross-broadcast boundary) PXE booting becomes problematic at best. This is because you must specify a boot filename in DHCP option 67; this is the network boot program (NBP) and is architecture-specific and UEFI-specific. This problem is not only specific to UEFI though, as the architecture-specific issue exists without using UEFI, but becomes more acute when you introduce UEFI systems due to the addition of UEFI-specific NBPs.

▶ Boot image selection is challenging in environments with mixed architectures and any ambiguity of which boot image to use. This occurs when multiple task sequences having boot images with different architectures are available or required by a device. ConfigMgr selects the boot image associated with the task sequence that has the highest deployment ID, effectively the most recently created deployment.

▶ With non-UEFI systems, x86 boot images can boot on any system and the task sequence engine automatically downloads, stages, and reboots the system into the correct boot image. However, with non-UEFI systems, x64 boot images can only boot on x64 capable systems. As very few systems in most enterprises are not x64 capable, this hasn't been an issue for some time. It is also controllable by creating a new dummy deployment on a task sequence with an x86-boot image to ensure that should any ambiguity exist, the x86-boot image is chosen.

▶ With UEFI systems, if the boot image doesn't match the architecture of the UEFI system, the boot image won't be able to start the system, and there is no fallback or manipulation possible. This means you should carefully control the deployments of your architecture-specific task sequence deployments to eliminate ambiguity. The authors recommend creating two new unknown computers collections: one for the x86 unknown computer object and one for the x64 unknown computer object, so that you can separately control the deployments targeted at each of these and thus the boot image architecture used.

TIP: BUILD AND CAPTURE DISK PARTITIONING

The default build and capture task sequence created by the New Task Sequence Wizard includes the two partitioning tasks discussed in this section: those for UEFI and for BIOS systems. As the image created is not specific to either system type, you can freely use either a BIOS or UEFI-enabled system to build your images. As using a VM generally produces the best image creation results and is easiest to work with, the BIOS task is typically used although there is no technical difference regarding the image that is created.

The default build and capture task sequence also includes additional required and optional partitions as discussed in this section. These are not explicitly needed when deploying an image so should generally not be captured, as they can bloat your WIM file and cause confusion. The authors recommend always using a BIOS-enabled VM to build your images and deleting the System Reserved partition included in the default Partition Disk 0 - BIOS task, leaving the single Windows partition.

Caveats, exceptions, irregularities, and differences always apply when any technology as significant as UEFI is introduced. Windows and ConfigMgr can gracefully deal with most (if not all) of these, but be prepared to research to learn the difference introduced with this technology and how to handle one-off or nonstandard scenarios.

One such scenario is the use of prestage media without an OEM vendor involved. Generally, prestaged media is shipped off to the vendor for mass imaging, but it can be useful for internal deployments as well. The challenge is delivering the WIM created by the prestaged process to UEFI systems, as these systems have the special boot requirements previously described in this section. The solution to this scenario is described at http://blogs.msdn.com/b/steverac/archive/2013/09/13/osd-pre-stage-and-uefi-systems.aspx.

Virtual Hard Disks and Windows To Go

Two new scenarios added to OSD in ConfigMgr 2012 R2 and SP 1 respectively are the ability to support Windows deployment to virtual hard disks (VHDs), and creation of Windows To Go (WTG) media. Both are slight variations on where the operating system is deployed and how it is used. The process is essentially the same, with several twists to account for the different requirements and unique destinations involved.

Deploying to and Maintaining VHDs

This feature enables ConfigMgr to deploy Windows to a new VHD and update an existing instance of Windows within a VHD it has previously created. In addition, it directly uploads a VHD to an instance of Virtual Machine Manager (VMM) for use within your enterprise. To take advantage of this new feature set, you must install the ConfigMgr administrative console on a 64-bit Windows 8 or 8.1 system, or on Windows Server 2008 R2, 2012, or 2012 R2 where Hyper-V is fully enabled and operational. To upload the VHDs to VMM, you must also install the VMM console on a system where the ConfigMgr console is loaded. This does not necessarily need to be the same system where you are creating and maintaining the VHDs.

All VHD management is performed from the Virtual Hard Disks node under Software Library -> Overview -> Operating Systems. This node is visible on all systems running the console; however, if that system does not meet the necessary OS requirements, you cannot perform any of the operations discussed in the following sections.

Creating a VHD

Before creating a VHD, you need a suitable task sequence. This could be any valid deployment task sequence; although the authors recommend one without any USMT or BitLocker tasks, as these aren't typically applicable when creating a VHD (but could be used depending on the scenario and goals for creating or using a VHD).

The Create Task Sequence Wizard, launched by selecting the Task Sequences node and then choosing Create Task Sequence from the ribbon bar or right-click context menu, includes a new option in ConfigMgr 2012 R2 for directly creating these slimmed-down task sequences: Install an existing image package to a virtual disk. If you choose this option, the wizard skips the pages and hides the options for the state migration tasks, BitLocker tasks, and the Install Software Updates task. In addition, a task is added to the end of the task sequence: a Run Command Line task that shuts down the VM using the shutdown command.

After preparing a deployment task sequence for your VHD, choose the Virtual Hard Disks node and select **Create Virtual Hard Disk** from the ribbon bar or right-click context menu to launch the Create Virtual Hard Disk Wizard, which contains four pages prompting for the following information:

> ▶ **General:** Supply metadata for the VHD including the name, version, and comment on this page. In addition, specify a target location in the form of a UNC, and filename for the VHD (including the .vhd extension). The site server's computer account must have NTFS and share Write permissions to the path specified.

▶ **Task Sequence:** Choose the task sequence to use on this page.

▶ **Distribution Points:** Choose an applicable DP containing the necessary content referenced in the task sequence.

▶ **Customization:** All choices made in this page are ignored by the VHD creation process, so this page should be skipped.

This process effectively creates prestaged media in addition to creating a local, temporary VM within Hyper-V; this explains the existence of the Customization page in the Create Virtual Hard Disk Wizard even though this page has no value. From there, it mounts the prestaged media in the VM, turns it on, and lets the prestage media deploy Windows to the VM.

The resulting VHD is listed under the Virtual Hard Disks node in the console, where it can be modified or uploaded to VMM. The VM created by the process is temporary and is deleted after the process completes.

Modifying a VHD

After creating a VHD as discussed in the previous section, it can be modified by running additional task sequences against it. This is accomplished with non-operating system-deploying task sequences, and can contain any valid tasks to update the operating system instance contained within a valid VHD. Examples include task sequences that install software or otherwise modify the OS using any of the following tasks:

▶ Install Application

▶ Install Software

▶ Run Command Line

Similar to the task sequence used to create a VHD, ensure that the last task of the task sequence shuts down the VM using the shutdown command in a Run Command Line task. You can copy the task from your VHD creation task sequence.

To run a custom task sequence on an existing VHD, select the VHD under the Virtual Hard Disks node in the console and choose **Modify Virtual Hard Disk** from the ribbon bar or right-click context menu. This initiates the Modify Virtual Hard Disk Wizard, which is identical to the Create Virtual Hard Disk Wizard. Ensure that you choose the proper custom task sequence on the General page. Finishing the wizard performs the same set of tasks as the VHD creation process, except that the created VM uses the existing VHD for its hard disk.

Updating a VHD with Software Updates

This process is nearly identical to the Offline Servicing option of image files in ConfigMgr, except that it operates on an existing VHD created by ConfigMgr rather than an operating system image contained within a WIM. It enables you to refresh or update the set of software updates in an existing VHD to keep it up to date. Only updates available in the software updates feature of ConfigMgr are available for this feature. In addition, the updates must be Component Based Servicing (CBS)-based, exactly like the Offline Servicing feature.

To initiate the process, choose the desired VHD under the Virtual Hard Disks node in the console, and then choose **Schedule Updates** from the ribbon bar or right-click the context menu. This opens the Schedule Updates Wizard, which allows you to choose applicable updates known to the ConfigMgr software updates feature and schedule them for installation. Behind the scenes, just like using Offline Servicing on an image file, DISM is used to inject the selected updates.

Uploading a VHD to VMM

The final task for working with VHDs in ConfigMgr actually uses the VHDs you have created. While you can certainly use the VHDs directly from the location you specified during creation (or manually copy them elsewhere), managing the VHDs using an enterprise virtualization product makes a lot of sense and brings synergistic value.

For an existing VHD created by ConfigMgr, choose the desired VHD under the Virtual Hard Disks node in the console and choose **Upload to Virtual Machine Manager** from the ribbon bar or right-click context menu. This starts the Upload to Virtual Machine Manager Wizard, where you specify the following:

▶ VMM server name

▶ VMM library share

▶ Use encrypted transfer

VHD-Specific Logs

There are two primary console-specific log files for VHD-specific operations (aside from the smsts.log described in the "Reviewing SMSTS.Log" section). Both are located in *%ProgramFiles(x86)%*\Microsoft Configuration Manager\AdminConsole\AdminUILog on the system running the console.

▶ **CreateTSMedia.log:** This log shows the creation of the prestaged media WIM.

▶ **DeployToVHD.log:** This log file shows all VHD and Hyper-V VM specific operations.

REAL WORLD: VIRTUALIZATION TEMPLATES AND CONFIGMGR

Creating and maintaining VHDs using ConfigMgr as discussed in this section is a great enabler for those using templates within VMM. However, using templates and a core VHD is roughly equivalent to using an archaic operating system imaging tool that deploys an all or nothing static image. This is completely contradictory to the dynamic nature and advantage of using OSD. When choosing your toolset, you should strongly consider using the normal OSD task sequencing process to deploy Windows to not only your physical systems but also your virtual systems to gain the same benefits across the board. An excellent article discussing this is located at http://blogs.msdn.com/b/steverac/archive/2014/03/29/the-suite-spot-of-imaging.aspx.

Deploying WTG Media

WTG is not extremely popular, but it has many capabilities and a lot of potential to solve unique and difficult business challenges. The only real requirement for WTG itself is that you have a certified USB drive; requirements are listed at http://technet.microsoft.com/library/hh831833.aspx#wtg_hardware. You could use a noncertified drive, but as with all things not supported (or certified), results could be unpredictable. The process supported by ConfigMgr is not intended for mass creation of WTG media; it enables an end user (or administrator) to build WTG media themselves, one at a time.

Deploying WTG drives using ConfigMgr requires the following:

1. A package to enable and configure BitLocker. This package should use the *<ConfigMgrInstallationFolder>*\OSD\Tools\WTG\BitLocker folder for its source location; no programs are necessary.

2. A fully functional Windows 8 or 8.1 deployment task sequence with one additional task that is placed immediately after the Setup Windows and ConfigMgr task. This is a Run Command Line task that references the package created in step 1 and uses the following command line:

```
i386\osdbitlocker_wtg.exe /Enable /pwd:[None|AD]
```

For the /pwd option, use AD to specify Active Directory as the key recovery location and None to place the burden of maintaining the key on the user. To use this task sequence with non-WTG deployment efforts, place a condition on this new task using the Options tab. Set the condition to check if the value of the _SMSTSWTG task sequence variable equals True as shown in Figure 6.22. It is not necessary to disable or otherwise change an existing Enable BitLocker task within the task sequence; these effectively are benign when executed for WTG scenarios.

3. An available, hidden deployment of the task sequence from step 2. This deployment should target all systems where WTG media creation is desired.

4. A prestaged media WIM created using the Create Task Sequence Media Wizard that is for the same Windows 8 or 8.1 deployment task sequence modified in step 2. When creating the media, check the **Allow unattended operating system deployment** option on the Select Media Type page as shown in Figure 6.23.

   In addition, set the value of the following two task sequence variables on the Customization page of the Create Task Sequence Media Wizard:

   ▶ **SMSTSPreferredAdvertID:** Set this to the Deployment ID of the deployment created in step 3. To find the ID, see the procedures discussed in the "Deployment Control" section.

   ▶ **OSDBitLockerPIN:** WTG media requires the use of a PIN or passphrase for BitLocker. The value of the OSDBitLockerPIN variable is used for this purpose; the user is required to enter this every time a system starts using the generated WTG media.

   You could also use a prestart script to set the values of these variables.

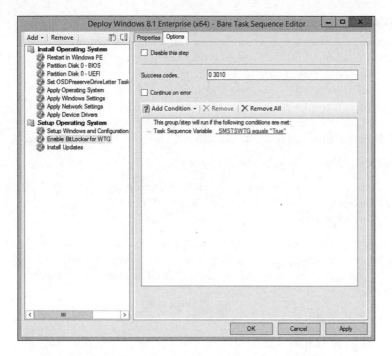

FIGURE 6.22   Task condition for the task to enable BitLocker in a WTG-enabled task sequence.

FIGURE 6.23   The Allow unattended operating system deployment option.

This WIM should be placed in its own folder within the source file repository. You should also copy the WTGCreator.exe file from *<ConfigMgrInstallationFolder>*\OSD\ Tools\WTG\Creator to this folder.

5. A WTG creator package used to initiate the WTG media build on a target system. The package should reference the folder containing the prestaged media WIM from step 4 and contain a single program with the following command-line where `PrestageName.wim` is the name of the WIM from step 4:

```
WTGCreator.exe /wim:PrestageName.wim /enableBootRedirect
```

The `enableBootRedirect` option is optional but adds the capability for a Windows 8 or 8.1 system with the WTG media present to automatically boot to the WTG media without having to change the boot order of the system.

6. An available deployment for the WTG creator package targeting applicable users or systems; the deployment should actually target the same systems, or a subset of the systems targeted by the task sequence deployment from step 3; otherwise, the task sequence is not allowed to run.

Although this list involves several steps, it is not that complicated. Essentially, the user kicks off the WTG creator package, which copies the prestaged WIM to the WTG device (assuming the user inserted it into their system). Once the system reboots to the media, the prestaged task sequence on the media automatically kicks off, deploying Windows 8 or 8.1 to the WTG media. The WTG creator displays a reboot prompt as its final action so that the user doesn't have to manually initiate this. When the reboot completes, users are free to use the WTG media or reboot back to their original operating system.

Other Improvements

Although most of the functionality changes and improvements in SP 1 and R2 support changes and improvements in Windows itself, several smaller changes directly improve upon or tweak OSD making it even better; these are covered in the next sections. None are groundbreaking or game changers; they improve overall usability and core functionality or directly address acute pain points felt at various ConfigMgr shops.

Offline Servicing

The main change to this feature is that it no longer pulls update source files from the software deployment package source locations, which could be remote from the site server (causing the process to take longer or be disrupted because of network issues) or even offline which causes the process to fail completely. Instead, the update source files are pulled directly from the content library on the site server. In addition, the process of image servicing continues even if failures occur, ensuring that the process is not completely derailed for a single missing or troubled update.

> **TIP: OFFLINE SERVICING STAGING**
>
> During the offline servicing process, the target image file is temporarily copied (staged) to a working folder, named ConfigMgr_OfflineImageServicing by default, and located at the drive root on the site server where the ConfigMgr binaries are installed. If this volume was not planned properly, there may not be enough free space for this staging operation, causing a failure. You may have other reasons to move this folder to an alternate volume; to move the folder, follow the documentation at http://blogs.technet.com/b/configmgrteam/archive/2013/07/15/customizing-offline-servicing-of-operating-system-images.aspx. Alternatively, use the PowerShell code in Listing 6.2 (also available as online content, see Appendix C for information) to update the location in WMI.
>
> Antimalware products are a common cause of offline servicing failures. You should ensure that the product you are using explicitly excludes the ConfigMgr_OfflineImageServicing folder on the volume configured—whether it is the default volume or one configured using this procedure.

LISTING 6.2   Create the ConfigMgr OfflineImageServicing Folder in WMI

```
$siteCode = "one"
$newDrive = "E:"
$offlineSvcMgr = Get-WMIObject -namespace "root\sms\site_$siteCode" -class
  "SMS_SCI_Component" -filter "SiteCode='$siteCode' And ItemName like
  'SMS_OFFLINE_SERVICING_MANAGER%'"
$offlineSvcMgrProps = $offlineSvcMgr.Props
$offlineSvcMgrProps | ForEach-Object {if ($_.PropertyName -eq "StagingDrive")
  {$_.Value1 = $newDrive}}
$offlineSvcMgr.Props = $offlineSvcMgrProps
$offlineSvcMgr.Put()
```

To view or verify the current drive letter set, use the code in Listing 6.3. (Note that by default, no value is set and this equates to using the drive the ConfigMgr binaries are installed on.) This script is available as online content, see Appendix C for details.

LISTING 6.3   View the Current Drive Letter Set

```
((Get-WMIObject -namespace "root\sms\site_$siteCode" -class
"SMS_SCI_Component" -filter "SiteCode='$siteCode' And ItemName like
 'SMS_OFFLINE_SERVICING_MANAGER%'").props
| where-object{$_.PropertyName -eq "StagingDrive"}).value1
```

Driver Package Export and Import

The Driver Package Export and Import feature was available in ConfigMgr 2012 RTM for most other content types, including software packages, applications, and content referenced within a task sequence. Specifically, it enabled exporting the content to a folder and the metadata about the content into a ZIP file that you could import into an alternate hierarchy. Doing this is useful for organizations with a test or development hierarchy that have a content promotion process, for backup or archival purposes, or for content sharing between cooperative organizations. However, you could not do this for individual driver packages until ConfigMgr 2012 R2.

Exporting a package (or application or task sequence) creates a folder with the specified content and a ZIP file containing the necessary information for later creating, updating, or re-creating the exported objects and importing the content into a ConfigMgr site. This functionality is not meant for staging content into other sites or distribution points within the same ConfigMgr hierarchy; for that, you should use the content prestaging capabilities of ConfigMgr as discussed in the "Content Prestaging" section. Follow these steps to export a driver package:

1. Navigate to **Software Library -> Overview -> Operating Systems -> Driver Packages** in the console and select the package in the Details pane.

2. Click **Export** from the right-click content menu or choose it from the ribbon bar.

3. The Export Driver Package Wizard is launched, where the main option is to select the destination path. Remember this process creates a ZIP file and a folder.

To import a driver package, complete the following steps:

1. Select the actual Driver Packages node in the tree.

2. Click **Import Driver Package** from the right-click context menu or ribbon bar.

3. The Import Driver Package Wizard is launched, where you must specify the location of the ZIP file created in the previous procedure when you exported the content. This location must be a UNC and cannot be a local path, and must contain both the ZIP file and folder exported by the export process.

   If there are duplicates, the wizard presents options to ignore, overwrite, or append categories as appropriate for each of the object types contained within the specified location. This location is also set as the source location for the drivers imported in as well as the driver packages, so you should move the ZIP file and content folder to their final destination or your desired source files location before initiating the import.

Do not modify these files after the import is successful; they are directly referenced and used when a package update is initiated or a boot image is created that uses one of these drivers.

Unknown Computer Cleanup

If you have enabled unknown computer support, ConfigMgr creates a new Unknown resource each time an unknown computer boots using PXE or boot media. This Unknown resource is essentially a placeholder for that unknown computer. It is eventually converted into a normal system resource once the task sequence progresses far enough for the ConfigMgr client agent to be installed (during the Setup Windows and ConfigMgr task), at which point it becomes fully functional. If anything prevents the task sequence from getting to or successfully finishing this task, the unknown resource is abandoned and left to clutter up the Devices node and the All Systems collection, plus any other collections that might include it based on membership rules. The only way to remove these abandoned resources prior to ConfigMgr 2012 SP 1 was deleting them manually.

SP 1 added the Delete Aged Unknown Computers maintenance task to automatically cleanup these leftover resources (shown in Figure 6.24). This task, enabled by default, deletes all unknown resources that have had no activity updates within the period specified (30 days by default).

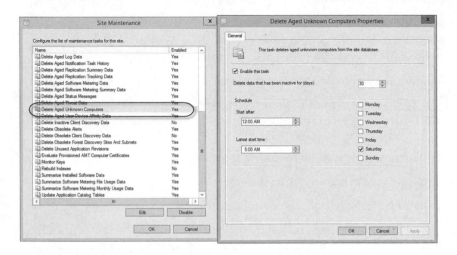

FIGURE 6.24   Delete Aged Unknown Computers task.

Prestaged Media

The two actual changes in prestaged media are subtle but greatly improve the overall process and experience. Both directly relate to the content referenced in and used by the task sequence when using prestaged media, and are discussed in the next sections.

Content Staging

The first change enables you to choose content directly to include in the resulting WIM. This allows the content to be prestaged onto the target systems by the OEM, in addition to the operating system image. The Create Task Sequence Media Wizard (shown in Figure 6.25) adds three pages where you can select this additional content for inclusion (each page is named for the content type added by it):

▶ Select Application

▶ Select Package

▶ Select Driver Package

By default, any content directly referenced within the task sequence is added automatically, although you can remove it to minimize the size of the WIM given to and used by the OEM when they prepare the systems. Content not included in the WIM is retrieved from your DPs during task sequence execution just as it would be during any other task sequence.

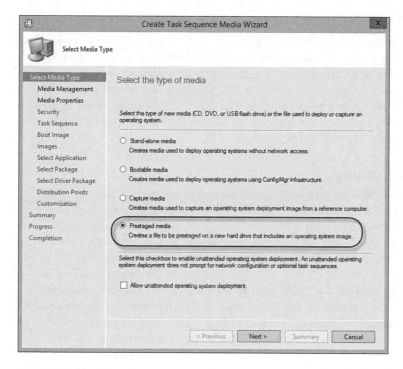

FIGURE 6.25   The Create Task Sequent Media Wizard.

Staged Content Use

The second change enables the task sequence engine to use this prestaged content directly instead of having to download it from a DP. In addition, the task sequence checks to see if a newer version of the content is available on a DP and uses that newer version instead of the locally prestaged version.

Content Prestaging

Content Prestaging (not to be confused with content prestaging in prestaged media, discussed in the previous section) was a new feature set in ConfigMgr 2012 RTM. This enables you to export content from one distribution point for direct import into another distribution point within the same hierarchy, without ConfigMgr using its own content distribution process to transfer the content over the network. How the content is transferred to the second distribution point is up to you. However, until R2, you could not export all the content within a single task sequence for use with this feature set. You now can quickly create a single prestaged content file for all the directly referenced content within a single task sequence. Right-click any task sequence, select **Create Prestaged Content File**, and follow the wizard. As with creating prestaged content files elsewhere in the console, content is pulled directly from a specified distribution point, thus you should use a DP in close network proximity to where you are running the console. Application dependencies are also resolved and included in the exported file. You can multiselect multiple task sequences for inclusion within a single exported file if desired.

A novel use of this new feature is to create a single content prestaging file quickly for content en masse. Although you can multiselect a single content type in the console such as Applications or Packages, you cannot directly select both Applications and Packages. However, you could create a dummy task sequence that includes tasks (such as Install Application, Install Package, Apply Driver Package) that reference these disparate content types. Then, you can create a prestage content file for this dummy task sequence that includes all of these different types of content.

Task Sequence Size Ceiling

The maximum size of an executing task sequence environment is increased from 10MB to 32MB in ConfigMgr 2012 R2. The task sequence environment is often equated to the size of the task sequence itself, although this is not accurate. The size of a task sequence directly affects the environment size, but it is only one factor. A more accurate description of the task sequence environment is the total memory footprint used by the task sequence during its execution. This includes the contents of all task sequence variables as well as any applicable ConfigMgr policies. Policies applying software updates are notorious for bloating the task sequence environment size, as are systems with extremely large numbers of complex applications or task sequences targeted at them. Note that the task sequence itself is actually stored in a task sequence variable, which is why it contributes to the memory footprint.

If you start running into 0x8007000E errors within your task sequence, you should examine not only the number of tasks within the task sequence, but also the complexity of those tasks, the complexity of the referenced applications, and the total number of deployments and software updates targeted at the system where the issue occurred. The 32MB limit is a hard-limit that cannot be adjusted.

> **NOTE: MEANING OF 0X8007000E ERROR CODE**
>
> 0x8007000E is a standard Windows error code that literally means not enough storage is available to complete this operation.

Troubleshooting Hints and Tips

The following hints and tips were solicited from the elite ConfigMgr OSD Masters (ECM MVPs). They are mostly specific to troubleshooting task sequences; only one of these is actually specific to R2. While none is particularly life changing, each can make your life a little easier when it comes to troubleshooting OSD and deploying Windows.

Reviewing SMSTS.log

This is the master and authoritative log file for task sequence execution; it exists on the system where the task sequence is running or has previously run. Nearly all troubleshooting efforts should start with an in-depth review of this log file. The log is moved around several times during the execution of a task sequence but is most commonly found in X:\Windows\Temp\SMSTSLog while in the Windows PE portion of the task sequence before the Setup Windows and Configuration task or %windir%\ccm\logs\SMSTSLog while in the Windows portion of the task sequence after the Setup Windows and Configuration task. If a task sequence finishes successfully, the log file is located in %windir%\ccm\logs.

Like with other log files within ConfigMgr, using the CMTrace tool makes life easier when combing through or watching a log file. A log file is ultimately just a text file, so if CMTrace is not available, any text editor or viewer, like Notepad, can work. CMTrace is a single, stand-alone executable and thus very portable. The additional functionality it provides includes automatic refresh as content is added to a log file, while filtering, merging, and error code lookup make it the preferred choice for viewing and reviewing all log files—even non-ConfigMgr log files. CMTrace.exe is located in the \Tools folder of the ConfigMgr installation folder on a site server and can be copied to any other system. CMTrace is automatically added to boot images in ConfigMgr 2012 and people often add it to their Windows images, making it is available anytime the need to read a log file arises. CMTrace is also available as part of the ConfigMgr toolkit, available from Microsoft for download at http://www.microsoft.com/en-us/download/details.aspx?id=36213.

Using SMSPXE.log

PXE booting a system is somewhat of a black box, particularly on the client side. This is because there is really no accessible or exposed diagnostics built into the network cards controlling the client side of the process. The server side, while also seemingly a black box, is actually logged quite well within SMSPXE.log. It explicitly details all PXE traffic sent to and seen by the PXE services on a PXE-enabled DP. It also logs what instructions are sent back to the client that is trying to PXE-boot. Included in the detail is the MAC address and SMBIOS GUID of the client system. In addition, the information used to query the ConfigMgr site for applicable task sequences and boot images is logged, along with the known state of the system requesting a PXE boot.

The following snippet (with line numbers added for reference) shows a known computer system with no applicable task sequences. Lines 1 and 2 clearly show that it is a known device, lines 3 through 6 show that there are no applicable task sequence deployments, and lines 7 and 8 show that the client essentially is ignored because there are no applicable task sequence deployments.

1. Client lookup reply: <ClientIDReply><Identification Unknown="0"
   ItemKey="16777222" ServerName=""><Machine><ClientID/><NetbiosName/>
   </Machine></Identification></ClientIDReply>

2. 00:15:5D:14:64:1E, 5ABDA92C-9237-4FDD-92B0-83E1F11D2122: device is in the
   database.

3. Client boot action reply: `<ClientIDReply><Identification Unknown="0"`
   `ItemKey="16777222" ServerName=""><Machine><ClientID/><NetbiosName/>`
   `</Machine></Identification><PXEBootAction LastPXEAdvertisementID="`
   `" LastPXEAdvertisementTime="" OfferID="" OfferIDTime="" PkgID=""`
   `PackageVersion="" PackagePath="" BootImageID="" Mandatory=""/>`
   `</ClientIDReply>`

4. `00:15:5D:14:64:1E, 5ABDA92C-9237-4FDD-92B0-83E1F11D2122:` no advertisements
   found

5. `00:15:5D:14:64:1E, 5ABDA92C-9237-4FDD-92B0-83E1F11D2122:` No boot action.
   Aborted.

6. `00:15:5D:14:64:1E, 5ABDA92C-9237-4FDD-92B0-83E1F11D2122:` Not serviced.

7. Client boot action reply: `<ClientIDReply><Identification Unknown="0"`
   `ItemKey="16777222" ServerName=""><Machine><ClientID/><NetbiosName/>`
   `</Machine></Identification><PXEBootAction LastPXEAdvertisementID="`
   `" LastPXEAdvertisementTime="" OfferID="" OfferIDTime="" PkgID="`
   `" PackageVersion="" PackagePath="" BootImageID="" Mandatory=""/>`
   `</ClientIDReply>`

8. `00:15:5D:14:64:1E, 5ABDA92C-9237-4FDD-92B0-83E1F11D2122:` no advertisements
   found

There are many other permutations of what might be logged in this log file; similar to this example, they typically are straightforward to decipher. Keep in mind that the only thing sent to the PXE services by the client is the client's MAC address and SMBIOS GUID. This means that the site must make all resulting decisions based on this information alone. Thus, if you are PXE-booting a system shown as `device is in the database` in this log file, it is always because there is an existing resource with either the same MAC address and/or SMBIOS GUID. How this other resource within ConfigMgr has the same MAC address or SMBIOS GUID is not something ConfigMgr can actually tell you; you must find the resource using a query, and determine what to do with it.

If your PXE-enabled DP is on a site server, the SMSPXE.log file is in the \logs folder of your ConfigMgr installation folder. However, if the PXE-enabled DP is hosted on a remote site system, the location of this log file changes in ConfigMgr 2012 R2 to the SMS_DP$\ SMS\Logs folder on the drive where the sccmcontentlib exists. If you upgraded from SP 1, the old log actually still exists but is no longer used. This can be confusing, as it seems to indicate something may be wrong.

SMSTSErrorDialogTimeout

This task sequence variable is set like any other. The value of this variable controls how long, in seconds, a task sequence displays a final, fatal error message before automatically rebooting a system. Depending upon where within the task sequence the fatal error occurs, the system may actually reboot into your deployed Windows image and it may look like everything was successful. If you (or someone else) were not explicitly paying attention to the system, you may not realize that the task sequence did not complete successfully. To prevent this from occurring, set the value of this variable to something higher than the default of 900 seconds (15 minutes).

Power Scheme

For longer running task sequences, the default Windows power scheme often causes the monitor to enter power saving mode. This is not a problem unless someone decides to take action on the system thinking that it is not powered-on because the monitor is blank. This includes turning the power off or closing the lid on a laptop to take it home. Both would disrupt the task sequence, causing it to fail.

To prevent this, add a Run Command Line task to the task sequence immediately follow-ing the Setup Windows and ConfigMgr task with the following (or similar, depending upon your needs) command line:

```
powercfg.exe -change monitor-timeout-ac 0
```

To restore the default power scheme, add another Run Command Line task at or near the end of the task sequence with the following command line:

```
powercfg.exe -restoredefaultschemes
```

For these tasks, do not specify any other options; none are necessary.

Pausing a Task Sequence

On philosophical grounds, a task sequence should only be paused when troubleshoot-ing. Pausing a task sequence to actually affect a deployed system or captured image is like pausing a fully automated widget factory to perform a manual step, and should be avoided at all costs as it limits (and even negates) the value of automating the entire process in the first place. However, pausing a task sequence for troubleshooting purposes is useful, as it allows you to manually simulate actions, test outcomes, and review or even update configuration in short order without having to change the task sequence or rerun it from the beginning. You could even pause the VM you are deploying to after the task sequence is paused, enabling you to quickly revert if one of your tests goes awry.

Pausing a task sequence involves adding a never-ending script into the set of tasks executed at the place where you wish the task sequence to pause. The VBScript in Listing 6.4 accomplishes this and also allows you to easily resume the task sequence from where it left off after you are finished with your manual operations.

LISTING 6.4   Pause a Task Sequence

```
Set fso = CreateObject("Scripting.FileSystemObject")
Set shell = CreateObject("WScript.Shell")
filespec = shell.ExpandEnvrionmentStrings("%systemdrive%") & "\go.txt"
'Check every 1 second to see if the file exists
While Not fso.FileExists(filespec)
        Wscript.Sleep 1000
Wend
'When it does exist, delete it and go on
fso.DeleteFile(filespec)
```

To use this script, complete the following steps:

1. Copy the code into a file named pause.vbs (or something similar). The file should be within its own folder within your source file repository. A parent folder for scripts within your source file repository for organizational purposes is also recommended.

2. Create a package under **Software Library -> Overview -> Application Management -> Packages** that uses the folder created in step 1 for its source location. No programs are needed.

3. Add a Run Command Line task to the task sequence at the point where you want the pause to occur. This can be anywhere within the task sequence. Set the package for this task to be the one you just created and the command line to be cscript.exe pause.vbs.

4. Execute your task sequence. When it gets to the pause task, it sits idly and does nothing. In fact, it is actually waiting for a file named go.txt to be created at the root of the drive containing the Windows installation; if the system is in Windows PE, this is the X: drive.

5. Press **F8** to get to a command prompt and complete the actions you deem necessary. This assumes that command support is enabled in the boot image being used; enable this by checking the **Enable command support (testing only)** check box on the Customization tab of a boot image, as shown in Figure 6.26.

6. Create a file named **go.txt** at the root of the Windows drive. An easy way to accomplish this from the command prompt is to enter the following:

   echo . > %systemdrive%\go.txt .

   Within 1 second, the script sees the file, deletes it, and exits, enabling the task sequence to continue. Having the script delete the file automatically at the end enables the use of multiple pause tasks within your task sequence as necessary.

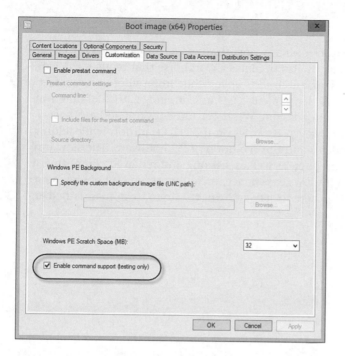

FIGURE 6.26   Enable command support option on a boot image.

Windows 8.1 Wireless Network Prompt

During a normal installation of Windows 8.1, the interactive user is prompted to connect to a wireless network if a wireless capable network adapter is detected in the system. By default, even during a deployment of Windows 8.1 that is configured to be completely unattended (like those used during OSD), this prompt is still shown. This brings the entire deployment to an unexpected stop. The fix is relatively straightforward and easy: Create or edit an unattend.xml file using the Windows System Image Manager tool installed as part of the ADK for Windows 8.1. You could edit the unattend.xml manually, but this is typically a nontrivial task that is easy to get wrong and thus further foul up your deployment. Add or update the following settings in the Pass 7 oobeSystem section as follows:

▶ **HideLocalAccountScreen:** true

▶ **HideOnlineAccountScreens:** true

▶ **HideWirelessSetupInOOBE:** true

If creating a new unattend.xml file, place it in a source folder within your source file repository and create a package that uses this folder for its source location (Software Library -> Overview -> Application Management -> Packages). Reference this new unattend.xml in the Apply Operating System Image task within the task sequence.

Summary

OSD continues to be a primary reason for many organizations to implement ConfigMgr. Once set up and configured correctly, it also becomes a workhorse that reduces the workload of IT administrators, engineers, and architects alike, while improving user satisfaction and the overall effectiveness of the IT department. OSD in ConfigMgr 2012 R2 does not dramatically change the paradigm for deploying Windows and does not add any spectacular new "must have" features; however, it carries on the OSD tradition while adding support for improvements in Windows and the evolution of PC hardware. The slow integration of MDT formally into the product, as well as a strong and renewed commitment by Microsoft to make the overall Windows experience, including setup and deployment, as painless as possible, means OSD is here to stay and will continue to be maintained and improved.

PART III

Journey to the Cloud

IN THIS PART

CHAPTER 7   Using the Intune Connector   199

CHAPTER 8   Mobile Device Management in
             Configuration Manager 2012 R2   243

Using the Intune Connector

IN THIS CHAPTER

▶ Getting Started with the Intune Connector

▶ Synchronizing AD with Microsoft Azure AD

▶ MDM Prerequisites

▶ Installing the Windows Intune Subscription and Connector

▶ Receiving Feature Updates Using the Extensions for Windows Intune

Integrating Windows Intune and System Center Configuration Manager (ConfigMgr) 2012 R2 requires that organizations determine those mobile platforms they plan to support and acquire the necessary technical components for configuring that interoperability. Companies must also establish a connection between their on-premise Active Directory (AD) environment and the Microsoft Online Services cloud environment, if this has not yet occurred. This chapter explains the configuration, prerequisites, and steps to install and verify proper installation of the Windows Intune connector role within the ConfigMgr architecture. For background on Windows Intune, including licensing and other uses of Intune, see Appendix A, "About Windows Intune."

Getting Started with the Intune Connector

The process of integrating Windows Intune with Configuration Manager consists of three components:

▶ Synchronizing the on-premise AD with Microsoft Azure Active Directory

▶ Completing required mobile device management (MDM) prerequisites

▶ Completing the Intune subscription and connector installation

Organizations choose the mobile device platforms to manage, but synchronizing the on-premise AD to the Microsoft cloud (Azure AD) is always required. When that synchronization occurs, Information Technology (IT) administrators can complete any requirements necessary to manage the mobile platforms before defining the Intune subscription and installing the Intune connector.

NOTE: NAMING CHANGE TO AZURE

On April 3, 2014, Microsoft changed the name of Windows Azure to Microsoft Azure to showcase the broader support of operating systems, programming languages, and platform interoperability available across Microsoft's public cloud offering.

Synchronizing AD with Microsoft Azure AD

Before integration of Windows Intune and ConfigMgr can be completed, an organization must purchase a subscription to Windows Intune and establish a connection between its on-premise AD and the Microsoft cloud. A "connection" in this context means that the organization must synchronize their on-premise AD to a Microsoft Azure AD namespace, also called an Azure AD tenant, using the Microsoft Azure Active directory synchronization tool (DirSync). DirSync copies user accounts, security groups, and those objects' attributes from the on-premise AD to Azure AD. This allows both cloud and on-premise services to work with common user objects, regardless of whether they use the cloud or on-premise AD. After the directories are synchronized the directories, you must also configure an authentication mechanism to avoid a situation where users entering their company user ID have a different password in cloud applications versus their on-premise applications. Following are common approaches to configure user passwords:

▶ Active Directory Federation Services (ADFS)

▶ Password synchronization using the DirSync tool

▶ Manually per user or via Windows PowerShell

ADFS is recommended for providing a true single sign-on solution. The example in the following section creates a Windows Intune trial account and installs DirSync to illustrate the overall synchronization process. Passwords are synchronized using the new Password Sync feature in the DirSync tool.

IMPORTANT DIRSYNC AND AUTHENTICATION NOTE

This chapter does not provide in-depth configuration and deployment considerations organizations require for directory synchronization and user authentication. Refer to the Windows Azure AD directory integration page on TechNet at http://technet.microsoft.com/en-us/library/jj573653.aspx for further information.

Creating a Windows Intune Instance and Azure AD Namespace

This section illustrates the DirSync process by explaining how to provision a trial account of the Windows Intune service and then use the DirSync tool to synchronize the directories. You can acquire Windows Intune in a number of ways. This example assumes an organization does not have other Microsoft Online Services, so it needs to configure Windows Intune and the Microsoft Azure AD namespace (tenant name). This is a common approach for organizations to acquire Windows Intune for their production environment. To configure DirSync, follow these steps:

1. Windows Intune offers a free 30-day trial account that can be used to test mobile device management with ConfigMgr integration, and then converted to a paid (for-fee) service. As shown in Figure 7.1, a trial account is created by completing the 30-day trial request form found at http://www.windowsintune.com.

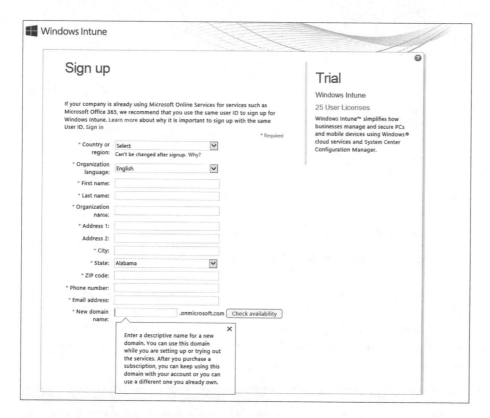

FIGURE 7.1   Windows Intune 30-day trial request form.

2. The value entered in the New domain name field (shown in Figure 7.2) is the Microsoft Azure AD namespace to be used for the Windows Intune service, as well as for other Microsoft Online Services added at a later date. Pay attention when creating this name, as it cannot be changed later. Once the name is entered and verified that it is not being used by another organization, the IT administrator can reserve the requested *.onmicrosoft.com name and create the initial global administrator account used to log in to the Windows Intune account portal (the Microsoft Azure AD portal used for Windows Intune).

FIGURE 7.2   Creating a new domain name and global administrator account.

3. After completing the request form, the initial global administrator account is created for the Azure AD namespace, and the IT administrator is redirected to the Windows Intune Account Portal (WIAP) where he can configure directory synchronization or perform other administrative tasks such as creating additional Azure AD administration accounts.

NOTE: USER ACCOUNT AND SERVICE MANAGEMENT PORTAL PAGES

The Windows Intune account portal located at https://account.manage.microsoft.com is for use with the Windows Intune service. Other Microsoft online services, such as Office 365, have their own user account management portal pages. While the portals currently use unique URLs for access, if the services use the same Azure AD namespace (*.onmicrosoft.com name), any user account management, including configuring DirSync, is seen in all portal sites. Microsoft is rumored to be planning to unify the portals into a single master Online Services dashboard; however, this solution is not yet deployed.

---

4. As shown in Figure 7.3, after logging in to the WIAP, IT administrators can access the Users section in the WIAP and choose the Set Up or Learn More option next to Active Directory synchronization.

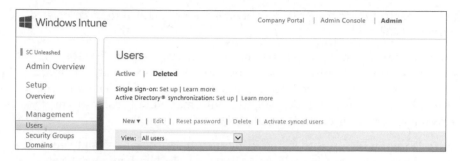

FIGURE 7.3   Configuring directory synchronization in the WIAP.

5. Once the Set up and manage single sign-on page appears (see Figure 7.4), there are multiple steps for enabling DirSync and adding a user account authentication mechanism, including the following:

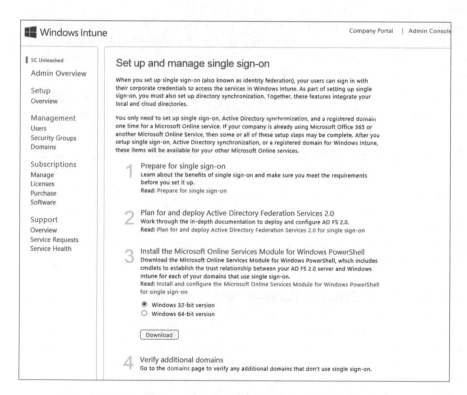

FIGURE 7.4   Setup and manage Active Directory synchronization.

▶ **Installing and configuring Active Directory Federation Services (ADFS):** Although not required to complete the Windows Intune connector installation, organizations are most likely to choose ADFS for their production environments. Configuring ADFS is generally recommended to be completed before DirSync.

▶ **Prepare for Directory Synchronization:** Use the **Prepare for directory synchronization** link (http://technet.microsoft.com/en-us/library/jj151831.aspx) to learn more about architecture and deployment considerations. The authors highly recommend reviewing this information to become aware of items relevant to your organization.

▶ **Verify Domain:** For users to log on using their organization's @company.com address (also known as the user principal name or UPN), there must be an Internet-facing domain name for that @company.com and the domain must be associated with this Azure AD namespace and verified by Microsoft. The domain name can only be associated with a single Azure AD namespace. Click the **domains** link to associate an Internet domain name with this Azure AD tenant.

▶ **Activate Azure AD for directory synchronization:** For Azure AD to allow authoritative changes from the on-premise AD, an organization must activate directory synchronization for its Azure AD tenant, accomplished by clicking the Activate button. Failure to do so causes an error when trying to use DirSync to synchronize directories.

▶ **Install and configure the Directory Synchronization tool:** Use the **Install the Directory Synchronization tool** link to view the latest information and download the DirSync tool.

▶ **Verify directory synchronization:** Inspect the WIAP to verify user accounts from the on-premise AD are displaying within the portal.

▶ **Activate synchronized users:** This step is not necessary to integrate Windows Intune and Configuration Manager. This step normally is used to associate the user account with the service and provide access for that user. ConfigMgr manages access to enroll and manage devices for users automatically through the Windows Intune subscription configuration.

Installing the Directory Synchronization Tool

Once the Azure AD environment is activated for DirSync, the tool can be installed and configured to synchronize directories. You can confirm that the Microsoft Azure AD namespace is activated for directory synchronization by returning to the Directory Synchronization setup page in the WIAP. The previous Activate button should now be replaced with the message **Active Directory Synchronization is activated** (see Figure 7.5). If this step is not completed, running the DirSync Configuration Wizard displays an error stating The Microsoft Azure Active Directory has not been activated for Synchronization and cannot continue. This section reviews several key items required to install the DirSync tool and configure synchronizing the directories.

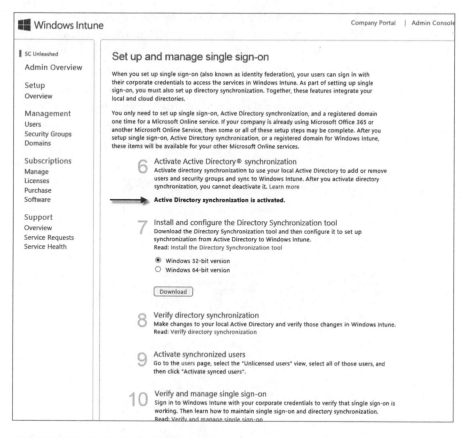

FIGURE 7.5   Verify in the WIAP that Azure AD has been activated for DirSync.

Assuming you previously followed the hardware and software requirements for the DirSync tool and verified your on-premise AD is ready for synchronization, installing the tool can be straightforward. The initial DirSync package is executed to install the Microsoft Azure Active Director Sync tool binaries, services, security groups, and supporting applications. The installation file is named Dirsync.exe; however, it leverages Microsoft Forefront Identity Management 2012 R2 components to perform the synchronizing functions. When installing this tool, it also grants the installer rights within the FIMAdminSync local security group so that the user account can create the synchronization configuration profile. The Microsoft Azure Active Directory Sync configuration wizard requires the installer to have knowledge of two key administrative-level accounts:

▶ Enterprise Administrator account from the on-prem Active Directory

▶ Global Administrator account from Microsoft Azure AD

As shown in Figure 7.6, the Windows Azure Active Directory Sync tool Configuration Wizard requires several tabs (pages) be configured:

▶ You must have credentials for an Enterprise Administrator account that the Windows Azure Active Directory Sync wizard uses to connect to the on-premise forest and create a service account that is used to read and synchronize the local Active Directory information.

▶ You must have access to a global administrator account to connect to the Microsoft Azure AD tenant to populate the imported user and security group objects.

▶ You must determine whether you plan to enable the password synchronization feature.

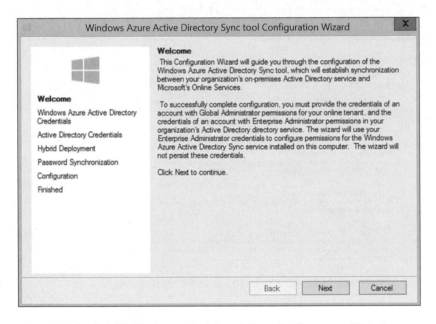

FIGURE 7.6   The Welcome page of the DirSync Configuration Wizard.

Figure 7.7 and Figure 7.8 show the account pages. Each administrator account must be entered correctly, as the DirSync tool verifies the user name and credentials before continuing to the next step.

Password synchronization (see Figure 7.9) is a relatively new feature of the Windows Azure AD Sync tool that synchronizes user passwords from your on-premise Active Directory to Windows Azure Active Directory. This feature enables your users to enroll their devices into management or log on via the company portal application using the same password used to log in to their on-premises domain. Password Sync is not implementing a single sign-on (SSO) solution because there is no token exchange and trust relationship as there is with ADFS. However, it mimics the experience and is relatively easily to configure, and may be an appropriate solution for small to midsize organizations.

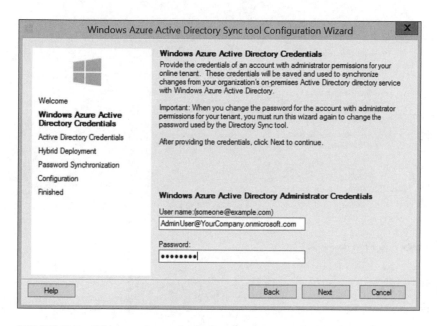

FIGURE 7.7 Windows Azure Active Directory Credentials page.

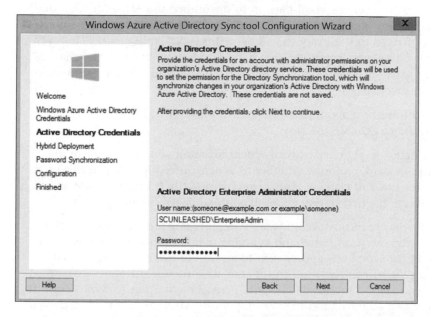

FIGURE 7.8 Active Directory Enterprise Admin credentials.

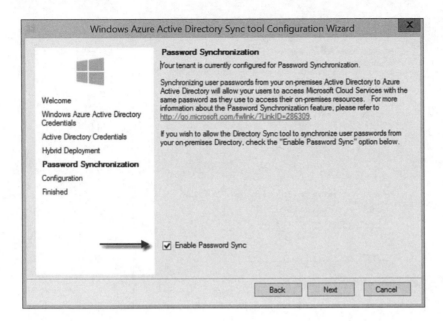

FIGURE 7.9   Enabling password synchronization.

Password Sync extracts the user password hash from the on-premise AD, adds some additional security information, and synchronizes this data with the other user account attributes. DirSync is configured to run every three hours; this is not configurable. However, passwords are synchronized on a more frequent basis. In addition, when a user changes his Active Directory password, the password synchronization feature detects and synchronizes the changed password to the cloud.

You can find more information about password synchronization at http://technet. microsoft.com/en-us/library/dn246918.aspx.

Once you choose whether to enable password synchronization you can complete the DirSync configuration wizard, choosing whether to **Synchronize your directories now** by checking the check box and clicking **Finish** (see Figure 7.10). If the check box is not selected, DirSync runs at the first refresh cycle, in approximately 3 hours.

The most convenient way to ensure accounts are synchronizing properly is by logging into the Windows Intune account portal and verifying new accounts are displaying, as shown in Figure 7.11. DirSync users appear next to an icon of two arrows in circular fashion. By selecting a user, you can confirm the user account and attributes are correct. Note the UPN is used to enroll mobile devices into management. After DirSync is running, you must verify that user accounts and their corresponding UPNs are accurate to prevent users from receiving errors during mobile device enrollment due to an invalid user configuration.

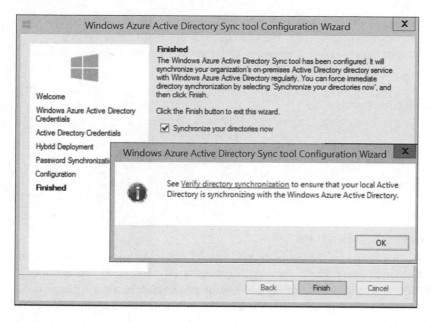

FIGURE 7.10   Finishing directory synchronization.

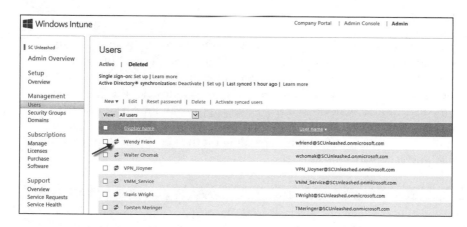

FIGURE 7.11   Successful directory synchronization.

MDM Prerequisites

Managing modern mobile platforms such as iOS, Windows Phone 8.x, and Windows 8.1 within ConfigMgr requires completing various prerequisites to integrate with Windows Intune for mobile device management. This section explains those items required before you can create the Windows Intune subscription and install the Windows Intune Connector site system role.

Shown in Table 7.1, three of the four modern mobile platforms available for mobile management have prerequisites. Some of these prerequisites are required to enable management of the mobile platform and some are only recommended, meaning they could be done later or in an alternate way.

TABLE 7.1   Mobile Platform Prerequisites

Prerequisites	Windows 8.1	Windows Phone 8.x	iOS	Android
Has prerequisite	Yes	Yes	Yes	No
Required or recommended	Recommended	Required	Required	N/A

Managing Windows 8.1 Devices

Managing a Windows 8.1 device as a mobile device, also known as using the OMA-Device Management (OMA-DM) channel, has no prerequisites to configure or complete before configuring the Windows Intune subscription and Intune connector. However, there are two recommended items to organize ahead of time to ensure the most efficient management experience possible:

▶ Sideloading key

▶ Code-signing certificate

The term *sideloading* is used when an organization wants to deploy a line-of-business (LOB) Windows Store application (.appx) directly to a Windows 8.x machine, rather than requiring the user to download the application from the public Windows Store. The ability to sideload is not available on every Windows 8.x edition. Windows 8, the basic edition targeted for home use, cannot sideload Windows Store apps. Windows 8.x Enterprise, Professional, and RT editions are capable of sideloading; however, this is not enabled by default. Enabling sideloading also differs depending on the version of Windows and whether the machine is domain-joined.

NOTE: SIDELOADING KEY LICENSING CHANGES

Microsoft has received considerable feedback on sideloading key requirements, and specifically regarding the cost of the keys. In April 2014, Microsoft announced new licensing changes with the release of Windows 8.1 Update that make it easier to enable sideloading for domain-joined machines. These changes also eliminate purchasing costs by providing the sideloading key at no additional charge for organizations with Microsoft volume license agreements. If your organization doesn't qualify for the sideloading key automatically, it could purchase the key for an unlimited number of devices at one low cost. A brief overview of the sideloading enhancements is at http://blogs.windows.com/windows/b/springboard/archive/2014/04/03/windows-8-1-sideloading-enhancements.aspx. For more detailed information, see the Microsoft Windows volume licensing guide at http://download.microsoft.com/download/9/4/3/9439A928-A0D1-44C2-A099-26A59AE0543B/Windows_8_1_Licensing_Guide.pdf.

Domain-joined Windows 8.x Enterprise and Windows 8.1 Professional (if the Professional machine is updated with Windows 8.1 Update) systems can enable sideloading via a straightforward group policy setting named Allow all trusted apps to install. Enabling this setting (found under Computer Configuration -> Administrative Templates -> Windows Components -> App Package Deployment) configures the Windows machine for sideloading after the group policy object (GPO) is applied.

If the Windows 8.1 Enterprise or Professional version is not domain-joined, or if the organization is enabling sideloading for Windows 8 RT versions, a sideloading key must be loaded and activated on the device along with setting the appropriate registry key settings, as shown in Figure 7.12. Configuration Manager and Windows Intune automate this configuration to save IT administrators the work of doing it manually for devices that are not domain-joined.

Requirements for Sideloading	Devices Managed by ConfigMgr + Intune
Sideloading Key Activation	1. Obtain a sideloading key from Microsoft.
	2. Load the sideloading key on the device.
AllowAllTrustedApps Registry Key	Set the following registry key value on the device: **HKEYLOCAL_MACHINE\Software\Policies\Microsoft\Windows\Appx\AllowAllTrustedApps=1**
Code-Signing Certificate	1. Obtain a code-signing certificate used to sign Modern UI applications that will be deployed by the company.
	2. Deploy the code-signing certificate.

FIGURE 7.12   Requirements for sideloading applications.

Sideloading keys are obtained from Microsoft or a software large account reseller (LAR) from which an organization purchases Microsoft software, and can be loaded within Configuration Manager when the ConfigMgr administrator creates the Windows Intune subscription (recommended by the authors), or later by using the Create Sideloading Key process within the Software Library node in the ConfigMgr console (shown in Figure 7.13).

Windows requires Windows Store apps be digitally signed to ensure the integrity of the software—that it hasn't been tampered with, it came from the correct publisher, and so on. Windows verifies the integrity of the file when it is loaded into memory (also known as kernel-mode code signing enforcement). Therefore, any sideloaded application must be signed with a key from a certificate that is trusted on the device. If the application was signed by a certificate obtained by a public certificate authority (CA) such as VeriSign, you won't need to trust that certificate on the local device as it is already there. However, if you are using an internal CA you must trust the certificate. The Windows Intune subscription properties prompt the ConfigMgr administrator to upload the code-signing certificate used to digitally sign applications the organization plans to sideload. As a best practice, companies should sign (and manage) all of their LOB applications with the same certificate because this makes application and certificate management easier.

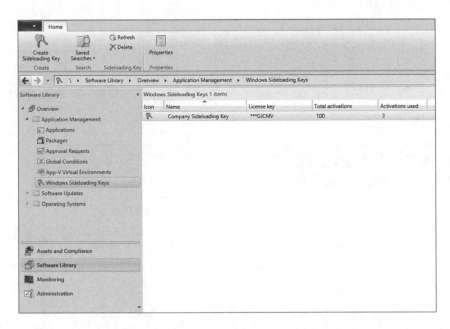

FIGURE 7.13   Windows Sideloading Keys node in ConfigMgr console.

> **NOTE: DEVICE ENROLLMENT**
>
> If configured at the time of creating the Windows Intune subscription, Windows Intune automatically activates the sideloading key, loads the code-signing certificate, and makes the appropriate registry entries on the device when it is enrolled. Otherwise, the code-signing certificate and sideloading key are installed at the next maintenance window on the device (up to 24 hours later) after the ConfigMgr administrator completes these steps.

Managing Windows Phone 8.x Devices

To enroll a Windows Phone 8 device into management via Windows Intune, you must complete certain prerequisites before creating the Windows Intune subscription. The three prerequisites follow:

▶ Obtaining an enterprise mobile code-signing certificate for Windows Phone 8

▶ Downloading and signing the Windows Phone 8.x company portal application

▶ Creating a ConfigMgr application for the Windows Phone 8.x company portal

The Windows Phone 8 platform includes the application programming interfaces (APIs) for organizations to create company hubs to deploy applications to their Windows Phone 8.x devices. These APIs are what Windows Intune (and other MDM vendors) leverages to sideload applications, and require organizations to follow specific steps to enable this functionality. Windows Phone 8 also contains APIs to enroll a device into a management service such as Windows Intune by using Company Apps under the phone's Settings. See Chapter 8, "Mobile Device Management in Configuration Manager 2012 R2," for more information on device enrollment.

The Windows Intune company portal application is actually a specific company hub for Windows Intune. In addition to application deployment, Windows Intune can enforce policy settings, gather inventory, and more. However, Microsoft engineered Intune to automatically deploy the company portal application at the time of enrollment. Therefore, even if you are not initially planning to deploy LOB applications, the company portal must still be properly configured and uploaded in the Windows Intune subscription.

To deploy the Windows Phone 8.x company portal application used by Windows Intune, you must first obtain an enterprise mobile code-signing certificate from Symantec (which owns VeriSign). This certificate is used to create an application enrollment token (AET) and also digitally sign the company portal application (SSP.XAP). The AET is used to enroll Windows Phone 8.x into the Windows Intune service when the user uses the Company App node in the Settings Application on the device, and must be in place to install applications. Every application an organization plans to sideload must be digitally signed with the same Symantec code-signing certificate used to generate the AET. The benefit of this approach is when the AET is removed, all sideloaded LOB applications (and cached data) are also removed from the Windows Phone 8.x device. This is the basis on which Microsoft built its selective wipe solution for this platform.

Only one Symantec enterprise mobile code-signing certificate is issued to an organization; this is linked to the Windows Phone developer account associated with that organization. If your organization is planning to deploy Windows Phone 8.x applications, more than likely the developers have registered your organization within the Windows Phone 8 development site and have followed the process to obtain the code-signing certificate. You can find the latest version of the Windows Intune company portal application for Windows Phone 8 that is signed by the code-signing certificate at http://www.microsoft.com/en-us/download/details.aspx?id=36060.

Microsoft Intune Support Services has published a guide for obtaining the Symantec certificate and signing the company portal app in the event that an organization has not yet obtained the certificate and is looking for assistance. This guide is posted to the Windows Intune team blog at http://blogs.technet.com/b/windowsintune/archive/2013/08/09/windows-intune-walkthrough-windows-phone-8-management.aspx?ocid=aff-n-we-loc--ITPRO40922. The guide was written for users of the Intune cloud-only service. However, the Symantec code-signing certificate and company portal steps are the same for Intune, regardless of whether or not it is integrated with ConfigMgr.

After the company portal application has been signed, the ConfigMgr administrator needs to do the following:

1. Create a Configuration Manager application in the Software Library node with a deployment type of Windows Phone app package (.xap).

2. Change the application name.

You can accept all defaults when adding the signed company portal Windows Phone 8.x application. However, the authors recommend that you change the name on the General Information tab. The Name field is automatically imported from the .xap file and is not descriptive (see Figure 7.14). Changing the name makes it easier to view the device in the ConfigMgr console. Regardless of the name in this field, the Windows Phone 8.x device always displays the application name as company portal. After changing the name, click **Next** and accept the defaults on the remaining pages. At this point, the prerequisites for Windows Phone 8 are complete because the company portal application is automatically deployed once the Windows Intune subscription is created.

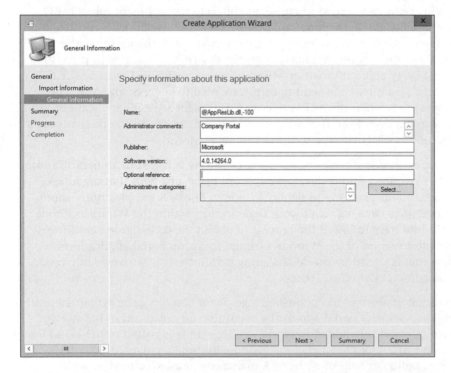

FIGURE 7.14   Changing the display name of the Windows Phone 8 application.

TIP: TESTING WINDOWS PHONE 8.X MANAGEMENT BEFORE ACQUIRING CERTIFICATES

For those organizations that are testing management of Windows Phone 8.x devices but have not purchased the Symantec enterprise certificate (or don't want to), Microsoft released the Support Tool for Windows Intune Trial Management of Windows Phone 8. Don't let the name fool you to think this was an afterthought: Microsoft did a great job on this tool, which provides a sample application enrollment token, signed company portal app, and two sample applications with which to test Windows Phone 8.x. Look for periodic updates by Microsoft, usually several months after an updated company portal application is released. Download the tool from http://www.microsoft.com/en-sg/download/details.aspx?id=39079.

Managing iOS Devices

As with Windows Phone 8.x, you must complete certain prerequisites to enroll iOS devices into management, either while creating the Windows Intune subscription or beforehand.

Like other major MDM vendors on the market, Configuration Manager and Windows Intune leverage the Apple MDM framework that is built into iOS. Prior to iOS 4, MDM vendors had to deploy a full MDM agent to the iOS devices to perform the limited capabilities supported at the time. With the release of iOS 4, Apple included enterprise management features within the operating system (OS) that integrated with the Apple Push Notification service (APNs), potentially alleviating the need for an agent to be deployed to the device (see http://www.infoworld.com/d/mobilize/iphone-management-tools-step-it-ios-4-751).

APNs is an Apple hosted certificate-based service that allows Configuration Manager and Windows Intune to communicate with the iOS device by sending notifications directly to the device (push). Using the Apple iOS MDM platform and APNs, ConfigMgr via Intune interacts with the Apple Push Notification server for pushing any notifications to the iOS mobile device and for device enrollment. When the APNs server receives the information, it pushes the message to the iOS device, alerting the user to items such as new MDM settings or application deployments.

To establish management of the iOS devices from ConfigMgr and Intune into the APNs and Apple MDM framework, your organization must register for an APN certificate. To complete the iOS section within the Intune subscription follow these steps:

1. Create a certificate signing request (CSR) in the ConfigMgr console and download it to a secure location.

2. Log in to the Apple Push Certificate Portal with a verified Apple ID.

3. Choose **Create Certificate** and agree to the Terms of Use.

4. Upload the signed CSR and download the APNs certificate.

5. Upload the APNs into the Windows Intune Subscription properties to create a secure communication management channel to iOS devices.

7

The APNs certificate associated with Configuration Manager and Intune (named MDM_ Microsoft Corporation_Certificate.pem) must be annually renewed and reloaded into the Intune Subscription. A single Apple ID can request and manage multiple APNs certificates. In general, Apple makes this process very straightforward and painless, especially because they no longer charge for requesting the APNs certificate. To begin the APNs certificate process, follow these steps:

1. In the Administration workspace of the ConfigMgr console, access the Windows Intune Subscription node and select **Create APNs certificate request** from the ribbon bar.

2. Browse for a download location and choose a name for the Certificate Signing Request form (*.csr) and click **Download**, as shown in Figure 7.15.

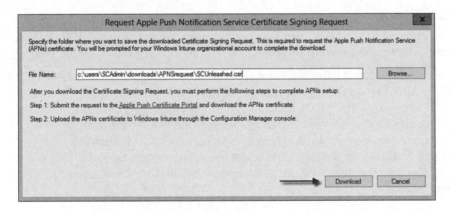

FIGURE 7.15   Downloading the CSR.

3. Use the URL listed in the CSR creation screen (see Figure 7.16) or access http://identity.apple.com/pushcert to log in with a valid Apple ID.

4. You are now at the root portal page, which shows all APNs certificates you have requested, including ones that have expired (see Figure 7.17). You can renew, download, and revoke existing certificates or choose **Create a Certificate** to create a new one.

5. You now are prompted to upload the CSR previously downloaded into the Create a New Push Certificate window and choose **Upload** (shown in Figure 7.18). Once done, accept the Apple terms and conditions regarding the use of Apple Push Certificates (shown in Figure 7.19).

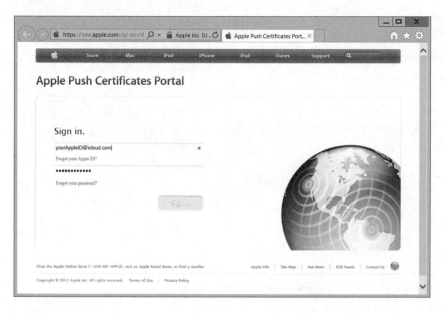

FIGURE 7.16   Log in to the Apple Push Certificate Portal.

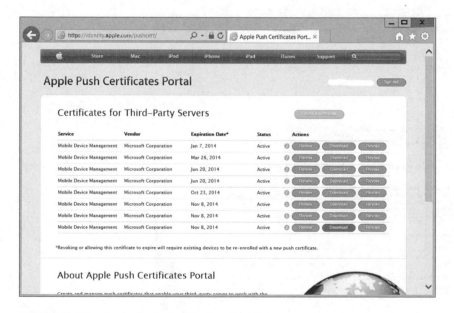

FIGURE 7.17   Apple Push Certificates Portal.

FIGURE 7.18   Creating a new push certificate.

FIGURE 7.19   Accepting the terms and conditions.

6. An Apple push certificate is now created and you can download it from the main portal. If you close the browser or have issues at this step, return to the main Apple Push Certificate Portal page. The certificate is listed on the screen with the current date. If you click **Download**, the certificate named MDM_Microsoft Corporation_ Certificate.pem is available and Internet Explorer prompts you to save the file (see Figure 7.20).

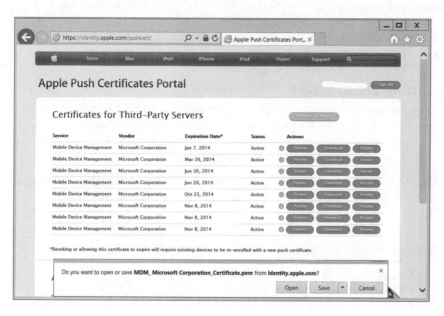

FIGURE 7.20   Download the APNs and store in secure location.

7. Store this file in a secure location until it is needed to create the Windows Intune subscription.

NOTE: CREATING THE APNS CERTIFICATE AND THE .JSON FILE WITH INTERNET EXPLORER

When using Internet Explorer to log in to the Apple Push Certificate Portal site and create the APNs certificate, you may be prompted to save a *.json file after completing your certificate creation request and uploading your .CSR file. JSON is the file extension for Java Script Object Notification and used as a bookmark to return you to the main portal page. Internet Explorer may interpret this file incorrectly and prompt you to download and save the file because it cannot open and interpret it. The file is not needed in the process; however, it does require you to manually return to the main portal page by browsing back to the previous page. Safari and Chrome browsers do not generate this file download prompt error and are returned to the main portal page automatically.

Installing the Windows Intune Subscription and Connector

With directory synchronization running and the mobile platform prerequisites completed, you can create the Intune subscription and install the Intune connector site system role. When the subscription is created, ConfigMgr also adds a new site system server, named \\manage.microsoft.com, which represents the cloud distribution point used by Configuration Manager when distributing applications to mobile devices. The Windows Intune Connector site system role performs the actual connection to the Intune cloud service to gather or deliver mobile device related content via a secure connection.

Creating the Intune Subscription

The Intune subscription represents the information necessary to connect to the Windows Intune online service, the mobile device platforms that are supported (including prerequisite information), and other information that is provided to users within the mobile device company portal application. To add the Intune subscription, follow these steps:

1. In the ConfigMgr console, navigate to **Administration -> Cloud Services -> Windows Intune Subscriptions** and select **Add Windows Intune Subscription** from the ribbon bar (see Figure 7.21).

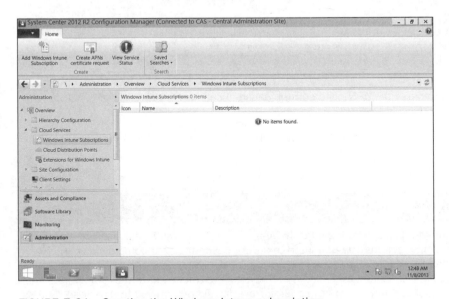

FIGURE 7.21   Creating the Windows Intune subscription.

2. Review the information on the Introduction tab, and then click **Next**.

3. On the Information tab, review the overview of the steps required to complete the subscription and click **Next**.

4. On the Subscription tab, have the global administrator username and password ready for the Azure AD tenant used with the Intune instance and then select **Sign In**. This opens a page that prompts you to accept the configuration change of making Configuration Manager the mobile device management authority. Since Windows Intune can manage mobile devices in a stand-alone configuration or integrated with ConfigMgr (but not both at the same time), you must accept this action by checking the box acknowledging that this action is irreversible after finishing this step of the Intune subscription (see Figure 7.22).

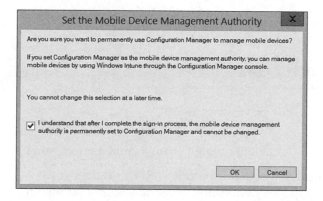

FIGURE 7.22   Setting the mobile device management authority.

A browser opens where you must sign in with a global administrator account username and password for the Azure AD tenant used for the Intune service (shown in Figure 7.23).

Upon successful sign in with the Azure AD global admin account, the browser window automatically closes and returns you to the Subscription tab. Click **Next** to continue.

CAUTION: SETTING THE MANAGEMENT AUTHORITY

Setting the mobile device management authority to Configuration Manager is an irreversible process.

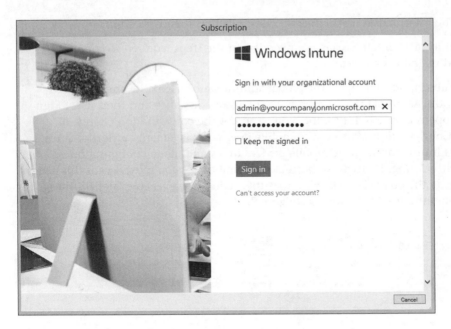

FIGURE 7.23   Sign in to the Intune tenant as a global administrator.

5. The General tab appears (see Figure 7.24). Enter the following required information:

▶ **ConfigMgr user collection:** This is a user collection used by ConfigMgr to authorize the users to enroll mobile devices into the Intune service. ConfigMgr analyzes the users within this collection every 5 minutes to check for new users or changes in membership. It then connects to the Windows Intune service and Azure AD to search for a corresponding user, based on the user principal name (UPN). Upon locating a UPN match, ConfigMgr synchronizes that user to the Intune cloud, authorizing the user to enroll devices and setting a Cloud User ID value in the ConfigMgr database and the Intune service. If a user is not in this collection, he is not authorized to enroll devices, regardless of whether he is placed in the Windows Intune Azure AD group, as that group has no bearing on device enrollment.

▶ **Company name:** This is the name shown in the company portal application on mobile devices. It can be placed next to the company graphic defined in the Company Logo tab if you use a logo in conjunction with the company name.

▶ **Configuration Manager site code:** This is the primary site code defined to associate with the mobile devices. The only time you would choose from multiple primary site codes is if the organization leverages a central administration server (CAS) and multiple primaries.

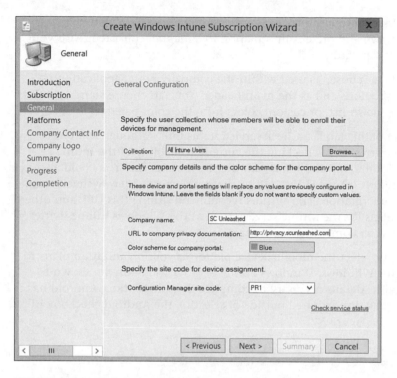

FIGURE 7.24   The General tab of the Windows Intune Subscription Wizard.

NOTE: USER REMOVAL FROM COLLECTION

If a user is placed in the appropriate user collection defined in the General tab of the Intune subscription and has enrolled mobile devices and is later removed from the ConfigMgr user collection, she cannot enroll any new devices, and her devices are eventually groomed from the ConfigMgr database.

Devices are not selectively wiped as a function of removing a user. The ConfigMgr administrator must perform that action on a user's devices; otherwise, they become orphaned without wiping any sensitive company data remaining on the device.

The other fields on this tab (URL to company privacy documentation and Color scheme for company portal) are not required, although both are relevant and should be defined.

▶ The privacy documentation URL is available to access within the company portal application on the mobile device and represents a standard web URL to direct users, when on their mobile devices, to privacy information from the company as well as a way for the organization to emphasize the management features deployed through Intune. Since it is only a web page, you have the freedom to design and present information in a manner consistent with your organization's standards.

▶ The color scheme chosen is used within the company portal application to highlight applications and as the main header. You can choose standard colors from the drop-down list, or custom colors from the color palette.

In the lower corner of this tab is a Check service status link. Although somewhat hidden, if you are interested in checking the current availability of the Intune service, you can click the link and bookmark the site for later use. You could also right-click the Windows Intune Subscriptions node and choose View System Status to access the same information. The authors recommend storing this URL and other communication outlets for the Intune service, such as the Windows Intune twitter account at http://twitter.com/windowsintune.

6. On the Platforms tab, select the mobile device platforms your organization plans to manage. By selecting Windows, Windows Phone 8, or iOS, sub-tabs are shown to supply the prerequisite details necessary to complete the subscription. Android has no additional configuration required outside of selecting the Android checkbox in Device type (shown in Figure 7.25).

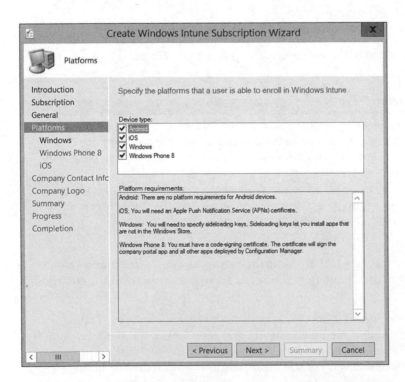

FIGURE 7.25   Mobile device platforms supported within Windows Intune.

The tabs listed under Platforms leverage the prerequisites previously covered in the "MDM Prerequisites" section.

▶ Selecting Windows on the Platforms tab displays the Windows tab (see Figure 7.26) and prompts you to enter the following information:

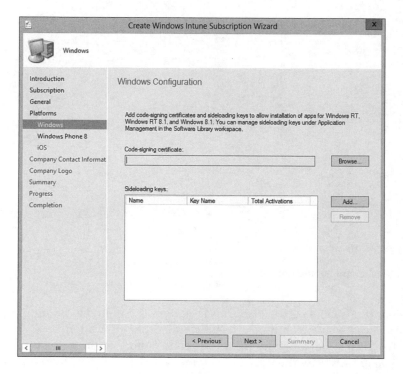

FIGURE 7.26   Adding the code-signing certificate and sideloading keys.

▶ Code-signing certificate

▶ Enterprise sideloading keys

These items are not required to continue creating the Intune subscription; however, the authors recommend entering the necessary information now so the Windows devices are fully provisioned as soon as possible after enrollment. If configured later, the certificate and sideloading key are transferred and installed on the device at the next policy polling interval (every 24 hours on the device).

To load the code-signing certificate, select **Browse** and navigate to the location of the X.509 certificate used to sign internal Windows 8.x applications (.aapx). To add the enterprise sideloading key, select **Add** and enter an appropriate Name, the 25-digit Key, Total activations, and optional Description, and then click **OK** (see Figure 7.27). With the volume licensing changes that Microsoft made in May 2014 in conjunction with the release of Windows 8.1 Update, there generally is only one key to enter at this step to represent your organization's entire mobile device population.

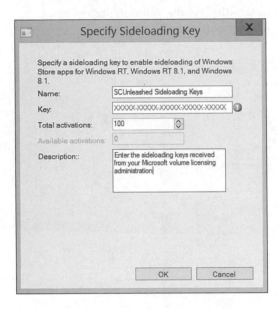

FIGURE 7.27   Entering the sideloading key details.

▶ Selecting Windows Phone 8 on the Platforms tab causes the Windows Phone 8 tab to be displayed; you are prompted to enter either the Application Enrollment Token (.aet file) and .xml file, or the code-signing certificate (.pfx). In addition, you must specify the ConfigMgr application package that represents the signed Windows Phone 8 company portal app created in the prerequisite steps previously outlined in the "Managing Windows Phone 8.x Devices" section (see Figure 7.28).

New in ConfigMgr 2012 R2 is the option to specify the Application Enrollment Token instead of the code-signing certificate and password used to secure the certificate when it was exported to a .pfx file. You may prefer to leverage the AET files and not expose the .pfx and the security password to this process. Microsoft released the AETGeneratorTool as part of the Windows Phone 8 SDK used with the code-signing certificate to generate the .aet and .xml files needed to complete this step. The command line to run the tool is straightforward:

```
AETGenerator.exe  PFXfile  password
```

Where PFXfile is the code-signing certificate obtained from Symantec, and the password required is the password used to secure the certificate when it was exported to a .pfx file.

After running the tool, the AET.AET and AET.XML files are placed in the root of the command prompt folder currently in focus. See http://msdn.microsoft.com/en-us/library/windowsphone/develop/jj735576(v=vs.105).aspx for more information.

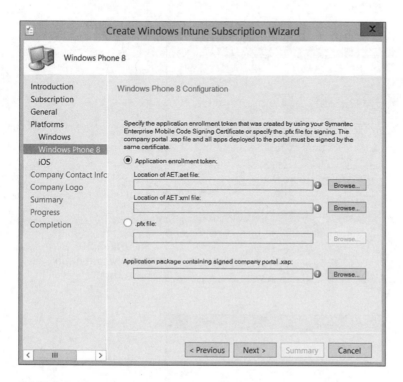

FIGURE 7.28   Windows Phone 8 configuration components.

If specifying the .pfx file directly, browse to the location of the .pfx file and click **Open**. Enter the security password for the .pfx file and then click **OK** (shown in Figure 7.29). After all items are completed, click **Next** to continue entering the subscription.

▶ Choosing iOS on the Platforms tab displays the iOS tab. After completing the iOS prerequisites, the Apple Push Notification service (APNs) certificate, named MDM_Microsoft Corporation_Certificate.pem by default, can be specified. Select **Browse** and navigate to the location of the .pem file. Click **Open** and then **Next** to continue (see Figure 7.30).

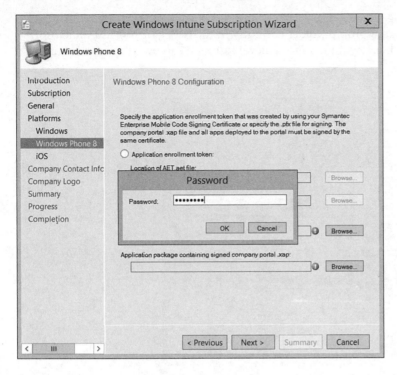

FIGURE 7.29
Specifying the .pfx
password.

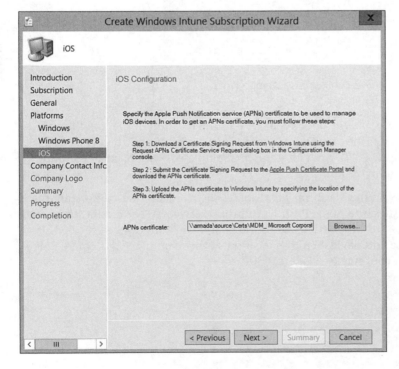

FIGURE 7.30
Specifying the APNs
certificate.

7. Use the Company Contact Information tab to define additional information that is displayed inside the company portal applications on the mobile devices.

No fields are required, but the authors recommend they be configured, especially the support website URL and website name, along with the Additional information field (see Figure 7.31).

FIGURE 7.31   Entering the company contact information.

8. On the Company Logo tab, enter the logo graphic for your organization, in JPEG or PNG format, to use against a white background or the selected color scheme chosen on the General tab. These fields are not required, and both can be defined. Each graphic must fit within the parameters defined, which requires the graphic is not more than 750KB and 400x100 pixels in size (see Figure 7.32).

9. Use the Summary tab to review the entered information before clicking **Next** and adding the subscription.

10. When you finish, the wizard displays a Completion tab. A warning message is listed (see Figure 7.33); however, this is to draw attention to the fact that while the subscription is created, the Windows Intune Connector site system role has not been added and needs to be done next to fully provision mobile device management.

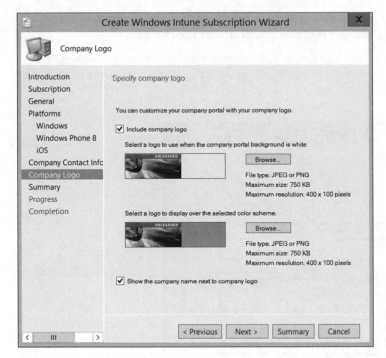

FIGURE 7.32   Entering the company logo information.

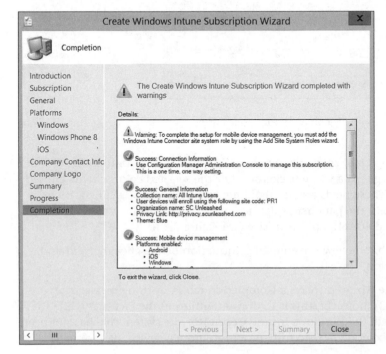

FIGURE 7.33   Completion pane highlighting a warning to the administrator.

Adding the Windows Intune Connector Site System Role

This section discusses adding the Windows Intune Connector site system role. This site system role installs the component on the CAS (or single primary site) server that makes the secure connection to the Windows Intune cloud service. The Intune subscription defines the Intune tenant and mobile device details; however, it is the connector site system role that performs the communication functions. Follow these steps to install the connector:

1. In the ConfigMgr console, navigate to **Administration -> Servers and Site Systems**. Right-click the CAS server or primary site server (in a single-site hierarchy), and choose **Add Site System Roles**, as shown in Figure 7.34. Similar to the Intune subscription, the Intune connector can only be installed on the CAS or primary site server.

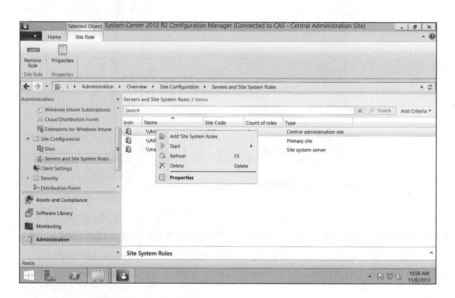

FIGURE 7.34   Adding a site system role.

2. On the General tab of the wizard, accept the defaults and click **Next**.

3. On the System Role Selection tab, choose **Windows Intune Connector** (shown in Figure 7.35), click **Next**, and proceed through the Summary tab to complete the site system role addition.

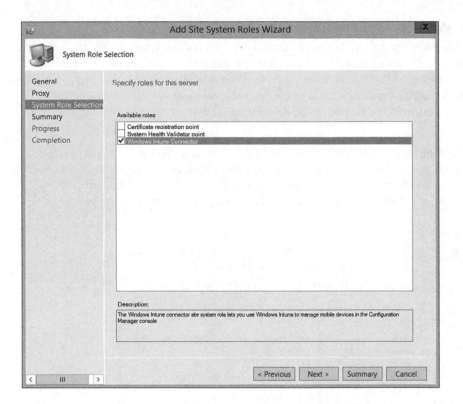

FIGURE 7.35   Adding the Windows Intune Connector site system role.

Confirming the Installation of the Subscription and Connecter Role

Now that the subscription is added along with the connector, you should verify the installation to ensure proper operation before enrolling devices. Verification includes the following tasks:

▶ Evaluating ConfigMgr logs

▶ Verifying network access

You can find the list of Configuration Manager 2012 R2 log files and explanations at http://technet.microsoft.com/en-us/library/hh427342.aspx. Navigating under the Windows Intune Connector node of the console displays the logs that interact with the Intune connector. Attention should be given to logs listed in Table 7.2.

TABLE 7.2   Important ConfigMgr Logs for Intune

Log Name	Description
Cloudusersync.log	Records license enablement for users
Dmpdownloader.log	Records details on downloads from Windows Intune
Dmpuploader.log	Records details for uploading database changes to Windows Intune
outgoingcontentmanager.log	Records content uploaded to Windows Intune
ConnectorSetup.log	Records the installation of the Intune connector

Check the ConnectorSetup.log file to ensure the proper installation of the connector. It confirms the start of the installation by verifying prerequisites for the connector, and then proceeds to install the components. Verify there are no errors that prevented the Installation was successful entry at the end of the log, shown in Figure 7.36.

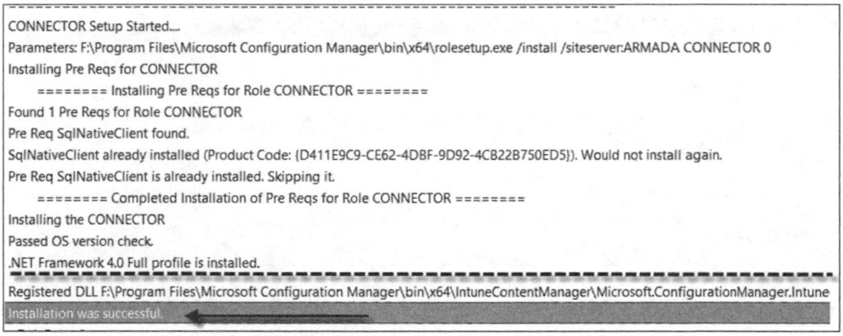

```
CONNECTOR Setup Started....
Parameters: F:\Program Files\Microsoft Configuration Manager\bin\x64\rolesetup.exe /install /siteserver:ARMADA CONNECTOR 0
Installing Pre Reqs for CONNECTOR
       ======== Installing Pre Reqs for Role CONNECTOR ========
Found 1 Pre Reqs for Role CONNECTOR
Pre Req SqlNativeClient found.
SqlNativeClient already installed (Product Code: {D411E9C9-CE62-4DBF-9D92-4CB22B750ED5}). Would not install again.
Pre Req SqlNativeClient is already installed. Skipping it.
       ======== Completed Installation of Pre Reqs for Role CONNECTOR ========
Installing the CONNECTOR
Passed OS version check.
.NET Framework 4.0 Full profile is installed.
Registered DLL F:\Program Files\Microsoft Configuration Manager\bin\x64\IntuneContentManager\Microsoft.ConfigurationManager.Intune
Installation was successful.
```

FIGURE 7.36   ConnectorSetup.log entry.

The Cloudusersync.log located on the CAS or primary site server records actions taken by ConfigMgr to evaluate users in the collection specific in the Windows Intune Subscription properties, and either successfully enables the user to enroll mobile devices or raises an error. ConfigMgr evaluates the ConfigMgr collection every five minutes to ensure a fast provision/deprovision of users. By default, any errors syncing users to the cloud are shown by listing the user ID and reason the user was not enabled. In the example in Figure 7.37, users failed to be enabled because there was no corresponding user account found in the Azure AD tenant used by Windows Intune that ConfigMgr was searching against.

Barring errors, users can enroll devices when synced by ConfigMgr. Successful enablement of users is listed in the log under the entry Total Successfully added users to the Cloud = xxx. However, the actual user name is not displayed by default. When troubleshooting to ensure a specific user can now enroll devices, the authors recommend enabling verbose logging on the cloudusersync.log to view all the user details. To enable more verbose logging, open regedit.exe on the CAS or Primary site server and add a DWORD entry named `Verbose Logging` with a value of `"1"` under the following:

```
HKEY_LOCAL_MACHINE\SOFTWARE\Microsoft\SMS\Components\SMS_CLOUD_USERSYNC
```

In addition to the log listing successful additions of users into the cloud, you can view the MDMUserProperty table in the site server SQL Server database. When the user is successfully enabled, she is given a cloud user ID and listed as a cloud user. You can also view the users with a cloud user ID GUID defined within the ConfigMgr console by navigating to the Users node and adding the Cloud User ID column to the display, as shown in Figure 7.38.

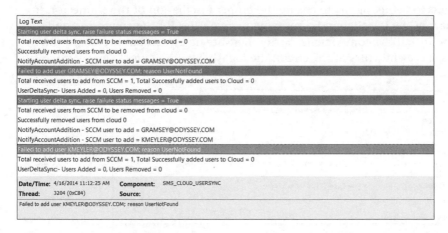

FIGURE 7.37   Default Cloudusersync.log entries.

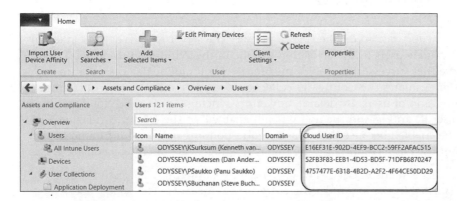

FIGURE 7.38   Cloud User ID column.

NOTE: CLOUD USER ID COLUMN IN THE CONFIGMGR ADMIN CONSOLE

In the user collections, including the one defined for the Windows Intune subscription, ConfigMgr console users can add the Cloud User ID column view. However, the console does not display values in this column unless you are at the top-level Users node.

The Dmpuploader.log and the Dmpdownloader.log files are used to record transmitted information to and from the Intune service. Ensure that no communication errors are found in the log and that the connector certificate and tenant ID are resolved. Figure 7.39 illustrates the Dmpdownloader.log functioning properly and downloading state message information.

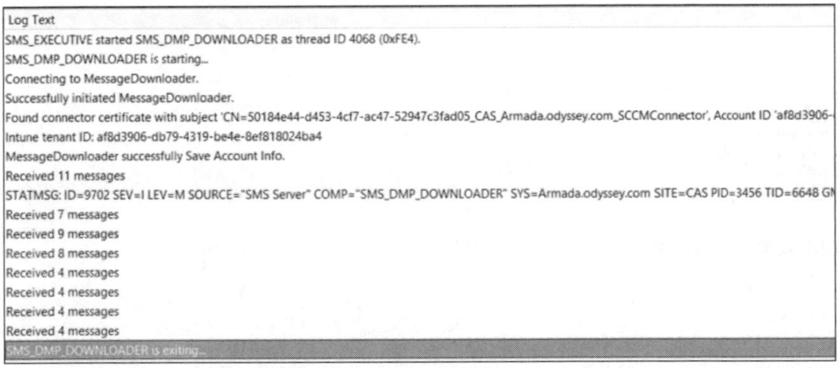

FIGURE 7.39   Dmpdownloader.log example.

The outgoingcontentmanager.log contains information on packages being distributed to the Intune service (where the distribution point is manage.microsoft.com). Confirm that there are no communication errors and that packages have successfully been transmitted to the Intune service. A good example to use is the company portal app for Windows Phone 8.x (ssp.xap). This app is automatically distributed to manage.microsoft.com when Windows Phone 8 is configured within the Windows Intune subscription. If you configure management of Windows Phone 8.x, verify the outgoing package communication is successful by searching the outgoingcontentmanager.log for **ssp.xap**. Figure 7.40 illustrates how the log displays a package communication into the Intune cloud distribution point. Notice how packages are stored encrypted in the Intune service.

Windows Intune provides 20GB of storage space for mobile device packages. Only content for LOB applications is distributed to the cloud distribution point (manage.microsoft.com). An organization might also want to understand how much space their mobile device LOB packages have consumed over time. A simple way to check the storage is to log in to the Windows Intune administrator console at https://manage.microsoft.com. If not already granted permissions, you must use an Azure AD global administrator to get into this console as it is not used for the ConfigMgr and Intune solution. Although this web administrative portal is not required for mobile device management, it still records how much space the Intune tenant has used in Azure storage. Navigate to the Administration node and check the Cloud Storage Status for the space used to date (see Figure 7.41).

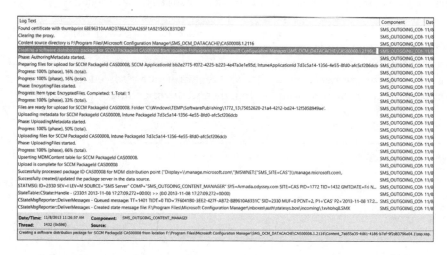

FIGURE 7.40   Outgoingcontentmanager.log uploading the company portal app.

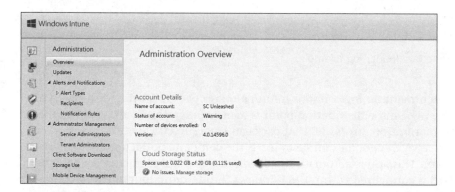

FIGURE 7.41   Windows Intune storage space status available for MDM packages.

If an organization is out of available Azure storage space associated with their Intune service, the outgoingcontentmanager.log should show this exception: The operation failed because a server-side limit was exceeded.

Removing or Overriding an Existing Intune Subscription

Microsoft provides a straightforward approach if you need to remove the Intune subscription or recreate a connection after a system failure. Situations like this might also arise if you were testing the Intune subscription in an Intune trial tenant and need to migrate to a production environment, or during a merger or acquisition. To remove the Intune subscription, follow these steps:

1. In the ConfigMgr console, navigate to **Cloud Services -> Windows Intune Subscription**.

2. Highlight the subscription and select **Delete** from the menu or right-click and choose **Delete**. You are prompted that the deletion also automatically removes the Intune connector site system role (see Figure 7.42). To proceed with the removal, click **Yes**.

3. To confirm the removal, check the status in the ConnectorSetup.log before reinstalling.

FIGURE 7.42   Removing the Windows Intune Subscription.

There are times when the subscription and Intune connector need to be reinstalled into an Intune tenant that previously had a subscription configured. An example would be using a ConfigMgr lab environment and migrating to your production ConfigMgr environment while keeping the same Intune tenant, or for disaster recovery situations. To re-add an Intune subscription to a previously used Intune tenant, navigate to the Cloud Services node and begin the process to add the Intune subscription previously described in the "Creating the Intune Subscription" section of this chapter. On the Subscription tab, after logging in to the Windows Intune tenant with an Azure AD global administrative account, a dialog box is displayed to confirm that you want to install the subscription and set it as the active management authority (as shown in Figure 7.43) for the Intune tenant, even if that tenant had a subscription previously configured.

FIGURE 7.43   Re-adding the Windows Intune subscription.

Receiving Feature Updates Using the Extensions for Windows Intune

The rapid pace at which new mobile devices are developed and released, along with their corresponding operating system updates, required Microsoft to develop a new mechanism to import MDM feature updates. Following the ConfigMgr 2012 R2 release in October 2013, Microsoft released additional MDM features in February and May 2014. To deploy new features that do not require site system or client upgrades, Microsoft has introduced the Extensions for Windows Intune function.

The Extensions for Windows Intune tab is located under the Cloud Services tab in the Administration node. It remains empty until an Intune subscription is defined and the connector site system role is installed. From then on, whenever Microsoft releases new MDM updates, the updates are displayed in this tab, as shown in Figure 7.44. Console users are also prompted that new extensions are available and can be enabled (see Figure 7.45). Microsoft's goal is to deliver as many MDM updates as possible through this channel, assuming the updates can be delivered in this manner. Device policy and configuration settings are good examples of features that can be released this way.

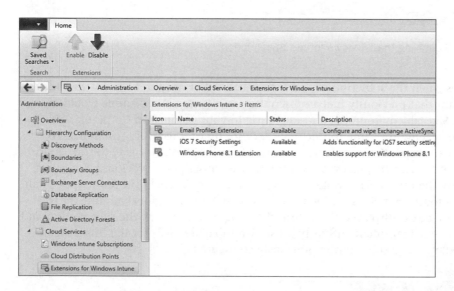

FIGURE 7.44   Extensions for Windows Intune.

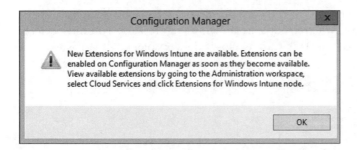

FIGURE 7.45 Console prompt that new Intune extensions are available.

To enable a new extension in the ConfigMgr console, complete the following steps:

1. Navigate to the extension listed in the console and right-click the extension and select **Enable**, or highlight the extension and choose **Enable** from the console menu.

2. The Microsoft license terms are displayed for the selected extension. Check the **I accept the license terms and privacy statement** check box and click **Yes** to enable the extension (see Figure 7.46). Configuration Manager then downloads the extension via the Intune connector and replicates it across the site hierarchy.

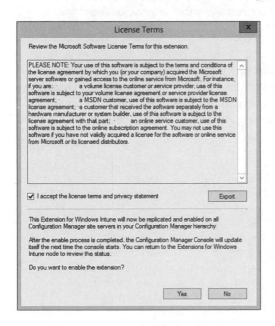

FIGURE 7.46 Accepting the license agreement to enable an Intune extension.

3. Now that the extension is enabled in the console, close the console and reopen it to be prompted to install the new extensions, as shown in Figure 7.47. You must select **OK** to install the extensions; selecting **Cancel** closes the console.

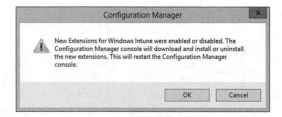

FIGURE 7.47   Message that new extensions are to be loaded.

To bypass installing the extension, open the Configuration Manager console using the /SMS:IgnoreExtensions switch. The next time the console is opened, you are prompted to install the extensions, unless you use the IgnoreExtensions switch again.

NOTE: UPDATING THE CONSOLE REQUIRES ADMIN RIGHTS

When updating the ConfigMgr console with the Intune extensions, you must be logged on as a local administrator, or use administrator rights to run the ConfigMgr console. This may pose problems within organizations with administrators that are not local administrators or with Citrix/RemoteDesktop environments.

To disable a Windows Intune extension that was previously enabled, right-click the enabled extension listed in the Extensions for Windows Intune node and select **Disable**. This action is replicated to the site hierarchy in several minutes, after which you must close and reopen the console to complete removing the features from the console view (see Figure 7.48).

FIGURE 7.48   Disabling an Intune extension.

Summary

Integrating System Center 2012 R2 Configuration Manager and Windows Intune provides organizations great value through a single pane-of-glass approach that maximizes common ConfigMgr skill sets and device management functions while lowering costs. The integration between these products involves planning, especially if an organization isn't already integrated with Microsoft Azure Active Directory. There are also mobile device platform prerequisites that must be completed as part of the integration process.

This chapter explained how to install and configure the Windows Intune subscription and Intune connector site system role. Chapter 8 explains how to use the integration with Intune to manage mobile devices within ConfigMgr.

Mobile Device Management in Configuration Manager 2012 R2

IN THIS CHAPTER

▶ Understanding Mobile Device Management Challenges

▶ Prerequisites of Mobile Device Management

▶ Enrolling Mobile Devices

▶ Inventorying Mobile Devices

▶ Managing Mobile Device Settings

▶ Deploying Applications to Mobile Devices

▶ Retiring/Wiping Mobile Devices

▶ Troubleshooting

Microsoft planned mobile device management as one of the features of System Center 2012 Configuration Manager (ConfigMgr), and the base or RTM (release to manufacturing) version of Configuration Manager 2012 included two methods of mobile device management:

▶ **Light management:** This model uses Exchange ActiveSync (EAS), enabling broad support for different mobile platforms, but with a limited feature set.

Light management requires either on-premise Exchange 2010 or Exchange 2013 or Office 365. Exchange ActiveSync can be used on any ActiveSync enabled device and requires an existing Exchange client access license (CAL). However, Exchange ActiveSync only provides limited inventory and settings management features.

▶ **In-depth management:** The in-depth management model includes more functionality for device management. This model is supported only for a limited range of devices because it requires a client on the mobile device.

The client can be installed to Windows Mobile 6.x devices and Nokia Symbian Belle devices. In-depth management also requires Internet-facing server roles to support the mobile clients.

These capabilities seem rather limited today; the mobile device market saw dramatic changes while Configuration Manager 2012 was being developed, and these changes were not incorporated into the released product. Microsoft closes that gap in ConfigMgr 2012 Service Pack (SP) 1 and R2 through enhancements to Configuration Manager and integration with Windows Intune. These changes are the focus of this chapter.

Because light and in-depth management were discussed in *System Center 2012 Configuration Unleashed* (Sams, 2012) and the features are unchanged from ConfigMgr 2012 RTM, they are not discussed here. This chapter covers Configuration Manager mobile device management when integrated with Windows Intune. Microsoft calls this *hybrid management*.

Understanding Mobile Device Management Challenges

Mobile device management has changed considerably in the last several years. The bring your own device (BYOD) strategy has become quite popular in corporate environments. This, along with the consumerization of Information Technology (IT), is changing how mobile devices are managed: IT no longer can dictate those devices used by end users, yet remains responsible for ensuring that the organization's data is protected under all circumstances. Microsoft's vision for mobile computing (http://blogs.technet.com/b/in_the_cloud/archive/2014/01/29/a-people-first-approach-to-mobile-device-management.aspx) is to enable individuals to be productive on the devices they love while helping IT ensure that corporate assets are secure and protected.

Microsoft utilizes a cloud-based mobile device management strategy to address the challenges of managing mobile devices. Because these devices use cloud-based resources, it makes sense to manage them using a cloud-based architecture. Microsoft addressed this by adding mobile device management support to Windows Intune. This capability was first introduced in January 2013 with the release of System Center 2012 Service Pack (SP) 1.

Windows Intune can be integrated with ConfigMgr 2012 SP 1/R2 to provide a single management console for all devices, as shown in Figure 8.1. This hybrid approach is known as unified device management (UDM). Having a single solution for managing traditional PCs and mobile devices helps organizations reduce management efforts, software, and training costs.

NOTE: INTUNE-ONLY AND HYBRID ENVIRONMENTS HAVE DIFFERENT CAPABILITIES

Mobile devices can also be managed using Windows Intune only, providing a similar feature set to ConfigMgr/Intune hybrid management but with a different user interface (UI). Intune-only management is targeted to those customers that do not have ConfigMgr 2012 R2 installed.

Even though Microsoft tries to provide the same management features with Intune only and hybrid management, some features are first introduced in Intune-only management or in hybrid management.

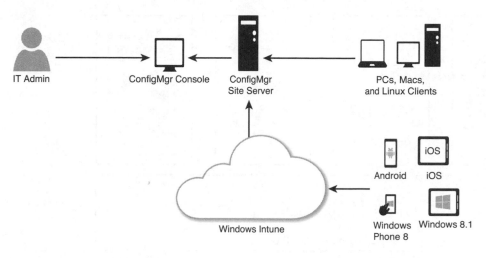

FIGURE 8.1   Windows Intune and Configuration Manager 2012 R2 integration.

To be successful in today's mobile device management market, a mobile device management product must support the most popular platforms: Android and iOS devices. Microsoft must also support its own operating systems: Windows Phone 8.x and Windows RT. New devices and operating systems are continually appearing on the market, and Microsoft has committed to update Windows Intune frequently to support new mobile operating systems and to provide new features. The integration between Intune and ConfigMgr means that after Microsoft updates its Windows Intune cloud service, on-premise ConfigMgr 2012 R2 environments must also be updated. ConfigMgr 2012 R2's new Extensions for Windows Intune feature provides a simple and fast update mechanism for this purpose.

Figure 8.2 illustrates the challenges of mobile device management. Users have a wide selection of differing mobile devices from different vendors that must be managed. The users need the appropriate applications and secure access to company data to be productive with their mobile device.

Organizations require the following features from a mobile device management solution:

▶ **Inventory:** It is important to know which devices are actually used.

▶ **Settings management:** Mobile devices must have the appropriate security settings to access corporate data.

▶ **Applications:** Organizations might have created their own applications for different mobile device architectures and want to deploy the correct versions to the devices.

   There are also many potentially useful applications in different application stores (App Store, Google Play, and Windows Store). However, users could have challenges finding the correct applications, due to the sheer volume of different application titles in these stores. With application management, IT professionals could easily point the right applications to the right users.

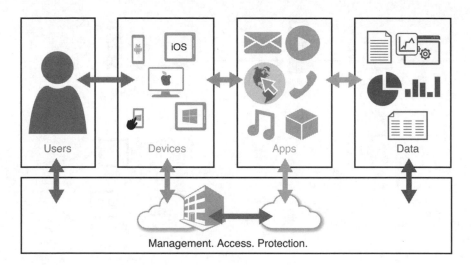

FIGURE 8.2   Mobile device management challenges.

▶ **Email:** Email is the most commonly used work-related application on mobile devices. Organizations want to centrally manage email account settings on these devices.

▶ **Data:** If users are accessing company data on mobile devices, there must be a way to ensure that sensitive data cannot be misused on a device and remove the data if a device is stolen.

Microsoft emphasizes that a mobile management solution must provide secure access to a company's data, email, and other resources, and has invested heavily to accomplish these goals in Windows Intune and System Center 2012 R2 Configuration Manager. Microsoft will continue to improve the mobile device management features in future releases.

> **NOTE: FOLLOW MICROSOFT'S BLOGS ABOUT NEW CAPABILITIES IN MOBILE DEVICE MANAGEMENT**
>
> Microsoft releases significant updates to its mobile device management capabilities about every three months. You should follow the blogs listed here to learn about the new features in the upcoming releases:
>
> http://blogs.technet.com/b/windowsintune/
>
> http://go.microsoft.com/fwlink/?LinkId=191941
>
> http://blogs.technet.com/b/configurationmgr/

Prerequisites of Mobile Device Management

Following are prerequisites for using the new hybrid mobile device management features with Configuration Manager:

▶ **Windows Intune account:** The organization must create a Windows Intune account. Microsoft has a separate Windows Intune license (Windows Intune Add-on for System Center Configuration Manager) exclusively for mobile device management for existing Configuration Manager customers.

Note that normal Windows PCs managed on the same Windows Intune account are not synchronized to the Configuration Manager database.

▶ **User account synchronization:** Local Active Directory (AD) users must be synchronized to Microsoft Azure Active Directory (AAD), using the DirSync utility. DirSync synchronizes user accounts and optionally password hashes to AAD. If password hashes are not synchronized to AAD, the users would need different passwords to the local AD and to AAD.

Some organizations are uncomfortable with password hashes stored in a cloud service. With Active Directory Federation Services (ADFS), the user's password authentication request is forwarded to the local AD. Thus, the password hashes are not stored on AAD, but the user can logon to Windows Intune with the same password used in the local AD.

▶ **Security certificates:** Each mobile device platform might have its own requirements for management; for example, Apple devices require an Apple Push Notification service (APNs) certificate, and Windows Phone 8.x devices require specific certificates.

▶ **Windows Intune connector:** Configuration Manager includes a new site system role, the Windows Intune Connector role. This role synchronizes content from the local Configuration Manager to a Windows Intune account and vice versa.

These prerequisites are discussed in more detail in Chapter 7, "Using the Intune Connector."

Windows Intune hybrid management supports the following operating systems:

▶ **Windows RT 8.0 or 8.1:** Microsoft has not created a Configuration Manager agent for the Windows RT operating system. You must use Windows Intune to manage Windows RT devices centrally, using the OMA-Device Management (OMA-DM) interface.

▶ **Windows 8.1 Professional/Enterprise (x86/x64):** You can manage Windows 8.1 Professional/Enterprise devices with a full Configuration Manager client or the OMA-DM interface (that is, like a mobile device). OMA-DM based management is a new feature of Windows 8.1 targeted to BYOD scenarios; it provides the same management features offered to other mobile devices. OMA-DM managed clients cannot be members of a domain.

▶ **Windows Phone 8 or 8.1:** Windows Phone versions 8 and 8.1 can be managed with Windows Intune. Management features are part of Windows Phone 8.x OS. Windows Phone 8.1 management capabilities are significantly improved from

Windows Phone 8. The authors recommend you upgrade existing Windows Phone 8 devices to 8.1 to utilize the new features.

▶ **Android:** Android version must be version 4.0 or later. Because Google has not provided a management agent to Android OS, Microsoft has built its own OMA-DM based agent for Android 4.x devices. It is part of company portal application.

Samsung KNOX Standard devices are also supported. Intune automatically identifies KNOX devices and uses KNOX APIs to manage those devices instead of generic Android OMA-DM agent. KNOX Premium features are not currently supported.

▶ **iOS:** All devices running iOS version 6.x or 7.x are supported. These include iPhones, iPod Touches, and iPads. Microsoft uses the built-in management agent within iOS devices.

ConfigMgr 2012 R2 customers require the Windows Intune Add-on for System Center Configuration Manager license to manage users' mobile devices. Each user license covers managing up to five devices for a licensed user.

Enrolling Mobile Devices

Before Configuration Manager can manage a mobile device, the user must enroll it. The enrollment process associates the device with a specific Windows Intune account.

To log on to Windows Intune successfully, the user account must be associated with the correct user principal name (UPN) and be a member of a collection allowed to enroll devices. This collection is specified when adding the Windows Intune subscription.

The enrollment process is the same regardless of the platform; the company portal application is needed on the device, and the user must provide the correct credentials to the Windows Intune.

NOTE: CANNOT RENAME DEVICES IN CONFIGMGR CONSOLE

After a device is enrolled, you cannot rename it from the ConfigMgr console. The device can be renamed in the company portal, but the new name is displayed in the company portal only, not in the ConfigMgr console.

Microsoft will support bulk enrollment of Android and iOS devices by the end of 2014 with the new Windows Intune version. See the following blog article for more information: http://blogs.technet.com/b/windowsintune/archive/2014/05/12/what-s-coming-next-with-windows-intune.aspx.

The next sections discuss enrolling specific device types.

Enrolling Windows Phone 8 Devices

To enroll a Windows Phone 8.1 device, the user should follow these steps on the device:

1. Go to **Settings -> Workplace**, select **add account**, and provide credentials to Windows Intune, as shown in Figure 8.3. (For Windows Phone 8 devices, go to **Settings -> Company Apps**.)

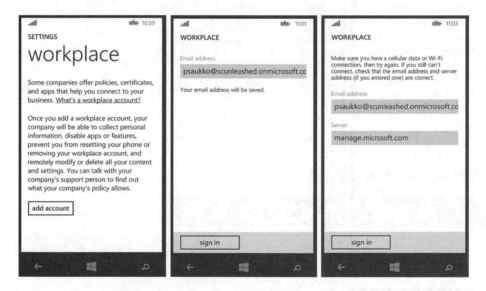

FIGURE 8.3   Providing credentials when enrolling a Windows Phone 8.1 device.

2. During enrollment, the device must contact manage.microsoft.com. If the company has not created a CNAME record from enterpriseenrollment.*your-domain-name* to manage.microsoft.com, the user must manually type in the server address of **manage.microsoft.com**.

3. The user must then accept installing the company app (see Figure 8.4). The company app is defined when you enable Windows Phone 8 support in Windows Intune subscription properties with the ConfigMgr console.

When the device is enrolled, it appears in the Configuration Manager console as *username*-WindowsPhone-#, such that psaukko-WindowsPhone-1 is the name for the first Windows Phone 8.x enrolled by the user psaukko.

TIP: UPDATING REFRESH POLICIES ON WINDOWS PHONE 8.1 DEVICES

Windows Phone 8.x devices refresh policies every 8 hours. You can update policies immediately on Windows Phone 8.x devices: Select **Settings -> Workplace ->** *<environment name>* and select the refresh icon shown in Figure 8.5.

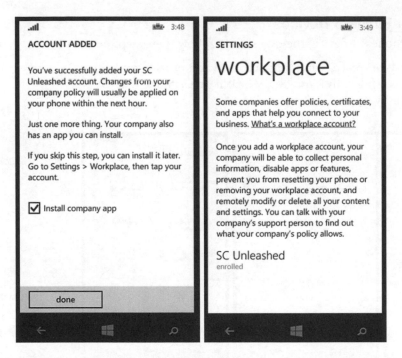

FIGURE 8.4   Installing the company app when enrolling a Windows Phone 8.1 device.

FIGURE 8.5   Refresh policy on Windows Phone 8.1.

Enrolling Windows 8.1 Devices

Users can enroll Windows 8.1 devices through **PC Settings -> Network -> Workplace**. Have the user follow these steps:

1. Type in the Windows Intune username and select **Turn on**.

2. Enter the credentials to Windows Intune, and agree that the device is to be managed as seen in Figure 8.6.

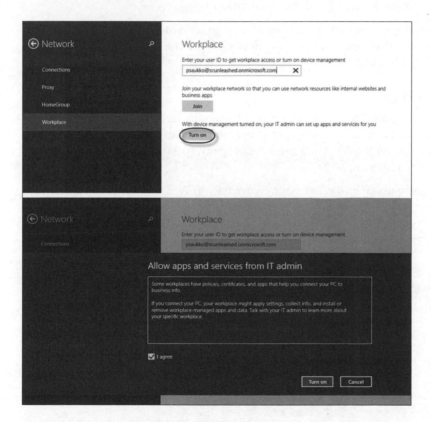

FIGURE 8.6   Enrolling a Windows 8.1 device.

The process is the same for Windows 8.1 RT and Professional/Enterprise devices. Joining the Windows 8.1 computer to a domain causes the device management option to disappear. Typically domain joined computers are managed with the full ConfigMgr client.

When you click **Turn on**, the Windows 8.1 device tries to connect to enterpriseenrollment.*your-domain-name*. Consequently, you should have defined a CNAME record of enterpriseenrollment.*your-domain-name*, which points to manage.microsoft. com. You cannot manually enter the server name when enrolling a Windows 8.1 device as during the Windows Phone 8 enrollment process. If you are unable to create a CNAME record, you can create the following Registry parameter:

```
HKEY_LOCAL_MACHINE\SOFTWARE\Policies\Microsoft\Windows\CurrentVersion\MDM:
DiscoveryService (REG_SZ) = manage.microsoft.com
```

After the device is enrolled successfully, the computer appears with its computer name in the ConfigMgr console.

Differing from Windows Phone 8, Windows 8.1 devices refresh policies every 24 hours by default. To refresh policies on Windows 8.1 devices manually, start a command prompt with administrative permissions and run the command `mdmagent.exe`.

The user should install the company portal application from Windows Store. Without the company portal, the user cannot install any applications. The company portal can be installed before or after turning on the management features.

Enrolling iOS Devices

The first part of enrolling an iOS device is to install the company portal application from App Store. You can find the application by searching for **company portal**. The official name of the application is "Windows Intune Company Portal." After the portal is installed, complete the following steps:

1. Start the company portal and enter your credentials to Windows Intune. After a successful login, the main window of the company portal displays. Your new iOS device is displayed under My Devices with a small Information icon. Select the device, and then select **Add device** to start the enrollment process. This is shown in Figure 8.7.

FIGURE 8.7   Starting the enrollment process for an iOS device.

2. Confirm the addition of the device and approve the installation of the management profile. Enter the passcode to accept the installation (see Figure 8.8).

FIGURE 8.8   Adding the iOS device and approving installation of the management profile.

3. A warning appears stating that by adding a management profile, your iOS device can be managed. When the process is complete, the iOS device is shown normally in the company portal as in Figure 8.9, under My Devices without the information icon.

FIGURE 8.9   Completing enrollment of an iOS device.

The iOS device appears in the ConfigMgr console with the name configured in the device's General settings. This is shown in Figure 8.10.

TIP: GIVE A UNIQUE NAME TO AN iOS DEVICE BEFORE ENROLLING

Because you cannot rename a device after it is enrolled, you should provide a unique name for all iOS devices before enrolling them. Include instructions for renaming an iOS device before enrollment in the same user document that discusses enrolling the device.

---

iOS devices check policies every 24 hours. You cannot manually refresh policies on iOS devices.

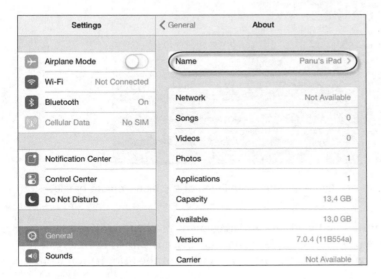

FIGURE 8.10   iOS device name.

Enrolling Android Devices

Enrolling Android devices is similar to enrolling iOS devices:

▶ Install the Windows Intune company portal from Google Play.

▶ Start the company portal application, log on with your Windows Intune credentials, and from the company portal's main window, select your new device -> **Add device**.

Android devices follow the same naming standard as a Windows Phone device:

username-AndroidDevice-#

In this example, psaukko-AndroidDevice-1 would be the name of the first Android device that user psaukko enrolls.

Android devices check policies every 8 hours. You cannot manually refresh policies on Android devices.

Inventorying Mobile Devices

The ability to inventory mobile devices is one of the primary benefits of mobile device management. Inventory provides organizations with a better understanding of the types of mobile devices being utilized by their users. The following information is typically needed from the mobile devices:

▶ Manufacturer and model of the device.

▶ Operating system and version.

▶ Unique identifier of the device. This could be the IMEI (International Mobile Equipment Identity) of a mobile phone or the serial number of a device.

▶ Information about the mobile phone's SIM (subscriber identity module) card (for example, telephone number and carrier).

After the enrollment process is complete, the device sends the discovery data record and hardware inventory to Windows Intune; ConfigMgr's Windows Intune connector then downloads the information from Intune to the Configuration Manager database.

Mobile devices follow the same inventory schedule as other Configuration Manager clients. Unlike normal ConfigMgr clients, hardware inventory cannot be forced from mobile devices. The device reports its inventory only during the defined schedule.

Available Discovery and Inventory Data

Mobile devices also report discovery data. Table 8.1 lists available and relevant discovery items for the different mobile platforms (Windows Phone 8.x, iOS, Android). The discovery data from a mobile device is slightly different than that of a full ConfigMgr client.

TABLE 8.1   Discovery Information from Windows Phone 8.x, iOS, and Android Mobile Devices

Discovery Information	WP 8.x	iOS	Android
Agent edition	✓	✓	✓
CPU type	—	✓	✓
Client version	✓	✓	✓
Client type	✓	✓	✓
Exchange device ID	✓	✓	—
Hardware ID (MAC address)	—	✓	—
Name	✓	✓	✓
NetBIOS name	✓	✓	✓
OS name and Version	✓ (No version)	✓	✓ (No version)

The Client Type field is naturally Mobile for the mobile devices, with a numeric value of 3. The numeric value is needed should you want to query all mobile devices.

> **NOTE: MAC CLIENTS ARE ALSO "MOBILE" CLIENTS**
>
> Remember that all OS X clients have Client Type = Mobile.

Because mobile devices do not install the ConfigMgr client, the Client Version field contains the operating system version of the mobile device. This might be confusing if you run the Count of Configuration Manager clients by client version report or create a query for a specific client version (see Figure 8.11).

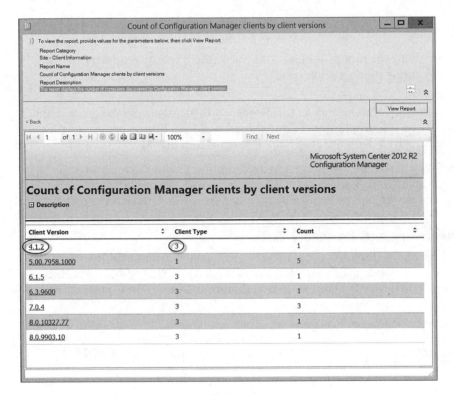

FIGURE 8.11   Client versions of mobile clients.

Because each operating system can report slightly different data, you do not get exactly the same inventory information from different operating systems. Figure 8.12 shows those inventory classes that are collected from different mobile device platforms.

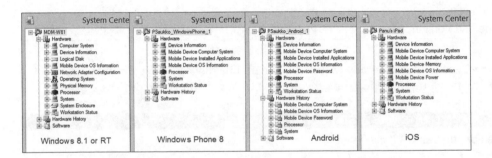

FIGURE 8.12   Hardware inventory from different mobile device platforms.

Notice in Figure 8.12 that hardware inventory history from mobile devices shows classes that have not changed from the previous inventory. All mobile devices always report the full inventory, and the site server does not process the delta between two hardware inventory cycles.

Table 8.2 lists the information available from different mobile operating systems:

▶ Windows Phone 8.x devices do not report IMEI information as a part of hardware inventory. However, you can get the IMEI from these devices with the Exchange ActiveSync connector. This is a benefit of using both Windows Intune and the Exchange ActiveSync connector with ConfigMgr.

▶ Android devices should report both Phone Number and Subscriber Carrier Network, although this depends on the combination of Android model, OS version, and firmware version.

   Android devices display a specific class: Mobile Device Password, which contains information about device's password settings. Mobile Device Power shows the battery's charge percent; this class is only for iOS devices.

▶ iOS devices provide the most complete hardware inventory of the three mobile platforms (Android, iOS, and Windows Phone 8.x).

▶ Windows 8.1 devices report slightly more information than Windows Phone 8.x, Android, and iOS devices. You can get information about logical disk partition, network adapter information (IP and MAC addresses), and physical memory. However, this is significantly less than what you can get from a Windows 8.1 device with a full ConfigMgr client.

TABLE 8.2   Inventory Information from Windows Phone 8.x, iOS, and Android Mobile Devices

Mobile Device Computer System	WP 8.x	iOS	Android
Product	—	✓	—
Product version	—	✓	—
Cellular technology	—	✓	✓
Device client ID	—	✓	—
Device manufacturer	✓	✓	✓
Device model	✓	✓	✓
DM version	✓	—	✓
Firmware version	✓	—	✓
Hardware version	✓	—	✓
IMEI	—	✓	✓
MEID	—	✓	—
OEM	✓	✓	✓

8

Mobile Device Computer System	WP 8.x	iOS	Android
Phone number	—	✓	✓
Platform type	✓	✓	✓
Processor architecture	✓	—	—
Processor level	✓	—	—
Processor revision	—	—	—
Serial number	—	✓	✓
Software version	✓	✓	✓
Subscriber carrier network	—	✓	✓
Jailbroken or rooted device	—	✓	✓
Mobile Device OS Information			
Language	✓	—	✓
Platform	✓	✓	✓
Version	✓	✓	✓
Mobile Device Memory			
Storage free (KB)	—	✓	—
Storage total (KB)	—	✓	—
Mobile Device Password			
Require device password	✓	—	✓
Device password minimum length	✓	—	✓
Mobile Device Power			
Battery percent	—	✓	—
Processor			
Description	✓	✓	✓
Device ID	—	—	—

Hardware inventory shows you which Android and iOS devices have been jailbroken or rooted. Jailbreaking usually refers to iOS devices and permits root access to the device's file system and manager, allowing the download of content that is unavailable through the official application store. Rooting is the process to get full access to Android devices. Those devices could introduce a security risk and you might want to block access from rooted devices. ConfigMgr includes a built-in query and a report to help you easily find jailbroken or rooted devices.

Root detection is run periodically on devices. It uses multiple different tests to find rooted devices. Microsoft continuously updates the detection logic to identify new ways to identify compromised devices.

Personal Versus Company-Owned Devices

Configuration Manager 2012 R2 lets you define an enrolled device as either personal-owned or company-owned. All mobile devices are personal-owned by default after enrollment. The ConfigMgr administrator can change the device from personal to a company device or vice versa by using the Change Ownership action, as shown in Figure 8.13. The option is available by right-clicking a mobile device in the ConfigMgr console.

FIGURE 8.13   Editing device ownership.

All devices with full ConfigMgr clients or that are domain-joined are considered company devices; the Change Ownership action is not available for those devices.

Hardware inventory from personal devices contains only that software installed by ConfigMgr. Android and iOS devices marked as company-owned report all software titles on a device. Windows Phone 8.x devices report only applications installed by ConfigMgr, regardless of the device ownership setting.

Device ownership affects software deployments to mobile devices. Required deployments are only available when the device is defined as company-owned.

Managing Mobile Device Settings

Perhaps the most common business reason for implementing mobile device management is to ensure that the necessary security settings (password settings) are enabled on mobile devices. This can be achieved by utilizing ConfigMgr's settings management feature.

Each management technology (Exchange ActiveSync, in-depth management, and Windows Intune/ConfigMgr hybrid management) supports different selections of the available settings. Exchange ActiveSync has the most limited set of potential settings, although it includes the most commonly used password settings. Microsoft has not improved the feature set of Exchange ActiveSync or in-depth management since ConfigMgr 2012 RTM. Hybrid management has the most complete selection of settings.

Settings management is located in the ConfigMgr console under Assets and Compliance -> Compliance Settings. Mobile device settings can be defined using configuration items or configuration baselines; ConfigMgr 2012 R2 has new options under Company Resource Access, as highlighted in Figure 8.14.

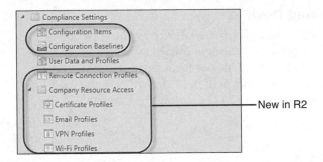

FIGURE 8.14   Mobile device-related settings.

Compliance status of mobile devices is found in the ConfigMgr console under Monitoring -> Deployments, similar to that of any other deployment. You could also use reports from Reporting -> Reports -> Compliance and Settings Management.

Certificate, VPN, and Wi-Fi profiles are only available using Intune-integrated management. Windows 8.1 mobile devices, Windows Phone 8.1, and iOS support all three profiles; Android devices support only certificate and Wi-Fi profiles. Windows Phone 8 cannot utilize these new management features.

As of mid-2014, Microsoft has released three extensions for Windows Intune:

▶ **Email profiles extension:** This enables configuring email profiles to Windows Phone 8.x and iOS devices.

▶ **iOS 7 security settings:** These are new configuration items for managing iOS 7-specific settings.

▶ **Windows Phone 8.1 extension:** This extension is required to support Windows Phone 8.1 devices.

Installing Windows Intune extensions is discussed in Chapter 7.

Configuration Items for Mobile Devices

To create a new configuration item for a mobile device, select **Configuration Items -> Create Configuration Item -> Mobile device**. Figure 8.15 shows the different settings categories for mobile devices.

Although some settings are visible in the ConfigMgr console, this does not mean you can force a setting to all mobile device platforms. If the operating system doesn't support the setting, it cannot be enforced on the platform. Two categories (Email Management and Peak Synchronization) include settings supported only on Windows Mobile 6.x or Symbian Belle devices. Ignore these categories if you don't have one of those devices.

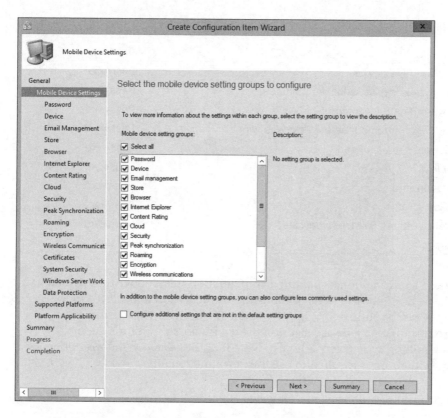

FIGURE 8.15   Mobile device configuration item categories.

Configuration item based certificate management is only supported on Windows Mobile 6.x, Symbian Belle, and Windows 8 devices. Use Company Resource Access -> Certificate Profiles to manage certificates on other devices such as Android, iOS, Windows Phone 8.1, and Windows 8.1.

In addition, many settings in other categories affect only Windows Mobile 6.x or Symbian Belle devices. The following tables list what configuration items could be deployed to Windows Phone 8, Windows Phone 8.1, Android, iOS, or Windows 8.1 devices.

Windows Phone 8 and Android have quite a limited number of supported settings as shown in Table 8.3 and Table 8.5. Most settings are related to passwords. Samsung KNOX devices support many oth'er settings; Microsoft will add support for additional Samsung KNOX settings in future releases of ConfigMgr.

TABLE 8.3   Supported Configuration Items for Windows Phone 8 Devices

Setting	Category
File encryption on mobile device	Encryption
Idle time before mobile device is locked (minutes)	Password
Minimum password length (characters)	Password
Number of failed logon attempts before device is wiped	Password
Number of passwords remembered	Password
Password complexity	Password
Password expiration in days	Password
Allow simple password	Password
Require password settings on mobile devices	Password
Removable storage	Security

Windows Phone 8.1 has additional supported configuration items above those available in Windows Phone 8. Windows Phone 8.1 adds the configuration items listed in Table 8.4. Settings can be pushed to Windows Phone 8.1 devices. This means that a setting is enforced sooner on a device, because the device doesn't wait for the next scheduled policy polling cycle (every 8 hours). Note that the related Windows Phone 8.1 Windows Intune extension is required to use the new functionality.

TABLE 8.4   Additional Configuration Items for Windows Phone 8.1 Devices

Setting	Category
Default browser	Browser
Microsoft Account	Cloud
Settings synchronization	Cloud
Copy and paste	Device
Diagnostic data submission	Device
Geolocation	Device
Screen capture	Device
Camera	Security
Bluetooth	Security
Near field communication (NFC)	Security
Disable application store	Store
Offload data to Wi-Fi when possible	Wireless Communication
Wi-Fi hotspot reporting	Wireless Communication
Wi-Fi tethering	Wireless Communication
Wireless network connection	Wireless Communication

TABLE 8.5   Supported Configuration Items for Android and Samsung KNOX Devices

Setting	Category
File encryption on mobile device	Encryption
Idle time before mobile device is locked (minutes)	Password
Minimum password length (characters)	Password
Number of failed logon attempts before device is wiped	Password
Number of passwords remembered	Password
Password expiration in days	Password
Password quality	Password
Require password settings on mobile devices	Password
Camera (Android 4.1 or later)	Security

Using ConfigMgr 2012 R2, you can set a large number of different iOS-related settings as listed in Table 8.6.

TABLE 8.6   Supported Configuration Items for iOS Devices

Setting	Category
Accept cookies in browser	Browser
Allow AutoFill in browser	Browser
Allow Browser	Browser
Allow JavaScript in browser	Browser
Allow pop-ups in browser	Browser
Force fraud warning in browser	Browser
Cloud backup	Cloud
Document synchronization	Cloud
Encrypted backup	Cloud
Photo synchronization	Cloud
App rating	Content Rating
Explicit content in media store	Content Rating
Movie rating	Content Rating
Rating region	Content Rating
TV show rating	Content Rating
Add game center friends	Device
Diagnostic data submission	Device
Multiplayer gaming	Device
Personal wallet software while locked	Device
Screen capture	Device
Video chat client	Device

8

Setting	Category
Voice assistant	Device
Voice assistant while locked	Device
Voice dialing	Device
Allow simple password	Password
Idle time before mobile device is locked (minutes)	Password
Maximum grace period	Password
Minimum complex characters	Password
Minimum password length (characters)	Password
Number of failed logon attempts before device is wiped	Password
Number of passwords remembered	Password
Password complexity	Password
Password expiration in days	Password
Require password settings on mobile devices	Password
Allow data roaming	Roaming
Allow global background fetch when roaming	Roaming
Allow voice roaming	Roaming
Allow Application Installations	Security
Camera	Security
Infrared	Security
Application store	Store
Force Application Store password	Store
In-app purchases	Store
User to accept untrusted TLS certificates	System Security

The settings in Table 8.7 are available if the iOS 7 security settings Windows Intune extension is deployed.

TABLE 8.7   iOS 7 Security Settings

Setting	Category
Lock screen control center	System Security
Lock screen notification view	System Security
Lock screen today view	System Security
Fingerprint for unlocking	System Security
Open managed documents in unmanaged apps	Data Protection
Open unmanaged documents in managed apps	Data Protection

There is also a wide selection of settings that can be targeted to Windows 8.1 devices, listed in Table 8.8.

TABLE 8.8   Supported Configuration Items for Windows 8.1 Devices

Setting	Category
Allow AutoFill in browser	Browser
Allow JavaScript in browser	Browser
Allow pop-ups in browser	Browser
Force fraud warning in browser	Browser
Allow plug-ins	Browser
Credentials synchronization	Cloud
Settings synchronization	Cloud
Settings synchronization over metered connections	Cloud
Diagnostic data submission	Device
File encryption on mobile device	Encryption
Always send Do Not Track header	Internet Explorer
Go to intranet site for single word entry	Internet Explorer
Intranet security zone	Internet Explorer
Namespace exists for intranet zone	Internet Explorer
Security level for internet zone	Internet Explorer
Security level for intranet zone	Internet Explorer
Security level for restricted sites zone	Internet Explorer
Security level for trusted sites zone	Internet Explorer
Idle time before mobile device is locked (minutes)	Password
Minimum complex characters	Password
Minimum password length (characters)	Password
Number of failed logon attempts before device is wiped	Password
Number of passwords remembered	Password
Password complexity	Password
Password expiration in days	Password
Allow convenience logon	Password
Allow data roaming	Roaming
Bluetooth	Security
Network firewall	System Security
SmartScreen	System Security
Updates	System Security
User Access Control	System Security

8

Setting	Category
Virus protection	System Security
Virus protection signatures are up-to-date	System Security
Work folders URL	Windows Server Work Folders

You must select **Remediate noncompliant settings** while creating a new configuration item if you want to force a setting (see Figure 8.16). All configuration items related to mobile devices support remediation.

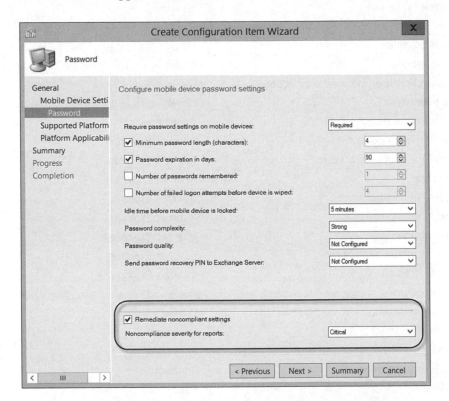

FIGURE 8.16   Mobile device configuration item remediation settings.

Configuration items must be added to a configuration baseline and the baseline deployed to the correct collection. Select **Remediate noncompliant rules when supported** for the deployment.

NOTE: DO NOT SET DIFFERENT VALUES TO CONFIGURATION ITEMS AND ASSIGN THEM TO THE SAME DEVICES

When mobile devices evaluate configuration items from multiple configuration baselines that have conflicting values, the order in which they are evaluated is nondeterministic.

Creating Custom Configuration Items for Mobile Devices

Mobile devices can support settings not visible in the ConfigMgr console. ConfigMgr allows administrators to create custom settings based on Registry or Open Mobile Alliance - Unified Resource Identifier (OMA-URI) settings. This is a useful feature for enhancing mobile device management capabilities.

The correct OMA-URI values can be found from the manufacturer's technical documentation. As an example, Microsoft has published the "Windows Phone 8.1 Enterprise Device Management Protocol" whitepaper (see http://go.microsoft.com/fwlink/?LinkID=279003), which lists OMA-URI values of possible settings in Windows Phone 8.1.

Complete the following steps to create a new custom OMA-URI based configuration item to disable the unenrollment of a Windows Phone 8.1 device:

1. In the ConfigMgr console, navigate to **Assets and Compliance -> Compliance Settings -> Configuration Items**. Select **Create Configuration Item**.

2. Provide a name and optional description for the new configuration item. Select **Mobile device** as the type of configuration item.

3. On the Mobile Device Settings page, select **Configure additional settings that are not in the default settings groups**.

4. On the Additional Settings page, click **Add**. In the Browse Settings dialog box, select **Create Setting**.

5. On the Create Setting page, provide a name and an optional description for the new setting. Select **OMA URI** in the Setting type drop-down and select an appropriate Data type. Provide the correct OMA-URI value; this value is case-sensitive. Figure 8.17 shows an example of a new setting that allows/disallows the manual unenrollment of a Windows Phone 8.1 device.

6. After creating the new setting, select it from Browse Settings dialog box.

7. On the Create Rule page, configure the correct value for the rule. Figure 8.18 shows that unenrolling Windows Phone 8.1 devices is not allowed.

8. On the Supported Platforms page, select the correct supported platforms.

Creating a custom configuration item is a simple process if the right OMA-URI value is known. After the setting is created, it can be added to a baseline and deployed to collections.

Remote Connection Profiles

Remote connection profiles are new with ConfigMgr 2012 R2; they enable users to start a remote desktop connection to their primary devices. If the organization has implemented a Remote Desktop Gateway server, the user can connect to his primary device from any Windows workstation or Android/iOS device with a remote desktop client outside the organization's internal network.

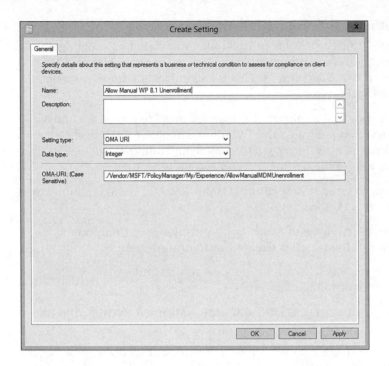

FIGURE 8.17   Creating a custom setting to allow/disallow manual unenrollment of a Windows Phone 8.1 device.

FIGURE 8.18   Disallow manual unenrollment of Windows Phone 8.1 devices.

On-premise Windows workstations with a full ConfigMgr client require a remote connection policy that enables the remote desktop service and grants Remote Desktop permission to the primary users of the device. When the policy is compliant on the device, ConfigMgr informs the Intune service of those users with compliant primary devices and the server name of the Remote Desktop Gateway. When a user logs on to the company portal, the user sees his primary devices on the portal and can start a remote desktop connection directly from the company portal as shown in Figure 8.19. While the source client must be a Windows client, it doesn't have to be managed by ConfigMgr/Intune. The user can log on to any Windows computer or Android/iOS device with a remote desktop client, sign in to the company portal website, and initiate a remote connection from there. The remote desktop client can also be initiated from the company portal application on a managed device.

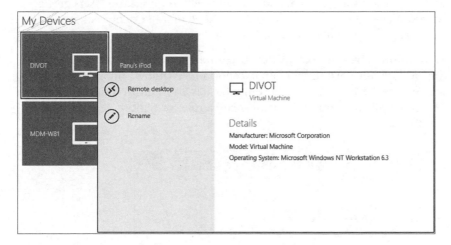

FIGURE 8.19   Starting a remote desktop connection to a primary device from the company portal.

Follow these steps to create a new remote connection profile:

1. In the ConfigMgr console, navigate to **Assets and Compliance -> Compliance Settings -> Remote Connection Profiles**. Select **Create Remote Connection Profile** from the ribbon bar to create a new profile.

2. Give a name to the new profile.

3. Define the settings for the profile (see Figure 8.20):

   ▶ **Full name and port of the Remote Desktop Gateway Server (optional):** Enter the fully qualified domain name (FQDN) of the remote desktop gateway server and the port. Port 443 is the default port to connect to the gateway server.

   If the name of the gateway server is not provided, the profile enables remote desktop services and grants primary users the right to connect using Remote

Desktop. In this case, users outside the company's internal network must initiate a VPN connection to access their primary devices.

▶ **Allow connections only from computers that run Remote Desktop with Network Level Authentication:** Because this setting improves security and all current client computers support Network Level Authentication, this should be enabled.

▶ **Allow remote connections to work computers:** Enables remote desktop services on a client.

▶ **Allow all primary users of the work computer to remotely connect:** Grants the primary users of a computer the right to start a remote desktop connection. ConfigMgr creates the Remote PC Connect local group for this purpose. In addition, the primary users are added to the Remote Desktop Users group. Do not manually add or remove users from the Remote PC Connect group, because this group is managed by the ConfigMgr client.

▶ **Allow Windows Firewall exception for connections on Windows domain and on private network:** Creates an exception to Windows firewall to enable remote desktop connections. If the computer has another firewall beside the Windows firewall, you must manually create a rule for remote desktop connections (port 3389).

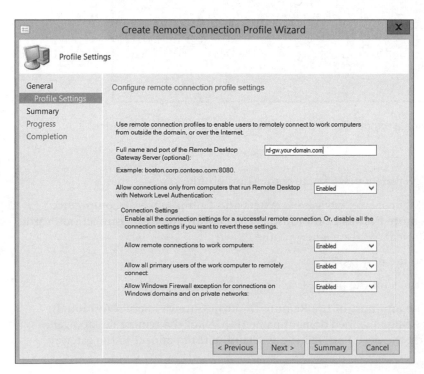

FIGURE 8.20   Creating a remote connection profile.

The last three connection-related settings must all be either enabled or disabled. You cannot have one setting enabled and two settings disabled or vice versa.

NOTE: REMOTE CONNECTION PROFILE SETTINGS ARE STORED IN THE LOCAL POLICY

You can also modify remote desktop settings with group policy or using ConfigMgr's client settings. Remote connection profile settings and ConfigMgr client settings are stored in the local policy of the client computer. Because group policy settings override local policies, you should not target the same settings with group policy if you want to manage remote desktop settings using ConfigMgr. Do not enable Remote Desktop with a Remote Connection profile and disable Remote Desktop with client agent settings or vice versa.

Deploy remote desktop profiles to those device collections containing Windows workstations with a full ConfigMgr client. Select **Assets and Compliance -> Compliance Settings -> Remote Connection Profiles**. Right-click the profile you created, and select **Deploy**. You must define a collection for the policy. You must enable the **Remediate noncompliant rules when supported** option when creating a new deployment. Only compliant devices are reported to Windows Intune and appear in the company portal.

Company Resource Access

Under Company Resource Access, you find three new ConfigMgr 2012 R2 features: certificate, VPN, and Wi-Fi profiles. Email profiles are available if the corresponding extension for Windows Intune has been deployed. These are discussed in the following sections.

Certificate Profiles

Mobile devices might require certificates to initiate VPN and wireless connections or with email profiles. With certificate profiles, you can deploy one of the following:

▶ **Trusted CA certificate:** You can deploy a trusted root certificate authority (CA) or intermediate CA certificate to form a certificate chain of trust when the device must authenticate a server.

▶ **Simple Certificate Enrollment Protocol (SCEP) settings:** This feature allows users or devices to request a certificate by using SCEP protocol. This requires that the Network Device Enrollment Service role is running on a Windows Server 2012 R2 server. You must have at least one trusted CA certificate profile before you can create a SCEP certificate profile.

Certificate profiles can be deployed to iOS, Windows 8.1, Windows RT 8.1, Windows Phone 8.1, and Android devices.

Before creating a Trusted CA Certificate profile, you must have exported your certificate as a .CER file and have Read access to the file. Then point to the certificate file and select the destination store as shown in Figure 8.21.

8

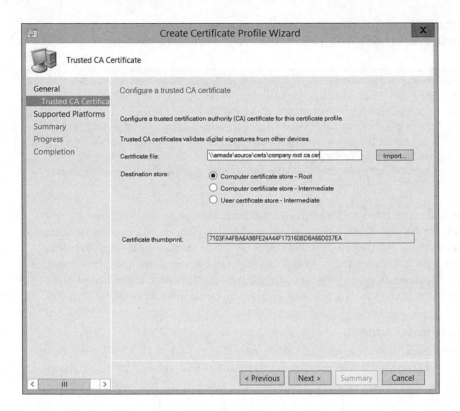

FIGURE 8.21   Creating a new trusted CA certificate profile.

The SCEP settings profile is more complex to implement, because it requires a Windows Server 2012 R2 server with the Network Device Enrollment Service role. This scenario requires at least two different servers:

▶ **Active Directory Certificate Services (AD CS) based-enterprise issuing certification authority server:** The CA server can be Windows Server 2008 R2, Windows Server 2012, or Windows Server 2012 R2. The certificate templates used to issue certificates must be configured for Supply in the request for the certificate subject. ConfigMgr automatically supplies the correct subject name.

▶ **Network Device Enrollment Service role server:** Windows Server 2012 R2 is the only supported operating system for this role, and mobile devices must be able to access this server from the Internet. Only the default HTTPS (TCP 443) or HTTP (TCP 80) ports are supported.

The Certificate Registration Point site system role must be installed before SCEP certificate profiles can be used. The role cannot be installed on the same server that runs the Network Device Enrollment Service role. Additional information about configuring certificate enrollment profiles is available with the ConfigMgr documentation at http://technet. microsoft.com/en-us/library/dn270539.aspx.

ConfigMgr automatically revokes user and computer certificates deployed by certificate profiles if the device is retired, wiped, or blocked from the ConfigMgr environment.

Three reports in the Company Resource Access folder relate to certificate profiles:

▶ History of certificates issued by the certificate registration point

▶ List of assets by certificate issuance state for certificates enrolled by the certificate registration point

▶ List of assets with certificates that are close to their expiration date

Email Profiles

Email profiles are available if the email profiles extension is enabled. This feature can automatically configure Exchange ActiveSync email profiles to iOS and Windows Phone 8.x devices. The Exchange ActiveSync host can be Exchange Server 2007 - 2013 or Office 365.

Complete the following steps to create a new email profile:

1. In the ConfigMgr console, navigate to **Assets and Compliance -> Compliance Settings -> Company Resource Access -> Email Profiles**. Select **Create Exchange ActiveSync Profile**.

2. Provide a name and an optional description for the new profile.

3. On the Exchange ActiveSync page, configure the correct account settings. The following settings are available and displayed in Figure 8.22.

   ▶ **Exchange ActiveSync host:** FQDN of the ActiveSync host. The host name is outlook.office365.com when using Office 365.

   ▶ **Account name:** The name of the email account. An account name makes it easier for users to distinguish their corporate email account from their personal email accounts.

   ▶ **Account user name:** The user account name is either the user's UPN or an alias. The alias refers to the user logon name (sAMAccountName attribute) in Active Directory. Exchange Server supports both methods. Office 365 supports only UPNs.

   ▶ **Email address:** The email address is either the user's primary SMTP address or UPN in Active Directory.

   ▶ **Account domain:** The value is automatically populated and cannot be changed.

   ▶ **Authentication method:** There are two authentication options: Certificates and Username and Password.

   Certificate-based authentication requires an identify certificate. This method of authentication is currently only supported in iOS and only for on-premise Exchange servers.

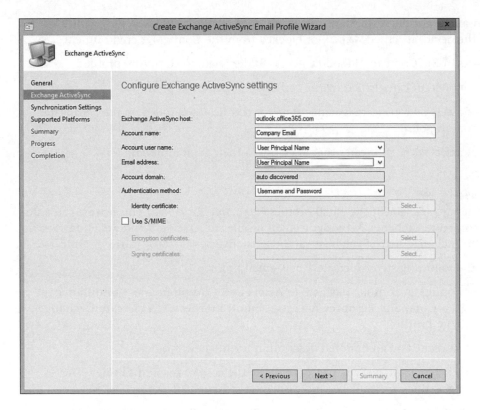

FIGURE 8.22   Exchange ActiveSync settings.

If Username and Password is selected, the user must provide a password to connect to Exchange ActiveSync. If the user's email address is not the same as his UPN, then domain\username and password are required as credentials.

▶ **Use S/MIME:** S/MIME protocol allows a sender to encrypt email content and digitally sign messages. This feature is supported for iOS and Windows Phone 8.1 devices.

4. On the Synchronization Settings page, configure the email client settings. The following settings are available (see Figure 8.23):

▶ **Schedule:** Specifies how often new emails are checked on a device.

▶ **Number of days of email to synchronize:** Defines the number of days the emails are stored on a mobile device.

▶ **Allow messages to be moved to other email accounts:** If selected, users can move email messages between different email accounts. The setting affects only iOS devices.

▶ **Allow messages to be sent from third-party applications:** Users can send email from other email applications. This setting affects only iOS devices.

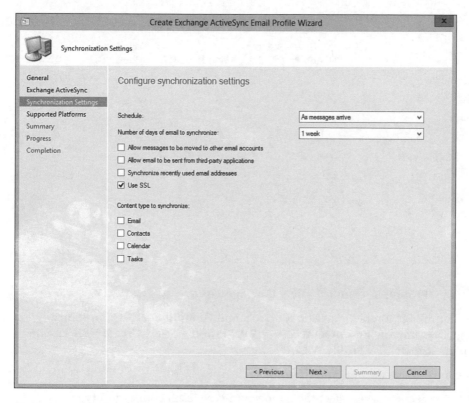

FIGURE 8.23   Exchange ActiveSync synchronization settings.

▶ **Synchronize recently used email addresses:** Allows users to synchronize the list of recently used email addresses. The setting affects only iOS devices.

▶ **Use SSL:** The device must use SSL to connect to ActiveSync server.

▶ **Content type to synchronize:** Select which content types are synchronized to Windows Phone 8.x devices. Available options are Email, Contacts, Calendar, and Tasks. By default, no content type is selected.

Email profiles must be deployed to user collections.

VPN Profiles

Administrators can define VPN profiles for users. This makes it easy for users to connect to corporate resources that require a VPN connection.

Some VPN profiles might need certificates for server validation or client authentication. You can deploy these certificates to devices by using ConfigMgr's certificate profiles.

VPN profiles are supported on Windows 8.1, Windows RT, Windows RT 8.1, Windows Phone 8.1, and iOS devices. ConfigMgr supports multiple different VPN technologies. Table 8.9 lists technologies supported on the various platforms.

TABLE 8.9   Supported VPN Connection Types

Connection Type	Windows 8.1 or Windows RT 8.1	Windows RT	Windows Phone 8.1	iOS
Cisco AnyConnect	—	—	—	✓
Juniper Pulse	✓	—	✓	✓
F5 Edge Client	✓	—	✓	✓
Dell SonicWALL Mobile Connect	✓	—	✓	✓
Check Point Mobile VPN	✓	—	✓	✓
Microsoft SSL (SSTP)	✓	✓	—	—
Microsoft Automatic	✓	✓	—	—
IKEv2	✓	✓	✓	—
PPTP	✓	✓	—	✓
L2TP	✓	✓	—	✓

To create a new VPN profile, complete the following steps:

1. In the ConfigMgr console, navigate to **Assets and Compliance -> Compliance Settings -> Company Resource Access -> VPN Profiles**. Select **Create VPN Profile** to start the Create VPN Profile Wizard.

2. Provide a name for the new connection.

3. On the Connection page, select the connection type. Each connection type has slightly different options. All connection types have two options in common:

   ▶ **Server list:** Define one or more VPN servers by entering a friendly name and IP address. If the connection type allows entering multiple VPN servers, iOS devices only use the default server.

   ▶ **Send all network traffic through the VPN connection:** All network traffic is sent through the VPN connection by default. If this setting is not selected, you can define that traffic for specific networks only is routed through a VPN connection. This is known as split or VPN tunneling. Automatic VPN connections require this setting be disabled.

   Figure 8.24 shows connection options when creating a L2TP-based VPN connection.

4. On the Authentication Method page, select the correct authentication method for the VPN connection. Available authentication methods differ between connections types. The following authentication methods and their supported connection types are available:

   ▶ **Certificates:** Cisco AnyConnect, Juniper Pulse, F5 Edge Client, Dell SonicWALL Mobile Connect, Check Point Mobile VPN

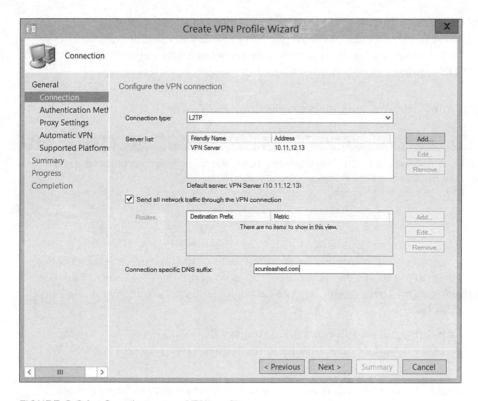

FIGURE 8.24   Creating a new VPN profile.

- ► **User name and Password:** Juniper Pulse, F5 Edge Client, Dell SonicWALL Mobile Connect, Check Point Mobile VPN

- ► **Microsoft EAP-TTLS:** Microsoft SSL (SSTP), Microsoft Automatic, IKEv2, PPTP, L2TP

- ► **Microsoft protected EAP (PEAP):** Microsoft SSL (SSTP), Microsoft Automatic, IKEv2, PPTP, and L2TP

- ► **Microsoft secured password (EAP-MSCHAP v2):** Microsoft SSL (SSTP), Microsoft Automatic, IKEv2, PPTP, and L2TP

- ► **Smart Card or other certificate:** Microsoft SSL (SSTP), Microsoft Automatic, IKEv2, PPTP, L2TP

- ► **MSCHAP v2:** Microsoft SSL (SSTP), Microsoft Automatic, PPTP, L2TP

- ► **RSA SecurID:** Microsoft SSL (SSTP), Microsoft Automatic, PPTP, L2TP

- ► **Use machine certificates:** IKEv2

5. Specify optional proxy server settings on the Proxy Settings page.

6. A VPN connection can be established automatically if needed; settings are defined on the Automatic VPN page of the wizard. If enabled, you must define the DNS suffixes, DNS server addresses, and the necessary action. Any network traffic to defined DNS suffixes automatically establishes the VPN connection.

VPN profiles can be deployed only to user collections.

> **NOTE: REMOVING A VPN PROFILE DOES NOT REMOVE THE PROFILE FROM DEVICES**
>
> A VPN profile is not removed from client devices when the deployment is removed. Users must manually remove the VPN profile.

Wi-Fi Profiles

Using Wi-Fi profiles, you can deploy wireless network settings to users. With this feature, users can easily connect to the wireless access points and have the correct authentication settings. Similar to VPN profiles, Wi-Fi profiles may need certificates for server validation or client authentication. These certificates can be deployed to devices using ConfigMgr's certificate profiles feature.

Wi-Fi profiles are supported on Windows 8.1, Windows RT, Windows RT 8.1, Windows Phone 8.1, iOS, and Android devices. Complete the following steps to create a new Wi-Fi profile:

1. In the ConfigMgr console, navigate to **Assets and Compliance -> Compliance Settings -> Company Resource Access -> Wi-Fi Profiles**. Select **Create Wi-Fi Profile**.

2. Provide a name for the new connection. You can also import settings from a configuration file that has been created on Windows 8.1 device. By default, the noncompliance severity for reports is Warning.

3. Enter information about the Wi-Fi profile as shown in Figure 8.25.

   Network name and SSID are required parameters.

4. On the Security Configuration page of the Create Wi-Fi Profile Wizard, select the appropriate Security type. You can select from the following security types:

   ▶ No authentication (Open)

   ▶ WPA - Personal

   ▶ WPA2 - Personal

   ▶ WPA - Enterprise

   ▶ WPA2 - Enterprise

   ▶ WEP

   ▶ 802.1x

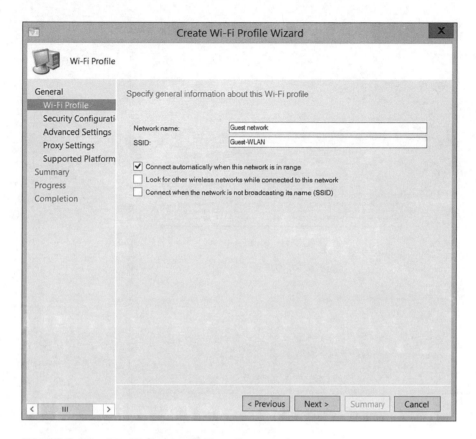

FIGURE 8.25   Creating a new Wi-Fi profile.

TIP: WI-FI PROFILES WITH A PRESHARED KEY

You cannot provide a preshared key using the graphical user interface. If you have WLAN access points that utilize preshared keys, you must first configure the correct key to a Windows 8.1 device. Then, export the policy using the following command:

```
netsh wlan export profile wlan-profile-name
```

Finally, create a new profile and use the option **Import an existing Wi-Fi profile item from a file.**

5. Define encryption and/or EAP types for most security type options. Depending on the selection, there might be additional options available.

For some security types, you must run the ConfigMgr console on the correct operating system version, because the setting might not be supported on an older version. For example, some EAP types are only supported on Windows Server 2012 R2 and Windows 8.1. If you run the console on Windows Server 2012, you receive the error message shown in Figure 8.26.

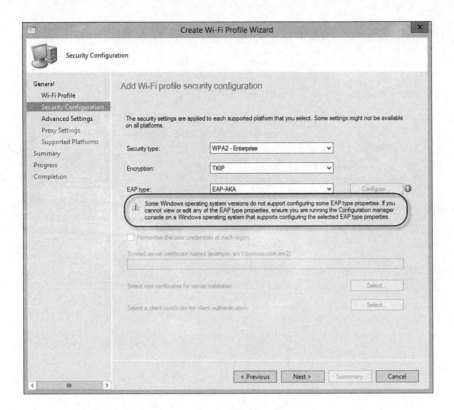

FIGURE 8.26   Wi-Fi profile security configuration.

6. Enter the any optional proxy settings for the Wi-Fi profile.

7. The last step of the wizard is to select supported platforms.

NOTE: REMOVING WI-FI PROFILES

Wi-Fi profiles are not removed from client devices when the deployment is removed. Users must manually remove these profiles.

You must have specific permissions to be able to create, modify, or deploy different profiles under Company Resource Access. There are new security permissions for Certificate Profile, Trusted CA Certificate Profile, Wi-Fi Profile, and VPN Profile. In addition, there is a new security role, Company Resource Access Manager, which has full permission to create and deploy profiles to the clients. Figure 8.27 shows these permissions.

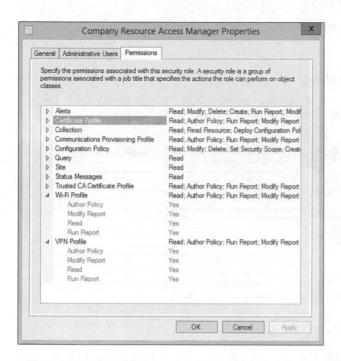

FIGURE 8.27   Permissions of Company Resource Access Manager security role.

Deploying Applications to Mobile Devices

Using ConfigMgr/Intune integrated management, you can deploy applications to all supported mobile devices: Android, iOS, Windows Phone 8.x, Windows RT, and Windows 8.1. All platforms support the following application types:

▶ **Applications from public application store (Google Play, App Store, and Windows Store):** The user must have an account to the store to be able to install applications. ConfigMgr only provides a link to an application in a store; the user must manually install the application from the store. This feature makes it easier for users to find the right application.

▶ **Organization's custom in-house applications:** If a company has created its own application for mobile devices (.appx packages for Windows 8 and Windows Phone 8.1 devices, .apk packages for Android devices, .ipa packages for iOS devices, and .xap packages for Windows Phone 8.x devices), they can be deployed with ConfigMgr.

▶ **Web application:** A web application is just a URL to some website. This could be a public website or an internal website that might need a VPN tunnel to access it.

A web application installs a shortcut to Windows 8.1, iOS (web clip), and Android (widget) devices. On Windows Phone 8.x devices, a web application is launched from the company portal.

Chapter 4, "New Application Deployment Types," discusses creating different application types.

Defining Application Information

When you create a new application, it is useful to provide information about the application on the Application Catalog tab of the application shown in Figure 8.28.

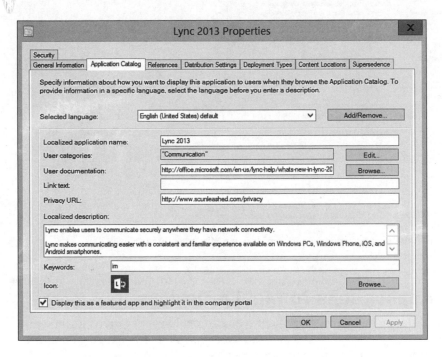

FIGURE 8.28   Application Catalog settings.

The following fields are shown in the company portal:

▶ **Localized application name:** The name of the application.

▶ **User categories:** Applications can be grouped with categories.

▶ **User documentation:** Additional information about the application. You can browse for a file, but the file must be accessible from mobile devices. A web link is typically the best solution.

▶ **Privacy URL:** An optional privacy information about the application.

▶ **Localized description:** A short description about the application.

▶ **Keywords:** Keywords are used when users search for specific applications. These are useful if many applications are published to users.

▶ **Icon:** If no icon is defined, a general icon is displayed in the company portal.

▶ **Display this as a featured app and highlight it in the company portal:** Most commonly used applications can be tagged as featured applications. Featured applications are displayed on the company portal's home page.

Application catalog information can be defined in multiple languages. The company portal on mobile devices displays the information using the display language of the mobile device if you provided information using the same language.

Figure 8.29 shows how the example application is displayed in the company portal.

FIGURE 8.29   Application details on the company portal.

The More Information and Privacy Statement links in the figure are not visible if the administrator has not defined anything for the User documentation or Privacy URL fields.

All mobile device platforms support Available Install deployments to user collections. If required, you can enable the Require administrator approval if users request this application option. This option is possible for in-house and web applications, but not for store applications.

> **NOTE: AVAILABLE .IPA APPLICATIONS ARE NOT DISPLAYED ON COMPANY PORTAL APPLICATION**
>
> The user must start a web browser on iOS devices and log on to the company portal website (https://portal.manage.microsoft.com) with the correct credentials to install available .ipa applications. Those applications are not displayed on the iOS company portal application, because Apple doesn't allow applications to install within another application. An exception to this rule is a native web browser.

Windows 8.x, Windows Phone 8.1, iOS, and Android devices support required installation deployments for in-house applications to users and devices. The application is installed automatically to Windows 8.x and Windows Phone 8.1 devices, but the user is prompted for approval on iOS and Android devices before installation.

Store applications do not support required installations.

Required uninstall works automatically on Windows 8.x, Windows Phone 8.1, and iOS devices, but an approval is prompted on Android devices before uninstallation.

Mobile devices support the following requirement rules:

▶ **Android:** Device ownership; minimum operating system version is automatically detected

▶ **iOS:** Minimum operating system version, operating system (different selection for iPad or iPhone), operating system language, and device ownership

▶ **Windows 8.x:** Operating system version, language, and device ownership

▶ **Windows Phone 8.x:** Operating system version, language, and device ownership

Deployments to mobile devices appear in the ConfigMgr console under Monitoring -> Deployments, similar to any other application deployment. You can also utilize the same reports.

Windows Phone 8.x, Windows 8, and iOS applications require code-signing certificates. If the certificate expires, users can no longer install applications. The administrator must renew the certificate and upload the new certificate to the corresponding Windows Intune Subscription tab in the ConfigMgr console.

> **NOTE: USE THE SAME APPLE ID TO RENEW THE APNS CERTIFICATE**
>
> When renewing the APNs certificate, remember to use the same Apple ID that you used with the original certificate request. If the certificate is renewed with a different Apple ID, the iOS devices must be reenrolled. You should create a specific a company Apple ID for this purpose and not use a personal Apple ID.

Using the Company Portal

The company portal is the primary ConfigMgr-related application for users on mobile devices. It has four main features:

▶ **Installing software:** The user can start the installation of deployed software from the company portal. Applications can be searched for by application name or keywords, or software can be browsed from different categories.

▶ **Managing mobile devices:** The user sees his mobile devices from the company portal and can manage them. Operations for mobile devices include renaming, removing, and resetting a device.

▶ **Initiate remote desktop connection to a primary device:** The user can start a remote desktop connection to her primary device, if remote desktop profiles are defined. Remote desktop connection works from Windows 8.x, iOS, and Android devices with a remote desktop client.

▶ **Contacting IT:** If the administrator has defined contact information as Windows Intune subscription properties, the contact information and details are displayed to users. This information is shown in Figure 8.30.

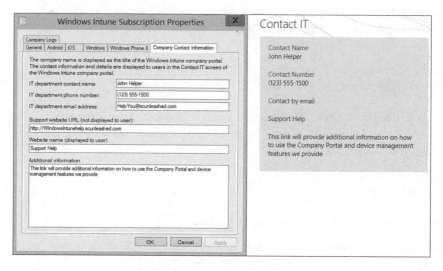

FIGURE 8.30   Contact IT information.

The company logo and name are displayed on the upper-left corner of the company portal. On Windows 8.1 and iOS devices, the company portal displays a small flag icon if there are any notifications to users, as shown in Figure 8.31.

FIGURE 8.31   Notification on the company portal.

Company Portal on Windows 8.1 Devices

Two different versions of the company portal are available for Windows 8.1.

▶ If Windows 8.1 is managed as a mobile device, the company portal is available from the Windows Store.

▶ You can also install the company portal to Windows 8.1 devices running the full ConfigMgr client. This requires downloading the company portal application from the Microsoft download center at http://www.microsoft.com/en-us/download/details.aspx?id=40795. The machines must also be domain-joined and the user must be logged on with domain credentials.

The company portal can be deployed like any other .appx package to your Windows 8.1 clients using the ConfigMgr client. Before installing the application, set the following Registry value:

```
HKEY_LOCAL_MACHINE\SOFTWARE\Policies\Microsoft\CCM: PortalPackageFamily (REG_SZ)
= Microsoft.CorporateAppCenter_8wekyb3d8bbwe
```

You must also enable the group policy **Computer Configuration -> Administrative Templates -> Windows Components -> App Package Deployment: All trusted apps to install**. Alternately, you can set this value in the Windows Registry:

```
HKEY_LOCAL_MACHINE\SOFTWARE\Policies\Microsoft\Windows\Appx:
AllowAllTrustedApps (REG_DWORD) = 1
```

Several differences exist between the two company portals:

▶ The Windows Store company portal lets you manage your mobile devices, but you can deploy only Windows 8 and web applications (see Figure 8.32).

▶ From the company portal for ConfigMgr clients, you can deploy any supported application types (.msi, exe, .appx), but you don't see your mobile devices (see Figure 8.33).

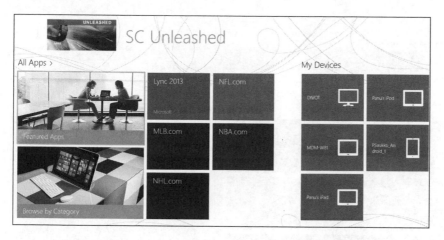

FIGURE 8.32   Windows 8.x company portal from Windows Store.

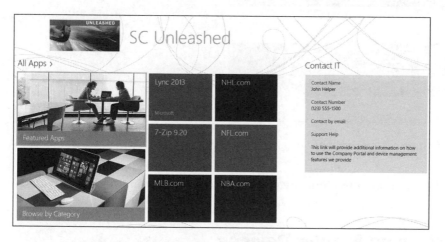

FIGURE 8.33   Windows 8.x company portal for full ConfigMgr clients.

Company Portal Website

You can access the company portal website from any device, even from devices not managed by Windows Intune/ConfigMgr. Browse to the website https://portal.manage. microsoft.com and log on with your credentials as shown in Figure 8.34. From here, you can see the applications and devices. You cannot install applications to an unmanaged device. However, you can rename, remove, and wipe managed devices from an unmanaged device. This is useful if one of your devices was stolen recently and you need to wipe it quickly.

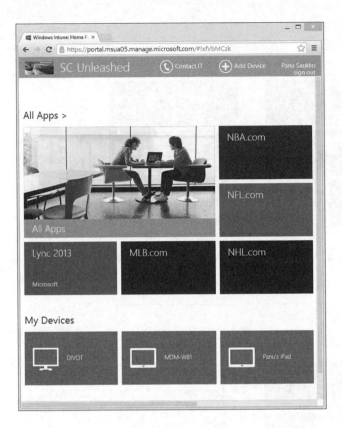

FIGURE 8.34   Company portal website.

A remote desktop connection to a primary device is also possible from the company portal website.

Retiring/Wiping Mobile Devices

Two options exist for a mobile device that no longer needs to be managed:

- ▶ **Retire (Selective Wipe):** Disables management of the device and removes company-related information from the device. Any software, data, or settings transferred to the device are removed. The user can initiate this operation from the company portal, or the administrator can do so using the ConfigMgr console. This option is useful when the user leaves the company or the device is given to another user.

  If email profiles are defined on a retired device, corporate email is removed only from the iOS native email client application and from Windows Phone 8.1. Windows Phone 8 does not support this feature.

  All personal data and applications are retained on the device.

▶ **Wipe:** The device is reset to factory defaults. This means that all data, settings, and applications are lost. This is useful when the device is stolen. The operation can be initiated either by a user from the company portal or by an administrator from the ConfigMgr console. This option is not available for Windows 8.1 devices.

Table 8.10 lists the company content that is removed while retiring a Windows-based device and Table 8.11 lists the same information for non-Windows devices.

TABLE 8.10   Company Content Removed When Retiring a Windows-Based Device

Content	Windows 8.1 or Windows RT 8.1	Windows RT	Windows Phone 8.1
Company apps and associated data	Apps are uninstalled and sideloading keys are removed. Data is no longer accessible.	Sideloading keys are removed, but apps remain installed.	Apps are uninstalled and application data is removed.
VPN and Wi-Fi profiles	Removed.	N/A.	Removed.
Certificates	Removed and revoked.	N/A.	Removed.
Settings	Removed.	Removed.	Removed.
Email	Removes emails from Encrypting File System (EFS)-enabled email. The native Windows Mail app is EFS-enabled, but Outlook is not.	N/A.	Email account and emails are removed from Intune-provisioned accounts.

TABLE 8.11   Company Content Removed When Retiring an Android or iOS Device

Content	iOS	Android	Samsung KNOX
Company apps and associated data	Apps are uninstalled and company data is removed.	Apps and data remain installed.	Apps are uninstalled.
VPN and Wi-Fi profiles	Removed.	VPN: N/A, Wi-Fi: Not removed.	Removed.
Certificates	Removed and revoked.	Revoked.	Revoked.
Settings	Removed.	Removed.	Removed.
Management Agent	Management profile is removed.	Device Administrator privilege is revoked.	Device Administrator privilege is revoked.
Email	Email account and emails are removed from Intune provisioned accounts.	N/A.	N/A.

Selective wipe is not effective on native Android devices, because Android requires prompting the user for every action.

Figure 8.35 shows the options to Retire/Wipe a device from the ConfigMgr console.

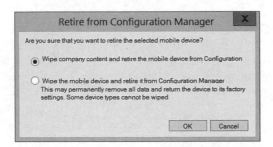

FIGURE 8.35   Retire/Wipe a device from the ConfigMgr console.

A user can also retire/wipe his mobile devices from the company portal (see Figure 8.36). The Retire option is called Remove, and Wipe is called Factory Reset. Icons are the same on different platforms, but command names might be missing on the mobile phone's smaller screen.

FIGURE 8.36   Retire/Wipe a device from the company portal.

Troubleshooting

Multiple log files can be helpful when troubleshooting mobile device management problems. One set of log files can be found on a server with the Windows Intune connector. Android, iOS, and Windows Phone 8.x devices have only one log file that is related to the company portal. Windows 8.1 devices report information to the Windows event log in addition to the company portal log file.

Log Files on Site Server

The main log files for Windows Intune and ConfigMgr integration, located in *<ConfigMgrInstallPath>*\Logs on a server where the Windows Intune connector site role is installed follow:

▶ **Cloudusersync.log:** Provides information about the synchronization process of enrollment user collection members to Windows Intune.

▶ **Dmpdownloader.log:** This log file displays information about the messages coming from Windows Intune to ConfigMgr.

▶ **Dmpuploader.log:** This log file shows how policies flow from ConfigMgr to the Windows Intune device management point.

▶ **Outgoingcontentmanager.log** and **distmgr.log:** Distmgr.log shows the basic process of content distribution, and outgoingcontentmanager.log the actual copying from ConfigMgr to Intune.

Should you have problems with the Windows Intune connector and need to contact Microsoft CSS, provide the following information to CSS:

▶ **Tenant ID:** Tenant ID is the unique identifier of Windows Intune account.

▶ **Transmission ID:** Uniquely identifies the transmission between ConfigMgr and Intune. It can be found in dmpdownloader.log and dmpuploader.log.

The IDs make it easier for Microsoft Support to find the necessary debugging information from Intune's internal log files.

Log File on iOS Devices

By default, there is no log file on an iOS device. To get a log file on an iOS device, you must shake the iOS device, which then shows the options displayed in Figure 8.37.

You can easily email the log files to the proper individuals. You need to have at least one email account configured on the device.

You can disable the shake gesture from **Settings -> Comp Portal -> Shake gesture: off**.

Log File on Windows Phone 8.x Devices

Logging is enabled by default on Windows Phone 8.x devices. User can touch the option for additional options (... icon) and then select send logs (shown in Figure 8.38). To send the logs files using email, you need to have email accounts configured.

Log File on Android Devices

To access the company portal log files on Android devices, select **Contact IT -> Menu -> Send Diagnostic Data**. Send the log file with Bluetooth, email, Gmail, or Wi-Fi Direct.

8

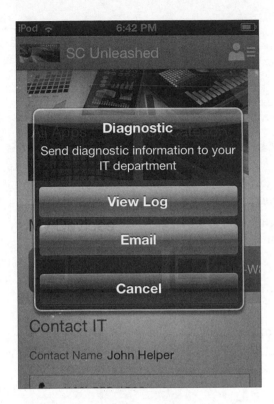

FIGURE 8.37   Log file options on iOS devices.

FIGURE 8.38   Log files on Windows Phone 8/8.1 devices.

Troubleshooting Windows 8.1 OMA-DM Devices

If you are used to the extensive logging provided with a full ConfigMgr client, you may be disappointed with how little logging OMA-DM managed Windows 8.1 offers.

To find more information about the enrollment process of the device from Event Viewer, look under **Windows Logs -> Applications and Services Logs -> Microsoft -> Windows -> System Settings -> Operational**.

The company portal has its own log files, SSPLog*.log. These are located in the *%SystemDrive%*\Users\username\AppData\Local\Packages\Microsoft. CompanyPortal_8wekyb3d8bbwe\LocalState folder.

You can find additional application deployment information primarily in the Registry, under the following key:

```
HKEY_CURRENT_USER\SOFTWARE\Microsoft\Windows\CurrentVersion\MDM
```

If you deploy .appx applications, some information is available in the Event Viewer under **Windows Logs -> Applications and Services Logs -> Microsoft -> Windows -> AppXDeployment-Server -> Microsoft -> Windows -> AppXDeploymentServer/ Operational**.

In addition to the information presented in this chapter, there is an excellent blog post at http://blogs.technet.com/b/configmgrteam/archive/2013/03/13/troubleshooting-windows-rt-client-software-distribution-issues.aspx, which steps through the in-depth debugging information of the software deployment process to OMA-DM managed clients. The blog article was written for Windows 8 RT, but the process hasn't changed in Windows RT 8.1 or OMA-DM managed Windows 8.1.

Summary

Organizations can extend ConfigMgr 2012 R2 with Windows Intune to unify traditional PCs and mobile device management with a single infrastructure. Windows Intune integrated mobile device management offers a comprehensive feature set that includes application deployment, settings management, inventory, lifecycle management, and access to a company's internal resources. This solution can differentiate between user and company owned devices. Windows Intune integrated mobile device management supports all major mobile device platforms: Android, iOS, Windows Phone 8.x, Windows RT, and Windows 8.1.

With the extensions for Windows Intune feature, you can dynamically add new Windows Intune features to the ConfigMgr environment with several clicks.

Exchange ActiveSync is another option for mobile device management. It is a simple and cost-effective solution for customers that are satisfied with a basic inventory and the ability to set key security settings on mobile devices.

Microsoft will continue to improve the feature set of mobile device management and support upcoming operating systems. A key area is improving security and data protection within different applications like Microsoft Office. By utilizing a cloud-based solution, Microsoft can rapidly release new versions to its customers. ConfigMgr 2012 R2 with Intune integration provides comprehensive mobile device management for all major smartphone and tablet environments.

PART IV

Appendixes

IN THIS PART

APPENDIX A   About Windows Intune   297

APPENDIX B   Reference URLs   315

APPENDIX C   Available Online   335

APPENDIX A

About Windows Intune

IN THIS APPENDIX

▶ Introduction to Windows Intune

▶ Mobile Device Management Features

▶ Windows Intune Licensing and Supported Architectures

▶ The Windows Intune Connector and Subscription

By now, you may have heard the terms *consumerization of Information Technology* (IT) and *bring your own device* (BYOD, which is where devices are purchased by users and used at work) and understand that there are productivity benefits to supporting this new style of work. The IT department has to manage those devices, almost all of which are mobile devices, in a way that still meets IT security and compliance requirements. This appendix explains the genesis of Windows Intune, its history, licensing, and architecture for integrating with System Center 2012 R2 Configuration Manager to deliver a unified mobile device management solution.

Introduction to Windows Intune

Consumerization of IT makes it necessary to incorporate user and mobile device management as part of the IT experience, something with which Configuration Manager (ConfigMgr) and Systems Management Server (SMS) have historically struggled. Users have an unprecedented amount of consumer devices at home, which leads to higher expectations of technology usage at work. This increased pressure on IT to allow these devices to access corporate apps and data, and forced them to purchase multiple products to manage and secure them as ConfigMgr 2007/2012 lacked the functionality. However, it wasn't enough to add mobile device support in Configuration Manager (remember ConfigMgr already supported legacy devices such as Windows Mobile and Exchange ActiveSync devices with the Exchange connector). Microsoft also needed new agility to react quickly to industry trends and new mobile device features that enter the market. This is where Windows Intune comes in.

Intune Comes Into Focus

What exactly is Intune? Windows Intune, billed as Microsoft's first cloud-based PC management solution, released to market in April 2011. In seeing that Configuration Manager was not penetrating the SMB (small medium business) market as well as it would have liked, Microsoft was interested in offering an alternative lightweight solution for customers. Data from that market segment showed customers were concerned with the amount of infrastructure needed to support ConfigMgr and the steep learning curve associated with the product. Their preference was PC management functionality delivered via the cloud. Through Intune and the licensing for Windows Client Software Assurance (SA), Microsoft offered SMB customers a current desktop experience (Windows 7) and the ability to manage their PCs from the cloud. This became the basis for the initial vision of Intune for customers:

- ▶ **Stay current:** Upgrade rights to Windows 7

- ▶ **Easy to use:** Cloud-based infrastructure and fast deployment

- ▶ **Smart parity:** Deliver core management features not duplicating ConfigMgr

- ▶ **Rapid release:** Deliver new features and updates every 6 months

After the product's second release in October 2011, Microsoft saw opportunities emerging for adoption by larger customer installations. While the SMB market adopted Intune well, other customer segments representing larger customers were just starting their evaluations. Intune had technical limitations that posed challenges for larger enterprise customers, as it leveraged Windows Live IDs for administrative accounts, which most customers viewed as a consumer-rated service rather than a corporate one. Intune also had scalability limitations governing the number of PCs that could be managed in a single Intune cloud instance. To expand the appeal and reach of the product, Microsoft decided in the third release to align Intune with Microsoft Online Services, the commercial offering including products such as Office 365 and Microsoft Dynamics. This changed the back-end account directory from Windows Live ID to Windows Azure Active Directory (formerly called Microsoft Online Directory Service). Azure Active Directory (AD) specifications and requirements for use with ConfigMgr and Intune are explored in depth in Chapter 7, "Using the Intune Connector."

In addition to the change to Azure AD, the third release of Windows Intune (June 2012) included the following features:

- ▶ **Antimalware:** Windows Intune Endpoint Protection based on Forefront Endpoint Protection 2010 and leveraging the same scan engine as System Center Endpoint Protection

- ▶ **Software updates:** Capable of delivering both operating system (OS) and third-party updates

- ▶ **Software distribution:** .MSI/.EXE based packages with content residing in Azure blog storage encrypted and compressed

▶ **Proactive monitoring:** Operating system and application monitoring leveraging System Center Operations Manager 2007 R2

▶ **Inventory:** Hardware and software inventory

▶ **Monitor and track licenses:** Upload or search for Microsoft Volume Licensing details and the ability to add third-party license information

▶ **Reporting:** Software updates, inventory, and license reports

▶ **Policy management:** Security policies to control configuration of the Intune agent and security configurations

▶ **End user self-service portal:** New user accounts available for self-service application provisioning and PC enrollment

▶ **Mobile device management and application delivery:** Supported applications delivery to Android and iOS devices and management of Microsoft Exchange ActiveSync policies

The final bullet, "Mobile device management and application delivery," contained a very significant feature that at the time flew generally under the radar. Intune was the first Microsoft product that could now perform application deployment to modern smartphone platforms. This was the beginning of an important shift of focus for the product.

Microsoft Strategic Direction Announcement

Following Intune's third release, customers noticed its ability to deliver applications to Android and iOS devices, something not included within System Center 2012 Configuration Manager. This prompted customers to question the direction of both products and what Microsoft's roadmap would be to support the next generation of "smart" devices: mobile phones and tablets. According to a recent IDC study, worldwide total unit shipments for smart connected devices, projected at 1.2B in 2012, would grow 16% to over 2B units in 2016.[1] After Intune's third release, it was unclear to customers which solution to use for their overall management needs. Smaller customers would continue to expect a cloud-delivered solution, while larger enterprise customers wanted to leverage ConfigMgr.

Released to Microsoft's Server and Cloud blog (http://blogs.technet.com/b/server-cloud) in September 2012, the company clarified its management vision by detailing some of the features in the fourth release of Intune (December 2012) and Service Pack (SP) 1 of System Center 2012 Configuration Manager, thus setting the direction for integration between the two products.

---

[1] *IDC Press Release, "IDC Expects Smart Connected Device Shipments to Grow by 14% Annually Through 2016, Led by Tablets and Smartphones," September 26, 2012*

NOTE: STRATEGIC DIRECTION ANNOUCEMENT

Microsoft is committed to a unified device management solution that combines cloud and on-premise capabilities, creating a premium offering that provides customers with scalability and infrastructure choice for their device management needs.

Unifying the management, security, and compliance of devices, a single infrastructure improves administrative efficiency and reduces the costs of tools and processes to support the organization. By delivering applications using a single application definition with multiple deployment types within ConfigMgr, it becomes easier to manage application lifecycles, and users become more productive as they have greater flexibility to use their choice of device. Microsoft has coined the phrase "Empowering People-centric IT." Simply put, that meant enabling IT to focus on managing at the user level and delivering applications to users' devices in a way that is optimized for each device and maximizes user productivity. IT can manage both corporate and personally owned devices with a unified infrastructure, now that all the devices can be seen and managed inside of ConfigMgr.

TIP: PEOPLE-CENTRIC IT

Microsoft now includes people-centric IT (PCIT) as part of their overall cloud OS vision. For more information on PCIT, see http://www.microsoft.com/en-us/server-cloud/cloud-os/pcit.aspx and download the PCIT whitepaper.

Mobile Device Management Features

With the December 2012 release of Windows Intune, the fourth release in less than 2 years, Microsoft shifted heavily into mobile device management. By integrating with Configuration Manager 2012 SP 1, organizations could now see mobile devices natively inside of the ConfigMgr console, and not just those devices discovered via the Exchange connector. The key features delivered in Configuration Manager are listed here, followed by an explanation of each feature:

▶ Device management

▶ Device inventory

▶ Policy settings management

▶ Application distribution

▶ Device retirement and remote wipe

For a detailed explanation of the use of the new features within ConfigMgr 2012 R2, see Chapter 8, "Mobile Device Management in Configuration Manager 2012 R2."

Device Management

One of the exciting features supported within Intune is the ability to perform direct device management of modern smartphones such as Windows Phone 8 and iOS. This over-the-air enrollment and management process no longer requires the need to use Exchange ActiveSync policies to manage settings on the devices.

The December 2012 release of Intune and the January 2013 release of ConfigMgr 2012 SP 1 accomplished mobile device management by leveraging a management channel that exists within the mobile OS, versus deploying a management agent (app) to the device to perform all the management functions. Therefore Intune did not support Android devices, and only supported Windows 8 RT (RTM). The Android operating system platform did not include the functionality of an embedded management channel to deliver the functionality wanted by Microsoft. For Android policy and settings management, Microsoft still required the use of Exchange ActiveSync (EAS). Configuration Manager administrators could still see Android devices within the console, however it required using the Exchange connector and the Android device must have Exchange ActiveSync configured.

With the release of Configuration Manager 2012 R2, a new version of Windows Intune, and the Windows 8.1 client OS, there are new options available to manage mobile devices. Android 4.x devices and Windows 8.1 (both x86 and ARM) can now be managed directly using the Intune management channel. To manage Android 4.x devices, users would install the new company portal application available for free in the Google Play Store, and enroll their device into Intune with this application. Windows 8.1 builds on the mobile management capabilities first added to Windows 8 RT. Using the embedded MDM agent, based on the Open Mobile Alliance–Device Management (OMA–DM) protocol, Windows 8.1 Intel x86-based machines can now be managed as mobile devices even though they are running a full Windows 8.1 OS. This is critical for Microsoft to expose since many BYOD scenarios include new full OS 8.1 devices. Without this option, companies would have to install the traditional ConfigMgr agent to manage the device. iOS and Windows Phone 8.x also added new enhancements to improve management functionality.

Device Inventory

Windows Intune supports gathering hardware inventory from the mobile device depending on mobile operating system support and settings defined within the ConfigMgr console. For devices that enrolled via Intune, Table A.1 identifies the attributes that are queried for and those devices that return the values.

TABLE A.1   Hardware Inventory Attributes from ConfigMgr R2 and Intune

Hardware Inventory Class	WP8	Windows 8.1	iOS	Android (Using the Company Portal App)
Name	✓	✓	✓	—
Unique Device ID	✓	✓	✓	—
Serial Number	—	—	✓	✓
Email Address	✓	✓	✓	—

Hardware Inventory Class	WP8	Windows 8.1	iOS	Android (Using the Company Portal App)
Operating System Type	✓	✓	—	✓
Operating System Version	✓	✓	✓	✓
Build Version	—	✓	—	—
Service Pack Major Version	—	✓	—	—
Service Pack Minor Version	—	✓	—	—
Operating System Language	✓	—	—	—
Total Storage Space	—	✓	✓	✓
Free Storage Space	—	✓	✓	✓
International Mobile Equipment Identity or IMEI (IMEI)	—	—	✓	✓
Mobile Equipment Identifier (MEID)	—	—	✓	—
Manufacturer	✓	✓	—	✓
Model	✓	✓	✓	✓
Phone Number	—	—	✓	✓
Subscriber Carrier	—	—	✓	✓
Cellular Technology	—	—	✓	✓
Wi-Fi MAC	—	✓	✓	✓

NOTE: HARDWARE INVENTORY

Review http://technet.microsoft.com/en-us/library/dn469411.aspx for the latest hardware inventory list from Microsoft. Also note that hardware inventory is controlled through the Client Settings node in the Administration pane of the ConfigMgr console. Not all hardware classes are enabled for mobile devices; you may need to review the settings if you are not receiving the inventory information you expect.

For those devices managed using EAS, the attributes are first returned to Exchange, and then they are placed into the ConfigMgr database if the ConfigMgr Exchange connector is configured. Without installing the Exchange connector role in ConfigMgr, the information only resides within Exchange. Mobile devices that are managed using Windows Intune and EAS would have duplicate information returned to ConfigMgr. In those instances, ConfigMgr merges the two data records together into the device object.

Prior to ConfigMgr 2012 R2, mobile device software inventory was limited to the line-of-business (LOB) applications that were installed on the devices. ConfigMgr could then be used to query and report the users and devices that installed various LOB applications. Windows Intune did not support querying for all the installed software in the

ConfigMgr 2012 SP 1 release. Microsoft added support for full software device inventory in ConfigMgr 2012 R2 by adding a device setting that defines whether the device is company or personal owned. Any mobile device that the ConfigMgr administrator defined as "company-owned" reports full software inventory to the extent that the device platform supports it. Currently, only iOS and Android support a full software inventory, which is returned during the hardware inventory cycle timeframe.

Policy Settings Management

Microsoft's vision of "people-centric IT" and unifying all device management inside of ConfigMgr is extremely attractive for organizations. A benefit of this approach is seen within mobile device policy settings. ConfigMgr administrators use similar skills and tasks for creating mobile device policies as for creating PC compliance items and baselines. Table A.2 enumerates the mobile device settings provided for unified device management in ConfigMgr 2012 R2.

TIP: COMBINING POLICY SOURCES

Users often configure the ActiveSync client to receive email. In the case where an EAS and ConfigMgr 2012 R2 mobile device policy overlap, the most restrictive policy is enforced.

Expect ConfigMgr to release mobile device features as rapidly as possible, as seen with the February 2014 release of new iOS 7 security and data-retention policies, the new Exchange email profile configuration capability, and the May 2014 Windows Phone 8.1 policies. For the latest policy and feature support list, review http://technet.microsoft.com/en-us/library/dn376523.aspx. To support the release of MDM features without requiring large architecture changes and system upgrades, Configuration Manager R2 includes a new node under Cloud Services called Extensions for Windows Intune. Chapter 7 includes additional information on how to receive and enable new MDM feature updates.

Application Distribution and the Windows Intune Company Portal

Windows Intune application distribution for mobile devices is a user-friendly approach to self-service provisioning. In ConfigMgr 2012 R2, Windows Intune added additional application delivery options, building on the SP 1 features, which now support the following:

- ▶ Internal LOB apps written by the company.
- ▶ External public store applications. Also call deep links, these are shortcuts to applications that reside in the public marketplaces of the device platform, such as the Windows Phone Store or Apple App Store.
- ▶ Web links for users to access web-based applications.
- ▶ Device-targeted application "push" deployments.

TABLE A.2 ConfigMgr R2 Unified Device Management Policy Settings

Device Setting Group	Settings	Values	Windows Phone 8.x	Windows 8.1 Enrolled via Intune	iOS	Android (Using the Company Portal App)
Browser	Default browser	Allowed / Prohibited	Windows Phone 8.1 only	—	✓	—
Browser	Autofill	Allowed / Prohibited	—	✓	✓	—
Browser	Plug-ins	Allowed / Prohibited	—	✓	—	—
Browser	Active scripting	Allowed / Prohibited	—	✓	✓	—
Browser	Pop-ups	Allowed / Prohibited	—	✓	✓	—
Browser	Fraud warning	Allowed / Prohibited	—	✓	✓	—
Browser	Cookies	Allowed / Prohibited	—	—	✓	—
Cloud	Encrypted backup	Allowed / Prohibited	—	—	✓	—
Cloud	Document synchronization	Allowed / Prohibited	—	—	✓	—
Cloud	Photo synchronization	Allowed / Prohibited	—	—	✓	—
Cloud	Cloud backup	Allowed / Prohibited	—	—	✓	—
Cloud	Settings synchronization	Allowed / Prohibited	Windows Phone 8.1 only	✓ (GET only)	—	—
Cloud	Credentials synchronization	Allowed / Prohibited	—	✓ (GET only)	—	—
Cloud	Synchronization over metered connection	Allowed / Prohibited	—	✓ (GET only)	—	—
Cloud	Microsoft Account	Enabled / Disabled	Windows Phone 8.1 only	—	—	—
Content Rating	Adult content in media store	Allowed / Prohibited	—	—	✓	—
Content Rating	Ratings region	Country of choice	—	—	✓	—

Device Setting Group	Settings	Values	Windows Phone 8.x	Windows 8.1 Enrolled via Intune	iOS	Android (Using the Company Portal App)
Content Rating	Movie rating	Rating	—	—	✓	—
Content Rating	TV show rating	Rating	—	—	✓	—
Content Rating	App rating	Rating	—	—	✓	—
Device	Voice dialing	Allowed /Prohibited	—	—	✓	—
Device	Voice assistant	Allowed /Prohibited	—	—	✓	—
Device	Voice assistant while locked	Allowed /Prohibited	—	—	✓	—
Device	Screen capture	Enabled /Disabled	Windows Phone 8.1 only	—	✓	—
Device	Video conferencing	Enabled /Disabled	—	—	✓	—
Device	Add game center friends	Allowed /Prohibited	—	—	✓	—
Device	Multiplayer gaming	Allowed /Prohibited	—	—	✓	—
Device	Personal wallet software while locked	Allowed /Prohibited	—	—	✓	—
Device	Diagnostic data submission	Enabled /Disabled	Windows Phone 8.1 only	✓	✓	—
Device	Geolocation	Enabled /Disabled	Windows Phone 8.1 only	—	—	—
Device	Copy and Paste	Enabled /Disabled	Windows Phone 8.1 only	—	—	—
Encryption	File encryption on mobile device	On/Off	✓	✓ (GET only)	—	✓, for Android 4
Internet Explorer	Go to intranet site for single word entry	Allowed /Prohibited	—	✓	—	—
Internet Explorer	Always send Do Not Track header	Allowed /Prohibited	—	✓	—	—

A

Device Setting Group	Settings	Values	Windows Phone 8.x	Windows 8.1 Enrolled via Intune	iOS	Android (Using the Company Portal App)
Internet Explorer	Intranet security zone	Allowed / Prohibited	—	✓	—	—
Internet Explorer	Security level for Internet zone	High, Medium-high, Medium	—	✓ (GET only)	—	—
Internet Explorer	Security level for intranet zone	High, Medium-high, Medium, Medium-low, Low	—	✓ (GET only)	—	—
Internet Explorer	Security level for trusted sites zone	High, Medium-high, Medium, Medium-low, Low	—	✓ (GET only)	—	—
Internet Explorer	Security level for restricted sites zone	High	—	✓ (GET only)	—	—
Internet Explorer	Namespace exists for browser security zone	Sites	—	✓	—	—
Password	Require password settings on mobile devices	Required	✓	—	✓	✓, for Android 4
Password	Password complexity	PIN, Strong	✓	✓	✓	—
Password	Idle time before mobile device is locked (minutes)	1 minute – 12 hours	✓	✓	✓	✓, for Android 4
Password	Minimum password length (characters)	4–18	✓	✓	✓	✓, for Android 4
Password	Number of passwords remembered	0–50	✓	✓	✓	✓, for Android 4
Password	Password expiration in days	1–365	✓	✓	✓	✓, for Android 4

Device Setting Group	Settings	Values	Windows Phone 8.x	Windows 8.1 Enrolled via Intune	iOS	Android (Using the Company Portal App)
Password	Number of failed logon attempts before device is wiped	0–100	✓	✓	✓	✓, for Android 4
Password	Password quality	Low security biometric, Required, At least numeric, At least alphabetic, Alphanumeric with symbols	—	—	—	✓, for Android 4
Roaming	Allow voice roaming	Allowed /Prohibited	—	—	✓	—
Roaming	Allow data roaming	Allowed /Prohibited	—	✓	✓	—
Security	Removable storage	Allowed /Prohibited	✓	—	—	—
Security	Camera	Allowed /Prohibited	Windows Phone 8.1 only	—	✓	✓, for Android 4.1
Security	Bluetooth	Allowed /Prohibited	Windows Phone 8.1 only	✓ (GET only)	—	—
Security	Allow app installation	Allowed /Prohibited	—	—	✓	—
Security	Near field communication (NFC)	Enabled /Disabled	Windows Phone 8.1 only	—	✓	—
Store	Application store	Allowed /Prohibited	Windows Phone 8.1 only	—	✓	—
Store	Force application store password	Enabled /Disabled	—	—	✓, this setting applies to iTunes only	—
Store	In-app purchases	Allowed /Prohibited	—	—	✓	—

A

Device Setting Group	Settings	Values	Windows Phone 8.x	Windows 8.1 Enrolled via Intune	iOS	Android (Using the Company Portal App)
System Security	User to accept untrusted TLS certificates	Allowed /Prohibited	—	—	✓	—
System Security	User access control	Always notify, Notify app changes, Notify app changes (do not dim desktop), Never notify	—	✓	—	—
System Security	Network firewall	Required	—	✓ (GET only)	—	—
System Security	Updates	Automatic updates is required	—	✓	—	—
System Security	Virus protection	Required	—	✓ (GET only)	—	—
System Security	Virus protection signatures are up-to-date	Required	—	✓ (GET only)	—	—
System Security	SmartScreen	Enabled /Disabled	—	✓	—	—
System Security	Lock screen control center	Enabled /Disabled	—	—	✓ (iOS 7)	—
System Security	Lock screen notification view	Enabled /Disabled	—	—	✓ (iOS 7)	—
System Security	Lock screen today view	Enabled /Disabled	—	—	✓ (iOS 7)	—
System Security	Fingerprint for unlocking	Allowed /Prohibited	—	—	✓ (iOS 7)	—
Data Protection	Open managed documents in other unmanaged apps	Allowed /Prohibited	—	—	✓ (iOS 7)	—
Data Protection	Open unmanaged documents in other managed apps	Allowed /Prohibited	—	—	✓ (iOS 7)	—

Device Setting Group	Settings	Values	Windows Phone 8.x	Windows 8.1 Enrolled via Intune	iOS	Android (Using the Company Portal App)
Windows Server Work Folders	Work folders URL	URL	—	✓	—	—
Email Management	Custom Email account	Enabled / Disabled	Windows Phone 8.1 only	—	✓ (iOS 7)	—
Wireless Communication	Wi-Fi Tethering	Enabled / Disabled	Windows Phone 8.1 only	—	—	—
Wireless Communication	Offload data to Wi-Fi when possible	Enabled / Disabled	Windows Phone 8.1 only	—	—	—
Wireless Communication	Wi-Fi hotspot reporting	Enabled / Disabled	Windows Phone 8.1 only	—	—	—
Wireless Communication	Wireless network connection	Enabled / Disabled	Windows Phone 8.1 only	—	—	—

A

To install the available self-service applications, users leverage a company portal application on their mobile device. In ConfigMgr 2012 R2, Microsoft shows their commitment to a consistent user experience by releasing updated company portal applications for Windows Phone 8 and Windows 8.1, along with new company portal applications for iOS and Android that bring parity to functionality and appearance. However, the company portal is used for more than just application delivery; it is designed to allow a user to have control over their devices and is tailored to each device platform. In addition to accessing applications that were published to that user, the company portal is used to enroll iOS and Android devices, and even control aspects of other devices linked to that user account. The exact functionality in the Company Portal depends on the device platform. Table A.3 lists company portal features.

TABLE A.3   Company Portal Features

Action Taken	Windows 8.1	Windows Phone 8.x	iOS	Android
Enroll local device	—	—	✓	✓
Rename devices	✓	✓	✓	✓
Retire local device	✓	✓	✓	✓
Wipe other devices remotely	✓	✓	✓	✓
Install company line of business apps	✓	✓	—	✓
Install deep-linked apps from Public Stores	✓	✓	✓	✓
Install or launch web-based application links	✓	✓	✓	✓

NOTE: SIDELOADING IOS APPLICATIONS

Apple currently restricts Microsoft from using a public store app, such as the Windows Intune company portal, to sideload LOB applications. Users must open their Safari browser and access the Windows Intune web portal on their device to view and install a company's LOB apps. In addition, iOS LOB applications requiring administrator approval are currently not supported using the Intune web portal.

Device Retirement and Remote Wipe

Windows Intune provides two distinct functions for a mobile device that is either lost/stolen or at end-of-life for management. Mobile devices can be retired from management, breaking the management channel where the device no longer receives management policies. Both administrators and users have the ability to perform this action, which could also be considered a "selective wipe" procedure, as it removes company applications, data, and management policies. Mobile devices can also be remotely wiped; for those devices that support that command, it is a factory reset of the device.

NOTE: RETIRING AND REMOTE WIPING DEVICES

In ConfigMgr 2012 R2, support for selective wipe and full factory resets vary by mobile device platform. There could also be longer time delays between when the administrator issues a wipe command and when it the device receives it. Refer to Chapter 8 for additional information, and ensure proper testing of the device platforms your organization plans to support.

Windows Intune Licensing and Supported Architectures

In addition to new mobile device features, the December 2012 release of Windows Intune changed the licensing model for the product, moving from a device-based license to a per-user model. The per-user licensing change aligned Windows Intune with other Microsoft Online Commercial Services that also leveraged per-user licensing, such as Office 365. For Windows Intune, a user license allows an organization to manage up to five devices. In addition to per-user licensing, the full Windows Intune SKU also includes the rights to System Center 2012 Configuration Manager R2 and System Center Endpoint Protection. For organizations that have already licensed Configuration Manager 2012 R2, options are available to license only Windows Intune, reducing organizational costs for the software.

With the unified device management and licensing options, organizations now have a wide variety of devices that can be managed by the unified device management solution. They can choose to deploy Configuration Manager to manage devices such as Macs, Windows Embedded, Windows PCs, and integrate with Windows Intune for their mobile device support. In addition, organizations could also deploy a cloud-only Windows Intune solution to solve their one-off PC management needs.

This book focuses solely on Configuration Manager R2, but it is important to take a moment to discuss the supported architecture environments for Windows Intune, discussed in the following sections

Unified Architecture

Unified device management (UDM) is the term used to describe an environment where Windows Intune and ConfigMgr are integrated together. *Hybrid cloud model* is another way to describe the UDM architecture because it leverages both on-premise and cloud components seamlessly. In this configuration, all device management is performed through the ConfigMgr administrator console. Achieving this interoperability requires both the on-premise Active Directory and a cloud Azure AD are synchronized together, in addition to having Configuration Manager R2 and Windows Intune licensed, deployed, and connected together. Therefore, customers need to plan to deploy the following technologies within their environment if they don't have this in place for other Microsoft cloud services:

A

▶ **Active Directory Synchronization (DirSync):** Used to synchronize user and security group objects and attributes from the on-premise AD to Azure AD

▶ **Active Directory Federation Services (ADFS):** Used as an authentication mechanism to reduce the user password complexity

Figure A.1 illustrates the key components used to support this solution. ADFS is not required for this solution; however, Microsoft highly recommends it as ADFS is used for other services such as the new Workplace Join feature and true single sign-on (SSO).

When installing the UDM configuration, ConfigMgr administrators install the Windows Intune connector site role within the CAS (or the single primary site), and define one of the primary sites as the location where devices are to be created. Only one Windows Intune connector per hierarchy is supported. Currently, the total number of mobile devices supported within the unified architecture is 100,000, based on the total supported number of devices that can be in a primary site. Therefore, if the ConfigMgr administrator dedicates a primary site to mobile devices and uses the Enterprise edition of Microsoft SQL Server for the site database, it can scale to the maximum supported limit.

Cloud-Only Architecture

Cloud-only architecture is the term used to describe an environment where only Windows Intune is deployed. Another name for this is the *Windows Intune stand-alone solution*. Outside of the removal of Configuration Manager 2012 R2, the major difference in the cloud-only solution is the number of devices supported and the limitations inside the product itself (as in fewer features). However, it is important to understand the future direction of the cloud-only solution. In a January 29, 2014 blog announcement (http://blogs.technet.com/b/server-cloud/archive/2014/01/29/new-enhancements-to-windows-intune.aspx), Microsoft reaffirmed its commitment to providing customers choice in management solutions by announcing new mobile device capabilities would be built in to the cloud-only architecture with a goal of striving for parity between solutions.

In this configuration, administrators might deploy Intune to manage PCs, mobile devices, or both. Even though Microsoft is striving for parity between both solutions, it is incorrect to assume that new Intune features work in both solutions. When System Center 2012 R2 Configuration Manager was released, nearly all the new capabilities initially required ConfigMgr 2012 R2. With the February 2014 update, Android management is now supported in both configurations, and Microsoft added new choices for policy settings. Integration with the local on-premise AD via DirSync is not required, unless an organization is interested in integrating with their on-premise Exchange environment. In that case, DirSync is a required component to install the Windows Intune Exchange connector.

Figure A.2 illustrates the key components used to support this solution. Related to PC management, the cloud-only solution supports fewer clients than ConfigMgr 2012 R2. Windows 8.x, Windows 7, Vista, and XP SP 3 are supported; missing, however, is support for OS X, Windows To Go, Windows Embedded, and Windows Server management. A customer that requires management of those devices would look to ConfigMgr.

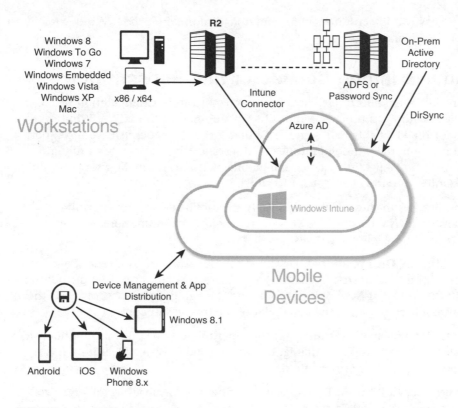

Windows 8
Windows To Go
Windows 7
Windows Embedded
Windows Vista
Windows XP
Mac

x86 / x64

Workstations

R2

Intune
Connector

ADFS or
Password Sync

On-Prem
Active
Directory

DirSync

Azure AD

Windows Intune

Mobile
Devices

Device Management & App
Distribution

Windows 8.1

Android   iOS   Windows
Phone 8.x

FIGURE A.1   UDM components.

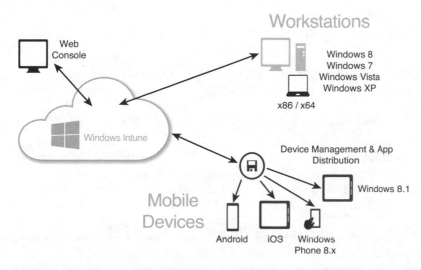

Web
Console

Workstations

Windows 8
Windows 7
Windows Vista
Windows XP

x86 / x64

Windows Intune

Device Management & App
Distribution

Windows 8.1

Mobile
Devices

Android   iOS   Windows
Phone 8.x

FIGURE A.2   Cloud-only components.

Refer to http://www.windowsintune.com for additional information about Windows Intune for cloud PC management.

The Windows Intune Connector and Subscription

Until this point, there have been references to a connector within Configuration Manager to integrate with Windows Intune, without fully explaining what this is. The Windows Intune connector is a ConfigMgr site system role that uses Secure Sockets Layer (SSL) port 443 to communicate to the Windows Intune cloud service. A Windows Intune subscription is created within ConfigMgr to define the mobile platforms ConfigMgr supports and the Microsoft Online Services cloud tenant to which to connect.

The subscription allows the organization to specify the mobile device configuration settings for the Windows Intune service. It is defined before the Intune connector is installed and contains the following items:

▶ **Windows Intune Organizational ID:** This is the actual Windows Intune service the organization must license (separately) and Azure AD namespace that defines the service in the format of *.onmicrosoft.com. The ConfigMgr administrator needs the service available to configure the remainder of the Intune subscription.

▶ **Setting the Management Authority:** This defines the way the organization manages mobile devices, either using ConfigMgr or Intune cloud-only. An organization can only choose a single authority method.

▶ **ConfigMgr User Collection:** This collection defines the users within the organization that can enroll mobile devices.

▶ **Company Portal Information:** Details on the color scheme and general information listed in the company portals.

▶ **Primary Site Code:** The ConfigMgr site code into which the Intune connector site system role is installed.

▶ **Mobile Device Platforms Provisioning:** Defines which mobile platforms users can enroll into the environment along with configurations necessary to support each mobile device.

After the subscription has been configured, the Windows Intune connector site system role is installed, and the connection to Intune is complete. On a set schedule, the connector site system role pushes device settings and deploys applications to the Windows Intune service, enables new users to be able to enroll their mobile devices, and pulls new data about existing managed mobile devices and stores it within the database.

Chapter 7 includes detailed information on installing and using the connector.

Reference URLs

IN THIS APPENDIX

► General Resources

► Microsoft's Configuration Manager Resources

► Other Configuration Manager Resources

► Blogs

► Public Forums

► Utilities

This appendix includes a number of reference URLs associated with System Center 2012 R2 Configuration Manager (ConfigMgr). URLs do change: Although the authors have made every effort to verify the references here as working links, there is no guarantee they will remain current. It is quite possible some will change or be "dead" by the time you read this book. Sometimes the Wayback Machine (https://www.archive.org/) can rescue you from dead or broken links. The Wayback Machine site is an Internet archive, and it takes you back to an archived version of a site...sometimes.

These links are also available "live" at Pearson's InformIT website, at http://www.informit.com/store/system-center-2012-r2-configuration-manager-unleashed-9780672337154, under the Downloads tab. Look for Appendix B, "Reference URLs."

General Resources

A number of websites provide excellent resources for Configuration Manager. This section lists some of the more general resources available:

► http://www.myITforum.com is a community of worldwide Information Technology (IT) professionals and a website established in 1999 by Rod Trent. myITforum includes topics on System Center and IT.

The list of blogs and other ConfigMgr-related articles at myITforum.com is enormous. This appendix includes some specific links and pertinent information, but it does not include everything.

The Windows IT Pro forums are now at http://myITforum.com/forums.

▶ A great source of information is for all things System Center related, including Configuration Manager, is System Center Central, at http://www.systemcentercentral.com.

▶ If you are not already receiving email notifications of new articles in the Microsoft Knowledge Base from kbalertz, you can sign up at http://kbalertz.com/! You just need to create an account and select those technologies you want to be alerted about.

 The System Center Virtual User Group is dedicated to providing educational resources and collaboration between users of System Center technologies worldwide. Meetings present topics from industry experts, including Microsoft engineers. These Live Meeting sessions are recorded for your convenience. To join the user group, go to http://www.linkedin.com/groupRegistration?gid=101906. You can also visit the System Center User Group website at http://www.systemcenterusergroup.net/.

▶ FAQShop.com, published by Enterprise Client Management (ECM) MVP Cliff Hobbs at http://www.faqshop.com/wp/, provides hints, tips, and answers to frequently asked questions (FAQs) related to Microsoft's various systems management technologies including the System Center components. Cliff has completely redeveloped FAQShop, which now includes System Center 2012 Configuration Manager content.

▶ Microsoft now includes people-centric IT (PCIT) as part of their overall Cloud OS vision. For more information on PCIT, see http://www.microsoft.com/en-us/server-cloud/cloud-os/pcit.aspx and download the PCIT whitepaper.

▶ People-centric IT enables each person you support to work from nearly anywhere on the device of their choice and gives you a consistent way to manage and protect it all (see http://www.microsoft.com/en-us/server-cloud/cloud-os/pcit.aspx#fbid=5bZ1uqqrqIt).

▶ With the release of System Center 2012, Microsoft bundles the previously different products as components in the System Center product. http://www.microsoft.com/en-us/server-cloud/system-center/datacenter-management-capabilities.aspx provides an overview of the System Center components and capabilities.

▶ Microsoft's jumping off point for System Center technical resources starts at http://technet.microsoft.com/en-us/systemcenter/.

▶ Microsoft has published a whitepaper on performance and tuning guidelines for Windows Server 2012 R2 at http://msdn.microsoft.com/en-us/library/windows/hardware/dn529133.aspx.

▶ Following are links to previous versions of performance and tuning guidelines:

  ▶ For Windows Server 2012, see http://msdn.microsoft.com/en-us/library/windows/hardware/dn529134.

  ▶ You can download the Windows Server 2008 R2 version from http://msdn.microsoft.com/en-us/windows/hardware/gg463392.

▶ You can download the Windows Server 2008 version from http://www.microsoft.com/whdc/system/sysperf/Perf_tun_srv.mspx.

▶ Read about monitoring and tuning SQL Server 2012 for performance at http://technet.microsoft.com/en-us/library/ms189081.aspx.

▶ http://technet.microsoft.com/en-us/ff657833.aspx provides information on SQL Server Reporting Services (SSRS).

▶ Michael Pearson has an excellent article discussing SSRS recovery planning, available online from the SQL Server Central community (SQLServerCentral.com) at http://www.sqlservercentral.com/columnists/mpearson/recoveryplanningforsqlreportingservices.asp. You must register with SQL Server Central to view the full article.

▶ http://technet.microsoft.com/en-us/library/ms156421.aspx discusses moving the SSRS databases to another computer.

▶ http://blogs.msdn.com/b/sqlserverfaq/archive/2014/02/06/how-to-move-databases-configured-for-sql-server-alwayson.aspx discusses moving databases configured for SQL Server AlwaysOn.

▶ For information on SQL Server best practices, see http://technet.microsoft.com/en-us/sqlserver/bb671430.aspx.

Read about the SQL Server 2012 Best Practice Analyzer at http://blogs.msdn.com/b/sqlsecurity/archive/2012/04/19/sql-server-2012-best-practices-analyzer.aspx, and download it from http://www.microsoft.com/download/en/details.aspx?id=29302.

▶ Use the SQL Server Profiler to view SQL requests sent to a SQL Server database. See http://msdn.microsoft.com/en-us/library/ms187929.aspx for information.

▶ Read about the SQL Server Service Broker at http://social.technet.microsoft.com/wiki/contents/articles/6598.sql-server-service-broker-at-a-glance.aspx.

To test Simple Mail Transfer Protocol (SMTP) using Telnet from a command prompt, follow the steps at http://technet.microsoft.com/en-us/library/aa995718%28EXCHG.65%29.aspx.

▶ A somewhat dated but still useful IDC whitepaper sponsored by Microsoft quantifies how businesses can reduce costs by managing the Windows desktop. This whitepaper is available for download at http://download.microsoft.com/download/a/4/4/a4474b0c-57d8-41a2-afe6-32037fa93ea6/IDC_windesktop_IO_whitepaper.pdf.

▶ According to the SANS Institute, the threat landscape is increasingly dynamic, making efficient and proactive update management more important than ever. http://www.sans.org/top20/ provides information.

Information regarding the Active Directory schema is at http://msdn.microsoft.com/en-us/library/ms675085(VS.85).aspx.

▶ Information on LDIFDE is located at http://technet.microsoft.com/en-us/library/cc731033.aspx.

▶ http://support.microsoft.com/kb/555636 describes the process of exporting and importing objects using LDIFDE.

▶ Requirements for Windows To Go are at http://technet.microsoft.com/library/hh831833.aspx#wtg_hardware.

▶ To learn more about the Microsoft Operations Framework (MOF)? Information about version 4.0 is at http://technet.microsoft.com/library/cc506049.aspx.

▶ Information on the MOF Deliver Phase is at http://technet.microsoft.com/en-us/library/cc506047.aspx.

▶ You can read about the MOF Envision SMF at http://technet.microsoft.com/en-us/library/cc531013.aspx.

▶ For information on MOF 4.0 and the Manage layer, see http://technet.microsoft.com/en-us/library/cc506048.aspx

▶ Information on the IO (Infrastructure Optimization) model is available at http://www.microsoft.com/technet/infrastructure.

▶ If you want to learn about Service Modeling Language (SML), see http://www.w3.org/TR/sml/. For additional technical information on SML from Microsoft, visit http://technet.microsoft.com/en-us/library/bb725986.aspx.

▶ Information on the IO (Infrastructure Optimization) model is available at http://technet.microsoft.com/en-us/library/bb944804.aspx.

▶ The Windows Server technical library is located at http://technet.microsoft.com/en-us/library/bb625087.aspx.

▶ Microsoft's Sysinternals website is at http://technet.microsoft.com/en-us/sysinternals/default.aspx.

▶ Download the Microsoft Security Compliance Manager (SCM) solution accelerator at http://www.microsoft.com/download/en/details.aspx?displaylang=en&id=16776.

▶ Silect Software (http://www.silect.com) offers CP Studio. CP Studio, like SCM, enables authoring of configuration baselines and configuration items outside the ConfigMgr console.

▶ To understand Unified Extensible Firmware Interface (UEFI), see http://en.wikipedia.org/wiki/Unified_Extensible_Firmware_Interface and http://technet.microsoft.com/en-us/library/hh824898.aspx. http://technet.microsoft.com/en-us/library/hh824839.aspx discusses configuring EUFI partitions. For a Windows and GUID Partition Table (FPT) FAQ, see http://msdn.microsoft.com/en-us/library/windows/hardware/dn640535(v=vs.85).aspx.

▶ XML Notepad 2007 is an intuitive tool for browsing and editing XML documents. Read about it at http://msdn2.microsoft.com/en-us/library/aa905339.aspx, and download the tool from http://www.microsoft.com/downloads/details.aspx?familyid=72d6aa49-787d-4118-ba5f-4f30fe913628&displaylang=en.

▶ The Windows Automated Deployment Kit (ADK) for Windows 8.1 is available at http://www.microsoft.com/en-us/download/details.aspx?id=30652.

▶ You can download the Windows Automated Installation Kit (WAIK) 3.0 from http://www.microsoft.com/en-us/download/details.aspx?id=5753, and the WAIK 3.1 Supplement is at http://www.microsoft.com/en-us/download/details.aspx?id=5188.

▶ Learn how to create a custom Windows PE image at http://technet.microsoft.com/en-us/library/dd744533(WS.10).aspx. Add drivers following the steps at http://technet.microsoft.com/en-us/library/dd744355(v=WS.10).aspx#AddDriverDISM.

▶ Understand PAE, NX, and SSE2 processor features used to run Windows 8.1 at http://windows.microsoft.com/en-US/windows-8/what-is-pae-nx-sse2.

▶ Windows IT Pro publishes online articles about System Center and other topics. See http://www.windowsitpro.com/ for information.

▶ Microsoft provides an entire portal on application compatibility at http://technet.microsoft.com/en-us/windows/aa905066.aspx.

▶ Microsoft's vision for mobile computing is at http://blogs.technet.com/b/in_the_cloud/archive/2014/01/29/a-people-first-approach-to-mobile-device-management.aspx.

▶ The whitepaper at http://go.microsoft.com/fwlink/?LinkID=279003 lists the Open Mobile Alliance - Uniform Resource Identifier (OMA-URI) values of possible settings in Windows Phone 8.1.

▶ Information about configuring certificate enrollment profiles is available at http://technet.microsoft.com/en-us/library/dn270539.aspx.

▶ An overview of the sideloading enhancements with Windows 8.1 Update is at http://blogs.windows.com/windows/b/springboard/archive/2014/04/03/windows-8-1-sideloading-enhancements.aspx. You may also want to see the Microsoft Windows volume licensing guide at http://download.microsoft.com/download/9/4/3/9439A928-A0D1-44C2-A099-26A59AE0543B/Windows_8-1_Licensing_Guide.pdf.

▶ Want to create drilldown SSRS reports? See http://technet.microsoft.com/en-us/library/dd207042.aspx.

▶ http://msdn.microsoft.com/en-us/library/ms157403.aspx provides a complete listing of SQL Server Report Server log files.

▶ An overview of Windows Azure Active Directory is at http://www.windowsazure.com/en-us/services/active-directory/.

▶ Read about directory integration at http://technet.microsoft.com/en-us/library/jj573653.aspx.

▶ Prepare for directory synchronization by reading http://technet.microsoft.com/en-us/library/jj151831.aspx to learn about architecture and deployment considerations.

▶ Information on password synchronization is available at http://technet.microsoft.com/en-us/library/dn246918.aspx.

▶ Information on Windows Management Instrumentation (WMI) is available at http://msdn.microsoft.com/en-us/library/aa394582.aspx.

▶ http://msdn.microsoft.com/en-us/library/aa394564(VS.85).aspx discusses WMI logging.

▶ For a discussion of User Account Control and WMI, see http://msdn.microsoft.com/en-us/library/aa826699(VS.85).aspx.

▶ Command-line tools to manage WMI can be downloaded at http://msdn.microsoft.com/en-us/library/aa827351(VS.85).aspx.

▶ See http://msdn.microsoft.com/en-us/library/aa394603(v=vs.85).aspx, http://technet.microsoft.com/en-us/library/cc180763.aspx, and http://blogs.technet.com/b/configmgrteam/archive/2009/05/08/wmi-troubleshooting-tips.aspx for information on WMI troubleshooting.

▶ For information regarding WMI Query Language (WQL), see http://msdn.microsoft.com/en-us/library/aa394606.aspx.

▶ Information regarding Windows network load balancing (NLB) is available in the Network Load Balancing Deployment guide at http://technet.microsoft.com/en-us/library/cc754833(WS.10).aspx.

▶ http://technet.microsoft.com/en-us/library/cc732906(WS.10).aspx provides information on requesting an Internet Server certificate (IIS 7).

▶ The best way to add a certificate to a certificate store en masse is to use group policy; http://technet.microsoft.com/en-us/library/cc770315(WS.10).aspx provides a step-by-step example.

▶ http://technet.microsoft.com/en-us/library/cc732597(WS.10).aspx provides information about acquiring a code signing certificate.

▶ Learn about USMT 8.1 at http://technet.microsoft.com/en-US/windows/dn168170.aspx.

▶ Microsoft provides solution accelerators, which are guidelines and tools to leverage the full functionality of Microsoft usage within your organization. These are available for download at no cost at http://technet.microsoft.com/en-us/solutionaccelerators/dd229342.

▶ Learn about using the Visual Studio Report Designer at http://msdn.microsoft.com/en-us/library/bb558708.aspx.

▶ Learn about Workplace Join at http://technet.microsoft.com/en-us/library/dn280945.aspx.

▶ Web Application Proxy is discussed at http://technet.microsoft.com/en-us/library/dn280942.aspx.

▶ In January 2014, Microsoft reaffirmed its commitment to providing customers choice in management solutions by announcing new mobile device capabilities would be built into the cloud-only architecture with a goal of striving for parity between solutions. Read the announcement at http://blogs.technet.com/b/server-cloud/archive/2014/01/29/new-enhancements-to-windows-intune.aspx/.

▶ See http://www.windowsintune.com for information on Windows Intune for cloud PC management.

▶ Listen to a TechEd 2014 presentation on what's new in 2014 in application management with Configuration Manager and Windows Intune at http://channel9.msdn.com/Events/TechEd/NorthAmerica/2014/PCIT-B323#fbid=qO-G9Ks6x0r.

▶ The Windows Intune administrator console is located at https://manage.microsoft.com.

▶ The Windows Intune Account Portal, located at https://account.manage.microsoft.com, is for use with the Windows Intune service.

▶ Learn how to generate an application enrollment token (AET) for Windows Phone 8 at http://msdn.microsoft.com/en-us/library/windowsphone/develop/jj735576(v=vs.105).aspx.

▶ Purchase a code-signing certificate for sideloading Windows Phone applications for Windows Phone from Symantec at http://www.symantec.com/verisign/code-signing/windows-phone.

▶ Microsoft provides the Support Tool for Windows Intune Trial Management for Windows Phone 8, which you can use to test application deployments to Windows Phone devices. Download the tool from http://www.microsoft.com/en-us/download/details.aspx?id=39079.

▶ Read about metered Internet connections for Windows 8.1 and Windows RT 8.1 at http://windows.microsoft.com/en-US/windows-8/metered-internet-connections-frequently-asked-questions.

▶ Trying to understand licensing?

   ▶ General licensing information is at http://www.microsoft.com/licensing/default.mspx.

   ▶ http://www.microsoft.com/calsuites/en/us/products/default.aspx discusses Server client access licenses (CALs) and the suites they may be included on. You can find the most current list of Microsoft CAL suite technologies at http://download.microsoft.com/download/3/D/4/3D42BDC2-6725-4B29-B75A-A5B04179958B/Licensing_Core_CAL_and_Enterprise_Suite.docx.

   ▶ System Center volume licensing is discussed at http://www.microsoft.com/licensing/about-licensing/SystemCenter2012.aspx.

▶ See Gartner Group's positioning of Configuration Manager in their magic quadrant at http://www.itbl0b.com/2012/06/gartner-says-microsoft-is-leader-of.html#.U2_9-HkU_Gh and http://www2.managedplanet.com/downloads/Gartner%20Client%20Management%20Magic%20Quadrant%202013.pdf for the article it references.

Microsoft's Configuration Manager Resources

The following list includes some general Microsoft resources available for System Center 2012 Configuration Manager:

▶ Microsoft's Configuration Manager website is located at http://www.microsoft.com/en-us/server-cloud/system-center/configuration-manager-2012.aspx.

▶ Find Microsoft's Configuration Manager TechNet main library page at http://technet.microsoft.com/library/gg682129.

▶ What's new in Configuration Manager 2012 Service Pack (SP) 1? See http://technet.microsoft.com/en-us/library/jj591552.aspx.

▶ For what's new in Configuration Manager 2012 R2, see http://technet.microsoft.com/en-us/library/dn236351.aspx.

▶ The System Center 2012 Configuration Manager documentation library with links to the different technical guides is at http://technet.microsoft.com/en-us/library/gg682041.

▶ For a list of technical publications for Configuration Manager, see http://technet.microsoft.com/en-us/library/hh531521.aspx.

▶ Information on supported configurations for Configuration Manager is available at http://technet.microsoft.com/en-us/library/gg682077.aspx.

 Microsoft introduced a full PowerShell provider with ConfigMgr 2012 SP 1. As of the R2 release, there are 560 cmdlets for ConfigMgr. The cmdlet reference is at http://technet.microsoft.com/en-us/library/jj821831(v=sc.20).aspx.

▶ http://support.microsoft.com/kb/2932274 describes the PowerShell changes in ConfigMgr 2012 R2 CU 1.

▶ Read about planning for communications in Configuration Manager at http://technet.microsoft.com/en-us/library/gg712701.aspx, including wake-up proxy for clients.

▶ Documentation on planning for software updates and Windows Server Update Services (WSUS) is at http://technet.microsoft.com/en-us/library/gg712696.aspx#BKMK_SUMCapacity, and http://technet.microsoft.com/en-us/library/dd939928(WS.10).aspx documents WSUS 3.0 system requirements. You may also want to view http://technet.microsoft.com/en-us/library/hh237372.aspx, which lists prerequisites for software updates.

▶ Software update improvements in Service Pack 1 are discussed at http://blogs. technet.com/b/configmgrteam/archive/2013/03/27/software-update-points-in-cm2012sp1.aspx.

▶ Read about creating software update points in an untrusted forest at http://technet. microsoft.com/en-us/library/gg712696.aspx#BKMK_SUP_CrossForest.

▶ Microsoft recommends installing the reporting services point on a remote site system server for improved performance. See http://technet.microsoft.com/en-us/ library/hh394138.aspx.

▶ SSRS should be installed in native mode for System Center 2012 Configuration Manager; this is discussed at http://msdn.microsoft.com/en-us/library/ms143711. aspx.

▶ You can script report backups using RS.exe. Documentation is available at http://msdn.microsoft.com/en-us/library/ms162839.aspx and http://msdn.microsoft. com/en-us/library/ms159720.aspx.

▶ You should always verify your reporting services installation before installing the reporting services point. http://msdn.microsoft.com/en-us/library/ms143773.aspx discusses the steps to take.

▶ Configuring reporting in ConfigMgr is discussed at http://technet.microsoft.com/ en-us/library/gg712698.aspx.

▶ ConfigMgr reports are now fully enabled for role-based administration. For information, see the "Planning for Role-Based Administration for Reports" section at http://technet.microsoft.com/en-us/library/7ca322fc-bbbf-42c8-82c9-6fc8941ef2e6#BKMK_RoleBaseAdministration.

▶ Hardware sizing information for site systems can be found at http://technet. microsoft.com/en-us/library/hh846235.aspx.

▶ Ports used by Configuration Manager are discussed at http://technet.microsoft.com/ en-us/library/bb632618.aspx. Information on configuring ports for Network Access Protection (NAP) is located at http://technet.microsoft.com/en-us/library/bb694170. aspx.

▶ See http://technet.microsoft.com/en-us/library/gg712701.aspx#Support_Internet_ Clients to plan for implementing Internet-based client management.

▶ Configuring a service principal name (SPN) for SQL Server site database servers is discussed at http://technet.microsoft.com/en-us/library/bb735885.aspx.

▶ Guidance for securing specific site system servers is at http://technet.microsoft.com/ en-us/library/gg682165.aspx#BKMK_Security_SiteServer.

▶ To configure proxy for site server roles, see http://technet.microsoft.com/en-us/ library/gg712282.aspx#BKMK_PlanforProxyServers.

▶ Best practices for collections are at http://technet.microsoft.com/en-us/library/ gg699372.aspx.

B

▶ Tips on installing and configuring distribution points (DPs) are at http://technet. microsoft.com/en-us/library/gg682115.aspx#BKMK_InstallDistributionPoint. You may also want to view http://technet.microsoft.com/en-us/library/hh272770.aspx, which discusses installing and configuring site system roles.

▶ Beginning with Service Pack 1, you can create a cloud DP in Windows Azure. Cloud-based DPs support both intranet and Internet-based clients, and automatically enable BranchCache on the DP to help you reduce content transfer from your cloud-based DP:

    ▶ See http://technet.microsoft.com/en-us/library/b2516212-e524-4031-9a1f-7b768084304d#BKMK_PlanCloudDPs for more information about cloud DPs.

    ▶ Also check out http://blogs.technet.com/b/configmgrteam/archive/2013/01/31/new-distribution-points-in-configuration-manager-sp1.aspx.

▶ http://technet.microsoft.com/en-us/library/gg712321.aspx discusses the automatic retry settings for a pull DP.

▶ When using HTTPS on a DP, you must import a certificate for the DP to use when it communicates with other site systems. This is discussed at http://technet. microsoft.com/en-us/library/230dfec0-bddb-4429-a5db-30020e881f1e#BKMK_clientdistributionpoint2008_cm2012.

▶ Learn how to customize Windows PE boot images for use in ConfigMgr at http://technet.microsoft.com/en-us/library/dn387582.aspx.

▶ http://technet.microsoft.com/en-us/library/hh427342.aspx#BKMK_OSDLog is a list of log files for operating system deployment (OSD).

▶ http://blogs.technet.com/b/inside_osd/archive/2007/12/13/troubleshooting-tips.aspx discusses OSD troubleshooting tips.

▶ http://blogs.technet.com/b/configmgrteam/archive/2013/07/15/customizing-offline-servicing-of-operating-system-images.aspx discusses customizing offline servicing of OSD images.

▶ For information about managing devices with write filters enabled using ConfigMgr, see http://blogs.technet.com/b/configmgrteam/archive/2012/11/26/managing-embedded-devices-with-write-filters-in-configuration-manager-service-pack-1.aspx.

▶ Read about integrating App-V into ConfigMgr; see the whitepaper at http://www. microsoft.com/en-us/download/details.aspx?id=38177.

▶ Read how to migrate user data from Windows XP to Windows 8.1 systems using ConfigMgr at http://blogs.technet.com/b/configmgrteam/archive/2013/09/12/how-to-migrate-user-data-from-win-xp-to-win-8-1-with-system-center-2012-r2-configmgr.aspx.

▶ Microsoft provides guidance on upgrading from Configuration Manager 2007 to System Center 2012 Configuration Manager at http://technet.microsoft.com/en-us/library/gg682006.aspx. Related is http://technet.microsoft.com/en-us/library/gg712336.aspx, which discusses security and privacy for migration to ConfigMgr 2012. http://technet.microsoft.com/en-us/library/gg712275.aspx discusses planning for content deployment during your migration.

▶ http://technet.microsoft.com/en-us/library/jj822981.aspx discusses upgrading from ConfigMgr 2012 RTM to SP 1 and then R2.

▶ Troubleshooting your ConfigMgr migration? See http://technet.microsoft.com/en-us/library/gg712297.aspx.

▶ Prerequisites for deploying the ConfigMgr client are discussed at http://technet.microsoft.com/en-us/library/gg682042.aspx.

▶ http://technet.microsoft.com/en-us/library/hh427342.aspx is a technical reference for ConfigMgr log files.

▶ See http://technet.microsoft.com/en-us/library/bb680409.aspx for information on configuring logging for Windows Mobile and Windows CE devices.

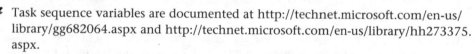

Task sequence variables are documented at http://technet.microsoft.com/en-us/library/gg682064.aspx and http://technet.microsoft.com/en-us/library/hh273375.aspx.

▶ Learn about remote profile connections at

  ▶ http://technet.microsoft.com/en-us/library/dn261225.aspx

  ▶ http://technet.microsoft.com/en-us/library/dn261201.aspx

  ▶ http://technet.microsoft.com/en-us/library/dn261199.aspx

▶ Microsoft's IT showcase for Configuration Manager is available at http://technet.microsoft.com/en-us/library/bb687796.aspx. It includes MSIT's early adopter experiences, best experiences, and lessons learned from their deployments of System Center Configuration Manager. You can also read about MSIT's upgrade of their user base from Windows 8 to Windows 8.1 at http://www.microsoft.com/en-us/download/details.aspx?id=40811 and http://www.microsoft.com/en-us/download/details.aspx?id=41965.

▶ To configure SQL Server site database replication, check out http://technet.microsoft.com/en-us/library/bb693697.aspx. http://technet.microsoft.com/en-us/library/bb693954.aspx discusses disabling database replication.

▶ A TechNet virtual lab introducing System Center 2012 Configuration Manager is available at https://msevents.microsoft.com/CUI/EventDetail.aspx?EventID=1032499898&culture=en-us.

B

▶ Following are some videos on System Center 2012 Configuration Manager:

  ▶ Wally Mead presents a ConfigMgr 2012 administration overview at the Belgian System Center Day 2011 on November 3, 2011; this was organized by the Belgian System Center User Group (http://scug.be/), see http://technet.microsoft.com/en-us/edge/Video/hh536213.

  ▶ Nico Sienaert discusses what's new in OSD at the System Center User Group in Belgium on March 22, 2012, available at http://technet.microsoft.com/en-us/video/sccm-2012-what-is-new-in-os-deployment.

▶ The different database roles used in Configuration Manager are discussed at http://technet.microsoft.com/en-us/library/bb632943.aspx. Although referring to ConfigMgr 2007 when this appendix was written, the information is still applicable.

▶ Information on managing mobile devices in Configuration Manager is at http://technet.microsoft.com/en-us/library/gg682022.aspx.

▶ To identify the Windows groups and accounts used in Configuration Manager and any requirements, see http://technet.microsoft.com/en-us/library/hh427337.aspx.

▶ http://technet.microsoft.com/en-us/library/gg712697.aspx discusses backup and recovery in Configuration Manager.

▶ Use the Set-CMSoftwareUpdatePoint PowerShell cmdlet, documented at http://technet.microsoft.com/library/jj821938.aspx, to change settings for a software update point (SUP).

▶ PKI certificate requirements for ConfigMgr are discussed at http://technet.microsoft.com/en-us/library/gg699362.aspx.

▶ Certificate profiles in Configuration Manager are discussed at http://technet.microsoft.com/en-us/library/dn248971.aspx.

▶ Package Conversion Manager (PCM) allows you to convert ConfigMgr 2007 packages into ConfigMgr 2012 applications. See http://technet.microsoft.com/en-us/library/hh531583.aspx for information.

▶ Prerequisites for Endpoint Protection are documented at http://technet.microsoft.com/en-us/library/hh508780.aspx.

▶ You can download the ConfigMgr 2012 R2 SDK from http://www.microsoft.com/download/en/details.aspx?id=29559.

▶ Classes available for hardware inventory for mobile devices are listed at http://technet.microsoft.com/en-us/library/dn469411.aspx.

▶ Compliance settings for mobile devices in Configuration Manager are documented at http://technet.microsoft.com/en-us/library/dn376523.aspx.

▶ A guide for obtaining the Symantec certificate and signing the company portal app, written by Microsoft Intune Support Services, is at http://blogs.technet.com/b/windowsintune/archive/2013/08/09/windows-intune-walkthrough-windows-phone-8-management.aspx?ocid=aff-n-we-loc--ITPRO40922. Although written for the Intune cloud-only service, the Symantec code-signing certificate and company portal steps are the same for Intune, regardless of whether it is integrated with ConfigMgr.

▶ Download the Windows Intune company portal for Windows Phone, which works with ConfigMgr 2012 R2 and Windows Intune, at http://www.microsoft.com/en-us/download/details.aspx?id=36060.

▶ The System Center Configuration Manager Company Portal App is available at http://www.microsoft.com/en-us/download/details.aspx?id=40795.

▶ ConfigMgr 2012 R2 allows you to do a selective wipe on mobile devices that only removes company content. Read about the content removed on various devices at http://technet.microsoft.com/en-us/library/2c6bd0e5-d436-41c8-bf38-30152d76be10#bkmk_dev.

▶ See http://blogs.technet.com/b/configmgrteam/archive/2013/03/13/troubleshooting-windows-rt-client-software-distribution-issues.aspx for troubleshooting Windows RT client software distribution issues.

▶ http://technet.microsoft.com/en-us/library/da15f702-ba6a-40fb-b130-c624f17e2846#BKMK_ClientDeployPrereqforLnU discusses prerequisites for client deployment to Linux and UNIX servers.

▶ Linux/UNIX and Macintosh client agents are not included with the installation files for ConfigMgr. You must download the appropriate agent from the Microsoft Download Center:

  ▶ For ConfigMgr 2012 SP 1, download the agent from http://www.microsoft.com/en-us/download/details.aspx?id=36212.

  ▶ For ConfigMgr 2012 R2, download the agent from http://www.microsoft.com/en-us/download/details.aspx?id=39360.

▶ Installing the Linux/UNIX client is discussed at http://technet.microsoft.com/en-us/library/jj573939.aspx.

▶ Read about Mac OS X 10.9 support at http://blogs.technet.com/b/configmgrteam/archive/2013/12/16/mac-os-x-10-9-support-for-sc-2012-config-manager-clients.aspx.

Other Configuration Manager Resources

Microsoft of course is not the only organization to discuss Configuration Manager. A number of websites provide excellent resources for Configuration Manager. Following are several you may want to investigate:

▶ Looking for training?

▶ Microsoft provides two courses on System Center 2012 R2 Configuration Manager:

10747D—Administering System Center 2012 Configuration Manager: Information on this 5-day class is available at http://www.microsoft.com/learning/en-us/course.aspx?id=10747d.

10748C—Deploying System Center 2012 Configuration Manager: Information on this 5-day class is at http://www.microsoft.com/learning/en/us/course.aspx?id=10748c.

▶ A great ConfigMgr trainer who teaches the ConfigMgr MOC is Michael Head. His current course schedule is located at http://www.HeadSmartGroup.com/.

▶ Infront Consulting Group offers System Center training; curriculum and syllabi are available at www.infrontconsulting.com/training.php.

▶ Microsoft Virtual Academy provides an overview course at http://www.microsoftvirtualacademy.com/tracks/overview-and-infrastructure-changes-in-sccm-2012.

▶ http://www.windows-noob.com/forums/index.php?/forum/92-configuration-manager-2012/ is a forum on System Center 2012 Configuration Manager.

▶ Configuration packs can be found at the System Center Marketplace. See http://systemcenter.pinpoint.microsoft.com/en-US/applications/search/configuration-manager-d10?sort=released&q=partnername%3aMicrosoft+System+Center.

▶ You can use Orchestrator to automate the client install on a Linux/UNIX system. For information on the process and sample runbooks to download, see http://blogs.technet.com/b/neilp/archive/2012/10/17/system-center-2012-automating-configuration-manager-client-deployment-to-linux-systems.aspx.

▶ Curious about the content library store? See Kent Agerlund's blog post at http://blog.coretech.dk/kea/understanding-the-new-content-library-store-in-5-minutes/.

▶ Don Jones discusses defining parameters in PowerShell scripts at http://technet.microsoft.com/en-us/magazine/jj554301.aspx.

▶ For information on the PowerShell execution policy, see http://4sysops.com/archives/powershell-execution-policy/?utm_source=feedburner&utm_medium=feed&utm_campaign=Feed%3A+4sysops+(4sysops).

▶ Read about using PowerShell to troubleshoot and repair WMI errors by the Scripting Guy at http://blogs.technet.com/b/heyscriptingguy/archive/2012/03/29/use-powershell-to-troubleshoot-and-repair-wmi-errors.aspx.

▶ CIM is the component information model that WMI is based on. To learn more about CIM, read the tutorial at http://www.wbemsolutions.com/tutorials/CIM/index.html.

▶ Need help with troubleshooting client push installation? Check out http://blogs. technet.com/b/sudheesn/archive/2010/05/31/troubleshooting-sccm-part-i-client- push-installation.aspx.

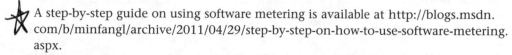 A step-by-step guide on using software metering is available at http://blogs.msdn. com/b/minfangl/archive/2011/04/29/step-by-step-on-how-to-use-software-metering. aspx.

▶ Steve Rachui discusses state messaging in depth at http://blogs.msdn.com/b/steverac/ archive/2011/01/07/sccm-state-messaging-in-depth.aspx.

▶ Steve Rachui has written a series of blog posts on the software updates process as viewed through the log files:

  ▶ http://blogs.msdn.com/b/steverac/archive/2011/04/10/software-updates- internals-mms-2011-session-part-i.aspx

  ▶ http://blogs.msdn.com/b/steverac/archive/2011/04/16/software-updates- internals-mms-2011-session-part-ii.aspx

  ▶ http://blogs.msdn.com/b/steverac/archive/2011/04/30/software-updates- internals-mms-2011-session-part-iii.aspx

▶ System Center Orchestrator is Microsoft's integration and automation tool. Steve Rachui provides runbooks as examples of using Orchestrator with ConfigMgr at http://blogs.msdn.com/b/steverac/archive/2013/04/16/mms-2013-orchestrator-and- configmgr-better-together.aspx.

▶ CoreTech provides an overview of cloud DPs at http://blog.coretech.dk/kea/ configmgr-cloud-distribution-points/.

▶ http://www.scconfigmgr.com/2014/02/27/monitor-osd-with-status-message-queries- in-configmgr-2012/ discusses using the status message viewer to determine the history of a task sequence deployment.

▶ Steve Rachui discusses OSD prestage and EUFI systems at http://blogs.msdn.com/b/ steverac/archive/2013/09/13/osd-pre-stage-and-uefi-systems.aspx.

▶ http://blogs.msdn.com/b/steverac/archive/2014/03/29/the-suite-spot-of-imaging.aspx discusses using OSD for imaging.

▶ http://www.itninja.com provides general guidance on software deployment and a forum for users to share their experiences testing whether software can be installed unattended. This site was previously known as AppDeploy.com.

▶ Read about open management infrastructure (OMI) at http://www.opengroup.org/ software/omi. You can find more in-depth information on OMI and how it works at https://collaboration.opengroup.org/omi/. Download the OMI getting started guide from https://collaboration.opengroup.org/omi/documents.php.

▶ Steve Rachui discusses Linux and UNIX support in ConfigMgr 2012 SP 1 at http://blogs.msdn.com/b/steverac/archive/2013/06/27/unix-and-linux-support-in- configmgr-2012-sp1.aspx.

▶ TechNet Magazine provides a look at Configuration Manager 2012's user-centric approach at http://technet.microsoft.com/en-us/magazine/gg675930.aspx.

▶ Niall Brady, an ECM MVP, publishes guides for ConfigMgr 2012 at http://www.windows-noob.com/forums/index.php?/topic/4045-system-center-2012-configuration-manager-guides/.

▶ Steve Rachui discusses operating system deployment to Linux operating systems http://blogs.msdn.com/b/steverac/archive/2014/01/02/osd-for-linux-imaging-yes-really.aspx. Note that this is not supported by Microsoft.

▶ For information about converting WQL to SQL, Brian Leary has a nice article at http://www.myITforum.com/articles/8/view.asp?id=9908. Written for web reporting with ConfigMgr 2007, the information is still applicable.

▶ Santos Martinez provides a walk-through to help you build reports that support role-based administration; his blog post is available at http://blogs.technet.com/b/smartinez/archive/2013/11/28/how-to-create-a-rba-capable-report-for-configmgr-r2.aspx.

▶ Marcus Oh writes about retrieving objects into a collection that does not exist in another collection at http://marcusoh.blogspot.com/2007/08/sms-selecting-objects-not-in-collection.html.

▶ Beginning with Configuration Manager 2007 R2, ConfigMgr can define a task sequence variable on a collection or individual resource without a value. Read about it in a posting by coauthor Jason Sandys at http://blog.configmgrftw.com/?p=44.

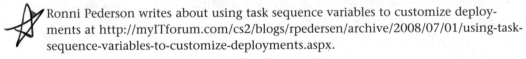

Ronni Pederson writes about using task sequence variables to customize deployments at http://myITforum.com/cs2/blogs/rpedersen/archive/2008/07/01/using-task-sequence-variables-to-customize-deployments.aspx.

▶ When a user with write permissions browses to a distribution point share on a Windows 7 system, he can accidentally modify the source for any package by simply viewing the contents. Windows 7 creates a thumbs.db that contains thumbnails of images in the folder. For additional information, see coauthor Greg Ramsey's post at http://gregramsey.wordpress.com/2012/02/13/interesting-issue-with-thumbs-db/.

▶ Flexera's AdminStudio (http://www.flexerasoftware.com/products/adminstudio-suite.htm) is a popular software packaging suite.

Adaptiva Software (http://www.adaptiva.com) extends Microsoft's technologies to enhance PC power management. 1E (http://www.1e.com) also has a number of products to assist with sustainability and energy efficiency.

▶ Symantec offers mobile device management software for iOS, Android, and Windows Phone devices; http://www.symantec.com/mobile-management#sccm provides details.

Blogs

Following are some blogs the authors have used. Some are more active than others are, and new blogs seem to spring up overnight:

▶ http://bink.nu is managed by Steven Bink, former MVP for Windows Server Technologies. According to the blog, it "watches Microsoft like a hawk."

▶ Garth Jones, a ECM MVP, posts articles at http://www.myITforum.com/contrib/default.asp?cid=116. He also is affiliated with the SMS User Group in Canada; those blogs are at http://smsug.ca/blogs/.

▶ http://sms-hints-tricks.blogspot.com/ is by Matthew Hudson, ECM MVP.

▶ Don Hite blogs at http://myITforum.com/cs2/blogs/dhite/.

▶ Ronni Pederson's blog is at http://ronnipedersen.com/. Older articles are at http://myITforum.com/cs2/blogs/rpedersen/.

▶ Ron Crumbaker, ECM MVP, blogs at http://myITforum.com/cs2/blogs/rcrumbaker/.

▶ Kim Oppalfens blogs at http://myitforum.com/cs2/blogs/koppalfens/default.aspx.

▶ Sherry Kissinger, ECM MVP, blogs at http://myITforum.com/cs2/blogs/skissinger/.

▶ Roger Zander blogs at http://myITforum.com/cs2/blogs/rzander/default.aspx.

▶ http://systemscentre.blogspot.com/ is maintained by MVP Steve Beaumont.

▶ Anthony Clendenen has a myITforum blog at http://myITforum.com/cs2/blogs/socal/default.aspx.

▶ By Carlos Santiago, a Premier Field Engineer at Microsoft, at http://blogs.technet.com/carlossantiago.

▶ The OSD Support Team blog is at http://blogs.technet.com/b/system_center_configuration_manager_operating_system_deployment_support_blog/.

▶ Microsoft's server and cloud blog is at http://blogs.technet.com/b/server-cloud/.

▶ The Microsoft "Deployment Guys" have a blog at http://blogs.technet.com/deploymentguys/default.aspx.

▶ Paul Thomsen blogs at http://myITforum.com/cs2/blogs/pthomsen/.

▶ MVP Scott Moss blogs at http://www.systemcentercentral.com/author/smoss/.

▶ http://blogs.technet.com/b/configmgrteam/ is the official blog of the Microsoft System Center Configuration Manager product group.

▶ Kevin Sullivan's Management blog is at https://blogs.technet.com/kevinsul_blog/. (Kevin is a Technology Specialist at Microsoft focusing on management products.)

▶ http://marcusoh.blogspot.com/ is a blog by MVP Marcus Oh.

▶ http://www.msfaq.se/ is Stefan Schürling's blog on Microsoft System Management. Stefan is an ECM MVP and contributor.

▶ Niall Brady, ECM MVP, blogs at http://www.niallbrady.com/. Former postings are at http://myitforum.com/cs2/blogs/nbrady/.

▶ Samuel Erskine blogs at http://www.itprocessed.com/.

▶ Torsten Meringer, ECM MVP, manages the German ConfigMgr blog http://www.mssccmfaq.de.

▶ http://myITforum.com/cs2/blogs/sthompson is the blog for Steve Thompson, ECM MVP.

▶ See http://blogs.msdn.com/b/shitanshu/ for information about Configuration Manager in Microsoft IT.

Following are our own blogs:

▶ Kerrie Meyler, MVP and lead author for *System Center 2012 Configuration Manager Unleashed*, maintains a blog at http://www.networkworld.com/author/kerrie-meyler/.

▶ Check out the blog at http://blog.configmgrftw.com/ by coauthor and ECM MVP Jason Sandys.

▶ Greg Ramsey, ECM MVP and a coauthor for this book, blogs at http://gregramsey. wordpress.com/.

▶ Panu Saukko, ECM MVP and a contributing author to this book, blogs at http://myITforum.com/cs2/blogs/psaukko/.

▶ Contributing author Kenneth van Surksum blogs at http://www.vansurksum.com.

▶ Contributing author Michael Wiles blogged at http://blogs.technet.com/b/mwiles/ while at Microsoft.

▶ Steve Rachui is a CSS guru on ConfigMgr and our technical editor. Check out his blog at http://blogs.msdn.com/steverac/.

Public Forums

If you need an answer to a question, the first place to check is the Microsoft public forums. A list of available TechNet forums is maintained at http://social.technet.microsoft. com/Forums/en-us/home. It is best to see whether the question has already been posted before you ask it yourself!

The link to all the System Center 2012 Configuration Manager forums is http://social. technet.microsoft.com/Forums/en-US/category/systemcenter2012configurationmanager. Following are the specific forums (English):

▶ Configuration Manager 2012—General (http://social.technet.microsoft.com/forums/ en-US/configmgrgeneral/threads).

▶ Configuration Manager 2012—Client and site deployment (http://social.technet. microsoft.com/Forums/en-US/configmanagerdeployment/threads).

- Configuration Manager 2012—Application management (http://social.technet. microsoft.com/Forums/en-US/configmanagerapps/threads).

- Configuration Manager 2012—Security and compliance (http://social.technet. microsoft.com/Forums/en-US/configmanagersecurity/threads).

- Configuration Manager—Operating System Deployment (http://social.technet. microsoft.com/forums/en-US/configmgrosd/threads).

- Configuration Manager—SDK (http://social.technet.microsoft.com/forums/en-US/ configmgrsdk/threads).

- Configuration Manager 2012—Migration (http://social.technet.microsoft.com/ Forums/en-US/configmanagermigration/threads).

- myITforum also has a discussion list for Configuration Manager along with a number of other discussion lists, see http://myitforum.com/myitforumwp/services/ email-lists-2/.

Utilities

Following are some utilities, both Microsoft and third party:

 The WMI Diagnosis Utility (WMIDiag) is available at the Microsoft download site, http://www.microsoft.com/downloads/details.aspx?familyid=d7ba3cd6-18d1-4d05-b11e-4c64192ae97d&displaylang=en.

 The WMI Administrative Tools are downloadable at http://www.microsoft.com/ download/en/details.aspx?id=24045.

 The Windows PowerShell Scriptomatic tool, created by Ed Wilson, enables you to browse WMI namespaces and automatically generate PowerShell code to connect to WMI objects. You can download the tool from http://www.microsoft.com/ download/en/details.aspx?displaylang=en&id=24121.

- Use Process Monitor to capture detailed process activity on Windows systems. For information and a download link, see http://technet.microsoft.com/en-us/ sysinternals/bb896645.aspx.

 NetDiag is a diagnostic tool that helps isolate networking and connectivity problems. For information, see http://technet.microsoft.com/library/Cc938980.

 Netperf is a benchmark that can be used to measure performance of many types of networking. It provides tests for both unidirectional throughput and end-to-end latency. For more information and to download the tool, see http://www.netperf. org/netperf/.

You can download and install add-ons and extensions for System Center 2012 Configuration Manager at http://www.microsoft.com/download/cn/details. aspx?id=29265. This includes the ConfigMgr toolkit and PCM.

Troubleshoot port status issues using PortQry and PortQryUI, downloadable from http://www.microsoft.com/downloads/details.aspx?familyid=89811747-C74B-4638-A2D5-AC828BDC6983&displaylang=en and http://www.microsoft.com/downloads/details.aspx?FamilyID=8355E537-1EA6-4569-AABB-F248F4BD91D0&displaylang=en, respectively.

 System Center Update Publisher (SCUP) enables third-party vendors and IT administrators to import, manage, and develop software update definitions that can be deployed with ConfigMgr. You can download SCUP from http://www.microsoft.com/download/en/details.aspx?id=11940.

 At times creating WMI queries can be quite cumbersome. There are a number of tools available for free to help ease the process. Following are some popular ones:

- **WMI Code Creator**: https://www.microsoft.com/download/en/details.aspx?displaylang=en&id=8572

- **WMI Code Generator**: http://www.robvanderwoude.com/wmigen.php

- **Scriptomatic**: http://technet.microsoft.com/en-us/library/ff730935.aspx; download it from http://www.microsoft.com/downloads/details.aspx?FamilyID=d87daf50-e487-4b0b-995c-f36a2855016e&displaylang=en.

- RSS Scripter, developed by SQL Server MVP Jasper Smith, simplifies creation of VB scripts for RS.EXE. Information is available at http://www.sqlservercentral.com/Forums/Topic1439847-150-1.aspx.

APPENDIX C

Available Online

IN THIS APPENDIX

▶ Setting SMSTSPreferredAdvertID

▶ Creating an OfflineImageServicing Folder

▶ Viewing the Current Drive Letter Set

▶ Pausing a Task Sequence

▶ Live Links

Online content is available to provide add-on value to readers of *System Center 2012 R2 Configuration Manager Unleashed: Supplement to System Center 2012 Configuration Manager (SCCM) Unleashed*. You can download this material, organized by chapter, from http://www.informit.com/store/system-center-2012-r2-configuration-manager-unleashed-9780672337154. This content is not available elsewhere. Note that the authors and publisher do not guarantee or provide technical support for the material.

Setting SMSTSPreferredAdvertID

Chapter 6, "What's New in Operating System Deployment," discusses how you could set the value of the SMSTSPreferredAdvertID task sequence variable. You could use the Set_SMSTSPreferredAdvertID.vbs VBScript in a prestart command to set this variable. It prompts the user for the deployment ID.

Creating an OfflineImageServicing Folder

Chapter 6 also discusses the offline servicing process. During this process, the target image file is temporarily copied to a working folder, named ConfigMgr_OfflineImageServicing by default. This folder is normally located at the drive root on the site server where the Configuration Manager (ConfigMgr) binaries are installed. The WMI_Create_OfflineImageServicing_folder.ps1 PowerShell script lets you update the location of this folder.

Viewing the Current Drive Letter Set

You can use the View_Current_Drive_Letter_Set.ps1 PowerShell script, discussed in Chapter 6, to verify the current drive letter set. By default, no value is set that equates to using the drive the ConfigMgr binaries are installed on.

Pausing a Task Sequence

Task sequences should only be paused when troubleshooting. Pausing the task sequence allows you to manually simulate actions, test incomes, and review or update configurations in short order without having to change the task sequence or rerun it from the beginning.

Pausing a task sequence involves adding a never-ending script into a set of tasks that are executing where you want the task sequence to pause. Use the pause.vbs VBScript, discussed in Chapter 6, to pause a task sequence and resume it after completing any manual operations.

Live Links

Reference URLs (see Appendix B, "Reference URLs") are provided as live links. These include nearly 300 (clickable) hypertext links and references to materials and sites related to Configuration Manager.

A disclaimer and unpleasant fact regarding live links: URLs change! Companies are subject to mergers and acquisitions, pages move, and change are made on websites, and so on. Although these links were accurate mid-2014, it is possible that some will change or be "dead" by the time you read this book. Sometimes the Wayback Machine (https://www.archive.org/) can rescue you from dead or broken links. The Wayback Machine site is an Internet archive, and it will take you back to an archived version of a site...sometimes.

Index

Numbers

0x80004005 error code, 172

0x8007000E error code, 190

0x80072ee2 error code, 176

1E, 332

A

accounts, Network Access, 32

Active Directory

  ADFS (Active Directory Federation Services), 203

  Azure AD, 17-18, 199-200

  DirSync

    Directory Synchronization Tool, installing, 204-208

    DirSync Configuration Wizard, 204-208

    installing, 204-208

    overview, 312

  integrating, 13

  overview, 318

  rights management services, 16

  synchronizing with Microsoft Azure AD, 200

    Azure AD namespace, creating, 200-204

    Directory Synchronization Tool, installing, 204-208

    Windows Intune instance, creating, 200-204

Active Directory Federation Services (ADFS), 203, 312

Active Directory Synchronization (DirSync), 312

AD. *See* Active Directory

Adaptiva Software, 331

Add Site System Roles Wizard, 233-234

ADFS (Active Directory Federation Services), 203, 312

ADK (Automated Deployment Kit), 148, 319

administration changes (ConfigMgr 2012 R2)

    automatic client upgrade, 31

    certificate profiles, 27

    client settings, 27-28

    database replication configuration, 20

        configuring interval for replication data summary, 23

        managing replication alerts, 23-24

        modifying SQL Server replication configuration, 20-21

        scheduling transfer of site data across replication links, 21-22

        support for distributed views, 22

    DPs (distribution points), 28-31

        cloud-based DPs, 28

        pull DPs, 28-31

    Internet proxy server configuration, 24

    Network Access accounts, 32

    PowerShell support, 32-34

    security, 28

    software update points, 25-27

        multiple software update points, 26

        specifying internal WSUS server as synchronization source, 26-27

        in untrusted forests, 26-27

    Windows Intune integration and extensions, 25

AdminStudio, 331

ADRs (automatic deployment rules), 40-41

Agerlund, Kent, 328

alerts, 43

Always On, Always Connected, 51-52

Android devices

    configuration items, 261

    enrolling, 254

    log files, 292

    mobile device management, 248

    retiring/wiping mobile devices, 289

    sideloading applications, 103

Apple App Store deployment type, creating, 90-91

Apple Developer License, 101

Apple devices. *See* iOS device management

Apple OS X computers. *See* OS X support

application compatibility, 319

application deployment

    to Apple OS X computers, 105-107

    application deployment type, 111

    best practices, 112-115

        applications in task sequences, 115

        software installation, 112-115

    definition of application, 77-78

    DTs (deployment types), 78

    to Linux and UNIX computers, 108-109

    to mobile devices, 85-86, 281-286

        Apple App Store deployment type, 90-91

        with company portal, 285-288

        defining application information, 282-284

        Google Play Store deployment type, 92-93

        sideloading applications, 93-103

        Windows Phone Store deployment type, 89-90

        Windows Store deployment type, 86-89

    new features, 78-79

    overview, 77

sideloading applications, 93-94

  for Android devices, 103

  for Apple iPhone, iPod, and iPad devices, 101-103

  certificate profiles, 96-97

  domain-joined machines, 95

  for Windows and Windows RT devices, 94-95

  Windows modern applications, 97-99

  for Windows Phone devices, 99-101

virtual applications, 81-82

  App-V 5 deployment type, 82-83

  App-V virtual environments, 83-85

VPN profiles, 104

web applications, 111

Windows Intune, 309-310

write filter support, 79-81

application deployment type, 111

Application Management, 38-39

  App-V virtual environments, 39

  overview, 38

  Windows sideloading keys, 39

applications

  definition of, 77-78

  deployment. See application deployment

  sideloading, 93-94

    for Android devices, 103

    for Apple iPhone, iPod, and iPad devices, 101-103

    certificate profiles, 96-97

    domain-joined machines, 95

    VPN profiles, 104

    for Windows and Windows RT devices, 94-95

    Windows modern applications, 97-99

    for Windows Phone devices, 99-101

  targeting, 13

App-V 5 deployment type, creating, 82-83

App-V virtual environments

  creating, 83-85

  overview, 39

.appx file format, 101

architecture

  cross-platform agent architecture, 119-120

  Windows Intune

    cloud-only architecture, 313-314

    unified architecture, 311-313

asset inventory. See inventory

Assets and Compliance (ConfigMgr), 34

  client notification, 36-37

  collections, 34

  company resource access, 37-38

  compliance settings, 37

  maintenance windows for software updates, 35

  Reassign Site option, 36

  Remote Connection Profiles, 37

  Resultant Client Settings, 34-35

  user data and profiles, 38

Authentication Method page (Create VPN Profile Wizard), 277

author's blogs, 332-333

Automated Deployment Kit (ADK), 148, 319

automatic client upgrade, 31

automatic deployment rules (ADRs), 40-41

Auto-Trigger VPN, 15

available discovery and inventory data, 255-258

Azure AD, 17-18, 199-200

  Azure AD Premium, 17

  namespace, creating, 200-204

  synchronizing AD with, 200

    Azure AD namespace, creating, 200-204

Directory Synchronization Tool, installing, 204-208

Windows Intune instance, creating, 200-204

B

Background Intelligent Transfer Service (BITS), 120

Beaumont, Steve, 331

best practices

    application deployment, 112-115

        applications in task sequences, 115

        software installation, 112-115

    overview, 317

Bink, Steven, 331

BITS (Background Intelligent Transfer Service), 120

/BITSPriority option (CCMSetup.exe), 54

blogs, 331-333

boot images, 151-155

    down-level boot images, 152-154

    optional components within, 154-155

boot partitions, 176-177

Brady, Niall, 330, 332

BranchCache downloads, 57

bring your own device (BYOD), 5, 10-11. *See also* mobile device management

built-in task sequence variables, 175-176

BYOD (bring your own device), 5, 10-11. *See also* mobile device management

C

CAS (central administration site), 47-48

CCMAgent-DATE-TIME.log file, 145

ccmexec command, 143

CCMNotification-DATE-TIME.log file, 145

CCMPrefPane-DATE-TIME.log file, 145

CCMSetup.exe, 54-55

central administration site (CAS), 47-48

certificate enrollment profiles, 271-273

    configuring, 319

    creating, 96-97

    new features, 27

Certificate Registration Point site system role, 272

certificates

    certificate enrollment profiles, 271-273

        configuring, 319

        creating, 96-97

        new features, 27

    Certificate Registration Point site system role, 272

    OS X requirements, 122

Change Ownership action, 259

changes, monitoring, 42

    alerts, 43

    client operations, 45

    deployment status, 43

    distribution status, 43

    reporting, 43

Check Readiness task, 170-172

chmod command, 127

CIM (common information model), 119

classes (hardware inventory)

    custom classes, 138

    default classes, 137

Clendenen, Anthony, 331

client agents

    client agent uninstallation/reinstallation

        Linux/UNIX client, 132

        OS X client, 134

    commands, 143

cross-platform agent components, 134

    hardware inventory, 136-142

    settings management, 134-135

    software inventory, 135

cross-platform client agents, 126

    Linux/UNIX client, 127-128

    OS X client, 129-132

downloading, 126

settings, 120-121

client enrollment. *See* enrollment (BYOD)

client notification, 36-37

client operations, monitoring, 45

client settings

    new features, 27-28

    Resultant Client Settings, 34-35

    wake-up proxy client settings, 27

Client-DATE-TIME.log file, 144-145

clients

    Always On, Always Connected, 51-52

    automatic client upgrade, 31

    BranchCache downloads, 57

    client agents

        client agent uninstallation/reinstallation, 132-134

        commands, 143

        cross-platform agent components, 134-135

        cross-platform client agents, 126-132

        downloading, 126

        settings, 120-121

    client experience, 55

    client notification, 36-37

    client operations, monitoring, 45

    company portal for Windows 8.x, 55-56

    device support through Intune, 54

    Linux and UNIX support, 49

    metered Internet connections, 52-53

multiselect in Software Center, 56

OS X support, 49

reassigning, 36

required deployment to devices, 57

selective wipe, 57

settings

    new features, 27-28

    Resultant Client Settings, 34-35

    wake-up proxy client settings, 27

setup/upgrade, 54-55

wake-up proxy client settings, 58

Windows 8.x modern applications, 54

Windows 8.x support, 51

Windows Embedded support, 49-51

Windows To Go (WTG), 54

cloud. *See also* Azure AD

    cloud-based distribution points, 28

    cloud-only architecture (Windows Intune), 313-314

Cloudusersync.log, 233-235, 291

cmdlets, 32-34

CMEnroll, 130-131

CMTrace, 191

collections, 34

commands

    ccmexec, 143

    chmod, 127

    client agent commands, 143

    su root, 127

    sudo, 129, 134

    tail, 144

common information model (CIM), 119

communication, cross-platform, 120

Company Contact Information tab (Create Windows Intune Subscription Wizard), 229

Company Logo tab (Create Windows Intune Subscription Wizard), 229-230 company portal websites, 287-288

company portals

    application deployment, 285-288

        company portal websites, 287-288

        on Windows 8.1 devices, 286

    company portal for Windows 8.x, 55-56

    Windows Intune, 309-310

company resource access, 37-38, 271

    certificate profiles, 271-273

    email profiles, 273-275

    Wi-Fi profiles, 278-280

company-owned devices, inventorying, 259. *See also* mobile device management

Completion tab (Create Windows Intune Subscription Wizard), 229-230

compliance

    ConfigMgr 2012 R2 settings, 37

    User Data and Profiles, 76

Computer rule type, 169

ConfigMgr 2012 R2

    administration changes

        automatic client upgrade, 31

        certificate profiles, 27

        client settings, 27-28

        database replication configuration, 20-24

        DPs (distribution points), 28-31

        Internet proxy server configuration, 24

        Network Access accounts, 32

        overview, 19

        PowerShell support, 32-34

        security, 28

        software update points, 25-27

        Windows Intune integration and extensions, 25

    application deployment. *See* application deployment

    Assets and Compliance, 34

        client notification, 36-37

        collections, 34

        company resource access, 37-38

        compliance settings, 37

        maintenance windows for software updates, 35

        Reassign Site option, 36

        Remote Connection Profiles, 37

        Resultant Client Settings, 34-35

        user data and profiles, 38

clients

    Always On, Always Connected, 51-52

    BranchCache downloads, 57

    client experience, 55

    company portal for Windows 8.x, 55-56

    device support through Intune, 54

    Linux and UNIX support, 49

    metered Internet connections, 52-53

    multiselect in Software Center, 56

    OS X support, 49

    required deployment to devices, 57

    selective wipe, 57

    setup/upgrade, 54-55

    wake-up proxy client settings, 58

    Windows 8.x modern applications, 54

    Windows 8.x support, 51

    Windows Embedded support, 49-51

    Windows To Go (WTG), 54

cross-platform support, 117

    client agent downloads, 126

    client agent settings, 120-121

    cross-platform agent architecture, 119-120

    cross-platform agent communication, 120

    firewall ports, 125

    Linux/UNIX requirements, 121

    OS X requirements, 121-125

    supported platforms, 117-119

data protection, 13-14

enabling for custom inventory providers, 141-142

enabling users with, 9-13

    BYOD registration and enrollment, 10-11

    consistent access to corporate resources, 11-12

    user connections to internal resources, 12-13

mobile device management

    challenges, 244-246

    company resource access, 271-280

    configuration items for mobile devices, 259-268

    deploying applications to mobile devices, 281-286

    in-depth management, 243

    enrolling devices, 248-254

    inventorying mobile devices, 254-259

    light management, 243

    prerequisites, 246-248

    remote connection profiles, 268-271

    renaming devices, 248

    retiring/wiping mobile devices, 288-290

    supported platforms, 247-248

    troubleshooting, 290-293

Monitoring, 42

    alerts, 43

    client operations, 45

    deployment status, 43

    distribution status, 43

    reporting, 43

overview, 19

public forums, 333

reference URLs

    Microsoft's Configuration Manager resources, 322-328

    other Configuration Manager resources, 328-331

setup and recovery

    CAS (central administration site), 47-48

    database configuration, 45

    migration capabilities, 47

    scalability enhancements, 46-47

    secondary sites, 48

    support for new operating systems, 45

    upgrade path, 47

Software Library, 38

    Application Management, 38-39

    OSD (operating system deployment), 41-42

    software updates, 39-41

unifying environment with, 13

write filter support, 79-81

configuration

    certificate enrollment profiles, 319

    clients, 54-55

    ConfigMgr 2012 R2

        CAS (central administration site), 47-48

        database configuration, 45

        migration capabilities, 47

        scalability enhancements, 46-47

        support for new operating systems, 43

        upgrade path, 47

    cross-platform agent components, 134-135

    database replication, 20

        interval for replication data summary, 23

        replication alerts, 23-24

        SQL Server replication configuration, 20-21

        support for distributed views, 22

        transfer of site data across replication links, 21-22

    Internet proxy server, 24

    mobile device settings

        Android devices, 261

        custom configuration items, 267-268

How can we make this index more useful? Email us at indexes@samspublishing.com

iOS configuration items, 263-264

iOS security settings, 264

remediation settings, 266

remote connection profiles, 268-271

Samsung KNOX devices, 261

Windows 8.1 configuration items, 265

Windows Phone 8 devices, 261

Windows Phone 8.1 devices, 262

MPs, 122

SMSTSPreferredAdvertID variable, 335

User Data and Profiles, 64

combined settings, 74

folder redirection, 64-67

offline files, 67-69

roaming user profiles, 70-74

Windows Intune subscriptions, 314

WinRM, 86

Configuration Manager. *See* ConfigMgr 2012 R2

confirming Windows Intune Connector site system role, 232-236

Connection page (Create VPN Profile Wizard), 276

connector (Intune). *See also* subscriptions (Windows Intune)

MDM prerequisites, 209-210

iOS device management, 215-220

Windows 8.1 device management, 210-212

Windows Phone 8.x device management, 212-215

overview, 199-200, 314

synchronizing AD with Microsoft Azure AD, 200

Azure AD namespace, creating, 200-204

Directory Synchronization Tool, installing, 204-208

Windows Intune instance, creating, 200-204

Windows Intune Connector site system role

adding, 231-232

confirming installation of, 232-236

ConnectorSetup.log, 233

consistent access to corporate resources, 11-12, 14-15

content prestaging, 189-190

content staging, 188

CoreTech, 329

corporate resources, consistent access to, 11-12, 14-15

CP Studio, 318

Create a New Task Sequence Wizard, 173

Create Application Wizard, 38

Create Deployment Type Wizard, 82-83. *See also* sideloading applications

Apple App Store deployment type, creating, 90-91

application deployment type, 111

Google Play Store deployment type, creating, 92-93

Mac OS X deployment type, 105-107

Windows Phone Store deployment type, creating, 89-90

Windows Store deployment type, creating, 86-89

Create Exchange ActiveSync Profile Wizard, 273-275

Create Package and Program Wizard, 108-109

Create Task Sequence Wizard, 156

Create Virtual Environment page, 83-85

Create Virtual Hard Disk Wizard, 180-181

Create VPN Profile Wizard, 276-278

Create Wi-Fi Profile Wizard, 278-280

Create Windows Intune Subscription Wizard

Company Contact Information tab, 229

Company Logo tab, 229-230

Completion tab, 229-230

General tab, 222-225

Information tab, 221

Platforms tab, 224-228

Subscription tab, 221

Summary tab, 229

CreateTSMedia.log, 182

cross-platform agent architecture, 119-120

cross-platform agent communication, 120

cross-platform agent components, 134

   hardware inventory, 136-142

      ConfigMgr site configuration, 141-142

      custom classes, 138

      custom inventory providers, 138-140

      default classes, 137

      non-Windows machine configuration, 140-141

      OMI (open management infrastructure), 136

      viewing results, 142

   settings management, 134-135

   software inventory, 135

cross-platform support, 117

   client agent commands, 143

   client agent deployment, 126

      Linux/UNIX client, 127-128

      OS X client, 129-132

   client agent downloads, 126

   client agent settings, 120-121

   client agent uninstallation/reinstallation

      Linux/UNIX client, 132

      OS X client, 134

   cross-platform agent architecture, 119-120

   cross-platform agent communication, 120

   cross-platform agent components, 134

      hardware inventory, 136-142

      settings management, 134-135

      software inventory, 135

firewall ports, 125

Linux/UNIX requirements, 121

OS X requirements, 121-125

   certificates, 122

   client enrollment, 124-125

   ConfigMgr Server, DP, and MP configuration, 122-123

   HTTPS site roles, 123-124

supported platforms, 117-119

troubleshooting with log files

   Linux/UNIX log files, 143-144

   OS X log files, 144-145

   verbose logs, 144

Crumbaker, Ron, 331

current drive letter set, viewing, 336

custom classes (hardware inventory), 138

custom configuration items (mobile devices), 267-268

custom inventory providers

   configuring non-Windows machines for, 140-141

   creating, 138-140

   enabling ConfigMgr site to support, 141-142

D

data protection

   with ConfigMgr and Windows Intune, 13-14

   Microsoft's philosophy, 9

   with Windows Server 2012 R2, 16

database configuration, 45

database replication, configuring, 20

   configuring interval for replication data summary, 23

   managing replication alerts, 23-24

   modifying SQL Server replication configuration, 20-21

How can we make this index more useful? Email us at indexes@samspublishing.com

scheduling transfer of site data across replication links, 21-22

support for distributed views, 22

deep linking, 78

default classes (hardware inventory), 137

defining application information, 282-284

deleting

subscriptions (Windows Intune), 236-241

Wi-Fi profiles, 280

Deploy Software Wizard, 80

deployment

ADRs (automatic deployment rules), 40-41

application deployment

to Apple OS X computers, 105-107

best practices, 112-115

definition of application, 77-78

DTs (deployment types), 78

to Linux and UNIX computers, 108-109

to mobile devices, 85-104, 281-286

new features, 78-79

overview, 77

sideloading applications, 93-103

virtual applications, 81-85

VPN profiles, 104

web applications, 111

write filter support, 79-81

certificate profiles, 96-97

client agent uninstallation/reinstallation

Linux/UNIX client, 132

OS X client, 134

cross-platform client agents, 126

Linux/UNIX client, 127-128

OS X client, 129-132

deployment status, 43

deployment types (DTs), 78

Apple App Store deployment type, 90-91

application deployment type, 111

App-V 5 deployment type, 82-83

Google Play Store deployment type, 92-93

Windows Phone Store deployment type, 89-90

Windows Store deployment type, 86-89

OSD (operating system deployment), 41-42

built-in task sequence variables, 175-176

content prestaging, 189-190

deployment control, 160-164

deployment monitoring, 164-166

Driver Package Export and Import, 186-187

offline servicing, 185-186

overview, 147-148

prerequisites, 148-155

prestaged media, 188-189

task sequences size ceiling, 190

task types, 166-173

troubleshooting hints and tips, 190-195

unknown computer cleanup, 187-188

VHDs (virtual hard disks), 180-182

Windows setup support change, 155-158

WTG (Windows To Go), 183-185

required deployment to devices, 57

UEFI (Unified Extensible Firmware Interface) support, 176-179

User Data and Profiles, 75

deployment status, 43

deployment types (DTs), 78

Apple App Store deployment type, creating, 90-91

application deployment type, 111

App-V 5 deployment type, creating, 82-83

Google Play Store deployment type, creating, 92-93

Windows Phone Store deployment type, creating, 89-90

Windows Store deployment type, creating, 86-89

DeployToVHD.log, 182

in-depth mobile device management, 243

device inventory

    overview, 13

    Windows Intune, 301-303

device retirements (Windows Intune), 310-311

devices

    application deployment, 85-86

        Apple App Store deployment type, 90-91

        Google Play Store deployment type, 92-93

        sideloading applications, 93-103

        Windows Phone Store deployment type, 89-90

        Windows Store deployment type, 86-89

    mobile device management, 268-271

        challenges, 244-246

        company resource access, 271-280

        configuration items for mobile devices, 259-268

        deploying applications to mobile devices, 281-286

        in-depth management, 243

        enrolling devices, 248-254

        inventorying mobile devices, 254-259

        iOS device management, 215-220

        light management, 243

        prerequisites, 246-248

        remote connection profiles, 268-271

        renaming, 248

        retiring/wiping mobile devices, 288-290

        supported platforms, 247-248

        troubleshooting, 290-293

        Windows 8.1 device management, 210-212

        Windows Phone 8.x device management, 212-215

    settings, enabling and enforcing, 13

    Windows Intune support, 54

direct device management (Windows Intune), 301

DirectAccess, 15

Directory Synchronization Tool, installing, 204-208

DirSync, 312

    Directory Synchronization Tool, installing, 204-208

    DirSync Configuration Wizard, 204-208

    installing, 204-208

DirSync Configuration Wizard, 204-208

disable deadline randomization, 27

disabling Windows Intune extensions, 236

discovery data (mobile device inventory), 255-258

disks

    online disk deduplication, 15

    partitioning, 176-177

distmgr.log, 291

distributed views, support for, 22

distribution points. See DPs (distribution points)

distribution status, 43

Dmpdownloader.log, 233, 235, 291

Dmpuploader.log, 233, 235, 291

domain-joined machines, sideloading applications, 95

down-level boot images, 152-154

downloading

    BranchCache downloads, 57

    client agents, 126

/downloadtimeout option (CCMSetup.exe), 54

DPs (distribution points), 28-31

    cloud-based DPs, 28

    configuration, 122

    pull DPs, 28-31

Driver Package Export and Import, 186-187

DSC (dynamic suite composition), 83

DTs (deployment types), 78

    Apple App Store deployment type, 90-91

    application deployment type, 111

    App-V 5 deployment type, 82-83

    Google Play Store deployment type, 92-93

    Windows Phone Store deployment type, 89-90

    Windows Store deployment type, 86-89

Dynamic Access Control, 16

dynamic resolution change, 15

dynamic suite composition (DSC), 83

E

ECM (Enterprise Client Management), 316

editing device ownership, 259

email profiles, 273-275

Enable BitLocker task, 173

enabling

    device settings, 13

    users, 14-16

    Windows Intune extensions, 238-240

Endpoint Protection, 40

enforcing device settings, 13

enrollment (BYOD), 248. *See also* cross-platform support; deployment

    Android devices, 254

    with ConfigMgr and Windows Intune, 10-11

    iOS devices, 252-253

    OS X requirements, 124-125

    Windows 8.1 devices, 251-252

    Windows Phone 8 devices, 249

Enterprise Client Management (ECM), 316

Enterprise Firmware Interface System Partition (ESP), 177

environment, unifying for people-centric IT

    with ConfigMgr and Windows Intune, 13

    Microsoft's philosophy, 8

    with Windows Server 2012 R2, 16

Error logging level, 144

Erskine, Samuel, 332

ESP (Extensible Firmware Interface System Partition), 177

Exchange ActiveSync page (Create Exchange ActiveSync Profile Wizard), 273-274

/ExcludeFeatures option (CCMSetup.exe), 54

extensions (Windows Intune), 25, 238-240

    disabling, 240

    enabling, 241-239

Extensions for Windows Intune tab, 238-240

F

FAQShop.com, 316

files

    .appx file format, 101

    install.wim image file, 155-158

    log files

        Linux/UNIX log files, 143-144

        mobile device management, 290-293

        OS X log files, 144-145

        SMSPXE.log, 191-192

        SMSTSErrorDialogTimeout, 192-193

        SMSTS.log, 191

verbose logs, 144

VHD-specific logs, 182

Windows Intune, 235-240

offline files, 67-69

scxcm.conf file, 144

filters, write filter support, 79-81

firewall ports, 125

Flexera AdminStudio, 331

folder redirection, 64-67

Folder Redirection Health Report, 76

folders

folder redirection, 64-67

Folder Redirection Health Report, 76

OfflineImageServicing, 186

OfflineImageServicing folder, 335

Work folders, 16

/forceinstall option (CCMSetup.exe), 54

/forcereboot option (CCMSetup.exe), 54

forums, 333

G

general resource reference URLs, 315-322

General tab (Create Windows Intune Subscription Wizard), 222-224

Get-Command, 33

Google Play Store deployment type, 92-93

H

hardware inventory

cross-platform agent components, 136-142

ConfigMgr site configuration, 141-142

custom classes, 138

custom inventory providers, 138-140

default classes, 137

non-Windows machine configuration, 140-141

OMI (open management infrastructure), 136

viewing results, 142

overview, 13

Windows Intune, 301-303

hidden task sequences, 164

Hite, Don, 331

Hobbs, Cliff, 316

HTTPS site roles, 123-124

Hudson, Matthew, 331

hypervisor support, 153

I

images

boot images, 151-155

down-level boot images, 152-154

optional components within, 154-155

install.wim image file, 155-158

thin versus thick images, 156

Info logging level, 144

Information tab (Create Windows Intune Subscription Wizard), 221

InformIT website, 315

Infrastructure Optimization (IO), 318

installation wrappers, 114

installing

Directory Synchronization Tool, 204-208

software. See application deployment

install.wim image file, 155-158

integrating Active Directory, 13

"Integrating Virtual Application Management with App-V 5 and Configuration Manager 2012 SP1" (whitepaper), 82 internal resources, user connections to, 12, 15-16

internal WSUS server, specifying as synchronization source, 26-27

Internet proxy server, configuring, 24

interval for replication data summary, configuring, 23

Intune. *See* Windows Intune

inventory, 13

    device inventory

        overview, 13

        Windows Intune, 301-303

    hardware inventory

        cross-platform support, 136-142

        overview, 13

        Windows Intune, 301-303

    mobile devices, 254-259

        available discovery and inventory data, 255-258

        personal versus company-owned devices, 259

    software inventory

        cross-platform agent components, 135

        personal versus company-owned devices, 259

IO (Infrastructure Optimization), 318

iOS device management, 215-220, 248

    enrolling devices, 252-253

    log files, 291-292

    mobile device settings

        iOS configuration items, 263-264

        iOS security settings, 264

    retiring/wiping mobile devices, 289

    sideloading applications, 101-103

iPad. *See* iOS device management

iPhone. *See* iOS device management

iPod. *See* iOS device management

IT Ninja website, 113

J

Jones, Don, 328

Jones, Garth, 331

K

kbalertz, 316

key licensing requirements (sideloading), 210-211

Kissinger, Sherry, 331

L

LDIFDE, 318

libraries. *See* Software Library

licensing

    reference URLs, 321-322

    Windows Intune, 311

    Windows Intune Add-on for System Center Configuration Manager license, 248

light mobile device management, 243

Linux support, 49

    client agent uninstallation/ reinstallation, 132

    cross-platform agent requirements, 121

    cross-platform client agent deployment, 127-128

    deploying applications to, 108-109

    log files, 143-144

live links (online content), 336

Location rule type, 169

log files

    Linux/UNIX log files, 143-144

mobile device management, 290-293

    log files on Android devices, 292

    log files on iOS devices, 291-292

    log files on site server, 291

    log files on Windows 8.x devices, 292

    Windows 8.1 OMA-DM devices, 293

    OS X log files, 144-145

    SMSPXE.log, 191-192

    SMSTSErrorDialogTimeout, 192-193

    SMSTS.log, 191

    verbose logs, 144

    VHD-specific logs, 182

    Windows Intune, 232-236

/logon option (CCMSetup.exe), 54

M

maintenance windows for software updates, 35

Make and Model rule type, 170

managing

    devices. *See* mobile device management

    replication alerts, 23-24

"Managing Embedded Devices with Write Filters in Configuration Manager Service Pack 1" (TechNet), 81

Martinez, Santos, 43, 330

MDM. *See* mobile device management

MDT (Microsoft Deployment Toolkit), 166

Mead, Wally, 326

Meringer, Torsten, 332

metered Internet connections, 27, 52-53

metro applications, 54

Microsoft Azure Active Directory

    overview, 199-200

    synchronizing AD with, 200

        Azure AD namespace, creating, 200-204

        Directory Synchronization Tool, installing, 204-208

        Windows Intune instance, creating, 200-204

Microsoft Configuration Manager. *See* Configuration Manager

Microsoft Deployment Guys blog, 332

Microsoft Deployment Toolkit (MDT), 166

Microsoft Operations Framework (MOF), 318

Microsoft Reserved Partition (MSR), 177

Microsoft Security Compliance Manager (SCM), 318

Microsoft server-cloud blog, 332

Microsoft System Center Configuration Manager product group blog, 332

Microsoft VDI (virtual desktop infrastructure), 15

migration capabilities (ConfigMgr 2012 R2), 47

mobile device management, 243, 300

    application deployment, 85-86, 281-282

        Apple App Store deployment type, 90-91

        with company portal, 285-288

        defining application information, 282-284

        Google Play Store deployment type, 92-93

        sideloading applications, 93-103

        Windows Phone Store deployment type, 89-90

        Windows Store deployment type, 86-89

    challenges, 244-246

    company resource access, 271

        certificate profiles, 271-273

        email profiles, 273-275

        VPN profiles, 275-278

        Wi-Fi profiles, 278-280

    in-depth management, 243

    enrolling devices, 248

        Android devices, 254

        iOS devices, 252-253

Windows 8.1 devices, 251-252

Windows Phone 8 devices, 249

inventorying mobile devices, 254-255

available discovery and inventory data, 255-258

personal versus company-owned devices, 259

iOS devices, 215-220

light management, 243

managing mobile device settings, 259-260

Android configuration items, 261

custom configuration items, 267-268

iOS configuration items, 263-264

iOS security settings, 264

remediation settings, 266

remote connection profiles, 268-271

Samsung KNOX configuration items, 261

Windows 8.1 configuration items, 265

Windows Phone 8 configuration items, 261

Windows Phone 8.1 configuration items, 262

prerequisites, 209-210, 246-248

iOS device management, 215-220

Windows 8.1 device management, 210-212

Windows Phone 8.x device management, 212-215

renaming devices, 248

retiring/wiping mobile devices, 288-290

company content removed when retiring Android devices, 289

company content removed when retiring iOS devices, 289

company content removed when retiring Windows-based devices, 289

supported platforms, 247-248

troubleshooting, 290-293

log files on Android devices, 292

log files on iOS devices, 291-292

log files on site server, 291

log files on Windows 8.x devices, 292

Windows 8.1 OMA-DM devices, 293

Windows Intune

application distribution, 309-310

company portal, 309-310

device inventory, 301-303

device retirement and remote wipe, 310-311

direct device management, 301

policy settings management, 303-309

Modify Virtual Hard Disk Wizard, 181

modifying

SQL Server replication configuration, 20-21

VHDs (virtual hard disks), 181

MOF (Microsoft Operations Framework), 318

monitoring changes, 42

alerts, 43

client operations, 45

deployment status, 43

distribution status, 43

OSD (operating system deployment), 164-166

reporting, 43

Moss, Scott, 332

MP configuration, 122

MP_ClientRegistration record, 127

MP_RegistrationManager.log file, 127

MSIs, repackaging, 113

MSR (Microsoft Reserved Partition), 177

multiple software update points, 26

multiselect in Software Center, 56

myITforum.com, 315

N

namespaces, Azure AD, 200-204

Network Access accounts, 32

Network Load Balancing Deployment guide, 320

O

offline files, 67-69

offline servicing, 185-186

OfflineImageServicing folder

   creating, 335

   overview, 186

Oh, Marcus, 330, 332

OMA-URI (Open Mobile Alliance - Uniform Resource Identifier), 319

OMI (open management infrastructure), 119, 136

online content, 335

   live links, 336

   pause.vbs script, 336

   Set_SMSTSPreferredAdvertID.vbs VBScript, 335

   View_Current_Drive_Letter_Set.ps1 PowerShell script, 336

   WMI_Create_OfflineImageServicing_folder. ps1 PowerShell script, 335

online disk deduplication, 15

open management infrastructure (OMI), 119, 136

Open Mobile Alliance - Uniform Resource Identifier (OMA-URI), reference URL, 319

operating system deployment. See OSD (operating system deployment)

operating systems

   cross-platform support, 117

      client agent settings, 120-121

      cross-platform agent architecture, 119-120

      cross-platform agent communication, 120

      Linux/UNIX requirements, 121

      OS X requirements, 121-125

      supported platforms, 117-119

   deployment. See OSD (operating system deployment)

   mobile devices. See mobile device management

   support for new operating systems, 43

   version support, 149-150

Oppalfens, Kim, 331

OS X Computer Enrollment Wizard, 131-132

OS X support, 49

   client agent uninstallation/ reinstallation, 134

   cross-platform agent requirements, 121-125

      client enrollment, 124-125

      ConfigMgr Server, DP, and MP configuration, 122

      HTTPS site roles, 123-124

   cross-platform client agent deployment, 129-132

      CMEnroll, 130-131

      OS X Computer Enrollment Wizard, 131-132

   deploying applications to, 105-107

   log files, 144-145

   OS X 10.9 (Mavericks), 119

OSD (operating system deployment), 41-42, 147

   built-in task sequence variables, 175-176

   content prestaging, 189-190

   deployment control, 160-164

   deployment monitoring, 164-166

   Driver Package Export and Import, 186-187

   offline servicing, 185-186

   overview, 147-148

prerequisites, 148

    boot images, 151-155

    operating system version support, 149-150

prestaged media

    content staging, 188

    staged content use, 189

task sequences

    pausing, 193-195

    size ceiling, 190

task types, 166-173

    Check Readiness, 170-172

    Enable BitLocker, 173

    Pre-provision BitLocker, 172-173

    Run PowerShell Script, 167-168

    Set Dynamic Variables, 168-170

troubleshooting hints and tips, 190-195

    pausing task sequences, 193-195

    power scheme, 193

    SMSPXE.log, 191-192

    SMSTSErrorDialogTimeout, 192-193

    SMSTS.log, 191

    Windows 8.1 wireless network prompt, 195

UEFI (Unified Extensible Firmware Interface) support, 176-179

unknown computer cleanup, 187-188

VHDs (virtual hard disks), 180

    creating, 180-181

    modifying, 181

    updating, 181-182

    uploading to VMM, 182

    VHD-specific logs, 182

Windows setup support change, 155-158

WTG (Windows To Go), 183-185

OSD Support Team blog, 331

OSDBitLockerPIN variable, 184

OSDPreserveDriveLetter, 175

OSs. *See* operating systems

outgoingcontentmanager.log, 235, 238, 291

overriding subscriptions (Windows Intune), 236-241

ownership of mobile devices, editing, 259

P

Package parameter (Run PowerShell Script task), 167

Parameters parameter (Run PowerShell Script task), 168

partitions, 176-177

password synchronization, enabling, 208

pause.vbs script, 336

pausing task sequences, 336, 193-195

PCIT (people-centric IT). *See* people-centric IT (PCIT)

Pearson, Michael, 317

Pederson, Ronni, 331

people-centric IT (PCIT), 6-9, 316

    data protection

        with ConfigMgr and Windows Intune, 13-14

        with Windows Server 2012 R2, 16

    enabling users for

        with ConfigMgr and Windows Intune, 9-13

        Microsoft's philosophy, 7-8

        with Windows Server 2012 R2, 14-16

    Microsoft Azure Active Directory, 17-18

    Microsoft's philosophy, 6-7

        data protection, 9

        enabled users, 7-8

        unified environment, 8

unifying environment for

with ConfigMgr and Windows Intune, 13

Microsoft's philosophy, 8

with Windows Server 2012 R2, 16

performance and tuning guidelines (reference URLs), 316-317

personal devices. *See also* mobile device management, inventorying, 259

philosophy of people-centric IT, 6-7

data protection, Microsoft's philosophy, 9

enabled users, 7-8

unified environment, 8

platforms. *See* operating systems

Platforms tab (Create Windows Intune Subscription Wizard), 224-228

policies

policy to enable sideloading on domain-joined machines, 95

PowerShell execution policies, 168

Windows Intune policy settings management, 303-309

ports, firewall, 125

power scheme, 193

powercfg.exe, 193-195

PowerShell

PowerShell Execution Policy, 27

support in ConfigMgr 2012 R2, 32-34

PowerShell Execution Policy parameter (Run PowerShell Script task), 168

Pre-provision BitLocker task, 172-173

prestaged media, content staging, 188

profiles

certificate enrollment profiles

configuration, 319

creating, 96-97

new features, 27

overview, 271-273

email profiles, 273-275

Remote Connection Profiles, 37

remote connection profiles, 268-271

roaming user profiles, 70-74

User Data and Profiles, 38

compliance reporting, 76

configuration, 64-74

deployment, 75

overview, 61-62

prerequisites, 62-64

settings, 27

VPN profiles, 104

Wi-Fi profiles, 278-280

protecting data

with ConfigMgr and Windows Intune, 13-14

Microsoft's philosophy, 9

with Windows Server 2012 R2, 16

Proxy Settings page (Create VPN Profile Wizard), 277

public forums, 333

pull DPs (distribution points), 28-31

Q-R

Rachui, Steve (blog), 329-330, 332

RDP (Remote Desktop Protocol), 15

Reassign Site option, 36

reassigning clients, 36

recovery (ConfigMgr 2012 R2)

CAS (central administration site), 47-48

database configuration, 45

migration capabilities, 47

scalability enhancements, 46-47

secondary sites, 48

support for new operating systems, 43

upgrade path, 47

redirection (folder), 64-67

reference URLs, 315

blogs, 331-333

general resources, 315-322

IT Ninja, 113

Microsoft's Configuration Manager resources, 322-328

online live links, 336

other Configuration Manager resources, 327-331

public forums, 332

utilities, 333-334

registration (BYOD), 10-11. See also mobile device management

reinstalling clients

Linux/UNIX client, 132

OS X client, 134

remediation settings (mobile devices), 266

Remote Access Role service, 14

remote applications, 15

Remote Connection Profiles, 37, 268-271

Remote Desktop Protocol (RDP), 15

remote wipe (Windows Intune), 310-311

RemoteApp, 15

removing

subscriptions (Windows Intune), 236-240

Wi-Fi profiles, 280

renaming devices, 248

repackaging MSIs, 113

replication alerts, managing, 23-24

reporting

overview, 43

User Data and Profiles compliance, 76

required deployment to devices, 57

Resultant Client Settings, 34-35

retiring/wiping mobile devices, 288-290

company content removed when retiring Android devices, 289

company content removed when retiring iOS devices, 289

company content removed when retiring Windows-based devices, 289

rights management services (Active Directory), 16

roaming user profiles

overview, 70-74

Roaming User Profiles Health Report, 76

Roaming User Profiles Health Report, 76

roles

Certificate Registration Point site system role, 272

Windows Intune Connector site system role

adding, 231

confirming installation of, 232-236

Run PowerShell Script task, 167-168

S

Samsung KNOX devices configuration items, 261

Santiago, Carlos, 331

Saukko, Panu, 332

scalability enhancements (ConfigMgr 2012 R2), 46-47

SCEP (Simple Certificate Enrollment Protocol), 271

scheduling transfer of site data across replication links, 21-22

Schurling, Stefan, 332

SCM (Security Compliance Manager), 318

Script Name parameter (Run PowerShell Script task), 168

scripts

pause.vbs, 336

Set_SMSTSPreferredAdvertID.vbs VBScript, 335

View_Current_Drive_Letter_Set.ps1 PowerShell script, 336

WMI_Create_OfflineImageServicing_folder. ps1 PowerShell script, 335

scxcm.conf file, 144

SCXCM.log, 143-144

scxcmprovider.log, 143-144

secondary sites, recovering, 48

security

    ConfigMgr 2012 R2, 28

    people-centric IT (PCIT)

        data protection with ConfigMgr and Windows Intune, 13-14

        Microsoft's philosophy, 9

Security Compliance Manager (SCM), 318

Security Configuration page (Create Wi-Fi Profile Wizard), 279

selective wipe, 57

session shadowing, 15

Set Dynamic Variables task, 168-170

Set_SMSTSPreferredAdvertID.vbs VBScript, 335

settings (mobile devices), 259-260. See also configuration

    Android configuration items, 261

    custom configuration items, 267-268

    iOS devices

        iOS configuration items, 263-264

        iOS security settings, 264

        Windows 8.1 configuration items, 265

    remediation settings, 266

    remote connection profiles, 268-271

    Samsung KNOX configuration items, 261

    Windows Phone 8 configuration items, 261

    Windows Phone 8.1 configuration items, 262

setup. See configuration

sideloading applications

    for Android devices, 103

    for Apple iPhone, iPod, and iPad devices, 101-103

    certificate profiles, 96-97

    domain-joined machines, 95

    key licensing requirements, 210-211

    overview, 78, 93-94, 210

    sideloading enhancements, 319

    for Windows and Windows RT devices, 94-95

    Windows modern applications, 97-99

    for Windows Phone devices, 99-101

sideloading keys (Windows), 39

Sienaert, Nico, 326

Silect Software, 318

Simple Certificate Enrollment Protocol (SCEP), 271

Simple Mail Transfer Protocol (SMTP), testing, 317

site roles (HTTPS), 123-124

size ceiling for task sequences, 190

/skipprereq option (CCMSetup.exe), 54

SMSPXE.log, 191-192

SMSTSAssignmentsDownloadInterval, 175

SMSTSAssignmentsDownloadRetry, 175

SMSTSDownloadRetryCount, 176

SMSTSDownloadRetryDelay, 176

SMSTSErrorDialogTimeout, 192-193

SMSTS.log, 191

SMSTSPostAction, 175

SMSTSPreferredAdvertID variable

    overview, 160-164, 184

    setting, 335

SMSTSSUdaUsers variable, 115

SMTP (Simple Mail Transfer Protocol), testing, 317

Software Center, multiselect, 56

software installation. *See* application deployment

software inventory, cross-platform agent components, 135

Software Library, 38

   Application Management, 38-39

      App-V virtual environments, 39

      overview, 38

      Windows sideloading keys, 39

   OSD (operating system deployment), 41-42

   software updates, 39-41

software update points, 25-27

   multiple software update points, 26

   specifying internal WSUS server as synchronization source, 26

   in untrusted forests, 26-27

software updates

   maintenance windows for software updates, 35

   Software Library, 39-41

   software update points, 25-27

      multiple software update points, 26

      specifying internal WSUS server as synchronization source, 26-27

      in untrusted forests, 26-27

   VHDs (virtual hard disks), 181-182

solution accelerators, 320

SQL Server

   replication configuration, modifying, 20-21

   SQL Server Service Broker port, 21

   SSRS (SQL Server Reporting Services), 317

SQL Server Service Broker port, 21

SSRS (SQL Server Reporting Services), 317

staged content use, 189

status

   deployment status, 43

   distribution status, 43

storage tiering, 15

su root command, 127

Subscription tab (Create Windows Intune Subscription Wizard), 221

subscriptions (Windows Intune)

   creating, 220-230

      Company Contact Information tab, 229

      Company Logo tab, 229-230

      Completion tab, 229-230

      General tab, 222-224

      Information tab, 221

      Platforms tab, 224-228

      Subscription tab, 221

      Summary tab, 229

   overview, 314

   removing or overriding, 236-240

sudo command, 129, 134

Sullivan, Kevin, 332

Summary tab (Create Windows Intune Subscription Wizard), 229

Support Tool for Windows Intune Trial Management, 321

SUPs. *See* software update points

Symantec, 331

Synchronization Settings page (Create Exchange ActiveSync Profile Wizard), 274-275

synchronizing AD with Microsoft Azure AD, 200

   Azure AD namespace, creating, 200-204

   Directory Synchronization Tool, installing, 204-208

   Windows Intune instance, creating, 200-204

Sysinternals website, 318

System Center 2012 Configuration Unleashed, 244

System Center Central, 316

System Center Orchestrator, 129

System Center Virtual User Group, 316

T

tail command, 144

Task Sequence Variable rule type, 170

task sequences

applications in, 115

built-in task sequence variables, 175-176

hidden task sequences, 164

new task types, 166-173

Check Readiness, 170-172

Enable BitLocker, 173

Pre-provision BitLocker, 172-173

Run PowerShell Script, 167-168

Set Dynamic Variables, 168-170

pausing, 336, 193-195

size ceiling, 190

SMSTSPreferredAdvertID task sequence, 160-164

templates, virtualization, 182

Tenant ID, 291

testing SMSTSPreferredAdvertID variable, 317

thick versus thin images, 156

thin versus thick images, 156

Thompson, Steve, 332

Thomsen, Paul, 332

Trace logging level, 144

training, 328

transfer of site data across replication links, scheduling, 21-22

Transmission ID, 291

troubleshooting with log files

Linux/UNIX log files, 143-144

mobile device management, 290-293

log files on Android devices, 292

log files on iOS devices, 291-292

log files on site server, 291

log files on Windows 8.x devices, 292

Windows 8.1 OMA-DM devices, 293

OS X log files, 144-145

OSD (operating system deployment), 190-195

power scheme, 193-195

SMSPXE.log, 191-192

SMSTSErrorDialogTimeout, 192-193

SMSTS.log, 191

Windows 8.1 wireless network prompt, 195

verbose logs, 144

trusted CA certificates, 271

tuning, 316-317

U

UDA (user device affinity), 115

UDM (unified device management), 311-313

UEFI (Unified Extensible Firmware Interface), 42, 176-179, 318

unattended software installation, 113

unified architecture, 311-313

unified device management (UDM), 311-313

Unified Extensible Firmware Interface (UEFI), 42, 176-179, 318

unifying environment

with ConfigMgr and Windows Intune, 13

Microsoft's philosophy, 8

with Windows Server 2012 R2, 16

uninstalling clients

Linux/UNIX client, 132

OS X client, 134

UNIX support, 49

client agent uninstallation/ reinstallation, 132

cross-platform agent requirements, 121

cross-platform client agent deployment, 127-128

deploying applications to, 108-109

log files, 143-144

unknown computer cleanup, 187-188

untrusted forests, software update points, 26-27

updating

software

maintenance windows for software updates, 35

Software Library, 39-41

VHDs (virtual hard disks), 181-182

upgrade path (ConfigMgr), 47

upgrading

automatic client upgrade, 31

clients, 54-55

ConfigMgr 2012 SP 1, 47

Windows 8 to Windows 8.1, 158

uploading VHDs (virtual hard disks), 182

URLs. See reference URLs

User Data and Profiles

compliance reporting, 76

configuration, 64

combined settings, 74

folder redirection, 64-67

offline files, 67-69

roaming user profiles, 70-74

deployment, 75

overview, 38, 54, 61-62

prerequisites, 62-64

settings, 27

User Data and Profiles Health Report, 76

user device affinity (UDA), 115

users

enabling for people-centric IT

with ConfigMgr and Windows Intune, 9-13

Microsoft's philosophy, 7-8

with Windows Server 2012 R2, 14-16

user connections to internal resources, 15-16

User Data and Profiles, 38

compliance reporting, 76

configuration, 64-74

deployment, 75

overview, 61-62

prerequisites, 62-64

remote connection profiles, 268-271

settings, 27

user experience, 55

VPN connections, 12-13

USMT 8.1, 320

utilities, 333-334. See also specific utilities

V

van Surksum, Kenneth, 332

variables, built-in task sequence variables, 175-176

VDI (virtual desktop infrastructure), 15

verbose logs, 144

VHDs (virtual hard disks), 42, 180

creating, 180-181

modifying, 181

updating, 181-182

uploading to VMM, 182

VHD-specific logs, 182

View_Current_Drive_Letter_Set.ps1 PowerShell script, 336

viewing

current drive letter set, 336

hardware inventory results, 142

virtual applications, deploying, 81-82

App-V 5 deployment type, 82-83

App-V virtual environments, 83-85

virtual desktop infrastructure (VDI), 15

virtual environments. *See* App-V virtual environments

virtual hard disks. *See* VHDs (virtual hard disks)

Virtual Machine Manager (VMM), uploading VHDs to, 182

virtualization templates, 182

Visual Studio Report Designer, 320

VMM (Virtual Machine Manager), uploading VHDs to, 182

VPN connections, 12-13

VPN profiles, 104

W-X-Y-Z

WAIK (Windows Automated Installation Kit), 153, 319

wake-up proxy client settings, 27, 58

Warning logging level, 144

Wayback Machine, 336, 315

WBEM (web-based enterprise management), 119

Web Application Proxy, 14, 15, 16, 321

web applications, deploying, 111

web-based enterprise management (WBEM), 119

websites. *See* reference URLs

Wi-Fi profiles, 278-280

Wiles, Michael, 332

Windows 8.x support, 51

   company portal, 55-56

   company portals, 286

   device management, 210-212, 247

   enrolling devices, 251-252

   log files, 292

   mobile device configuration items, 265

   retiring/wiping mobile devices, 289

sideloading applications, 94-95

upgrading Windows 8 to Windows 8.1, 158

Windows 8.x modern applications, 54

Windows 8.1 0MA-DM devices, troubleshooting, 293

wireless network prompt, 195

Windows Automated Deployment Kit (ADK), 319

Windows Automated Installation Kit (WAIK), 153, 319

Windows Embedded support

   overview, 49-51

   write filter support, 79-81

Windows Intune

   data protection, 13-14

   device support through Intune, 54

   enabling users with, 9-13

      BYOD registration and enrollment, 10-11

      consistent access to corporate resources, 11-12

      user connections to internal resources, 12-13

   extensions, 25, 238-340

      disabling, 240

      enabling, 239-240

   integration with ConfigMgr 2012, 25

   Intune connector

      adding Windows Intune Connector site system role, 231-232

      confirming installation of Windows Intune Connector site system role, 232-236

      overview, 199-200, 314

   licensing, 311

   log files, 232-236

   mobile device management features, 300

      application distribution, 303-310

      company portal, 303-310

      device inventory, 301-303

How can we make this index more useful? Email us at indexes@samspublishing.com

device retirement and remote wipe, 310-311

direct device management, 301

policy settings management, 303-309

mobile device management prerequisites, 209-210

iOS device management, 215-220

Windows 8.1 device management, 210-212

Windows Phone 8.x device management, 212-215

overview, 297-300

reference URLs, 321

subscriptions

creating, 220-230

overview, 314

removing or overriding, 236-241

supported architectures

cloud-only architecture, 313-314

unified architecture, 311-313

synchronizing AD with Microsoft Azure AD, 200

Azure AD namespace, creating, 200-204

Directory Synchronization Tool, installing, 204-208

Windows Intune instance, creating, 200-204

unifying environment with, 13

Windows Intune Add-on for System Center Configuration Manager license, 248

Windows Intune Connector site system role

adding, 231

confirming installation of, 232-236

Windows IT Pro, 319

Windows Management Instrumentation (WMI), 320

Windows modern applications, sideloading, 97-99

Windows Partition, 177

Windows Phone 8.x devices

device management, 212-215, 247

enrolling, 249

mobile device settings, 261-262

sideloading applications, 99-101

Windows Phone Store deployment type, creating, 89-90

Windows RT devices

mobile device management, 247

sideloading applications, 94-95

Windows Server 2012 R2

data protection, 16

enabling users for people-centric IT, 14-16

BYOD registration and enrollment, 14

consistent access to corporate resources, 14-15

user connections to internal resources, 15-16

VDI (virtual desktop infrastructure), 15

unifying environment with, 16

Web Application Proxy, 14

Workplace Join, 14

Windows Server technical library, 318

Windows sideloading keys, 39

Windows Store deployment type, creating, 86-89

Windows To Go (WTG), 42, 54, 183-185, 318

Windows XP, end of support, 147

WinRM configuration, 86

wiping mobile devices, 288-290

company content removed when retiring Android devices, 289

company content removed when retiring iOS devices, 289

company content removed when retiring Windows-based devices, 289

wireless network prompt, 195

wizards. *See specific wizards*

WMI (Windows Management Instrumentation), 320

WMI Query Language (WQL), 320

WMI_Create_OfflineImageServicing_folder.ps1 PowerShell script, 335

Work folders, 16

Workplace Join

   overlapping ranges, 14

   reference URLs, 321

WQL (WMI Query Language), 320

wrappers (installation), 114

write filter support, 79-81

WTG (Windows To Go), 42, 54, 183-185

WTGCreator.exe, 185

XML Notepad 2007, 318

UNLEASHED

Unleashed takes you beyond the basics, providing an exhaustive, technically sophisticated reference for professionals who need to exploit a technology to its fullest potential. It's the best resource for practical advice from the experts and the most in-depth coverage of the latest technologies.

informit.com/unleashed

Unleashed titles are available in print and eBook formats. InformIT provides eBooks in PDF, MOBI, and EPUB formats.

System Center 2012 Orchestrator Unleashed
ISBN-13: 9780672336102

OTHER UNLEASHED TITLES

Microsoft System Center 2012 Unleashed
ISBN-13: 9780672336126

Microsoft Lync Server 2013 Unleashed
ISBN-13: 9780672336157

Windows Server 2012 Unleashed
ISBN-13: 9780672336225

Microsoft Dynamics CRM 2013 Unleashed
ISBN-13: 9780672337031

Microsoft Exchange Server 2013 Unleashed
ISBN-13: 9780672336119

SharePoint 2013 Unleashed
ISBN-13: 9780672337338

Microsoft SQL Server 2012 Unleashed
ISBN-13: 9780672336928

Windows 8.1 Apps with XAML and C# Unleashed
ISBN-13: 9780672337086

Windows 8.1 Apps with HTML5 and JavaScript Unleashed
ISBN-13: 9780672337116

WPF 4.5 Unleashed
ISBN-13: 9780672336973

Windows Phone 8 Unleashed
ISBN-13: 9780672336898

ASP.NET Dynamic Data Unleashed
ISBN-13: 9780672335655

Microsoft Visual Studio 2012 Unleashed
ISBN-13: 9780672336256

C# 5.0 Unleashed
ISBN-13: 9780672336904

Visual Basic 2012 Unleashed
ISBN-13: 9780672336317

HTML5 Unleashed
ISBN-13: 9780672336270

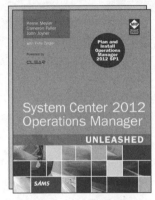

System Center 2012 Operations Manager Unleashed
ISBN-13: 9780672335914

informit.com/sams

System Center 2012 Service Manager Unleashed
ISBN-13: 9780672337079